FRITZ PERLS

Here and Now

Jack Gaines

Illustrations by G. Russ Youngreen

INTEGRATED PRESS
P. O. Box 666
Tiburon, CA 94920

Copyright © 1979 by Jack Gaines

INTEGRATED PRESS
P . O. Box 666
Tiburon, CA 94920

Celestial Arts is indebted to John O. Stevens of Real People Press for his
permission to quote extensively from *In and Out the Garbage Pail*
throughout this book.

First Printing, July 1979

Made in the United States of America.

Cover design by Robert Hu

Library of Congress Cataloging in Publication Data

Gaines, Jack, 1918–
    Fritz Perls, here and now.

    Bibliography: p.
    Includes index.
    1. Perls, Frederick S.   2. Psychiatrists—
United States—Biography.   3. Gestalt therapy.
I. Title.
RC339.52.P47G34   616.8'9'00924   [B]   77-90020
ISBN 0-9610310-0-X Hardback
ISBN 0-9610310-1-8 Paperback

1 2 3 4 5 6 7—85 84 83 82 81 80 79

Contents

Photographs following page 440

Author's Note

Acknowledgment is herewith made to the many trusting, cooperative, gracious people and to the suspicious, uncooperative and wary as well, who allowed me into their homes and lives and participated in my addiction to Fritz stories. Their names appear on these pages and in the index. I am deeply grateful to them and to the others whose history and experience could not be included.

"The main tool for a therapist," Fritz told a professional group, "is the ear. When somebody talks, you have two choices—either you let your computer listen, which means you get the details, the statistics and the facts, or you can let your ears listen and get the personality behind the words. . . ."

I have listened to those willing to talk about Fritz. *Their* personalities as well as his are here, for in sharing their experiences with Fritz they have inevitably also shared private details of their own lives. I am deeply grateful to all of them.

Transposing their spoken words into immutable print was, in its way, like being involved in a theatrical presentation. As the stage manager might shift a prop or a character, I have moved material around on the stage of this book. And like the director, I have taken great care to present the statements faithfully.

Foreword

When Fritz was "on," he was the most exciting therapist who ever lived. His was the unique ability to pierce
down into a person and grasp what was most basically
awry: where grief, fury, death lay deeply hidden; to
specify the arena where the battle could emerge and be
fought; to limn the two opponents; and, with precision
and grace, to direct the battle . . .

Joen Fagan*

I never knew Fritz Perls. That probably had more to do with
writing this book than anything else. Each time I was to meet
him, something intervened. The last time, I was sitting in an
auditorium in Manhattan awaiting his arrival when it was
announced to the overflow crowd that Fritz was ill, and that
our tickets would be honored at another time when Fritz got
better. Fritz never got better.

A short time later I found myself in a mid-life crisis of
sorts. I had sold the business I'd founded and run for over
twenty years. I was suddenly alone and uncertain of what to
do with my life. Inexplicably despondent, I wanted help.
Somehow Fritz was the only therapist I trusted, and when I
heard that a man who had worked with Fritz for many years
would be leading a workshop in Big Sur, California, I flew
there.

I went to Big Sur for a week and stayed a year. By that
time, at the age of fifty-three, the corporation president,
mini-philanthropist, and man-about-New-York I had been
had dissolved into a guy groping for his identity. I moved to

*"The Importance of Fritz Perls Having Been," *Voices:* The Art and Science of Psychotherapy (Journal of the American Academy of Psychotherapists) Spring 1971.

a house on top of a mountain in Big Sur, at the edge of the ocean. It could not have been in greater contrast with my life in New York City. My nearest neighbor was visible only with binoculars. The small dirt road to the rest of the world was sometimes impassable.

I lived in quiet turmoil, dwarfed by the majestic beauty that surrounded me, wrestling with the ideas of life and of suicide. Some of that time I spent at Esalen Institute, where Fritz had lived and taught only a year before. Anecdotes and legends of this man still circulated around the institute as if the roly-poly curmudgeon were still alive walking the grounds, distributing his erratic blessings and verbal blasts as he had always done. They spoke of him—and often still do—in the present tense.

The stories had the quality of the Sufi tales of Nasruden, the foolish, sad, outrageous, wise man. They fascinated me and before long I found myself with a tape recorder in hand. a faithful hagiographer of the legend of Fritz Perls. I was entranced by this man who seemed to be both satyr and shepherd, both vagrant and wizard. In a sense, Fritz became my roommate; his wrinkled forehead, his frown and his deep, gravelly voice became part of my life.

Kind and cruel, compassionate teacher and indifferent son-of-a-bitch, devil and saint, Fritz Perls allowed himself to be what he was. When he was sad, he was unquestionably sad; when he was happy or angry or moved, he did not deny himself or those around him his experiences. As I interviewed his former associates, and students, relatives and acquaintances, Fritz would sometimes float in and nod approvingly, or blast "Bullshit!" when someone talking about their relationship with him was laying it on too thickly. There is, after all, an element of self-aggrandizement in eulogizing a great man. The truth, however, began to flow and to become this book about Fritz Perls. Those who worked with him found that they came to a fork in the road; their lives changed; they became wholer, more themselves. I, too, saw myself more clearly.

The book traces his career from his early obscurity in Germany to his belated acclaim in America, and finally it follows him, tired amid celebrity, to his deathbed. The many voices in the book speak with candor and intimacy, but just as no two historians ever agree on the way something happened, so, too, no two people agree on who Fritz was. Each offers his or her own distinct and partial attitude, like the five blind men who each touched a different part of the elephant and saw that part as the whole.

Fritz Perls was one of those rare people who stirred fresh interpretations from each person who met him. The universal quality is diversity. There are many Fritzes. What emerges very sharply from these varied tellings is the vitality of the man and the wide range of individual reactions to his influence. There is an intrinsic rightness about this, for Fritz abhorred what he called "carbon-copy" people. His genius was that he could catalyze the unfolding of someone else's personal uniqueness.

Fritz was, of course, not without faults. He was described as crazy, irresponsible, reckless, radical, impulse-ridden, narcissistic, sexually promiscuous. And, at least at certain times, he was most of these. But he was also capable of stunning events in that special learning situation called psychotherapy. In his humanity, he taught us.

Fritz was never anybody but himself. He neither wanted to please you nor did he necessarily want you to please him. If we meet, beautiful; if not, let's accept that and go on. Being easy with each other, letting life unfold at our individual pace, in harmony with everyone else and with the universe.

So, here, no attempt has been made to create one picture of Fritz Perls. You will be given many. There *are* many. You will make your own, as indeed we each do in all of our relationships and experiences and thereby determine the quality of our lives. Fritz urged us to allow ourselves to live fully. He did.

I give you what I have of Fritz.

Jack Gaines
Tiburon, California, 1979

His height. . . .

LEO ZEFF
When I talked to Fritz I had to look down just a little. I'm 5'7", so he was about 5'4". . . . a little gnome. . . .

VIRGINIA SATIR
He was a massive, big man, my height at least. I'm 5'10". . .

ROLLO MAY
I always took him as being more or less my size. I'm 5'11". I knew him in 1948, and back in those days I had the impression he was quite a big man, not fat but heavy. *Not* short; there was nothing short about him. He may have shrunk a bit in his old age but I'd be doubtful about that. . . .

FRITZ PERLS
When I walked in a crowd (in Japan) I felt like a giant among dwarfs and I am only 5'9".

What did he look like?

BARRY STEVENS
He could change his appearance. Sometimes he would puff himself up and be huge and sometimes he was quite small. I have seen Fritz look like a tired, thin, shriveled old man with watery blue eyes, and I have seen him look stout and strong and vigorous, with coal black eyes shot with fire. Mostly his eyes were warm brown.

GIDEON SCHWARZ
My inside reaction when our eyes met for the first time was "How dare you!" He was making so much contact it was almost obscene.

WILLIAM QUINN
He had a voice like a cello; it was rich and vibrant. . . .

SEYMOUR CARTER

Fritz' face could change from a cruel Arab prince, that whole Semitic cast of cruelty and kingliness, to being a very soft and blubbery old man within seconds. Many times he would be feeble and shaking, and he would allow himself the tremors of energy running through him.

HUNTER CULP

He walked sort of with a little Japanese shuffle.

KEN STEVENS

The first time I saw him I thought for sure it was Santa Claus — a big belly standing on two little stalks which were his legs.

BERNARD GUNTHER

He had the worst fucking tense body I have ever seen on anyone! He had hammer toes you could've pulled nails with. He was like a hard old alligator. His back was absolutely rigid. He was very flexible in his mind but his body was just knots. Yet he'd look so marvelous. Sometimes he'd put on a pair of tennis shoes without socks. With those spindly legs and his big pot belly and beard, he looked just like a little kid—proud of his belly the way kids are.

Yet he was as messy as a hastily folded road map forever trailing ashes. . . .

MICHAEL MURPHY

You could just see him filling out. He was, I would say, so shameless in showing the girls that he had one of these incredible, marvelous bodies. He would just put out the body and strut around. Panache! Once, when there was a bunch of people filming at Esalen, Fritz strutted around for all the world like one of those big cats in the zoo. Stark naked. It was incredible!

The details, the statistics and the facts. . . .

Friedrich Saloman Perls was born in Berlin on July 8, 1893. His father, Nathan, was a wine salesman who had no affection and little interest in any of his three children, and he particularly despised his youngest child, Fritz (as he was known even then). The boy loved acting, hated school, and resented the anti-Semitism that was endemic to life in Germany then. World War I interrupted his training as a medical student; he became a soldier, was wounded and awarded the German Cross, which he threw away.

After the war, he resumed his medical studies. He received his M.D. in 1921 in Berlin and started practice as a neuropsychiatrist there. In 1926, he moved to Frankfurt. There he met Lore Posner, a psychology student. They married in 1930. From 1927 to 1933, Fritz continued his studies at various psychoanalytic institutes in Berlin and Vienna, continued his own analysis, in which Karen Horney and Wilhelm Reich were the key figures, and from 1928 to 1933 had private practices in Frankfurt, in Vienna, and in Berlin—where he was also a consultant to a private mental hospital.

In 1933, when the nazis took over Germany, Fritz and Lore and their two-year-old daughter fled the country. A period of destitution in Amsterdam was terminated in 1934, when Fritz got a position as an analyst in South Africa. For the next twelve years he and his family (which by then included a second child, a son) lived a busy and prosperous life in Johannesburg: Fritz founded the South African Institute for Psychoanalysis in 1935; had his first book, *Ego, Hunger and Aggression,* published in Durban in 1942; and from 1942 to 1946 served as a psychiatrist with the South African Army.

Released from the army, concerned over the authoritarian and racist trends in South Africa, Fritz decided on a move to the United States in 1946. There, in cooperation with the William Alanson White Institute in New York, he practiced as a psychoanalyst from 1946 to 1950. Then the friction between Fritz and Lore (who had Americanized her name to Laura) led to their separation: Laura stayed in New York with the children, and Fritz, who had found acceptance neither for himself nor for his gestalt therapy, became a somewhat disgruntled Johnny Appleseed, planting gestalt therapy institutes and giving workshops wherever he could around the country for the next fourteen years.

From 1950 to 1955 he moved from New York to Los Angeles, back to New York, to Miami, then to Columbus, Ohio, involved in private practice and in the establishment of Gestalt Institutes both in New York (1952) and Cleveland (1954). From 1955 to 1964 he practiced in San Francisco and Los Angeles and was a consultant in Mendocino, Metropolitan, and Patton State Hospitals. This constant change and movement was reflective of his continuing rebellion against the mainstream of current psychiatric practice.

It was not until 1964, when he was already 71, that he discovered a place in Big Sur, California which provided the aesthetic sphere and the climate of freedom to work and to live as he wanted. There, at Esalen Institute, his work, his reputation as a therapeutic genius, and his health flourished.

Although at the outset he felt that he would stay at Esalen for the rest of his life, Fritz left there for Canada after five years. His departure was motivated in part by fears that, under Nixon, America was moving irreversibly towards fascism, and in part by his desire to found his own gestalt kibbutz

In June 1969, he opened the doors of his Gestalt Institute of Canada at Lake Cowichan on Vancouver Island. He had become internationally known as the founder of the "most effective innovation in psychiatry since Sigmund Freud." He was conducting and recording seminars and professional training workshops in gestalt therapy. He had plans for enlarging the scope of his Lake Cowichan institute and was working on a multimedia textbook. Upon returning from a European tour to a crowded schedule, he died of a heart attack in Chicago on March 14, 1970.

The stories must be placed in their proper light for those who fail to see the relation between fantasy and reality, the past and the present. Everything is related and interactive but at times we fail to see how, and consequently fail to make a higher synthesis.

Anais Nin
From *Under a Glass Bell*

Germany

Fritz says in In and Out the Garbage Pail*:

> *I was close to my sister Grete. She was a tomboy, a wildcat with stubborn curly hair. . . Grete has adjusted herself. She is very nervous, very talkative and very worried. In spite of this we love each other and she takes great pride in the fact that her black sheep of a brother is becoming famous. "If only Mama could have experienced it." She is always sending me the most expensive and delicious candies.*

She is in her 80s. Her name—Gutfreund, "good friend'—suits her. "Have some more cookies," she urges. We sit at a small round table with her sister-in-law, Laura Perls. Her kitchen in upper Manhattan is European and spotless. She has put out a bowl of fruit and some freshly baked cookies, and as I eat a few she smiles and quietly puts some more onto the plate. Her fondness for her brother is evident from the pleasure with which she talks about him. But I am her guest, and she gently pushes the plate towards me. . .

MARGARITE GUTFREUND

My parents were married eleven years before they had children. My mother couldn't have them; then she had an operation and they came every year, one after another! There were two girls before Fritz; Fritz was the last. He was the baby; he was spoiled. He was a wild child—wild, wild!

When we were children in Germany, Fritz didn't really

---

*Hereafter, Fritz' quotes from *In and Out the Garbage Pail,* his autobiography, appear throughout the book in the indented small italic.

have any intimate friends. Most of those who came to our apartment were my friends—girl friends. We had a large apartment and there was always much laughter. We had little gatherings and Fritz would often come down to join us.

Fritz and I were very close together. We always went ahead, hand in hand, but our sister, Else, would hang onto Mother. She couldn't go by herself. No one knew until much later that she had congenital neo-blindness. All the doctors told her to sit around, take care of herself and do nothing. Finally a doctor in Thuringen prescribed special, large, thick glasses which enabled her to read. Then she finally started living.

My father wanted children but when they came he didn't care much . . . he wasn't a good father. Most of the time he was not home. He wanted to be the leader, to rule over everybody in the family as he did in the Freemason Lodge; there he was the Grand Master.

Once, when Fritz did something wrong Ma ran after him with a carpet beater. To get away he threw a glass at her and slammed the door in her face. Father was away on a trip, but still she wouldn't tell on Fritz when Father returned. She would protect him, which explains part of the tension between Ma and Pa. Another thing was that Ma was religious. She kept kosher, as she had in her parents' home; she had separate dishes and lit the Friday night candles. But Father would want to eat ham and butter with meat. She told me she couldn't do it . . . but what could she do? She buried her feelings.

I'll tell you, though Fritz and Pa didn't get along, in *this* way Fritz followed in his footsteps. After a while, he too denied Judaism. He was even less religious than Father. I think he rejected religion on Marxist, intellectual grounds.

Fritz loved the theater; he always wanted the theater. Whenever we went to the home of Grandma and Grandpa, he would go in the kitchen and behind closed doors, while the adults were out there talking or eating, he would entertain the maid and me with very theatrical persiflages he had made of big poems by Schiller and Goethe, or little parts from plays.

I remember one night he came home very late from the theater. Father had always said to be home by such and such a time, no matter what. But Fritz loved the theater so, he had to stay to the end of the performance. When he got home Father had locked him out, so Fritz hid outside in the bushes. Mother waited till Father went to sleep and then opened the door for him.

When he was a teenager, enrolled in the Gymnasium, he saw that Reinhardt was giving classes. He signed up, and had small parts in plays. Once he played *Mephisto* for Reinhardt. He took a lot from the theater for his workshops later.

The teachers at the Mommsen Gymnasium in Berlin where he went were very anti-Semitic. And, being a sensitive boy, he *felt* it and he was infuriated by it. Fritz was a brilliant student, for spite he wouldn't learn. They kept him back three times. As a result Pa took him out of school and put him into business . . . clothing, I think, or materials. That lasted only a few weeks, but for Fritz that was enough! It was a disaster, worse even than school had been. But it taught him a lesson: He got scared, I guess, that he'd be stuck in something he detested as much as business. So he signed up for a new school which he chose himself. It was a classical high school—Latin, Greek and one other language.

He did absolutely brilliantly. He did so well, in fact, that they let him skip the course work; all he had to do was the written work for the final exams, and then he graduated right away at the top of his class.

He got his M.D. from Frederick Wilhelm University in Berlin in 1921. He had a good practice. His patients gave him meat and things which he could no longer obtain.

When things got tough with money in Germany he went to New York. That was in 1923, when he was thirty. Always, when things became hard in life, Fritz would go away. When everything was well again, Mama wrote to him, "The market has stabilized with the mark and you can come back now." He could not become independent in America, anyway, because he didn't have an American medical license; and so he came back in '24. He was a neurologist and psychologist in Berlin . . . doing very well . . . and he was still very young.

Ach! The years go so quickly by. It seems all that was only a few hours ago. I feel that Fritz is still here today. It's really true . . . you only live now . . . he knew.

There are a few glimpses of Fritz' war experiences . . .

LEO ZEFF
He was a medical officer in the first World War, and he was heavily involved in gas warfare. And what he saw, he said one time, utterly, utterly embittered him all his life.

JACK DOWNING
Fritz was very much shaped by his four years in the trenches. He was with a chemical warfare company and he told a story about the "knockers"—these were men in his company who were given hammers with iron heads and rubber on them (my picture is of something like mechanics use for tires). Their job was to go over after the gas attacks and kill by hand any of the French or British soldiers felled by the gas. They'd knock them over the head like you'd knock an animal on the head. Fritz wasn't one of these; he was the medical officer.

I was a medic attached to the 36th Pioneer Battalion . . . especially trained for attacking the enemy with poison gas. I had to go to the more dangerous front trench. We were supported by two companies of poison gas-throwers. At three o'clock a.m., we made the gas attack, and within minutes we got the full barrage of the British guns. Two hours of hell . . . I got a superficial wound on my forehead. . . .

I had already succeeded in hardening and desentizing myself, but there [are] deaths I could hardly face . . . One happened . . . the night we made a gas attack . . . the wind changed direction. We . . . get the gas into our trenches! . . . the masks fail with many. And many, many get slight to severe poison and I am the only medic . . . I have only four small oxygen flasks . . . everyone is desperate for some oxygen . . . clinging . . . I have to tear the flask away from one to give some comfort to another [soldier]. More than once I was tempted to tear my mask off my sweating face.

FRITZ FAISS

When you listen to Fritz, you would believe that he was quite untouched. I would say the soft side of Fritz was very tender. . . .

He never elaborated on his experiences during the war, but I believe being in the field of medicine, the casualties brought from the battlefield caused a tremendous aftershock. As long as he was busy on the operating table and taking care of the patients, the casualties, he was all right. He kept himself very much in form, but when it was over—this extreme waste and the injuries to his own inner self—it was a shock he had to overcome. It was not easy. He was not able to do it on his own. He needed an analyst and he couldn't find one. Later he met a man he trusted—I think it was Wilhelm Reich—and he said that that was the first time that he trusted a man.

He had lost interest in medicine. It was not reaching deep enough for him. By trying to find out about it, he discovered his own self, quite fascinating aspects which did not fit at that time in any school and still do not fit into it well.

Even with the immense basic training he had received in Germany, he was in all respects a self-taught man.

Besides his beloved sister, Grete, Laura Perls, nee Lore Posner, knew Fritz longer than anyone I met. Their relationship spanned more than forty years of love, parenthood, collaboration, bitterness, catastrophe, uprootings, partings, and, always, reunions.

In his autobiography Fritz wrote:

> *Most of all, I felt more and more uncomfortable with Lore, who always put me to a disadvantage, and who at that time never had a good word to say about me. . .*

Yet there are over three hundred references to her in that autobiography, including.

> *. . .as Lore once pointed out to me, "good" habits are life supportive. . .*

> *I don't feel good writing about Lore. I always feel a mixture of defensiveness and aggressiveness. . . .*

> *Maybe one day I will feel like sorting myself out and will write about my voyeuristic compulsions centered around Lore, about her sometimes brilliant insights and her care for me when I was sick. . . .*

Evidently Lore Posner was a small compact dynamo of a woman when she was in her twenties. At 70, Laura Perls is still lithe and dynamic. I first met her in 1972 when I was in a Jim Simkin workshop. There were six therapists in training at Simkin's house in Big Sur then. When you're depressed and have seven sadists therapizing, you're really in trouble. I was.

One day, Laura Perls visited the Simkins and Jim asked her to lead the group. She knew nothing about what had been happening, and within twenty minutes of being in her presence, I felt restored. She was like fresh air. It was not so much that she was kind as that she was just human. "Allow yourself to be," she told me, and it was as though she had freed me from captivity.

The following year, Laura Perls and I spent some sixteen hours together talking about Fritz. . . .

LAURA PERLS

In the fall of 1926 I was a student at Frankfurt University. My Professor Adhémar Gelb and Kurt Goldstein were giving a joint seminar on the research they were doing in gestalt psychology, which was then a new field. I was bored. As I turned my attention from the speakers I saw this man sitting there whom I had never seen before. I didn't know who he was. I had the feeling: "There *he* is!"

A month later, through a friend who was also an assistant of Goldstein's, I met this man. Of course, it was Fritz. He had had his M.D. and was working with Goldstein in the Institute for Brain-injured Veterans from the first World War. Goldstein was working with the whole organism, not just parts of the human being. He was very avant-garde at that time. Gestalt psychology had then been largely concerned with sensory perception, and not as yet with personality. In working with brain lesions they discovered that when a particular organ is damaged or missing, the whole person changes and reorganizes through this loss.

Fritz was thirty-three when I met him and I was twenty-one. I was very young, naive, inexperienced . . . yah, he was *very* impressive!

He started to hang around, often with the friend who introduced us. He also came to some of Gelb's lectures and we had dinner afterwards.

Our relationship was always a very on-and-off affair. We were together and apart. He left Frankfurt and went to Vienna for a few months and then he went to Berlin; and in '28 he returned to Frankfurt for six months or so. I think he came back because I was there. When he was in Frankfurt we saw each other all the time. When he was not in Frankfurt, we met every few weeks somewhere for a weekend. We met in all kinds of places—in Würzburg and in Goslar and in Weimar. We went on vacations together. We were mostly in beautiful places where one could see a lot. We would walk around in the city and look at Goethe's garden house or the

beautiful old houses in Goslar. I still take these little walks
whenever I go to Germany

My mother loved Fritz. She was terribly impressed with
him. My father, however, was worried. I was his favorite
daughter. He said, "This man will never be able to look after
her."

I don't need anyone to look after me. I can look after myself,
I always could. I'm still doing it—and looking after a lot of
other people as well. I certainly looked after Fritz!

In *Garbage Pail* Fritz writes that I was pressing for marriage. It simply was not true. I never expected that he would
marry me, or that he would marry at all. And I didn't care.
For more than three years before we were married I was his
lover, and still I certainly didn't press. Actually, it was the
other way around. Fritz wanted to have a child. For a long
time he had the fear that he was sterile. I think he got married to a great extent to find out if he *could* have a child.

We were married in Berlin in 1930. Our wedding was not a
big, plush kind of thing. My sister had had that two years before and, though my father really wanted a big wedding for
us, too, we persuaded him to give us a car and a small wedding in City Hall.

When we got married my father got so sick that we
couldn't leave for our honeymoon! We stayed in a hotel in
my hometown for about three days until he had somewhat
recovered.

> *After World War II we visited the grave of Lore's
> father, and I had a grief explosion. And I mean an ex-
> plosion. Unexpected, taken completely by surprise as if
> some boil had broken open . . . I don't understand the
> outburst . . . my father-in-law and I were never close. As
> a matter of fact, if I was a black sheep for my family
> during my puberty years, I was a pitch black monster
> sheep for the Posner family.*

I know very little about Fritz' childhood. I know that his
father was a peculiar man who, like Fritz, was not, in the
long run, a family man. I saw him only a few times; he was

an old man then. He was tall and at one time probably very good-looking. He had a long white beard; in his old age Fritz looked not so different from him. He was a wine merchant. He traveled a lot selling Palestinian wines, and he founded Freemason lodges all over the place. Apparently he made quite a good living, but he didn't give much for the family. He didn't support Fritz' studies adequately either. Fritz worked most of the time, either in the theater or tutoring, and financed his studies mostly himself. His father contributed only in a very niggardly way. I think he never supported the family adequately because he was spending a lot of money traveling and working on his lodges.

He was quite into his own thing. He lived in the same house with his wife and the older daughter who did not get married, but he had a room to himself and meals were brought to him, and he went out by himself. Fritz hated his father. They were not on speaking terms when Fritz was growing up.

> *My father lived mostly outside the family boundary. At home he was a guest, to be served and respected.*
>
> *My father and mother had many bitter fights, including physical fights, when he beat her and she grabbed his magnificent beard. He often called her a piece of furniture or a piece of shit.*

Fritz did something similar to his father, I think, although on a different level. He would start an institute somewhere with a whole group of trainees and stay there for a while and then go to another place and start another one and another one. But when I once said, "You know, you are in many ways like your father," he got very mad. Somehow though, he mellowed. Years later he told me, "You know, I think in many ways I am like my father"—as if he had just discovered it!

Fritz' mother was a very down-to-earth person. She did her own housework, but she had vacuum cleaners and all the modern machines that came out. She was a very good person and a concerned mother. When there were free days in the museum or any kind of free concerts, she took her children. She came from a cultured family. Her brother was a doctor and her cousin was a famous lawyer.

> Mama . . . was very ambitious for me and not al all the "Jewish mother" type. But then my father kept her short of money and were glad if we had enough to eat. . . . Her father was a tailor and considering her background, her interest in art—especially in the theater—was amazing. . . .

> In Germany all apartment houses had front and court apartments. The front apartments with the view on the street had marble staircases and carpets and an extra entrance for servants. The court apartment in the Ansbacher Strasse had at least a little garden and a rod where the servants beat the dust out of the carpets. There was no electricity, thus no vacuum cleaners or refrigerators.

Her cooking was good, decent home cooking, but nothing special. Fritz wasn't really spoiled with eating; he ate mostly anything all the time. When you grew up in Germany during the first war and through the depression you ate what was available. He liked a lot of things—things like herring and sweet things. He liked marzipan. Whenever he came to visit me, I bought sticks of marzipan.

In many ways I am similar to Fritz' mother. Physically,

she was a small woman, too. And both of us looked after him. Actually, Fritz wasn't brought up to do anything. (Most men weren't, of course.) He slept in the dining room on a couch and Mama picked up whatever he left around. I was quite taken aback when I visited them the first time. His mother was sitting there sewing and dropped something. None of her three children picked it up. I did. In the beginning when we were married Fritz just let everything lie around. There was usually cigarette ash all over the place in spite of ashtrays. He dropped whatever he didn't use anymore, just anywhere. I felt like the clown in the circus who goes after the elephant with broom and shovel to clean up the shit!

Fritz had a good relationship with his mother, but he was also spiteful. He told me several times about how he had done something that got his mother terribly angry and she went after him with a carpet beater. He ran away and she couldn't catch him. He slammed the door in her face and turned the lock and then banged through the glass on the top of the door and made faces at her. He kept on doing that all his life in one way or another—annoying people until they went after him in some way and then he'd bang the door in their faces as if to say, "You can't do anything to me."

Fritz had always had this "you-can't-do-me-anything" attitude, and he often seemed inconsiderate. In school he was a very good mathematician but a lazy student. In one class, for example, there was a kind of proof that he was supposed to do and he did it brilliantly but in a different way from the way the teacher taught it. He got an "A" for the result but an "F" for attention. He was very proud of this. He called himself an *enfant terrible*. He liked to be where he could really do what he liked and not do what he didn't like, and where everybody did things for him. In this kind of community he could live.

Disapproval always provoked his spite. I remember his Uncle Eugene, his mother's brother, who was a doctor, was so against psychoanalysis. Of course, that didn't stop Fritz.

He had this ideal of being independent and self-sufficient. But it's adolescent to say, as he did in the gestalt prayer, "I am doing my own thing" or "I am my own person," because the adolescent comes home, drops his dirty clothes, changes into clean ones and goes out, and takes for granted that Mother takes care of everything. Talking about taking total responsibility for one's life is arrogance: One's life is always interdependent with the lives of other people and to ignore that means to ignore contact. I think Fritz ignored that to a great extent. . . .

Karen Horney was Fritz' first analyst in the early 'twenties. When he came to Frankfurt he went into analysis with Clara Happel. I started analysis with Happel because I wanted to be in on what Fritz and the friend who introduced us were talking about. The original motivation, really, was to get closer to him. Later, he was in analysis with Harnick, but Harnick said the marriage would prevent me from getting my doctorate and he wouldn't go on working with Fritz if he married me. And when we got married, he did break off that analysis. I was supposed to be rewriting my thesis at the time but I couldn't be bothered. For a while I thought I would just leave it, but later, after I had a baby, I went back and finished. Harnick had been mistaken and he apologized.

Fritz started with Reich after we got married, I think around the end of 1930, and Reich was his analyst for two or three years.

We left Germany in April of '33. It was just beginning then: The Reichstag fire was in February; the boycott day when they closed all the Jewish businesses and broke the windows was the first of April. We were living in Berlin at the time. Many thought that the persecution would last only a year or two (how could an idiot like Hitler last?) but when we saw this developing we thought we would leave Germany.

We left more for political reasons than because we were Jews, although there was already a lot of anti-Semitism. The *Eignet,* under which the Jews were deprived of ownership of their businesses, and the *Gleichschaltung,* where they put gentiles into Jewish businesses as so-called supervisors, had been put in effect. At the time Fritz was teaching a course at the *Arbeiterhochschule,* the Worker's University. We were members of the anti-fascist league and were very left-oriented.

Much earlier, in 1919, when Fritz was an advanced medical student at the University of Freiburg, he had to leave there because of leftist activities. He was involved with the *Arbeiter* and *Soldatenrat,* which was the political advisory council. They were people from the army, ex-officers like himself, sympathizing with the workers. I think he was afraid of being killed and he left Freiburg and went back to Berlin and finished his degree there.

When things started up in 1933 we applied for passports to play it safe. And just as soon as we got the passports we got threatening letters, probably through somebody in the passport office: "Are you getting the jitters, *Juden schweine* (you Jew pigs)?" When we got the visa to leave, Karen Horney gave a guarantee for us. We also had an affidavit from Dr. Brill, then president of the Psychoanalytic Association. Our last few nights in Berlin we slept in a different place every night. People were getting pulled out of their beds between two and four in the morning—not only Jews but also people who were active in any leftist or communist movement.

We knew that if the fascist regime really did develop, we couldn't live there and work the way we wanted to work. Economically, too, things were getting much worse. I had always received an allowance from my father, as much after I got married as before, but in 1933 I was reduced to half because his jewelry manufacturing and wholesale business was getting shaky. It had been very prosperous, one of the two big firms in Pforzheim. . . Fritz had an institute in which he did a lot of physical therapy, massage and radiation therapy, but one didn't get patients.

Amsterdam

LAURA PERLS

On the 25th of March my father died in Berlin. The funeral was in my hometown. We had planned to move into a new apartment, a somewhat cheaper one, on the first of April. My father had paid for the first one. I had the most wonderful modern furniture that was specially designed for me. Everything changed. We decided to leave Germany and we shipped the furniture to Holland.

I had already had my first child and in April I went with the baby, Renate, to my mother's house in Pforzheim, and Fritz went to Amsterdam. He had only two twenty-mark notes stuffed into a lighter. He stayed at a refugee camp there, and then finally, when he took an apartment together with some other refugees, I didn't want to be separated any longer so I simply arrived with the baby in September. We were twelve people living in a four- or five-room apartment on Amstelkade along the canal. It was a fairly nice neighborhood then. The apartment was actually rented by a divorced German woman with some money. I believe she had something with Fritz before I came and had gotten him out of the refugee camp. He had not been able to get a permit to work.

JACK DOWNING

The Dutch Jews set up places where they could get some minimum shelter, living with others in an attic. They had a very bad winter. They had no money.

LAURA PERLS

It was an unbelievable period. The furniture was held up at the border by the people from whom we were supposed to

15

rent the new apartment in Berlin until we paid them for the "damage" we did them by not moving in. I paid for it with the last little bit of money that I had. And we had no money in Amsterdam at all. When we finally got the furniture it was badly damaged from standing in open sheds on the border, and we had to sell it for almost nothing. We practically ate our furniture and had hardly anything left. We had over a thousand volumes in our library and we sold it for next to nothing. It was just too awful. We lost everything—our library—everything. It was. . . Ach! I can't even talk about it anymore.

My mother was horrified when she visited me in Amsterdam for a few days and found me washing the stairs with my bare hands. I had never done anything like that before—I was on my hands and knees. I didn't mind a bit. I wasn't a good cook, and another woman in the house cooked and I mainly washed and cleaned. I remember how it was that winter—fifteen degrees below zero! I can still see Fritz' long johns standing on the kitchen balcony to dry, frozen stiff!

I was pregnant again and the woman from whom we rented the place gave me the name of a doctor and I had an abortion there. Somebody denounced me to the police for having an illegal abortion; it could only have been her. Fritz was away. . . I had to go to the district office. I threw an hysterical fit so they would think that if I had had the child I would have probably gone crazy. I think that was the only real performance I ever gave in my life!

Those months were the hardest we ever had. We really didn't know what was going to happen and we lived from day to day. I had always had everything and so, for me, it was nearly a sport to see how little I could get along with. I did much better than some of the others. There were a few girls in the house where we lived who had been salesladies in a department store and they were horrified with the way they had to live now. I think, too, in a way, it was much harder for Fritz because he never had much. Our home in Berlin was the first place where he had really had good things. He had just started the practice there a few years before, and he had to leave behind all that equipment. I do think it was much more of a wrench for him to leave than it was for me.

We tried to get work permits in Amsterdam but we couldn't because there were too many refugees already. Actually, it was good luck that we didn't get them, because the ones who stayed all perished. My sister, her family who lived in Holland, all died.

Fritz went to London for a few days to ask Ernest Jones, Freud's biographer, if he knew of an opening anywhere. Jones had had an inquiry for an analyst and a training analyst from someone who had worked with Theodore Reik and was doing analysis in South Africa. The more famous analysts were already established; they wanted to come here to America, not to South Africa. We would have gone anywhere we could live and work. Fritz already spoke English and apparently we were the only ones who responded favorably to Jones' inquiry, so at the end of December we went to South Africa.

Johannesburg

The image of Africa fashioned by Johnny Weissmuller in Tarzan movies was not the Africa that the Perls came to in 1934. It was instead the metropolitan city of Johannesburg, populated by 288,000 people, and was in total contrast to the oppression of nazi Germany and the difficulties of Amsterdam.

In his new home, Fritz soon became a successful psychiatrist.

LAURA PERLS

It was really a godsend. They were good years for us in many ways. We prospered immediately and we developed independence without interference and without having to follow party lines, either politically or psychoanalytically. We probably became much more creative than we could have if we had stayed. We lived as comfortably as I ever had in Germany, and remember, I come from a well-to-do family. Fritz had never lived so comfortably before. The whole time we had house servants and, for four years, my mother's maid from Germany as nurse for the children.

From 1935 to 1939, Sylvia Behrmann was a five-times-a-week, lie-on-the-sofa patient of Fritz'.

SYLVIA BEHRMANN CONRAD

Fritz spoke more during our sessions than most psychoanalysts did, except when we had a battle of wills and I wouldn't talk nor would he. Usually I gave in first. The relationship always had an element of non-patient in it.

He had trouble with Dr. Wulf Sachs, the man who considered himself a psychoanalyst and who had been instrumental

18

in bringing Fritz to South Africa. The trouble was that Fritz
was contemptuous of Sachs, as he was of everyone else, and
Sachs didn't like being put down. I agree with Fritz that
Sachs was incompetent—he tried to treat me psychoanalytically at the same time he was treating my whole family and
me physically. I walked out after two weeks. I did not know
any of Fritz' other patients. There were no groups in those
days. I think Fritz was regarded as rather a queer duck by the
general community. He built the first "modern" house with
a flat roof and that sent the neighbors up the wall because it
stood out from the conventional ones around it.

LAURA PERLS
We were terribly in love with each other and the baby—those
were very good years. He acknowledged then that I was his
wife, his lover, and the mother of his child. At first he was
crazy about Renate. For the first three or four years of her
life she hung on his neck all day long, and he loved it.

> *When Renate, our elder child, was born, I was fond of*
> *her and even began to reconcile myself somewhat to*
> *being a married man. But when later I was blamed for*
> *anything that went wrong, I began to withdraw more*
> *and more from my role as a* pater familias. *They [Lore*
> *and Renate] lived, maybe still do, in a very peculiar*
> *clutching symbiosis.*

Her face is a perfect blending of Fritz and Laura. Her voice
is deep and has a decided British quality. Her laugh is
hearty—it shakes walls. She lies on the couch in her living
room in Leonia, New Jersey, and talks about her father with
anger.

RENATE PERLS
Fritz left me out of his whole life. . . .
  Since I was four years old, I've actually had only a pretend
father. I've always had a terrible need for Fritz to love me.
All along there was the hope that he would, and that's been
going on for forty-odd years.

I've tried to make peace with him. I wrote him a long letter at a time when I was very ill and thought I was going to die. But I did not hear one word. All I got back from that, somewhere along the way, was, "Ren always wants something."

For once a letter from Ren without asking me for something, but I'm sure the letter is an overture for a request that likely will come via Lore.

I guess I did always want something. I wanted a father. I always wanted a father. I kept looking for him and looking for him: Obviously, I built my own idea of what he should have been. He was a father figure for a lot of people, but dammit, I was his daughter.

He didn't have time for his own kids. The only time he had time for my brother, Steve, was when he got his Ph.D. "Be somebody! Be somebody! Be somebody!" Did I have to prove I was somebody in order for him to understand me and be with me?

I tried very hard to be somebody—I tried to be *Fritz!* And the more I tried the less he cared for me. And the more he pushed me away, the more I tried to be like him.

He taught me to smoke when I was four years old in hopes that I would not smoke. He evidently gave me only one cigarette. Perhaps if he'd given me a whole pack it might have made me violently ill, but I liked it, and for a long time I smoked like a fiend. (I don't now and haven't for years.)

One day when Mother wasn't around Fritz got angry with me for something I can't remember, and he locked me in the garage for the whole afternoon. I was terrified in there—there was very little light. John, the manservant we had then, said to me, "I want to let you out, but I don't dare." And at the age of three and a half I understood that he couldn't let me out or he would lose his job.

It wasn't something that happened all that frequently, it's just that they were so memorable. Another time Fritz had bought a package of flags, little flags from all over the world, wrapped in cellophane—this was at the beginning of the war. He left them lying around the house; he didn't say we couldn't have them or anything, so my girl friend and I decided to wear a flag of a different country every day. We had been doing this for a few days and one morning, not knowing what it was, I put the swastika on. I guess Fritz really hadn't looked in the package, I don't know, but when I came in to have breakfast in my school uniform he took one look at me, tore the swastika off and shook me so hard that my bones rattled like a skeleton and I peed in my pants.

Now, as an adult, I can understand his violent reaction, but as a nine-year-old I was embarrassed, to say the least, to have this happen in front of someone. What did I do wrong? I didn't know what the swastika represented and he never explained. He should have told me; I just didn't know. I would never have had the guts to consciously provoke him. I didn't go against *anything* he said. I was petrified of him. The two of us could be in a room for two minutes and one or the other would walk out. We didn't have anything to say to each other.

I have beautiful and tender memories of Fritz, too. When I was four Fritz fell on the tennis court and pulled a tendon or something. Anyway, he was walking with a crutch on one side and a cane on the other. We lived in a very modern house with a swimming pool and tennis court and roof garden, in a lovely residential section; the area wasn't completely built up and the two of us took a walk through the fields. I was running back and forth a little ahead of Fritz, and back to him and so on. I remember the jump suit I was wearing that day. I was feeling absolutely marvelous.

He often took me to his favorite haunts—various restaurants. I'd get an ice cream soda, or sometimes lunch. But then he would read, or he would talk to friends. One time we were in an upstairs balcony- type cafe and I remember seeing a dog run over. I don't know what this has to do with Fritz, but he was there, and it's a vivid memory.

I also remember one of our trips to Pretoriaskop. Before Fritz was in the army he owned a laundry there with somebody else. We used to pick someone up in a one-horse town called Primrose. This guy had a son, and the two of us would

have a ball. We would crouch on the back seat of the car and
every time we went around a corner we'd fall down. Looking
back on it, I'm surprised Fritz permitted us to do this, but he
did.

One day there was this horrendous experience of not being
met after nursery school and having to walk home by myself.
It was a mile and a half or two miles and I decided to take the
long way around which Fritz sometimes took in the car, and
I got completely lost. I kept coming back to the same place
again and didn't know where the hell I was. Finally I got to
the main road, Oxford Street it was, and I saw a horse and
cart coming up the street. It was during the days when they
had horse carts for delivery and pickups. Anyhow, I heard a
terrible crack; and the horse had broken his leg! I stood
watching the whole thing!

When I got home I was an hour and a half late. Neither of
my parents were around and my nurse was not in the least
concerned. "How dare you come home an hour and a half
late!" She was a bitch on wheels, another one who locked me
up for a whole day once when my parents were away. I
couldn't tell them about her. I learned very, very early in life,
"You keep your mouth shut and do as you're told." All the
natural curiosity and spontaneity of childhood was just
completely knocked out of me.

As a child you don't realize the reasons for things. It's
only later when you grow up and have a nervous breakdown
and become a total wreck that you start to think of these
things. Every damned fear or phobia I ever had was brought
on by Fritz, in a way. Everything goes back to things that
happened with him, and whenever I think I'm rid of his
ghost, he's with me again.

SYLVIA BEHRMANN CONRAD
My nephew went to the same nursery school as his daughter,
Renate, who was then about five, and when I picked Stanley
up at school, I often picked up Renate too, as the Perls'
house was on my way to my sister's house. Once, Renate refused to come home with me. I told Fritz or Laura or the
nurse (I can't remember which—you're asking me to re-

member forty years back and that's a long time), and expected one of them to pick her up. But the next day I learned that she had walked all the way home—about two miles. Fritz didn't seem perturbed. He was only surprised that she could find her way home.

Once in his early days in the U.S., when Renate was having some kind of trouble I expressed some sympathy and concern; he shrugged it off, implying to me that his only responsibility was in having fathered her and the rest was none of his business

LAURA PERLS

We had our first really serious disagreement when I was pregnant with my second child. It was very early during our first year in South Africa when we were building the practice and a house, too. He was afraid another child would be too much of a burden. I told him, "If you don't want the child, I'll have it. It will be my child." And it was. For a while we were pretty cool because Fritz was not in agreement with my pregnancy. I had already had one abortion in Holland, and although we had both agreed on it, it was very traumatic for me and I refused to have another one. When the boy, Stephen, was born, he was a lovely child. Immediately, a very nice, bright boy, and Fritz was reconciled to the child. But he didn't really have anything to do with him. It was the European attitude that men never handled small babies, and that was more or less Fritz' attitude—it was a woman's job.

Steve was born in 1935, and Renate, who was four at the time, got jealous: She started sucking her thumb and wetting her pants. And Fritz simply dropped her. He could not stand her anymore. It was very traumatic for her, and remained so for a long time.

The following year Fritz went to Marienbad for the International Psychoanalytical Congress. He was away for about three months and when he came back he had completely lost interest in the children and was just involved in his own work. And then the war broke out and he got into the South African Army.

He was in the Army for four and a half years. During that

time we were involved with *Ego, Hunger and Aggression,* and with our practice. Though we had a nurse for the children, I spent quite a bit of time with them. He spent very little. Occasionally he might take them to the circus or the ice rink or something like that, but that was about all. We usually went on vacations alone; a few times we took the children.

RENATE PERLS
Around my tenth birthday we were on the Oribi tour about seventy miles outside of Durban, South Africa. In fact, it was my tenth birthday present from him. (That, and a pound note so I could buy all the junk I couldn't buy before, because my mother said, "No, you can't have that.") It's one of those things that will be with me forever. It's the most beautiful place I think I've ever been in my life—forests and rivers—a place of great beauty. There were some very steep drops, one of them about two thousand feet. There was a rock jutting out dropping into the middle of nothing. I was pretty far from the edge and I wanted to go just a little closer; I took a few steps and Fritz yelled at me. He scared me so much it ruined my day. I realized afterwards that he didn't want me to fall, but for a long time I was afraid of heights.

I think of other trips and of all the times I was sent away. What were supposed to be vacations for us, was, for me, being sent away, not to camps per se, but to places where they had children. Some friends of the family had a farm in Rustenberg which was very nice, but I was miserable there.

I found out afterwards that these were times my mother was having minor surgery. But nothing was ever talked about around the house. Everybody was very secretive; Steve and I were never told anything. When we sold that fantastic house I was eight years old. I went to the candy store one day and when I got back there was a "For Sale" sign on the house. That was it. I was hysterical, "My God, why doesn't somebody tell me something!?" We were never told anything. It was always, "Mind your own business."

LAURA PERLS

When we had been married a couple of years, Fritz had said to me, "You know, I am disappointed. I always thought if we lived together you would make me work. . . and you are just as lazy as I am." He didn't know that I made him work by supporting everything he did and keeping everything out of his way that could possible disturb him. Of course, the children very much resented that I kept *them* out of the way, too. He couldn't stand it when they got under his feet, and he wouldn't have stayed with the family as long as he did . . . he did stay, basically, until Steve went to college.

STEPHEN PERLS

A lot of people ask me what it was like growing up with a famous father. When I was growing up he wasn't famous. He was very much into his own things, but there wasn't any of the notoriety. It was only the last few years of his life and mostly since he died that there's been that influence.

We lived in three different houses in South Africa. The first one (where I was born) was white with lots of land around it. It was quite luxurious. Laura and Fritz had a tennis court and swimming pool built, which means both of them must have done well economically rather quickly. As you know, they had to get out of Germany fast and they arrived with hardly any money.

One flash I have of the period was Fritz making some paper boats. Then a heavy, fat woman (I don't know if she was a friend or a maid or what) came diving into the water and sank my little boats!

We moved from the first house—it was the beginning of World War II—because it was way out in the suburbs, and since there was gas rationing none of the patients could afford to go out there. The house in the city didn't have a swimming pool and tennis court and I felt very bad about that. I was still a little kid.

I vaguely remember my father coming home on weekends in his captain's uniform. He was a practicing psychiatrist in the South African Army. I must have been four or five years old. Other than seeing him in his army clothes and relaxing around the house, I don't remember doing much with him.

I remember spending a lot more time with my mother, but a couple of times the whole family went on longer vacations. We took trips up into the veldt area to look at the animals, or down to the ocean. But mostly I remember talking *about* my father, and him not being there.

We had nice grass and grounds where we lived so I'd bring my friends over occasionally. But one message was very clear in all the houses we lived in (because therapy and group rooms were part of the houses we lived in) and that was, "Quiet! Stay away! Don't bother us, kid. Take your friends elsewhere."

I didn't have angry feelings toward my father at any time when I was younger. I was a little angry as I got older, mostly comparing myself with some of the other kids. Other kids' parents would come to high school functions and that kind of stuff. It wasn't strong anger, it was more wondering "how come?" It wasn't, "Goddamn him, he should be more involved with me." It was more, you know, "They're not interested in me. I'll just leave them alone and go do my own thing." My father was never angry; he was simply so busy with his own things. It was more just kind of a non-involvement that became part of my lifestyle.

LAURA PERLS

Fritz did not really have any close, intimate relationships. He had admirers and disciples, but the friends were, at least initially, my friends. On his own, he hardly had any close, intimate relationships. I think I was, in a way, his only friend. He talked to me about other people, and lots of things he certainly never talked about anywhere else.

Fritz had talent for anything. So have I; but he didn't really follow up. He never worked hard at anything. And Fritz was never going to be anything but himself. What he did, he did! He did things just to prove that he could really do them, and then he gave up just at the point where he would have had to work at being *really good*. A lot of things

he did just to find out if he could do them. I think he got
married that way and had a child that way. He learned to
play the violin just to a certain point when we had a music
teacher—a German refugee who was a good violinist—actually staying in our house. And it was the same with his paintings. Some of his paintings were nice, but he didn't work at
it, you know, he played with it. He always loved to sketch in
the zoo; he liked animals, particularly the gorilla. He did ice
skating and later he learned flying. He loved to dance. We
danced very well together, and even in South Africa we
danced a lot at home. But I appreciated more the fact that he
did these things than what he did.

SYLVIA BEHRMANN CONRAD
He learned to fly and took me up in a two-seater. I was
scared and became airsick. He was a very good pilot and the
sickness was due to me, not to him. He worked on my fear of
the flight and some of my tension in therapy, and about ten
days later he took me up again and I was OK. Having had the
experience and expressing my fear helped me. As far as I
know he went out alone, though he may have taken up others
as he did me. He rented an open plane (a Piper Cub, I think).
Fritz loved to do anything different. When they built an ice
rink in Johannesburg he learned to skate. I went with him a
couple of times. At other times I acted as Fritz' secretary.

A group of us went for a weekend to Basutoland—now
Lesotho—and it was very good, just enjoying the scenery
and working a bit on his book, *Ego, Hunger and Aggression.*
On the drive back Fritz went 85 MPH. and he was very
excited about it, as he said he had never driven so fast before.

*It was during these rambunctious years that Fritz' major
contributions to psychotherapy began to take shape . . . .*

LAURA PERLS
In South Africa, Fritz first concentrated on the oral resistance. I became interested in feeding and weaning in connection with the birth and feeding of my first child. I started to

research that a bit and Fritz took it up and developed it with
the concept of resistance—and that later became part of *Ego,
Hunger and Aggression*. When Fritz was an army psychiatrist, he had a lot of free time; he came home on weekends
and we sat and worked on the book.

I actually wrote some of the chapters of *Ego, Hunger and
Aggression* and contributed a great deal to the book, but
Fritz always needed the acclaim and the fame. I didn't. I was
so much in love with him I gave *everything* to him, and he
took it and kept on taking it. In the first editions (South
African and British editions), he mentions in the foreword
that I contributed a lot and cites the particular chapters. But
later, in the American reprints, he wrote a new introduction
and conveniently forgot my contribution.

That original foreword read:
> *. . .In writing this book I have had much help, stimula-
> tion and encouragement from books, friends and teach-
> ers; but above all from my wife, Dr. Lore Perls. The
> discussions I have had with her of the problems brought
> forward in this book have clarified many issues; and she
> has made valuable contributions to this work; as, for in-
> stance, the description of the dummy attitude.*
>
> > *F.S. Perls*
> > *December 1944*
> > Ego, Hunger and Aggression, *1st Edition.*

Ultimately everything was discussed. He put in some things I
didn't agree with and which, later on, he didn't either, like
the extreme hostility to Freud. At the time it was called *A
Revision of Freudian Analysis, a Separation from Freud.*

Fritz had gone to Vienna from South Africa after the
Marienbad Congress to see Freud. He had an appointment
with him—I think the appointment was made by Anna
Freud, whom Fritz knew. But Freud was already old and
very sick with cancer. His lower jaw was artificial, and very
painful. He probably couldn't speak very much. He was no
longer teaching and was only seeing some of his old friends
and colleagues, so he was not at all interested. He saw Fritz
for only three or four minutes. Freud signed his picture for

him and that's all. *[The picture now hangs in a simple frame in Laura's study.]*

Fritz had a great respect for Freud, of course, but he didn't think of himself as a successor. He thought of himself as somebody who was pioneering psychoanalysis in Africa,* and he felt that Freud should have been interested in that. At the time, however, Freud was pulling in, he wasn't expanding anymore. I understand that now, and Fritz probably would now, too, but he didn't then. He was forty-three and really very successful as a therapist, and it offended his vanity. He was devastated, not because he idolized Freud— Fritz had no idols—but because he admired him.

I was hurt mostly by the repercussions that Fritz was, and still is, to a great extent, regarded as the sole founder of gestalt therapy. Fritz always needed a lot of support, although he didn't realize this. He either ignored the support he got, or he took it for granted.

Gestalt therapy has been developing through the years, you know, so it's not possible to sort out who thought or said what. Actually, there is also existential philosophy and a whole phenomenological and Eastern approach in gestalt therapy. In any case, Fritz and I began together. We started the Institute in 1952 after the publication of *Gestalt Therapy: Excitement and Growth* in 1950 and that is really when things started to jell. Up until then what we were doing didn't have any name.

You see, Fritz and I were both trained in psychoanalysis and started off doing straight analysis. Fritz was an analyst in our years in Germany. By then, of course, we were already influenced by Reich. Fritz had worked with Schilder at the Wagner-Jauregg Clinic; Schilder had already started combining analysis and gestalt concepts; but he didn't get into gestalt therapy.

Fritz became theoretically aware of muscular armor through Reich, but I knew that already from my own body

---

*Fritz had founded the South African Institute for Psychoanalytic Studies.

work. I saw all my patients as physical types—certain breathing types were associated with certain aspects of neurosis.
When we were in South Africa I worked twice a week with a
eurhythmics teacher from Frankfurt out on our big lawn,
and I wanted Fritz to join. He said at the time it was girls'
stuff and it was boring.

MOSHE FELDENKRAIS
I read the first book he wrote when he was still in South
Africa. I was very impressed because this was the first time I
saw an intelligent approach to the body manifestations, emotional and psychological, the way he understood them. I
found the technique he then used on his students already
more advanced than that in my work at home. At the time, I
didn't have much support from people around and I felt that
Perls was the kind of intelligence that could make therapy
much more efficient and more direct.

LAURA PERLS
Fritz stayed in South Africa for nearly thirteen years and I
for nearly fourteen. We were both in private practice except
for the years from 1942-1946 when Fritz was a psychiatrist in
the army. We started a psychoanalytical group there and we
started training a few people. . . .

After several years, our position as training analysts was
suddenly revoked by the International Association. It was
based on some kind of order that anyone who had not
already been training in Europe could not be a training analyst anywhere else. Fritz wasn't accepted as a full member of
the Psychoanalytic Association before because, actually, he
hadn't gotten through with his analysis.

Fritz' problems came about because he had given that lecture in '36 at the Psychoanalytic Conference in Marienbad,
Czechoslovakia. The paper was on oral resistances and it was
not well received. Most people didn't understand it. It was
more Reichian, and Reich was already suspect. In '37 or '38,
the man who had called us to South Africa made some kind
of *shtunk* at the Lucerne Congress. Fritz felt resentful about

the whole psychoanalytic movement, at not being understood and at being rejected.

One of the reasons we left South Africa immediately after the war was because, although he was accepted as an army psychiatrist, when he came back they didn't license him.

But we had never really intended to stay in South Africa. We had already applied for immigration to America, but the quota was filled. World War II broke out, and after the war, faced with the '48 elections, we didn't want to be there anymore. Smuts, the prime minister, didn't want to be re-elected because he was already in his 70s. Fritz had met Smuts only once, but he admired him and had been influenced by his book *Holism and Evolution*. And we could anticipate how the new elections would go with the mood in the country and the Union party more or less leaderless. A lot of people—particularly the artists and intelligentsia—were leaving. The intelligentsia was, by and large, democratic and radical, and working against apartheid, although apartheid didn't become a slogan until the Nationalists came to power. It was an intellectual task to aid the Blacks in South Africa, just as in Germany it had been an intellectual task to ally ourselves with the worker. Although the apartheid problem has come much more to the fore now, one wasn't very much directly touched by the political climate at that time.

STEPHEN PERLS
From the family's standpoint South Africa was a cultural desert. Nothing going on, just dull, dead. My mother particularly wanted my sister and me to grow up in an environment that was more culturally stimulating, and America seemed to be much more of a possibility. Secondly, the political climate in South Africa was changing around '46. The apartheid government was getting stronger. They hadn't come into power at that point, but things definitely seemed to be going in a fascistic direction. The Afrikaners were focusing on the Blacks of Africa, and their orientation did not seem to be that much different from the nazis' and naturally that was against both my parents' views. They wanted to get out of

there before they got into the same routine they had been
through in Germany. . . .

SYLVIA BEHRMANN CONRAD
I didn't see much of Fritz as I was pregnant and involved in
family. I did see him again in 1946. They had sold their very
modern house. He had changed a great deal. He was thinking of coming to the States, and did leave while I was still in
South Africa, I believe, though Laura did not come until
later.

LAURA PERLS
It was in '46 or '47, and I did all the breaking up in South
Africa. . . like selling things and the house. . . and I was so
busy, too. I had an enormous practice there. During the war
I worked ten, twelve, thirteen hours a day and six, seven days
a week. In addition, I had the family.

New York

As he had when they left Germany, the man of the house went ahead to scout things out. . . .

LAURA PERLS

Fritz came in '46 and he went first to Canada because he didn't have a residence permit here [in the U.S.] yet. He worked for about six months or so in Montreal and then visited my brother in Providence, who had come shortly before the war.

Fritz stayed with them for a few weeks and they advised him, wrongly, that he shouldn't try to settle in New York because there was so much competition there. I don't think they had any idea of his professional status and potential. Then Fritz went to New Haven for a few months and started a practice there. The psychiatric chair there had been vacated at that time and they apparently suspected that he was counting on that and there was a kind of concerted front against the outsider. He was very unhappy there and he nearly came back to South Africa where I had stayed with the children, because we didn't break up there completely until we knew that we could make it here.

Then he visited Erich Fromm in New York for a few days, and Fromm said, "I don't understand why you don't stay in New York. I guarantee you will have a practice in three months." And in three *weeks* he had a practice! He had gotten friendly with the people from the Washington School of Psychiatry, the William Alanson White Institute. Actually, they wanted him as a training analyst. But they wanted him to take his medical degree again here. Fritz was then already over fifty, and he said if he goes to school he goes as a teacher, not as a student. So instead he took over the practice of someone who had gone out to the West Coast.

33

When Clara Thompson suggested to me that I should become a training analyst in the Washington School, I declined. I refused to accept the notion of adjusting to a society which was not worth adjusting to. . . .

Among the people Fritz contacted when he came to New York was Charlotte Selver who had a well-established practice as a teacher of sensory awareness. . . .

CHARLOTTE SELVER

I didn't know anything about Perls. He called me one day in New York, saying that Erich Fromm had told him about my work and suggested that he visit me. Perls had just come from South Africa and he wanted to settle down in New York. He was very alone when he came. I helped him to furnish his first office. He visited me often, but I honestly must say that this man never appealed to me, although his ideas interested me. He started to take private lessons with me. He was often in despair. Later when I went to the Cape and gave courses in Provincetown, he took part in them. He studied for about one and a half years, often a few times a week.

He was very impressed with our work, and he asked me to work with him. He wanted me to take his patients before him and kind of open them up for what he wanted to work on with them later . . . a collaboration. I felt used. I did not want to work in this way. He offered a big salary, and said, "Charlotte, work with me and I will make you famous." I told him that if I wanted to become famous, I'd do it myself. He always had something in mind. My refusal was the end of his interest in me at that time, I would say.

Like all true agents of change, Fritz took a fairly deprecatory view of the psychiatric establishment. So it was not surprising that the psychiatric establishment held a similar view of Fritz.

Alexander Lowen is Executive Director of the Institute for Bioenergetics Analysis. . . .

ALEXANDER LOWEN

Fritz told me that when he came to this country for the first time, he went up to see his old analyst, Wilhelm Reich, in New York, and was quite put out about the reception he received from Reich. Reich asked him if knew about the energy that he had discovered —the *orgone*—but Fritz hadn't heard anything about Reich's later work since they broke contact many years earlier in Germany, when Reich had gone on to Norway and Fritz had gone on to South Africa.

Fritz was put off by the fact that Reich wasn't interested in what Fritz was doing, and I guess Reich, himself, was a little put off that Fritz had no awareness or interest in this whole big development that Reich was pursuing. It was a short meeting; there was a kind of lack of communication, and I don't think Fritz saw Reich again. He was a little bitter about the whole experience with Reich.

The story of his meeting with Freud sounds very similar to that.

Yes? It's very hard for Fritz to take a back seat to anybody. It's very surprising that he ever worked with Reich, because Reich is much more like that than Fritz.

Fritz and I didn't get along too well on a personal level, although we had a certain respect for each other. No, he wasn't abrasive with me because we never let it get to that, but he *was* abrasive—there's no question about that. I just kept a little distance from him. The reason was, I didn't respect his personal behavior; that's really true—I didn't respect it. He characterized himself as a dirty old man, and he *was* a dirty old man. To my way of thinking, it didn't go with being a leader in the field of therapy.

Another of the psychological professionals who disliked Fritz in those first years in New York was Rollo May. . . .

ROLLO MAY

In 1948, I rented an office from him in New York and he wanted me to buy a radio from him. He said that as a recompense he would send me a couple of ten-dollar patients. Ten dollars in those days was a fair amount of money—especially for those of us who were more or less beginning. It was kind of a bribe.

I didn't know him much in that period. He was a bona fide analyst who worked long periods with patients. I simply met him a few times. I didn't want to know him either. I didn't find him in the slightest bit attractive. I found him a boor— an authoritarian boor. To me as well as to others. An authoritarian boor.

Boor and unattractive though he was, and was to remain, for some, Fritz had his admirers. Marilyn Rosanes-Berrett was one of the early ones. . . .

MARILYN ROSANES-BERRETT
I first met Fritz about '51. He and Laura were giving lectures. They lived on Central Park West—not where she is now but a different apartment then. And I can remember Laura sitting in the park combing her little girl's hair, while Fritz was up there, in the apartment, demonstrating and lecturing.

I didn't have much contact with him at first. He had a horrible reputation for sleeping with his patients and I was told not to have anything to do with him. I met many patients who slept with him and said it was one of the greatest experiences they ever had and they were so happy for it.

There's no person outside of my husband, parents, or child who's had the effect that Fritz has had on me. There's no person like him who has done as much for me—who's been good, so kind and a bastard to me; nobody gave me as much in as many ways. I have tears and I'm all upset, and I have goose pimples, and I have every kind of reaction—and Fritz, I wish you were here right now, I've missed you so many times, you've left me such a richness. I've seen him in every way: mad, crazy, beautiful, one with God—everything that man had the ability to be. And he knew when I was phony, he knew when I was true. He could spot a person—one of the people, a psychiatrist named Marty, asked to come into our workshop. Fritz said to me, "I never want to see that man."

Fritz loved some types—open bastard-bitch—open defenses, that type. He didn't like anyone who would placate him or be too good to him or used good-girl or good-boy defenses—that drove him up the wall. I used those defenses for years. He did some very nice things for me, when I needed him. He was there for me. he did beautiful things when I was needing.

FRANK RUBENFELD
I first saw Fritz at an APA convention. Ruth Cohen, Albert Ellis, Marie Colman Nelson, Betsy Mintz, and a bunch of people were sitting around and talking about how they had grown personally and professionally. Fritz was the only man up there who wasn't wearing a tie or a jacket. Some guy was droning on and on, and Fritz interrupted him and said, "I may be a son of a bitch, but I'm not a masochist. You talk like a machine gun. I'm not going to listen to you." I cracked up. That was my first encounter with Fritz.

Fritz had published Ego, Hunger and Aggression *in South Africa, and once he was settled in New York, quickly realized the value of the printed word in getting his message to a greater audience. He turned to the Julian Press and Arthur Ceppos with his second book. In 1950, Art Ceppos took a chance in publishing the book that was off the beaten path. He gambled well. Sales of* Gestalt Therapy *increased from year to year and now, after eighteen years, it is still increasing steadily.*

ARTHUR CEPPOS
I was a father figure for Fritz (that seems very funny) because I was his publisher. I published Fritz' first American book, *Gestalt Therapy: Excitement and Growth in the Human Personality*. The name of the firm was Julian. It was

my firm, I was the president. I had been working closely with William Alanson White Psychiatric Foundation and that's why Erich Fromm, Freda Fromm Reichman, Clara Thompson, all came to me.

At that time I was working within the orthodox body of psychiatry and only the really imaginative ones would dig what the hell gestalt therapy might possibly do for them. Well, of course, they also rejected Reich. Incidentally, when the book first came out it didn't sell; it was very hard to push it because Fritz was not accepted in any way.

I met Fritz when he just got over here; I met him through Paul Goodman. It must have been 1950. They had rented a brownstone somewhere in the seventies or eighties and I signed a contract with him; Paul did all the work and he got the advance.

Paul Goodman was not a psychotherapist. He had been a patient of Laura's. In the beginning Paul was tremendously fascinated by Fritz. I don't know whether he would have admitted it at that time but certainly the work he did with Fritz in this book is just about the best work, the most discriminating that Paul ever did. Paul wrote the last section and he edited the first two sections, which are based on philosophical evaluations that I think emerged out of Fritz' concepts and not out of Paul's. The first section is completely Fritz. Fritz needed nobody else to write for him, he was a highly articulate guy and a damn good writer.

Fritz wrote afterwards; he had written *Ego, Hunger & Aggression* before he wrote this book. Paul certainly was a writer. Hefferline was merely used because he had the teaching position at Columbia University.

Fritz always said that I was an oddball, that I would pick up what nobody else would pick up. He meant this as a recommendation. I think in paperback the sales are over half a million; it is still available in hardback. That is considered the central book. Fritz wasn't too fond of it because he felt as though Laura had a share in it. She didn't though, really; it was Fritz' work. That was the book that brought it all out.

MARILYN ROSANES-BERRETT
I resented it when Fritz told me to work with Jim Simkin.
"Fritz," I said, "I could teach him. I don't need him."
What he was saying in his lecture sounded like an old rehash.
Fritz said, "Let yourself go to him," and I did. He's no
Fritz, but I got something.

*In time, Fritz was to be the catalyst in changing the lives and
careers of many of those whom he touched. In 1952, Fritz
touched Jim Simkin.*

JIM SIMKIN
When I started working at the Veterans Administration in
New York City, I was just thirty. Later, I became chief psychologist at the VA in Newark, New Jersey. I had worked
hard for this goal and finally got it and I felt like shit. I was
feeling empty and depressed; I kept looking for something.

I couldn't find what I wanted. Finally, in the spring of '52
I went to the Gestalt Therapy Institute* to meet Fritz Perls,
whom I had heard about from a friend. I liked what I saw
and I stayed with him. Most of the time he was right on. I felt
I was working with somebody who was working mostly with
me and not with a theory or some idea. I found working with
him very difficult, but I'd get through some of my anger and
frustration and some of my life would come back.

Fritz and I had many differences. I was not an immediate
disciple, nothing like that at all. I was a skeptic all the way
through. And I'm still skeptical of some of the gestalt
therapy theory.

The gestalt he was doing then was quite different in the
sense that the couch was used—there was no face-to-face. In
those days I was on the couch and Fritz sat behind with the
dark glasses, Hollywood-style. I started therapy with him in
'52 and finished in early '55.

Incidentally, he used to con people with bargains. When I
first interviewed for therapy with him, for example, I could

---

*Fritz and Laura had opened the Gestalt Therapy Institute of New York a
few months earlier.

have one hour for fifteen dollars, or ninety minutes for
twenty.

When I finished with Fritz, I was still working at the VA in
Newark, and started private practice after I finished my
training. He suggested that I do some control work. So I saw
Laura a couple of sessions . . . I didn't like working with her.

LAURA PERLS
Jim Simkin worked a short while with me when Fritz left. He
was very hostile at the time and he didn't really want to work
with me . . . he was very resistant. He then went to Los
Angeles and it came out later in a group session that we had
in Los Angeles that actually he was very resentful that Fritz
had left him. And he took it out on me. He was bolder with
me than he was with Fritz. But then he worked very little
with me and we didn't really click. . . .

JIM SIMKIN
Fritz abandoned the Gestalt Institute in New York about '55
to Laura and the two Pauls, Goodman and Weisz. He got
restless and went to Ohio and did something there. Then he
went to Florida and started something there.

Florida

What brought me to Miami Beach I could not exactly say. I found nothing of . . . the color and excitement of Durban where I loved to vacation when we lived in South Africa . . . in plastic Miami Beach, but swimming, the only sport left to me, pulled me there from New York.

GERTRUDE KRAUSE

Bill Groman, a young businessman in Miami, got entranced with Fritz' book *Gestalt Therapy* and started to correspond with him. At some point Bill said, "Come down to Miami. I'll get a group for you." And Fritz said, "Fine."

At that time Bill's friends were primarily dentists, and the first group—a large group—consisted of dentists, their wives, their hygienists, and a few other people. Most of them were impressed with Fritz. However, he got no professional recognition or acceptance, except by one psychiatrist by the name of Earl Moore.

Earl was the only one in the establishment that greeted and welcomed Fritz. He was also the only psychiatrist who was doing group therapy, which nobody down there had every heard of, and he invited Fritz over.

I first met Fritz through Dr. Moore and what he did there as a therapist was most unusual. One incident is impressed on my memory. It had to do with a fellow of 35 or 40, who was unable to detach himself from his dead father. Fritz worked with him for about a half hour, even going to the extent, as I remember, of shaking him physically, which was unusual for Fritz. Finally, he had the fellow go back in fantasy to the grave site, to when his father had died, and bury his father and say goodbye to him.

41

I was so impressed by this particular bit because the fellow's whole appearance changed. He suddenly was a new man. His whole body loosened up. It was a most impressive display. Thereafter most of the groups that Fritz had were held at our house.

SYLVAN KRAUSE
Before the group gathered Fritz would come to our house and have dinner with us, so I also saw him in a social environment. I think that he was an incredible therapist. But I had very little respect for him socially. As a social person, I thought he was a 24-carat son of a bitch. I never heard him at any time say, "Please" or "Thank you." These were words which I did not find in his vocabulary.

I started off my social relationship with him with the prejudice that I had at that time against German refugees; I had met them in business. I found them untrustworthy and untrusting. I found them devious in their business relationships and completely unwilling—the ones that I met—to acknowledge that this country, which had received them with relatively open arms and had given them opportunities which they had been denied in their own country, was not a shit country: They felt that there were a thousand things wrong with it and damned few things, if any, that were good about it.

Fritz carried the same continuum along with respect to this country. He had, as far as I remember, nothing good to say about anything here, and he didn't hold it back. He said that he was scared to death of fascism which he had escaped in Germany, had run away from in South Africa, and now saw in this country. This was '54 and '55. And either it was the time of McCarthy, or shortly after McCarthy's time.

The one thing I liked about Fritz was that he liked Gertrude. This is the only thing I found in his favor. He treated her very well. She was very fond of him. She saw him in a completely different light from mine. She saw him as being soft and warm. He was a welcome guest in my house because of Gertrude.

GERTRUDE KRAUSE

I square danced with him once a week for a long time. He moved very well. There was one incident that was very shocking for me. He was my partner and we were to meet at the park at eight o'clock and I waited and waited. There was this old codger hanging around who always wanted to dance with me, and he asked would I be his partner. I said, "No, I'm waiting for my partner." And he would not go elsewhere. He just waited and waited and then when Fritz didn't show up, he said, "Your partner isn't coming," and he took my hand. I thought, fine, I wasn't going to wait indefinitely for Fritz. The caller started and Fritz appeared and came running up and grabbed me and said, "You're *my* partner." And the man said, "No, she's my partner," and they began to tear at me and Fritz went out of control, screaming with rage—mostly at the man, not at me. He was absolutely beside himself, he was so wild. As far as I was concerned, Fritz was late and I was going to dance with this man, and Fritz went away. I thought, well, I've done it; I've ruined my relationship with Fritz, you know, he's not my friend any more.

And then came a break and I noticed Fritz was sitting on a bench and I went over and sat with him. He said, "Can I get you a coke?" I didn't know about that kind of rage, you know: you just expend it and then it's finished.

SYLVAN KRAUSE

You can't hate a guy like that, you really can't.

Fritz was always interested in something that would bring him unearned income, which is not unusual; so he always looked for something where he could get income without having to do what he considered work. At that time I was setting up a new development, building business—a speculative business. I told him we were forming a syndicate of a group of people who would bring in their funds and, naturally, participate in the profits. And because he was very good to Gertrude—he was really fine to her—when he asked whether there was room for participation (I had more than adequate people already in with adequate money), I said to him, "If you want I'll find some room for you." Then, later, he said, no, that wasn't for him but he asked me what I thought about his buying into a grove of tung trees. (Tung nuts were a very important ingredient in the making of paint, and they grow in the northwestern part of Florida.) I said that from my experience in farming when I first came to Florida, it's a highly speculative thing. So he said, "Well, I bought in it."

He had asked me for my advice, then told me that he had bought a grove. To me, that's kind of an inverted way of operating. If I want advice, I want it before I go into something. I figure this is also part of this German-refugee syndrome.

Six months or so went by and again we were sitting at the dinner table—we saw each other weekly at our home during this time before the group would arrive—and he asked me out of the blue, "How are you doing with your subdivision?" I said, "Fabulously. We opened and sold thirty houses the first day and we've got a hundred houses under construction and so on, and it looks as though it's going to be a successful venture." He said, "Can I have a piece of it?" And I said, "I'm sorry."

He had lost whatever he put in on that tung thing—probably in the neighborhood of ten or fifteen thousand. At the time he went in tung was very scarce, so he probably paid top price for the grove and in six months' time DuPont or somebody else came along with some synthetic and used it to take the place of tung.

GERTRUDE KRAUSE

My general impression was that often he was very far ahead of a client. Not one step, *many* steps ahead. He changed gradually to being more in tune with the person. He picked up things very quickly, and his mind was so fast that he would be miles ahead. I know he did this with me and very often I was completely lost.

SYLVAN KRAUSE

I never saw Fritz work in the group without dark glasses. He always wore them. When he got bored with what was going on and somebody was repeating and repeating the same kind of nonsense, Fritz would go to sleep behind his glasses. I think he wore the glasses for that reason.

When Marty Fromm met Fritz she was a housewife and mother in her early thirties. . . .

MARTY FROMM

Fritz had come to Miami a few years before I met him. He had been diagnosed as having a heart condition and had come to Miami to die. That was his statement. He liked the sun and the water. He was living very, very, quietly. There were no women in his life for just about the first time in his life. He did his little trip around the growth centers every six weeks, but that was for his baby, gestalt therapy. In Miami, he didn't live with friends or with people around him; nor did he have any kind of spark or excitement or enthusiasm in his life. He lived a very isolated existence. Sometimes he had dinner at the home of one of his patients, or went out after group for coffee at one of the Jewish restaurants on the beach, or he went to the movies by himself. You can't really imagine how withdrawn he was. He *really* had come to Miami to die.

He lived very penuriously. He had some independent income and about a dozen patients, but he lived like a poverty-stricken person. He never spent money loosely and freely until the last few years of his life. He didn't want to charge his patients a lot. He didn't need money, nor did he want to get rich, but he did want to work and to see some patients. In Miami, the cost for individual therapy with Fritz Perls was twenty dollars a session and five dollars for group.

A few weeks before I met Fritz my six-year-old daughter had a breakdown. I had put her into therapy with a psychologist, and I had decided that I was totally responsible for her breakdown. I really *did* feel responsible. I was desperate for my child, not for myself. I knew something terrible was going on, and although I never shared it with the world I knew how bad and suicidal I felt.

I was living in Miami Beach at the time and someone told me about this crazy man who led groups there. I said, "How much?" and they said, "Five dollars a session." I went home and told my husband, "This sounds very cheap. Let's go and see together what we get for ten dollars."

There were eight or ten people gathered in this tiny room where Fritz was living then. It was dingy and depressing. I didn't work in the group but something really moved me, I was deeply touched. It was my first exposure to psychotherapy, my first exposure to a group. Fritz was rough. I vaguely remember something about a woman playing mommy. I went home and cried and cried and cried. My husband said he did not like it, and he did not go back.

I did want to go back and I pushed to do this thing that I wanted strongly. I was terrified to do anything that wasn't approved by the entire world. Of course, I had done a lot on my own that was very independent and ambitious and I was achievement-oriented for my day; by the time I was nineteen I was teaching high school; at twenty-one I had a master's degree and was teaching full time. Nevertheless, I played the game of being a nice little girl. I was totally scared of people and I lived a very isolated existence: a married, Jewish, professional middle-class life.

The Marty you see today is nothing like the Marty that existed when I met Fritz. That Marty really was terrified of the world and never told anyone what she felt, much less what she thought. I never said anything that was alive or real or true to anybody. I wanted to placate the world.

I didn't even tell psychologists and psychiatrists I knew socially in Miami that I was seeing Fritz as a psychiatrist. Sneakily I would ask them, "Ever hear of a guy in town named Fritz Perls?" And they'd say, "Yes, he's terrible." Whoever I asked would say just awful things about him. It was hard for me to see Fritz, hearing this kind of feedback from people who, though I only knew them superficially, were the only people in my life. Yet I knew he was a genius; there was never any doubt.

Fritz had come into town with a chip on his shoulder and he asked the Miami psychological and professional community to knock it off. His attitude, as well as the novelty of his approach, demanded that kind of attack. They really disliked him. They tolerated him only because he was alone and minding his own business; they knew he had half a dozen patients and was really not making waves—they could just ignore him. He was very bitter about his lack of professional status and prestige. It wasn't a matter of success because he was doing nice things for individuals and he knew that. But he got no professional recognition.

I was thirty-two and Fritz was sixty-five when we met in December 1957. Once I started, I saw Fritz anywhere from three to five times a week for individual therapy. I knew he was a super therapist and I knew that I wanted him for that. Around the fourth week when we said goodby Fritz put his arms around me and kissed me and I could feel myself respond. I drove home in an absolute tizzy, very sexually moved. I was a frigid, scared little lady. Nobody was touching me—my husband and I weren't making love, and I was isolated from any kind of contact, so I was pretty ripe.

I went in the next day for a session and when he kissed me I broke away and said (in my most icy tone), "I need a therapist, not a lover!" and walked right out of the apartment. In fact, my therapy might have been more effective if he had not become my lover, I don't know.

The Marty of fifty is a much more sophisticated woman of the world, but the Marty of thirty-two was a glacier. He used to call me the "Ice Queen." He came on very hard and strong at that time. He got to me simply by holding me and touching me. He was definitely the aggressor. And by any standards, he was absolutely the most magnificent lover I've ever had in my entire life. I don't know any man that is as sensitive and exciting and alive and knowledgeable, and a super performer and an artist simultaneously.

I tell Marty that I'd heard that Fritz was impotent, and Marty says. . . .

That sounds crazy to me. Every time I saw Fritz over the years he was never impotent. I'm talking about Fritz in Miami days; that's what I know about. We would spend hours and hours in bed together on an afternoon, and then I'd go home and attend to supper and take care of the kids or go to school or something. Often, I'd go back in the evening. We'd go to a movie, we'd take a walk, we'd do a therapy session, and before I left Fritz would say, "I don't feel very sexy, but let's just lie down and be near each other." And every single time we ended up making love in the same dramatic, fantastic fashion. In addition, he always masturbated by himself. We were together hour after hour, day after day that way. Fritz had a huge cock and adored it. He wasn't worried about his potency then. He was a magnificent lover. But there was also, Fritz said, something magical happening for him as well. He called what we had his "renaissance." Since I'd never had any good sex, it was more than that for me—it was a kind of bloom.

The Newsboy. . .

ALAN MARTIN

I knew Fritz before he met Marty Fromm. In fact, Fritz lived in Miami for a year, a year and a half, before he even met her. She wasn't in the initial group of seven or eight people who used to go to see him on a regular basis. I kind of resent Shepard* putting in a whole chapter about Miami and only talking to that one person. Marty Fromm was not the whole Miami. And Marty's interpretation that he came to Florida because he was dying is wrong. I never got that impression. I think he went to Florida more to retain his health. He never looked as if he was sickly. His expression was always cheerful. In fact, in later years he told me that he went down there to improve his health, not because he was dying. That's a distortion.

---

*Fritz, Martin Shepard.

I remember eating with him a number of times. He ate in this kind of dairy restaurant. I was about 15 or 16 years old and, to me, he seemed like a kindly man—a grandfather type or a benevolent uncle—not really benevolent, but nice. I was a newspaper boy then and I'd drop in after my route, like about 6:30. He'd sit there alone and I'd plan to meet him for dinner. Sometimes I'd see him, sometimes not. He wouldn't say, "I'm going to be there," you know; he'd say, "I might" even though he knew he probably would.

He liked his plain little diet—boiled fish or cottage cheese and a little salad. He didn't eat fancy foods. And he didn't sit in the limelight. He'd be sitting there alone before I got there, right near the corner. I can remember the table. He would be reading a book or a newspaper, and he'd put it aside when he saw me. He wouldn't talk much, but he would listen, you know; he would just *be* there.

I remember he wore a little beret, which was very cute. The thing I remember the most about that period is his face. He looked so beautiful then. He had a nice peaches and cream complexion, almost like Santa Claus. He dressed very neatly, sometimes a sport coat and an open-neck shirt. I had a very nice feeling about him. He didn't have his whole personal quality of "I'm Fritz." He was just a man. His hair was completely disheveled, going every which way. He looked a little like Einstein in those days. This was before he grew his beard. He was a better looking man without it.

He was kind of in retreat, you know what I mean? In a sense, he had been kicked out of New York. I mean, not literally, but he was ostracized by the whole William Alanson White crowd. Even though, I guess, some of them were really somewhat with him, the big shots, the real Sylvan-types, did kick him out of their group. In Miami, a Dr. Moore let him use his place. Dr. Moore was the kind of guy who would help the lowest sharecropper; he could be down and out and come to Dr. Moore and he'd help him. He didn't know who Fritz was, but he said, "Okay, you can do your thing in my place." It had a kind of medical aura; it wasn't just like working out of a shack, it was a regular psychiatric institute.

I think Fritz regained his whole self-image through having a
place to work and a little respect.

He lived in a very small two-room place for about two
years. It was very crude. You just sat on a folding chair or on
the edge of the bed. There wasn't a couch. It wasn't at all an
office. He didn't have his groups there—he had his groups at
Dr. Moore's place. It was definitely a man's bedroom and a
small one at that. Outside of the double bed and the chair,
there was really nothing much in the room. Definitely
austere. It was almost like a motel room of the 'fifties. He
lived like a transient. I got the feeling that he didn't care, that
that wasn't really his home; and he used it really to sleep with
women there. I believe he was fucking like crazy in that
place.

He used to have a lot of affairs. He didn't live too far from
me and I was very impressed because he was an old guy—at
least he looked old to me. He's *not* dying, but he's not young
either. He was clearly an old man, you know.

I had a couple of therapy sessions with him and there'd be
somebody waiting outside on the lawn in a lounge chair and
she'd be nude. You could see there was something going on.
The way he'd kiss 'em and grab 'em, you know, you knew it
wasn't therapy.

One of my memories is of a striking model. I can see this
woman today. Very, very charming. I mean the kind of
woman that if a thousand chicks walked down Fifth Avenue
in New York, she would stand out. She was really built. Like
she was an ex-model, but not flat-chested. She was *beautifully* built. And she had quite an elaborate car, a very sleek,
nice convertible. You know, it was impressive! What the hell
did this woman see in that old guy? To me, it was the big
mystery. Jesus Christ, how could he satisfy them? That was
my curiosity. I don't know how he got them, and I couldn't
understand how he kept them.

He had a personal style that some people found abrasive. I
didn't, because he was so much older and I kind of looked up
to him, but he wasn't polite and intellectual to people on his

own level. He thought that was all chicken shit. You know, if you've got something to say, say it, don't talk about it for hours, you know what I mean? One person told me he was working with him and Fritz gave him back the money 'cause he needed it more than Fritz did. That's the kind of thing that greatly impressed me, then and now, that he always had such a sense of spontaneity in the therapeutic sessions.

He was completely spontaneous when he was working with me. I had one session with him that's more valuable than any I've ever had. He asked me where I was for that day, and I told him some chit chat—chicken shit as he would say, but I didn't think of it as shit. He listened and he said, "When you're ready to work, call me," and he walked out of the room! I sat there dumbfounded, thinking, "What the hell is happening here? This guy is not interested in me." But it had such an effect! He was reading a magazine in the other room, just flipping the pages, just passing time by looking at the magazine. And when I said I wanted to work, he came back immediately. You know, I had the best session I've ever had in my whole life!

It was like I had incredible strength, almost like a psyche-delic trip. He said, "You like to write. Write. Write me a verbal story about where you are and what you feel." I suddenly got this realization that I was full of shit before. He had picked up on that, of course, and—ah, now, I was just giving him the internal essence of what I was about at that moment. I was in a real depression, down in the bottom of the pit reaching to get out, and I didn't think I could. He was with me the whole time. I really respect him for that. I remember coming out, and, you know, when I finished, not only did I thank him, I hugged him.

He was nice, he smiled, but he didn't reach out. He just did it in his way, you know. And then I went home and wrote a play about that session because I was so struck by it. I had a couple of other good sessions, but nothing as clearly powerful as what I got out of that one.

To me, Fritz is like a therapeutic ideal; a therapist who can be so honest, so intuitive, who can use a therapeutic device he created at just that moment with such powerful effect. I think that was his real strength: to come up *on the moment* with something, and fit it right in, and in a way that got the person going to other, deeper stuff. Many of the therapists I go to don't understand about spontaneity. They try to be too studied or calculating.

When you were in therapy with Fritz, it was kind of like an event. It had a suspenseful quality. You didn't know what was coming up next, which I think was beautiful because it got you really aware of what you are about right *there,* right at *that* very moment. I mean it got you to kind of cut off a slice of yourself. You know what I mean? You kind of cut right through yourself at that time and what the fuck you are *at this moment.* And that was the brilliance. Any time I hear these therapists say they use gestalt techniques, I know they don't know what they are talking about. To me, the essence was his being right there all the time. To me, gestalt is right here this very minute. Anything else is not gestalt.

SYLVAN KRAUSE
The next move he made was to share a house with Marilyn Rosanes-Berrett. She needed a tenant and she took Fritz. My impression is that Marilyn has taken the position she was momma to Fritz and the supportive influence in his life. As far as he was concerned, I think he regarded her as the land-lord and that was the end of it.

MARILYN ROSANES-BERRETT
Fritz was sick and he had to stay in Florida. He moved down there about '54 and he stayed until about '60. I was there for three years, and after I moved back to New York in '57, I used to go back twice a year because I still had a house there. He rented from me. I had a little apartment in back. And when I got back to Florida, he let me use it to see my patients. I also worked with him at a psychiatric clinic. There was a Dr. Moore who took him in. They parted not in a good way, but he worked with him there.

JIM SIMKIN
He used to wear horn-rimmed glasses before he worked with Marilyn Rosanes-Berrett in New York. She cured him of his visual problems and he discontinued the use of glasses.

In Florida, Fritz' patient, Marilyn Rosanes-Berrett, became his teacher. . . .

MARILYN ROSANES-BERRETT
I am a clinical psychologist. I wasn't in the beginning. After working with Fritz, I left Florida and went back to school in '57 to work toward my degree. I had no degrees before, but I had training as a Bates* technician.

In '54, Fritz was losing his sight. He had a horrible inflammation in one eye and myopia in the other, and was wearing dark glasses. And what it was like to teach him about vision . . . I pushed him into it! We fought, I forcefully pushed him into the chair (and he was much bigger than I) and I said, "Fritz, you do as I say!" and he did. Then his eyes opened up and he jumped up and threw his arms around me, kissed me and said, "I taught you well." The bastard, he didn't teach me that, I did it myself. But he taught me lots of other things well.

I was Fritz' patient and he was mine, in Florida, for three years. And then he would come back periodically from Florida and every trip to New York he came to see me. He slept in Laura's house, but he did his work here.

There was no fee between us. He worked with me and I worked with him. In Florida, before the eye work, I paid him. Then in New York, we exchanged; he'd give me a session and then I'd work with his eyes.

He was one of my best patients. Everything I said, he could do right away. He could let go. And then he would go back and hold on to his myopia again. It took him two years to let go of it completely, to know he could afford to give it

---

*A system for improving vision so that glasses are not necessary.

up. And then after the two years, we worked on putting the two eyes together, the fusion, and that took awhile, even though he understood the right-left split—the man-woman split—so well as a result of his work. Suddenly his whole head opened up. It was overwhelming to him to experience this. At the beginning I gave Fritz a few lessons in a row for his eyes and then he said, "Enough, I'm going to do it on my own."

It is hard work to improve vision in people with visual difficulties. When I first met him for our training, he was 62. He died at 77; he still had normal vision. Fritz didn't give me credit for it in his autobiography, *In and Out the Garbage Pail.*

I was not one of his favorites. I was not one he looked at. In Florida when I once asked him to tell me what he thought of me, well, he was vicious, absolutely biting and vicious and nasty. That was one of his very vicious periods. He was too caught up in a lot of things—too needy and too desperate, but he could be very nice.

He was ambitious, but his ambition arose from a different reason then. He really wanted to share with the world, and later, he really believed that he would cure people, get them to function better.

Eugene Schoenfeld, who for years wrote a popular newspaper column as "Dr. Hip Pocrates," had an early glimpse of Fritz' unorthodoxy. . . .

EUGENE SCHOENFELD
When I was a medical student at the University of Miami, Norman, my roommate then, had already gone through some traditional psychotherapy and he wanted to continue in some sort of therapy while he was in medical school. I believe it was his uncle who had heard of Fritz Perls and suggested Norman see him. Fritz Perls was practicing in Miami at that time—the fall of 1957.

Like all medical students, Norman was very intense and anxiety-ridden. A lot of it had to do with beginning medical school—how would we do? Would we get through it? etc. He was the kind of nervous individual who smoked three maybe four packs of cigarettes a day.

When he came back from his initial session with Perls I asked, "How did it go?" His mind was totally blown by the experience. Fritz Perls wanted Norman to do something like getting up and standing on a table and becoming a rooster. Norman thought it was completely far out and not helpful. As he described Perls, he sounded to me like he was another kind of strange charlatan. I remember the incident clearly because at the time it seemed such a departure from any kind of therapy that I had ever heard of. I forget if Norman went once or twice but he could not understand what Perls was doing. I remember thinking this certainly sounds like a strange and definitely a new technique. This was fall 1957.

When I think of it now, however, this kind of treatment would've been very good for Norman. It surely had a strong influence. It really provoked him. He has since completed psychoanalysis and is now a psychoanalyst himself.

NORMAN LITOWITZ
He did not help me. He did not help me.

I remember having a tremendous impulse to tell him I hated him, that he had wasted his talent. I would guess he was in a perpetual state of fragmentation.

He made no contribution at all. He will be forgotten quickly.

MARTY FROMM
After a couple of months in therapy, Fritz announced in his inimitable German accent, "The basis of your neurosis is boredom." I thought about that. I didn't know what to do about all the strings and patterns of my relationships with my children and husband, but I enrolled at the University of Miami and began a master's degree program in psychology.

Fritz enjoyed talking with me while I was in graduate school—and writing term papers. For him it was effortless,

and for me it was "A"s! He liked to listen to what traditional psychology was doing because he was so far away
from the academic field. It really drove him mad. He was
totally contemptuous. He threw a fresh light on anything
that I wrote and handed in.

By the time Fritz left Miami, I was so into gestalt therapy,
both as a patient and as a therapist (because Fritz was training me), that what I was learning in school had absolutely no
connection to the dynamics of clinical practice which I was
learning with Fritz. One day, when I was just short of another master's degree, I dropped out.

About six months after we were together, Fritz left Miami
for Columbus, Ohio, at the invitation of Vincent O'Connell
to train psychiatrists at a mental hospital there. Fritz was
very interested in that. I carried on terribly when he said he
was leaving because I knew I had just tapped into some idea
of how crazy I was and what a terrible lifestyle I was living.
And when Fritz said he was leaving I felt totally abandoned.
At that point, I really didn't understand the theoretical position of either Fritz or gestalt therapy, but I sure learned a lesson that has helped me enormously concerning the word "responsible." His statement was essentially, "I don't owe you
anything, Marty. I did what I could for you while I was
here." And he left.

I knew that for Fritz, gestalt therapy always came first. He
really was a missionary for his baby. There was no question
that it was absolutely the most important thing in his life.

A few weeks after he went to Columbus, Fritz asked me to
come up and help him get settled. He mentions that somewhere in *Garbage Pail*. I'm very well organized and efficient—those are the things I do well. I did a lot of work for
him all the years we were together. I spent just one weekend
in Columbus to help him set up housekeeping, and a couple
of months later he came back to Miami to stay.

At that point, there was no doubt that he didn't come back
to do me a favor—he came back for himself. I was still married and living at home and playing the Jewish mother-
housewife.

There are many advantages to having a lover older than my father. The age difference made it possible for us to be in public together and see friends in the community and he could come in and out of my home. My husband knew him as my psychiatrist and as a friend who occasionally came to the house or went to the movies with me. There were no overt hostilities between the two of them. My husband wasn't interested in playing the jealous-husband game. He really preferred not to see; that was his style.

On the surface, and in reality, we really were a family, but very superficially. We were divorced years later but Fritz had nothing to do with that; nobody can break up a good relationship. I had a live-in maid at home but I still ran the household, took care of the children, participated in a social life with my husband, went to school, attended concerts and theater, did homework, participated in individual and group therapy—and I ran Fritz' household and took care of him, too.

I'm a cleanliness-and-godliness lady and Fritz didn't care about these things. He really didn't care about being clean. He didn't mind being dirty and he didn't mind his smell. He laughed at my obsessive-compulsive cleanliness, and would tell me stories about how men loved body smells, and how Europeans are really a lot more earthy than Americans, and how terrible all the deodorant sprays on the market are that take away our natural body odors. Most people experienced Fritz' strong body odor and never dared to say, "Change your shirt; take a shower." Fritz was really so independent that if you didn't like his odor that was your tough luck. What I'm telling you is accurate in terms of Fritz, no matter what fantasies you may have about people preferring cleanliness and godliness. It was my obsession, not his. If I objected to his odor and his dirt, he would let me clean him up. I really appreciated that. The fact that he would let me bathe him, clean him and groom him and take care of him was so that it would be nicer for me to be near him and to smell him and to hold him; it was something I was delighted to do for *me*.

Whatever was happening with Fritz and me in our personal relationship was ongoing therapy for me. It has certainly paid off in all of my relationships—with my children and everyone. It's something I talk about in groups and in the classroom, and it's my way of life. I learned the importance of sharing every fantasy—every negative as well as every positive feeling—of eliminating mind reading about the other's intentions, of not playing "nicey" games because you're worried about what the other guy is going to think about you, and really coming on straight. I've internalized this in living my life and it saves enormous amounts of time and problems in communication. It's the only way I know to live and the only way I know how to maintain and develop a relationship. I learned it the hard way. . . .

> *Marty rejected the idea of my marrying her. I was too old. She did not want to give up the security of her marriage and to imperil the psuedo-security of her children.*
>
> *I wish I could simply say that Marty broke my heart, but that would be a great oversimplification. The fact is that I went through a period of suffering equal to the time in the trenches. The difference is that in the trenches I could experience myself as a victim of circumstances; with Marty, I carry the responsibility.*

NATALIE MANN

Fritz told me about Marty and that he had the same feelings toward me that he had toward Marty, and that he hadn't had feelings toward anyone since he had left Marty. He asked if I would live with him. I knew that I was very taken with him. What troubled me was feeling close to someone who I felt was old and close to death. This scared me because I'd just gone through a death. He gave me Marty's address and I went down to Miami and visited her. I didn't know her before. I called her to talk to her very specifically about this, and for advice as to how she felt about my going to Fritz and committing myself to live there. She told me some stories of her relationship with Fritz about Fritz' jealousy and how he used to park the car and follow her to see if she was going with someone else and that sort of thing, and just how nasty and brutal he was. And based on that, I decided not to, so I didn't.

For well over a year, in 1958, Fritz had practiced as a psychoanalyst in Los Angeles. He had roots there and early in 1960 he returned to the West Coast.

JIM SIMKIN
He had an invitation to consult at Mendocino State Hospital in California. The chief psychologist there, Wilson Van Dusen, was very turned on to gestalt therapy and the whole existential philosophy. He wrote an article in which he claimed that gestalt therapy was the only therapy which practices what existential therapy preaches. . . .

Mendocino

Until Fritz met Wilson Van Dusen, he had gotten little support from the professional community. From their first meeting Van Dusen recognized that Fritz' work was a far more effective treatment of mental patients than the traditional methods. It was he who gave Fritz his first opportunity to demonstrate his work to other professionals. It seems clear that the high regard of Van Dusen and his colleagues penetrated Fritz' resigned acceptance that his work would not flower. It marked another important step in Fritz' resurgence; a turning point in his life.

> *Wilson . . . suggested my coming to the West Coast and doing some work out of the Mendocino State Hospital. I welcomed the suggestion.*

WILSON VAN DUSEN

I went to a conference in San Francisco on psychodrama and Fritz was a participant in it, he was not one of the leaders. Jacob Moreno, who was the head of psychodrama, was there and his wife, too. Moreno was somewhat simpleminded alongside Fritz. Fritz did some beautiful imitations of Moreno, by the way. He'd say, "This is the way Moreno walked," and he would walk like a puppet hanging from a string; it really looked like Moreno when he did it. I gathered that Fritz had studied with Moreno. We were all professionals there of one type or another, social workers, psychologists, etc.

Everything else about the conference fades from my memory except for a single incident: A young psychiatrist was talking about the importance of peace in the world. He was trying to elicit aid in achieving international peace and Fritz interrupted him by saying, "Listen to the tragic quality in the man's voice." And suddenly, listening, we all heard it. Then the man broke down and cried. The tragedy really was that he was leaving his wife and family. World peace was a kind of blown-up exterior of the inner struggle. Fritz had heard it first. What struck me was that the man's dynamics were manifest in the voice quality, not in what was said, and none of us had been aware of it. It suddenly became apparent to some of us that a whole realm of the person was showing that we weren't paying much attention to. But Fritz was. There were several other situations after that where it was evident that Fritz could see in a way none of the others could. He was, to my mind, the greatest observer of body language I have ever known.

At the end of that conference, three or four of us, all young people, went to see him. He had a little hotel room near the conference site. This was in San Francisco; I don't know the year. I'm terrible about dates. I couldn't even guess what year it was. We went to see him as a guru.

I asked him to come up to Mendocino State Hospital as a consultant. My role there was Chief Psychologist. I was concerned with staff development and I believed that most of our lack of progress was due to our staff, not the patients; so at that point I was doing everything that was possible to improve the staff. I gather that Fritz was between engagements, so to speak. He told me later that he had just come out of depression—a depression that seemed to involve not having any sense of direction at all for his own life . . . what to do . . . where to go. He was open to anything and I hit him at the right moment.

So he came up to Mendocino and immediately fell into a rather extraordinary role. I had talked him up very big to my colleagues there, so he was given more than the usual consultant role. A consultant was usually there for one day and Fritz ended up spending at least thirty days there.

At that time we lived in a modest tract home and during the time he was there he lived with us. I drove him to work on my motorscooter, which he refers to in his book. He rode on the pillion seat, the afterseat on the motorscooter. I think that was something that was an adaptation for him.

At the hospital, we called together a group of all the key administrators and Fritz was going to train them. I remember the opening session very clearly. I was the only one present who knew Fritz at this point. He didn't know any of the others.

We were all sitting around—the chief of this and the chief of that, and all these dignitaries—we had worked together for years and knew each other well—and as people were chatting, Fritz raised his hand and asked for silence. Then he went around the group and told what he could see in each one. He just about blasted us out of our chairs because he saw what we knew to be the real nature of each person. He hit everyone with deadly accuracy. Paul Frey, a friend of mine who has an immense concern with eschatology (the ending of all things), is a theologian and a psychiatrist. As an expert in the cataclysmic ending of all things, Frey was concerned with everything, agonizing about how the world would be destroyed, and Fritz could see the whole thing there in Paul's face. He said, "Look at the agony in his face." When he said it, we could all see it. Before he said it, none of us had been aware of it. Then he got to a psychiatrist who started talking nervously and Fritz just sat back and waited. He gave him maybe ninety seconds and then he just raised his hand and said, "I feel you are dumping a load of garbage on me," which was actually very accurate. It was verbal garbage. It wasn't worth a damn and there was a great deal of it pouring forth. Everyone else was stunned because this particular psychiatrist always did that. It was, in effect, wordy garbage, but no one had ever had the clarity to see it or the callousness or the daring to say anything like that.

I remember another psychiatrist who was a very nervous, ambitious and uptight black. He was just blown out of the room.

"Know Fritz? If I hadn't, you'd probably be talking to some stumblebum New York nigger now." Andy Curry, professor

*of psychology and humanities at the California School of
Professional Psychology, dance and artistic director of
Tantra Feets Dance Ensemble, and a writer and poet. . . .*

ANDY CURRY

In those days at Mendocino, Fritz dressed in the fashion of
New York City in 1960. His thick Viennese accent seemed literally to ring, and I can recall him slurring, "Oh, you are full
of shit." You heard the words down in your toes, down to
the early sediments of shit which constituted the foundation
of your phoniness. He simply saw things truly, and knew
how to listen to a life, as one talked about life in disguised
terms. He was truly a phenomenon to watch.

I will never forget his gaze. Fritz' eyes were very unusual—commanding, almost mirror-like, and curiously forgiving. You saw that he saw what you were in relation to what
you were trying to be. There was no hypnotism or "charismatic magic," as some thought. His gift was that he saw the
truth and spoke the truth.

I came to Mendocino State Hospital at a time when they
needed group workers and I wanted to get as far away as I
could from Cleveland, Ohio. A hospital that would hire a
guy like Fritz then had to be far out. Mendocino was in the
boondocks, and my hunch is that they hired big names in
order to keep us there. Maxwell Jones came as a consultant
one year. Hayakawa and Haskell Norman were consultants
and Alan Watts, too; and there was Virginia Satir and the
regular big psychiatric names. I had been at Mendocino for
three years when I first met Fritz. Wilson Van Dusen was
chief psychologist then. He recognized Fritz early and got
him to Mendocino.

I was working with some heavy stuff. There weren't too
many black dudes struggling with psychotherapy in those
days. Van Dusen knew. I talked to Van daily for four years.
He told me that this man Perls was unusual and that if he
asked for someone to work it would be to my benefit to vol-
unteer. This made sense to me. But when Fritz got up there to
address us, he didn't ask. He just discussed his overall

approach. I thought he was pompous and, as I look back, I realize that he hooked the smart aleck part of me.

I thought he was slightly in error on some minor facts about Freud's early treatment approach. In those days, my whole way was to come in at you. I mean, if you made a little teeny mistake I'd come in and wrap you up. I was a sharp-shooter. My whole fucking life I asked the questions. My survival technique. I was the college prep, the reader always checking the footnotes, listening for fuckers to make mistakes so I could come in and say, "You weren't quite accurate there—it was 1914 that Freud said . . ." Playing that game was my whole life then. I'd always been the little kid who's got to catch up—second in the relays, never could anchor. I'd read all that shit the night before, and I guess I was looking for him to make a mistake. So during the question period, I asked him how what he was saying differed from what Freud and Breuer had said and he asked what I meant.

I said, "Well, he worked with those women. . . ."

"Vich vomen?"

"Dora and Anna O. and Fraulein somebody. . . ."

Who but a smart-ass, joe-peppermint quiz kid is going to bring up these cases? I picked nit for a minute or two; and, after a long silence, he asked me to the front—the "hot seat" he was to call it later.

I went up to the stage, very, very nervous because the patients were present. I was working in a back ward then, and I was thinking, "How am I going to work honestly with this dude in front of these people who are going to fry my ass next Monday?" There were fifty or sixty people there. But I soon forgot them completely.

He did an analysis of my hand. It's very hard to tell when black people blush because we don't show it, but I remember how sensitive he was to my discomfort. He stayed right with me, those eye things of his. I was doing pretty good there, man, I can remember feeling, "Keep that fucker off my ass." My whole thing apparently was keeping people off me,

no love, no tenderness, rather, you're going to have to fight
. . . Then something happened and he sort of caught me. I
tried to get him off me, to stop the thing and he said, "You
just felt something—come do to old ugly Fritz what you
feel."

I was angry—this very powerful authoritative, authoritarian man was in charge of me—and when I came off the chair,
what I was feeling was "I'm gonna . . . I'm gonna hit this
motherfucker in the mouth!" But when I got over there, that
rage and that anger wasn't anger. He had touched something
in me, and something in here went push-pull, click-click, and
all I could do was, just—you know, tears in my eyes—just
put my arms around him. And that old bastard sat there and
smiled, watching me fry while my fairy tale of the time dissolved in the grease. I remember myself hugging that son of a
bitch as hard as I have ever hugged anybody. And, while I'm
just standing there hugging that dude, he's whispering to me,
"Do you understand what we're working on?" and I said,
"Oh, fuck, yes, do I ever!" And my "yes" sounded like it
must surely sound the very first time you use the word in
relation to understanding. Crying, weeping, the whole thing.

I'd read in books that meaning arises in the process of interaction between people and at that moment I was reading it
in the very marrow of my being.

WILSON VAN DUSEN
We were all terribly impressed with Fritz, especially the su-
perintendent, Ernest Klatte. He remained impressed by Fritz,
and he had been a dyed-in-the-wool skeptic from way back.
Fritz did not think much of many psychiatrists and that was
a great compliment to me. It was odd, in the first place, that
I, a chief psychologist, would bring Fritz, a psychiatrist, to
the hospital as a consultant; and even odder that the psychologist adored the psychiatrist. It was a real weird combi-
nation for the rest of the staff. Normally a psychologist
would bring a psychologist or a psychiatrist would bring a
psychiatrist. There was a kind of status hierarchy to this.

Anyway, from then on, I think, for some thirty days, I worked with Fritz to attempt various things in the hospital. I used him everywhere that looked promising in the hospital. He gave a series of lectures on his cosmology, how he viewed things. He did interpretation of the dreams of staff members. I remember a technician would tell a dream about two lines long, Fritz would make a couple of comments, and the technician would break down and cry. They were just stunned. They had never seen anything as effective and as fast as this.

Watching Fritz work, almost in minutes I saw for the first time the inside of members of the staff whom I had worked with for years. One psychologist had a dream that he was bouncing a ball off the wall, it was bouncing and ricocheting all the way through the dream. It came out in Fritz' work with him that the real meaning was *he* was the ball, forever moving, bouncing from thing to thing and could never settle. And this was precisely the difficulty I had with him as his supervisor. The dream was the forerunner of what the man would be. He later left and got a position where he traveled endlessly; he never settled.

I would say almost none of us had any real skill with dreams until Fritz showed us his ways of working on them, including the heavy weight given the body language and voice qualities. This was a major revelation for me. In the book I published last year, *The Natural Depth in Man,* there is a whole chapter on the body language. I teach it now to counselors in training, but I never reckon myself as good as Fritz.

ANDY CURRY

I learned from Fritz that nobody is ahead of me.

"Put no head above your own." "Vy do you insist on quoting Freud?" "Vy is it you remind me of what you read last night?"

If you can understand the term *trickster-guru,* not as a put-down but as an accurate description of how a therapist-teacher can use himself in a situation, then you have some sense of Fritz back in the early '60s. His gestures were very slow. He would bring you down, calm you down. He would lean back in his chair very calmly, and you would see that *he's* not nervous, and, gee, I guess it's OK. Then you would notice that your breathing was slower. He was putting you at ease. He would say, "Oh, you think you're ugly? Vell, I'm ugly. Don't you think Fritz is ugly?" And every time you would say, "Dr. Perls," he would say, "Call me Fritz."

I lived in Berkeley at the time and Fritz was staying there too with Gene Sagan, another unusual and gifted therapist. Twice I drove Fritz to Berkeley.

Imagine Fritz and me, a black dude and an old European cat, in a little white MG, tearing ass down old Highway 101. I had scarves, goggles, the whole fantasy, and I drove too fast. He was very cool and very gentlemanly; it was just, "Slow down." He worked on my hyperaggressive driving—a "tearing into the air," he called it, as if there was somewhere I was going. He was always slowing me down. He liked to stop in Healdsburg at a little German place where they had Mozart on the jukebox.

Fritz had a kind of license over you. He could say whatever he wanted to and you'd go "OK." He said to me, "Vot's mit the gloves and scarf?" He had a sense of humor, you know. "The car von't go unless you. . . ." But the drives were helpful. I no longer drive a car in which it and I tear at the air.

Oh, man, that guy! Once during the three-hour drive, he said, "Slow down. Let's talk about your going to Africa." It was in the context of what I was going to do next—to stay or to go to Langley-Porter or go back to Cleveland or try an offer in Saskatchewan. He said, "Vell, if you're going that far, vy not Africa? You ought to go."

"I don't want to go over there."

"You should. People with master's degrees are ministers of health in some of those republics, heads of the whole thing."

It was like he was saying, "Here's the world. It doesn't stop in New York or Miami or at the Azores. There is this *whole* world." I think he knew what he was talking about because in the '60s a lot of black people from this country did go over there. He thought I should go and try to get some of this experience of authority in a country of blacks.

My identification with Fritz was very deep. Looking back on him and those times—his piercing gaze, the ever-present long ash on his cigarette, his rugged stone-to-the-bone funkiness—I know that I had the very special honor of encountering a truly unusual person. A phrase that pops into my head is Chaung Tzu's "the great and venerable teacher." He could speak with very few words about a great deal of human things, things that get wasted and lost in interpersonal lying, deceiving, and fantasy. Fritz seemed always to stand at the brink of life, at the point of love. The man is still resonating in me. I have all his books. I know many of the people he worked with. I keep his picture on my wall.

WILSON VAN DUSEN

If you detached Fritz from others and let him drift, he would have died. Once he got support and agreement that his work was important, then he began to see himself differently.

Even at that first conference when I was so struck by how much he was seeing and hearing, many other people were not as struck by him. There were just a few of us who appreciated his skill.

Fritz didn't have the normal fantasy overlay. He immediately saw to the bone of what was there. When he spoke of dating his "impotence" back to his World War I experience, he meant "impotence" in more than only the sexual sense: the inability to have any internal fantasy. At least this was reported as his major concern in analysis and during his contacts with me. Remember, he was a disdained Jewish medical orderly in the German Army—there was marked Jewish prejudice then, so he was a social outcast—having to take care of the injured and the dead. It was as though the shock of these scenes of war glued him to what was externally visible.

I have long felt that what he experienced as a negative condition was also what made him a consummate observer. If we amplified what was going on in normal social interaction we would hear things like "She is doing her usual thing, complaining." These projected attitudes lay over and obscure seeing what *she* is actually expressing. Fritz didn't have this "normal" fantasy overlay; so what we saw as his wonderful powers of observation he justifiably felt as an impoverishment that prevented him from fantasizing. This "impotence in fantasy" meant he was stuck to what was before him—hence his unusual skill. While it felt like a lack to him, to us it would be something of a gift. Pure seeing in the Zen sense. Actually, he never stopped working with the wounded, only the meaning of wound changed.

We lived with him. He had a little room in our house and he lived like a pig. He just dropped everything all over. He was a slob and my wife was cleaning up after him. He didn't leave anything with me when he left, just a room to clean up. We kidded him about it. He acknowledged it. That's the way he was. But he was good to our children. We have two young girls. They both have fond memories of his taking them uptown and buying them toys. He told me things that gave me a sense of a man without direction in his life.

Toward the end of that period, or maybe it was when he came back as a consultant the second time, I'm not clear, we had the Sagans over one night—Fritz, Sagan and his wife, and Marj, my wife—at a dinner gathering, and Fritz proceeded to kind of analyze my wife after dinner.

No, it wasn't solicited, no! My wife is anti-analytical, anti-therapy. He worked on her, her harshness, you know. It became a weird kind of evening. As I remember it, Sagan was splitting from his wife and he and his wife were kind of working on my wife and my relationship, and Fritz was in the midst of this. My wife didn't like any of that kind of prodding and for some reason Fritz persisted, which, in retrospect, I would say, was poor judgment. He should have

backed off because my wife got so mad. I have never seen her
so angry in my whole life before. I wasn't paying attention to
the argument; maybe it wasn't about anything. I just
watched the tension increasing. She just picked up the first
thing she could find, which was the sugar bowl, and threw it
at him.

MARJORIE VAN DUSEN

It was a social situation. Fritz was a guest at the time. We
had had dinner and were sitting around having coffee and
Fritz was especially abrasive and nosy, I'd guess you'd call it.
I don't really remember specifically what it was . . . I probably have repressed it. It was some question about my relationship with my husband. He was very hostile towards me.
He wouldn't stop. He really liked to get to people. I think he
was sort of the epitome of the original male chauvinist pig.
An ordinary person would have backed off and said, "Well,
gee, she's getting mad." He'd been a guest here for about six
weeks. It had been a long time, I think anybody wears thin
after six weeks but Fritz, particularly, didn't endear himself
over a long period of time. I finally got fed up. I let him have
it! I hit him with a sugar bowl! I actually broke his wrist
watch!

WILSON VAN DUSEN

It fell in pieces on the floor. I went and hid the gun, feeling
that she might kill him! He had triggered her full anger! I
was concerned with trying to keep this explosion from getting any more dangerous, because she had gone beyond what
I had ever seen before. Fritz picked his watch up off the floor
and the whole evening was a shambles. He left, and later sent
the watch back in pieces as though I was responsible for it. I
sent the pieces back to him with a note telling him he was responsible for his own mess. I assume he got another watch.
He had persisted beyond what was really wise. She never did
again feel good about Fritz. She always referred to him as
"that bum." She also referred to him as the devil. She meant

"*The* Devil" literally. It was as though she had flipped her lid.

The threat to Marj was clear. Her life revolved around me—housewife with two children. At that time she hadn't become a liberated teacher. She knew I was impressed by Fritz and emulated him in therapy. In a vague way Fritz wanted me to go off with him. I think it reasonable that Marj was threatened. He obviously cared for me, not her.

Marjorie Van Dusen
I've always thought that anger was a stimulant, that you do things when you're angry that you wouldn't ordinarily do. I don't know; I don't believe I've ever been that mad at anyone before. I think he was trying to provoke it. He liked to do that; that was his idea of kicks. I'm convinced of that. Now, many people would say I'm wrong, but I really feel that he liked to do that, though *he* was incensed that I got angry. I think he didn't expect open hostility.

Fritz was the original male with a capital M; women were really nothing, as far as he was concerned. He expected to be waited on and have everything done, all his personal laundry and all that sort of thing. He just expected it. He left things out for you to do. When he got up in the morning he expected breakfast to be ready. I was very accommodating. I was also very repressed. And Fritz was—how to put it?— well, he was very attracted to young girls. At the time he was staying with us he was involved with a very young girl; she was not as old as my children.

Did she stay with him?

Not in *our* house! But I knew about it. He didn't like women his own age. Fritz represented something to me that I didn't want my husband to be—running around with young girls, experimenting with drugs and that kind of life. I felt that Fritz was trying to influence Bill in this way, and I didn't like it. It was nothing obvious; it was subtle—setting an example, d be what I'd say. It sure as hell wasn't out of admiration for me! I don't think he cared what he was doing to me; and he was doing something to me!

Fritz was a user; he was a taker, not a giver. I had his number from the first day he came in. All the time that he stayed with me—he never brought anything to the house. He never contributed anything to the household. No wine, no food, no flowers, no nothing. I don't think it was a deliberate thing; I just think he had no manners. I always look upon manners as the grease of civilization—they help things along. If you're in somebody's house for a month or six weeks, you need a little grease, you really do. You need a few social amenities. Sometimes it's better not to let everything hang out; it's better to be a little more conservative and thoughtful to keep things going. I admit I was a very conventional person, but *he* didn't know how to say thank you.

Fritz always felt as though I was very repressed; he said as much. I think he felt that I didn't admire him and he very much wanted people to admire him. He liked to be worshiped. I think I just got fed up with him. Fritz loved to analyze everybody and everything. If you talked about a dream that you'd had, he'd immediately put you on the spot, and things like that. I guess that's why I got mad at him. Fritz saw everything as a therapeutic situation, and there we differed tremendously. He was very destructive. I just felt that he was evil, that he liked to provoke people.

He certainly was a very nosy man—he became involved in things that were not his business—like *my* personal problems. I didn't feel that they were his concern. After that length of time in my home, he should have—being the therapist that he was—been aware enough of me not to provoke me. I think he was doing it deliberately. He loved to divide people from their loyalties.

He was a troublemaker. I don't think he had any noble motivation at all, none at all! I'm convinced of that, and as I got to know Fritz I became more and more convinced of it. I think Fritz was the most attentive man to his own interests that I've ever met. He was completely concerned with himself, to the exclusion of everyone else. Obviously, I didn't like him. I felt he was unnecessarily cruel.

My feeling about Fritz was that his entire life was a super ego trip. If he didn't get adulation . . . I think that was why he got so upset with me, because, after all, he was supposed to be the Big Deal Therapist. He was *much* angrier with me than I was with him. In fact, I'm quite sure he never forgave me, because he mentioned it in his writing, in *Garbage Pail,* and it really was a very sort of nothing incident. However, it was obviously still on his mind, which kind of amazed me. I had forgotten the whole thing, until someone told me that it was in that book.

It's a quirk of my own personality but I don't believe in insulting my guests, much less my hostess. The dinner was a social rather than a psychological situation and a colossal affront of him to be so cruel and critical as he was to me. He was trying to work his therapy on me and bring me to some sort of enlightenment but I wasn't interested.

Wilson Van Dusen

I sometimes think I should have gone with him. The main reason I didn't was that I was to aid his reputation, not mine, at totally uncertain compensation. It would have been fine if I didn't have a family and didn't need to work. Even then I would have hesitated. I wasn't as sexually liberated as Fritz. Also I was a very different breed from Fritz.

I fully understand and sympathize with my wife's reactions to him. He once told me his wife had described him as a cross between a prophet and a bum. I still think that a very apt description. In a therapeutic setting I could see the great prophet. At home she just saw the bum. Both were very real. At first I tried to overlook the bum, but it weighed heavier as time went on. Our way of living was just too different to live together. I guess, in a way, we were lovers who found ourselves incompatible. After all, my first loyalty was to my family.

MARJORIE VAN DUSEN

I don't think he was a man you could leave alone; either you disliked him intensely or you thought he was really great. I'd probably get along fine with him now because I think I could laugh at him or with him now. I didn't feel like a person then; I felt like an extension of someone else. I'm a person now; there's really nobody that can touch me. He was a very interesting man. As I look back, I can understand that.

Fritz could be charming when he put his mind to it. He could be *very* nice. He was extremely worldly, had been all over the place and knew everything and everybody. I felt that he related a lot better to the kids than he did to me.

JOANNE VAN DUSEN

He used to always do magic tricks for my sister and me when he stayed at our house.

KATHY VAN DUSEN

He did them really well. He used cards. Once he put out his hands and the card was behind his ear. He never told us how he did it. That's about all I remember about it. He kind of scared me. I've always been really weird toward older men. Not all older men, but some of them just scared me sexually. You know, they just bother me, and *he* seemed to bother me in that way even though I was very young.

Once he gave me a little mosaic pin. It wasn't a piece of junk. I hung on to it for a long, long time, up until about three years ago and I lost it some way.

JOANNE VAN DUSEN

You gave it to me. He gave me a wooden doll house and a bunch of rooms of doll house furniture. I tell you, I have a rotten memory, but it was as if, you know, I could go in the toy store with him and pick out anything I wanted.

I think mainly I wasn't concerned with what went on between Fritz and Mom because I was more concerned with the hassles Mom and Dad were having. Kathy and I were really upset about that. I wasn't thinking about Fritz at the time, although I know Kathy and I were both sad that Fritz left because we liked him. He was fun and he was really nice to us.

San Francisco

Eugene Sagan was another who recognized Fritz' genius, and helped move him away from his relative obscurity. He was also among those who wanted to attach himself to Fritz. . . .

EUGENE SAGAN

Fritz had come out to the West Coast about the end of 1960. I was in New York that August when I read *Gestalt Therapy* and I wanted to contact the author. I called Laura Perls and she said Fritz was going to be in San Francisco about the time I was due to arrive back here.

At our first meeting in the San Francisco Bay area, Fritz suggested we have a therapy session. So I started having individual therapy sessions with him and going up to Ukiah to watch him work at the Mendocino State Hospital. It was like meeting an explosion.

Until that time, I'd never been taught very much as a psychotherapist. A little bit here, maybe, a little bit there, and then, all of a sudden, I meet a man from whom I can really learn. I wouldn't say that Fritz was actually teaching at this point in his career; he would let you observe and if you were able to figure it out and put it together, that was fine. He was a teacher and father figure for me almost from the beginning.

Working with Fritz, eventually, a person is going to get it through his head that the ways in which he presents himself are the parts of his total gestalt. And the purpose of therapy, as far as I'm concerned, is to become aware of these various ways or styles. Most analysts spend such a minimal part of the time pointing out a patient's style to him. That first meeting with Fritz made me aware of the importance of this. Fritz saved me twenty years. I've said publicly before that if I'd had to explore these techniques on my own, I might not be

too much further along today than I was with the two analysts I saw before Fritz.

As I remember him in 1960, I would not describe him as a
charismatic person. He was enormously insightful and very
sharp and bright, but it was not especially apparent that he
would make as great a contribution as he finally did. After
all, Fritz had been wandering around the country a hell of a
long time before people began to say, "My God, this man
really has something!"

Jack, I'd like to listen to a tape with you that I did with Fritz
somewhere back around 1964. I haven't listened to this for
awhile. It deals with my relationship with Fritz at a time
when he was my therapist. I normally wouldn't listen to this
by myself. Basically, I want to get a sense of the relationship
between Fritz and me.

I don't know exactly what I'm looking for but I've already
seen how I set up my relationship in what I've called my
"reverence contract" with Fritz: I seem to have felt a need to
tell him how wonderful he is and how important he is to me,
and as I'm saying it my voice sounds so phony on the tape.
Not that it wasn't true, but the setup of the admiring little
boy to the great big powerful daddy was a very contrived situation on my part.

What I was saying to him, in effect, was that at that point in our relationship I felt that his acting only like a therapist with me was just nonsense . . . Well, let's listen to some of this tape.

Gene has an excellent sound system and, sitting in his book-lined studio, watching his face change, it is almost as though he is now with Fritz seven years before. His expression is mildly defiant, yet deferential. Fritz' deep guttural voice and his presence come alive. It is somewhat eerie. The tape deals with Gene seeing himself as Fritz' son, and Fritz, most professionally it seemed to me, making clear that he was not. . . . At this point, Gene turned the tape recorder off and moved his hand across his chest.

Notice the thing that he didn't realize is that we've got the same body structure. It seemed to me that he was bringing in one label—disciple—and I was bringing in another—son—and we were coming from these two different positions. I was uncomfortable with the comment he made about a father having certain obligations to a son, because I could sense his discomfort there. But I didn't like the implications of "disciple" either.

After all, this is before things got so big for him. There hadn't been that many people in the professional field who recognized him yet as being important; I believe he enjoyed the validation he got from me. I think he was grappling with those voices inside him which kept insisting, "Am I a charlatan or am I a genius?"

Listening to the tape, it's clear that in part I was trying to get a group to say, "Fritz asks people to sign reverence contracts and he won't admit that and let's all make him admit it." These so-called reverence contracts actually called for a certain amount of hero worship, a certain amount of inauthentic admiration. And, in reality, I was very willing to give it to him. I'm trained. I was trained from a little boy to give reverence contracts . . . but I wanted him to be the kind of parent who wouldn't even ask for one.

What kind of relationship did you have with your own father?

Well, actually, my father is still alive. My relationship with
him is fairly complicated but, in general, I've been a quiet or
very accommodating son; and he has been domineering and
controlling toward me. Although there are some obvious
similarities between the two, Fritz would be a far more appealing father. Both of them are very bright. Both of them
are very complicated. Both of them tend to be quite isolated
from people on the whole, but *extremely* clear about how to
relate to people. I mean clear in the sense that they both became successful in their chosen professions: Both men
arrived at places in terms of reputation and accomplishment
which as children they never thought of in their wildest
dreams. Fritz was sometimes even heard to say, "What am I,
a little Jewish boy, doing here?". . . meaning, as the genius
of the gestalt movement.

I think it was as hard for Fritz to accept anything openly as
it was for him to accept his success inwardly. I remember an
incident when John Enright interfered as John Graham was
trying to give Fritz something and I hit Enright. That time
Fritz was working with Graham, and Graham began doing a
dance in which he was making a gift of himself to Fritz.
Graham was moving and talking to Fritz, and to break in
upon that, to distract either of them from what was happening, was totally inappropriate. Whatever Enright's need was
at that moment, I don't know, but he interfered, or
attempted to . . . and I got up, and I just hit him,
WHAMMO! Looking back on it, I can be clear that the reason I felt so much anger and did that was I felt I had to make
a very strong statement: "I want to take care of you." I
really did see him as my father.

WILSON VAN DUSEN
After he left Mendocino, he went to a hotel in San Francisco
and I got a letter from him saying, "Send me some patients; I
am dying of boredom in this hotel." I think he was still
somewhat lost after he left me. What he felt was that the
whole gestalt thing was so thin as not to be worth fiddling
with; he had kind of lost interest in it. But here I was at that

time sitting at his feet, adoring this man for his tremendous therapeutic powers and it was, in effect, he told me, that it was just boring to him. It was as though he didn't do anything. You know, a guy says something and Fritz does something and it's amazing, they'd pay him for this. It had no intrigue for Fritz. It was during a depressed period that he couldn't find any joy in his own methods. Later on he did.

In and Out of New York

Much as Fritz may have disliked New York, he'd still go back there from time to time. . . .

LAURA PERLS

He would arrive at the airport and telephone, "In half an hour I'll be home," after I hadn't seen him for a whole year!

Why did I let him come? I wanted to see him.

When he started giving workshops here again (after living in Florida and several other places for some years), he had one here in my house. Oh, yes, he asked my permission, but I *assumed* he would have it here. . . I took part in the workshop but he got so hostile toward me, it became so embarrassing also for some participants who were my friends that I said, "You know, I won't have that in my house!" After that he had the workshops at someone else's house.

I was here and he knew it. If I had really resented being available to him I would probably have finished it.

Marilyn Rosanes-Berrett was most willing to have Fritz use her home for his groups.

MARILYN ROSANES-BERRETT

Every time he came to New York, he would call me. He always told people—I'd get messages through the grapevine—"Call Marilyn, I'm coming on this and this day and she'll organize a workshop." They would last a whole week—four hours in the morning and four hours in the evening.

I organized a series for Fritz that was open to the public, but it didn't do well financially. He made maybe $1,000. I got him started on this whole lecture tour. He used to come to New York every year, and in '65 I organized workshops where people paid. I did all the work, and collected the money, and bought the food. He was always grateful. I earned a lot of money for him, and I got very little in return, monetarily. I didn't ask him for more. And whatever I asked for, he gave me. Toward the end I asked him to give me ten percent and he agreed gladly. He just did it. That was it.

Los Angeles

ANNE SIMKIN

I loved Fritz. To me he was part of our life, part of our house. To me Fritz *is* something that is alive and a part of myself.

I saw him, for the greater part, as a very shy person. And not open and vulnerable at all with people. Since I was not a professional, he could be himself with me; I trusted Fritz and I'm sure he trusted me. To me he was a human being. . . I can't describe what that is, except to say that he was somebody I could relate to.

Yes, I know he was capable of being cruel. To me he was kind. I was afraid to work with him because I figured he knew me so well. He asked me to come into his group. . . I felt that he was enticing me, so I didn't buy it. I didn't work with him, and I'm sorry that I didn't. . . on the other hand, I probably did work with him in my own way.

He was at our house during many of the Jewish holidays. . . he'd be with us at Passover and Chanukah.

He was very sloppy and he liked to be taken care of. That goes together. He *needed* to be taken care of, I think. And he was very good at having people do stuff he didn't like to do. Fritz was surrounded by helpers. And he liked being seen. He had to be the central attraction.

I just don't remember being unhappy very much around him.

I saw a beautiful moment when his son, Steve, was at our house in Los Angeles. Friz was very touched, very happy to be with Steve. Steve had passed his orals, or had just taken them, and it was very beautiful for me to watch them.

Another view. . .

STEPHEN PERLS

For a while there was very little contact between us. But then after I had my doctorate and I was a certified psychologist, I *seemed* to have value in his eyes.

That was the message he *seemed* to have given my sister. She had no value for him because she didn't go on in school. He had little contact with me when I was in high school and college, but when I got my doctorate and began to get involved in therapy as well as program development kinds of activities, he then made contact with me.

He flew to Albuquerque just on his own once and visited with Rae and myself. He had come to Oregon once because he was close by and wanted to come and visit. I'd last seen him before that about 1960 in Chicago. He phoned from the airport asking if we would like to visit with him, so Rae and I went over for an hour. Then he flew off to wherever else he was going.

Most of our meetings were a little strained—not really formal but not really warm either. We would chitchat a little but he didn't like chitchat. He wanted to get directly into issues and feelings, yet he knew that if he got into heavy talk about the family it would push me away. Fritz was critical of my mother and my sister; he often felt they were leeching on him. So I would wonder, "What does he say about *me* when I'm not around?"

I identified with them, and at the same time I agreed with much of what he was saying because I'd experienced similar kinds of things. He said he respected my independence—venturing off to Ohio when I was seventeen or eighteen, instead of staying back east and getting caught up in the little world of my sister and my mother.

When I was at Antioch College, he invited me to participate in a demonstration he was doing at the Dayton State Hospital. I was a little scared because I'd never been in a state hospital before. He talked to the people and had them talk to him. There wasn't any particular hot seat kind of activities. Though I really don't remember the content of that session, it seemed like he got people involved in whatever the issues were. But either I wasn't that much into psychology then, or I was generally scared being in that hospital with all those crazy people. I didn't then have the impression that I did later when I saw some of his films. He seemed quite mild, focusing on bodily movements but not pushing the participants. I don't know whether his skills improved over the years or whether I just wasn't tuned in earlier or what.

Stephen's sister, Renate, now married, was not tuned in either. . .

RENATE PERLS
There was a time we were working on a book together. (It was one he was writing after *Gestalt Therapy* which Goodman and Hefferline had worked on.) That was in 1953, shortly after the Gestalt Institute opened. I was 22; I was in terrible shape. I was so frightened taking the cab down to my parents' apartment, I would arrive paralyzed; I couldn't move. . . but I'd taught myself to type. I was a lousy typist but Fritz wanted some help putting his words into correct English without losing the gestalt feeling. He spoke excellent English but he *wrote* with a German accent! It could have been a very healthy experience because I enjoyed it and I felt I was useful. Fritz and I worked well together; the thought came from him but I did the writing. But then he gave it to somebody who had been a patient of his and supposedly knew gestalt and she fucked it up completely, lost the whole meaning of the book. By that time Fritz had lost interest and he threw it away. Burned it, I think. Of course, I was very resentful because I felt that this was also my baby. But I didn't say anything, I swallowed it again.

Art and I lived with them for a year while Art was going to the Art Students League in New York. One night the maid had made dinner but there was very little meat. Art and I wanted to eat early because we were going off to a movie or something, so we each ate just a little sliver. We left most of it for Laura and Fritz. Fritz came downstairs, took one look at the dinner and screamed at us, "Get out of my house, you parasites!" Of course, I went into hysterics. Laura came in and intervened. She told me afterwards that she said to him: "You can't throw her out, she's eight months pregnant."

I admired Fritz for his work, and I think that gestalt therapy is really the only one that's worthwhile. I've been in various types of therapy and didn't move at all until I worked with a gestalt therapist.

My quandary is between the way Fritz was with me and the way he was with "humanity." His was a humanitarian approach, but not a human family approach. The thing is, I'm much more myself because of my involvement with Fritz, or disinvolvement, whichever way. I have tremendous respect for his work. So Fritz had helped me in spite of himself.

If you had met me a year or two ago it would have been, "Oh, I'm Fritz Perls' daughter! Some of his greatness has rubbed off on me, whoopee!" I was so much into being Fritz and proud of being his daughter. In many ways I *am* like Fritz—I'm not denying it—but at this point it's a bore, it really is. I just feel, "Jesus Christ, let me be myself."

Marv Lifschitz became Renate's gestalt therapist . . .

MARVIN LIFSCHITZ
I learned my own way of working with resistance from watching Fritz dismiss people impatiently. I learned to patiently deal with the person who's dumping on you, or not wanting to work, and have them see what they're doing.

I suppose it was precisely this quality which contrasted so markedly with Fritz' attitude toward his daughter, Renate, that she liked most working with me. I never saw it that way before. She claims I'm the only one she didn't feel wiped out by or whom she didn't wipe out.

She'd called me because she was unable to travel to New

York. She said at the time, "I don't want to frighten you, but a lot of people are threatened by me; I'm Fritz Perls' daughter." I was very excited and very challenged by the prospect of working with her.

Both parents contribute to a child's upbringing, each, of course, in their own way. And in Renate's case, both the parents happened to have been brilliant therapists.

Fritz described her in *In and Out the Garbage Pail* as a phony. I found her to be dynamic, intelligent, sensitive, and with a good sense of humor.

During the first session, I remember she saw the gestalt prayer on my wall. It had tremendous impact. She went for it at one point; she felt like ripping it. I said, "Go ahead. If you want to rip it up, rip it up." And she got into some work on that. She's never fought me on the technique, although many times when I'd give her some kind of homework statement, she'd say, "No one's going to tell me what to do."

JIM SIMKIN
He wasn't finding what he was looking for and wound up on the West Coast again in 1960.

By 1961 we had two gestalt study groups going. By then Fritz had started a San Bernardino route and a Santa Ana route. He would go along the Santa Ana Freeway and the San Bernardino Freeway and stop at this hospital and that private practice group. It was typical of what Fritz did. He would reach out and start something.

He got some excitement out of this for a year and a half. Then he started feeling burdened.

> In spite of Jim Simkin's support . . . I could not get through to the profession and I could not get rid of a feeling of being condemned to life. I did not even have a depression. I was fed up with the whole psychiatric racket. I did not know what I wanted. Retirement? Vacation? Change of profession?

Possibly Fritz' state of boredom and depression at this time led him to Fritz Faiss, an art teacher, a naturopath and psychoanalyst.

FRITZ FAISS

Fritz was interested in the experimental workshops I was conducting at UCLA for developing new teaching techniques in art. I based my teaching on simple but effective exercises which helped to awaken imagination, fantasy, and creativity. As I said, Fritz was very interested in my workshops, but it was a difficult decision for him to join the activities. He attended several of these annual summer workshops as well as the shorter winter sessions. When he finally became part of the work group, he developed a sincere attitude for self-expression through painting. Since he was most often the oldest in the group, his achievements were quite remarkable.

For Fritz, my psychographic exercises, as I called them, were a great obstacle. It was difficult for him to let go, to relax . . . the exercises require a complete surrender: the hand and pencil are guided from within, from inward forces. Consciousness and will power can only disturb the flow of this inward force. Fritz' first reaction was to discontinue these exercises. When I first analyzed some of his psychographic drawings, he tried to hide them; he did not like to be analyzed. He made silly pictures to indicate that he was not willing to accept any directives at all. When I urged him to continue the exercises, he began to feel their therapeutic quality. He enjoyed the relaxing, and the contemplation and meditative mood they created. He had relapses, but he worked his way up again.

He spent much time painting and drawing. Whenever I suggested to my pupils at the end of a day's session that they should do some extra work, it was Fritz particularly who did surprising amounts of interesting works. With great pride he presented them next day. In time, Fritz became quite soft; he asked for criticism and for analysis of his new productions. It was a sure sign that his inner resistance had been overcome; he let me and other people peek into his inner self. I think it was a surprise for Fritz himself to let this happen.

When I was a little harsh and quite direct in my analysis he would send me—after the session—little pieces of paper, neatly folded and sealed. In few lines, in haiku form, he complained that I was too stern, too demanding, and that I asked for too much work. He asked me to be more considerate because he was actually just a "small boy" at this.

Fritz was thrilled and excited like a child that images formed in him, and that he could project them outward and onto the canvas. It was a first time experience for him. He was untrained. He took to painting rather late in his life.

The psychographic drawings show specific trends of the inner self . . . Fritz reflected a lack of coherence and design, restlessness, strong activity, and an industriousness which comes quick and stops fast. There was also expectation of a great happiness, related to sexual adventure, and to philosophies offering enlightenment and perfection. His drawings indicated a strong tendency to look ahead, toward the new, the unexpected, the "modern"—indicating that Fritz was looking for something to develop, for the yet unformed. When I elaborated on these drawings, when I analyzed them, he began to "see" them. They were symbolic. He had created symbols of his inner self—or seen from another angle, he had created archetypal images.

After the preliminary exercises with basically abstract elements, the pupils were given free rein to paint, draw, sculpt, or write whatever they liked. The subject matter was of no particular importance; only how you expressed it. Did your inner images find an outer gestalt or not? As it turned out, Fritz liked to paint romantic landscapes. They were quite acceptable. He showed meadows with flowers, hills and forests, mountains in the background and blue skies with fluffy clouds; all very sweet, very lovely. He also showed little creeks with silvery streaks of running water coming down the mountains.

Then as an afterthought he added, a female figure reclining in the midst of the meadows. Nude. He added a round disc in strong yellow to the blue sky. After some consideration, he added a snake heading toward the reclining nude. Now, so far, we have the archetypal symbols of nature: fertility in the form of a female nude and the link to the lost Paradise—the snake. The waters running down from the mountains represent the four rivers of life. In some pictures

Fritz depicted the snake biting the reclining nude. Over all these additions and layers of conscious and unconscious trends, he added—quite deliberately—the figure of Satan, the black-winged devil, hovering above the poor female and releasing his bowels onto the female. When I asked Fritz about the strange metamorphosis his pictures underwent from the sweetness of the romantic landscape to the action of the devil, he answered that this was the way he felt about life. And the female figure and the devil expressed how he conceived of his relationship to the other sex.

During one of the sessions of my workshop, together with Fritz' group, I mentioned that well-trained artists of Japan and China could define one's character and personality from a single line drawn with brush and ink. Fritz asked me if I could do it too. I had never tried it. He insisted that I should and I was ordered out of the room. After some time I was called back. A large number of single lines drawn with brush and ink on newsprint paper were spread out on the floor and on tables. I concentrated on one drawing. I put myself into a meditative mood, and put my feelings about the quality of the line into words: It told me that the person who drew the line was able to do managerial work, to lead people. I felt that the person would be successful in any profession, and in a variety of enterprises. The most striking fact was that the line carried a trend to penetrate into other people's minds—I described it as a serpent crawling at ease into holes. The line revealed considerable vitality, strong inner drive, will power, romanticism, intelligence, sensuality and materialism. Toward the end the line became fuzzy. There were indications of an attempt to mend these parts together. It indicated that the person lost interest fast and was often forced to go back and bring things to an end. I called it lack of consistency and continuity.

I was asked if I could read something in respect of health. There were indications of occasional spasms related to heart disorder.

Fritz, who had kept himself in the background, left the room. He was very upset. It was *his* line! Later he told me that he had felt a shock, particularly when I mentioned the heart condition. it was something he tried to ignore, to hide away, but as a medical doctor he was aware of the importance of the fact. . . .

Soon after this, Fritz went to Israel, the ancient homeland of the Jewish people. . . .

Israel

Aha, Aha, the old Jew's homecoming to the land of his ancestors. . . No, mine was not a Jew's homecoming, though for a while I played with the idea of making my home in Israel.

ABRAHAM ELIZUR

Fritz was the kind of a person who desired so much wandering around. Some people referred to him being like the hippie-type. In a sense, he was a hippie-type. On one occasion, his wife told me he was like a gypsy; he liked to wander around. It was so strong in him that nothing could have touched him. He apparently wanted to meditate, contemplace, wander around and be by himself. He felt at home; he enjoyed being there.

> *I hate the chrome-plated hotels where one is waited on all the time. I often feel somewhat paranoid in small, elegant hotels; the vulture-like bellboys and elevator boys and chambermaids hover over me and are ingratiating and nice in return for a tip . . . I decided to go . . . to Ein Hod, an art colony . . .*
>
> *Painting had become my preoccupation in Israel . . . I had never painted with so much enthusiasm and involvement. Painters like Van Gogh were stimulated and in search of landscapes. Here was living color: here where the Negev muzzles the Red Sea, flanked by the mountains of Jordan and Egypt; here where the sun stirs up color after color from the heights of the mountains and penetrates to the underwater life of corals and gorgeously colored fishes; here eyes could feast on colors and shapes varying every hour of the day . . . .*

*Painting became intense involvement, vaguely ap-
proaching an obsession. Soon I had one teacher after
another. In Ein Hod, Israel, I did likewise.*

*Ein Hod is an artist colony south of Haifa, the northern port
of Israel. Johanan Peter, a tall rangy craftsman of exquisite
jewelry, became Fritz' friend. . . .*

JOHANAN PETER
He painted with Hillel. He went with Hillel to the beach.
Hillel gave him a place and said, "Here you paint," and
Hillel went to fish (he likes very much to fish).

*I'd been told he might not talk to me. His sight was failing,
his wife was ill and his beloved country was at war again. I
knock. The door opens to an ancient time. I am suddenly in
the presence of a patriarch. I tell him I would like to talk to
him about Dr. Perls. The door opens wider.*

*"Come in, he says" you are welcome. Please spend the
night with us."*

ISHAIAH HILLEL
Balzac said, "A good storyteller starts from the end, goes to
the middle, and finishes at the beginning." So I will tell you
that the end came when he said, "I did not know that your
wife was a swine like you." I went up to him and said, "You
pack your things! I don't want to see you. If you're here in
an hour I'll break your neck!"

I went upstairs and laid in bed. I was so shattered . . . calling my wife and me swine . . . outrageous! Particularly my
wife. She treated him like royalty. When she was here, she
prepared his bed, furnished fresh sheets, straightened things
up for him. That was the tradition of her house, her father
was like that; their house was always full of Arabs, Chris-
tians and Jews—"Come and eat and drink . . ." Me, too,
I'm the same way. And he still owed me money for paints
and canvases he bought from me.

So when he said this, I said, "I don't know what burns you, but get out of my house! I don't want to have anything to do with you any more. Get out of here!"

While he lived with me he would always tell me when he was bringing a girl. He would say, "Tonight I need a woman," and he would go and fetch a girl from the hotel in Haifa, a *femme de chambre*. He paid her money—he was not stingy in this respect.

He had wanted a lamp in his bed for reading. We gave him one. But he hadn't put it in properly and he had gotten a little shock. That made him furious.

"I nearly got killed last night with that girl."

"But you were not killed," I said. And he exploded at me using that term "swine."

And, then, as I was lying in bed, he came up and tried to overcome this shocking disappointment I had in him. True, he paid what I asked for painting lessons, but I gave him more; I gave him my heart. We were intimate, so much so that we didn't need to talk because he read my thoughts and I read his thoughts. So he came up, put his hand on my knee and said in a very soft voice, "Are you feeling well, Hillel?"

I didn't answer him, and he kissed me on the forehead and said, "I owe you money."

I said, "Nothing! Leave me alone! Go away!"

That's all. Then he left the village.

I am a fifteenth-generation Israeli. My maternal ancestor, Hashlah Hakadosh, was one of the three leading figures of the Kabala.* He came to Israel in 1618 from Frankfurt where he was the chief Rabbi. We have three in our family with the name Kadosh, which in Hebrew means "saint." My grandmother was the first cousin of the Jewish German poet, Heinrich Heine, who was born in Dusseldorf. my grandfather, my mother's father was Isaiah Eash Horoviti which was exactly the name of Hashlah Hakodosh before he was sainted. You know, with Jews, it goes from grandfather to grandfather. We have many branches and the ramifications are great, but if you preserve the name of the first man, this is the stamp.

I inherited only the weight of this spiritualism. I was one of the eight or ten Jewish high officials in the British Mandate Government. I am one of the founders of this village of Ein Hod. I was the first mayor here. Again, the credit goes to my ancestors because both of my grandparents were the founders of Rishon-Lizion** in 1882. They founded the first Jewish settlements after the destruction of the Temple. Then, the Jews went back to work the land. Both my grandfathers were farmers. I speak many languages. I love the Arabic language no less than I love the Hebrew. If I met an Arab who speaks perfect Hebrew, I would rather speak Arabic with him because I love the language. Professor Kulcsar has lectured about my paintings at the International Convention of Psychiatrists at Madrid. My son is a chemical engineer. My daughter published a work which is a compulsory book at the university and at every university in the United States where Hebrew is taught.

What makes this impressive genealogical background even more interesting is that the man we are talking about actually insulted you.

Yes, and he insulted my wife . . . and it was not warranted.

---

*a sacred esoteric doctrine; a system of occult theosophy or mystical interpretation of the scriptures.
**a town near Tel Aviv.

At the beginning, Perls stayed in a hotel in Haifa. After he became my pupil he wanted to be near me so he asked to live in my house and I agreed. When we first met and he saw my paintings, he said, "Oh, these paintings were done under the influence of LSD." This brought us together in a way I cannot talk about now. I was just recently out of the hospital bed, where I was for two years in complete seclusion under LSD treatment . . . it was a terrible experience. Later, at Perls' request, I introduced him to Professor Kulcsar, and he also went once a week to take LSD in pills.

I had told Perls about a certain dream I had which repeated itself in various forms, but always the same dream. He asked me to come with him to the hospital to demonstrate his work on my dream for Professor Kulcsar's staff. We went a couple of times, but the third time I said, "Dr. Perls, I have had enough. I could stand your experiments and demonstrations once, the second time it was hard, the third time I absolutely refuse."

Once a week we would go out to the sea and I would tell him about composition and everything—how to pick out a piece of landscape or seascape—and then I went fishing about a hundred yards away. One day I saw him walking back and forth while I was still fishing, so I came to him to make my corrections. He continued walking back and forth, sometimes closing his eyes and crossing his hands behind his back. Then he said, "You know, Hillel (he called me Mr. Hillel in the beginning, then Hillel), "I've had eight art teachers in Los Angeles and I begin to think you are a bloody good teacher." I appreciated Perls as an average painter. He had talent but he had much work to do.

Another time, he said, "Hillel, Oscar Wilde said, 'What's the good of friendship if one can't say what one thinks.'" He said nothing for awhile. Then he said, "Hillel, I have left psychiatry. I don't want to go back to it. I want to devote myself to painting and music."

Actually, we didn't talk much—from time to time about music, painting and human behavior. Once, as we were about to go back, he turned to me and said, "Hillel, you have to go back to writing. But before you start, see that you have a writing place with a key and lock so that your wife won't put her hands on it."

When I think of that now, my head is bursting. I am a literary man more than a painter but I didn't tell him that I was a writer. I had stopped writing because of her but, you see, nobody in the world knew that; *nobody in the world*. I never spoke to anyone about my attitude to writing or why I stopped.

This is something too intimate to talk about. When my eyes are pinned down to writing I tend to the subject, but when I talk there are associations and ideas and they jump from one thing to another. I free myself to my thoughts. I don't pin myself down to development of an idea.

I felt Perls was a great man. He could see. I admired him, he had great intuition and intelligence . . . start talking to him and he will dissect you and tell you what's in and what's out. He always read my thoughts.

I felt he is Jewish but we never talked about this or about his opinion of the Jewish state. He was very vital. He had to have his drink and he had to have his women. He was, as the French say, a *bon viveur*. He made the impression of a strong big man who liked to enjoy all the things in life but still I felt at that time he was very low. He didn't show it, but I could see it in his paintings. He did tell me about his wife— she is a psychologist, too, in New York. In the car, going to the sea one day, he said, "Why didn't she answer? Why didn't she confirm that she received the three hundred dollars I sent her?" Another time he said, "I wish she's dead. I hope she's dead." There was a divergence between them, a very deep friction. I didn't ask him. I never ask unless someone tells me and then I make up my mind for myself.

After Perls left Ein Hod, he went to Eilat. Then about half a year later he came one day again as if nothing had happened between us to have my opinion of the paintings he made in Eilat.

I have no ill feelings towards him. My lasting impression is a favorable one.

A frail woman, she hung back as her husband spoke. She brought tea and cookies and gentleness. Only after her husband had gone to lie down—exhausted from talking about Fritz' insult—does she speak.

SARAH HILLEL

He was here the end of 1962, 1963. He liked the ambience and the interesting people of Ein Hod very much. He was here for two months, then left and came back for a month and went to Eilat and came back for a week, and then he suddenly disappeared.

We have a little place for people who want to stay overnight. He had nobody. I know he didn't like too much the place he stayed in Haifa. Where would he go to stay, to a hotel? I could afford to accommodate him, so that's what I did. He was downstairs—he took the two rooms, first one and then we gave him that other room as well.

On the one side, he could be very nice and kind, and on the other side, so rude. Sometimes, I was surprised. He was not stable at all. He was himself a sick man, I mean morally sick, in a very low spirit. He even got special treatment with LSD shots every week at the Psychological Department at Tel Hachomer-Shamair with Dr. Kulcsar. After his treatments, of course, he didn't drive, so they drove him back to Tel Aviv and I put him in my home there overnight. When he came to my house, he didn't feel well and was so pale. He would lay on the couch for hours, dozing. I always tried to give him some light food, some porridge or whatever. Then,

in the evening, I gave him better food. I never asked him to
pay for that or made any account. I received him as a guest.
In the morning we drove back to Ein Hod; it is about 70-80
kilometers away. He was so tense when he was driving, he
never liked to speak; you just couldn't ask him a word.

Here he didn't work, he didn't write; he wanted only to relax with conversation and painting.

He was certainly not a talkative person yet he could express himself with such grace . . . but sometimes with such
rude words! It was surprising that such an intelligent man,
himself a psychiatrist, didn't have control of what he was
saying or doing . . . No, he had no opportunity to say anything nasty to me. I didn't give any. I never discussed anything with him. I just observed; only quietly I did what I have
to do, as a human being. I never said the simplest word that
could hurt him. I let him be quiet and at ease. Nevertheless, I
think he was mentally ill, because of the way he behaved. He
took everything for granted. He was not grateful for
anything; he didn't express himself for something you did
for him.

When he stayed overnight in Tel Aviv after a treatment, he
got up early, and on Saturday they were opening the restaurant very late and he was hungry. He couldn't ask. I didn't
take any notice of that; if there were no restaurants where he
could go and get something, I was ready to serve him. So I
used to call him in. I gave him a nice helping because he was
a big person. He needed much food and he liked to eat. . . .

The more you were kind to him, the more he was rude. I
couldn't find out why. Was it something against his family
that put him against people, or was that his nature? I never
found him in a good mood. Never. Maybe he came after a
very bad shock. I don't know.

But we don't do things to get gratitude. We Israelis always
put up anybody who comes as a guest, you know. That is the
Oriental way of hospitality, even in the face of rudeness.
And he was rude. Sometimes it was inside him, and sometimes he just expressed it. I had pity on him. I really had pity
on him.

Professor Kulcsar (pronounced culture) *was head of the psychiatry department at the teaching hospital, where Fritz got his LSD shots. He was the only psychiatrist to examine Eichmann before his trial in 1961. He laughed when I told him I'd heard that Fritz had been a patient of his and had gotten special treatment because he was very depressed. . . .*

SHOLOMO KULCSAR

Dr. Perls was *not* a patient! There was *no* treatment! That didn't even come into the mind of anyone on our staff. I had then a stack of LSD and I gave it to him. I think it was a continuation of the methods which he used before. He liked it. He closed himself in a room and we weren't present—there was nothing peculiar. I didn't feel he was at all depressed. On the contrary, he was quite active; depressive people are not active. And the rate of his thoughts and of his speech was quite in contradiction to depression: To be depressed is to suffer from a depressive disease and he was not depressed.

Dr. Perls was with me in Tel Hachomer Hospital and we became friends. I had read his works and was very much impressed. He demonstrated his methods to me and to my staff and stayed with us for about four weeks.

He took a series of LSD, which was used medically in those days. He claimed that in the state of LSD ecstasy he was able to synthesize more of his ideas. It was a method for him. So in a sense, it *was* as a patient, but it was as a teacher too. We were all very impressed by his method. According to my knowledge, he was the first one to use the technique of analyzing each element of the dream as a split off part of the dreamer. I use this method in my work in psychodrama and it is very effective. His theory is well-known, but his living presentation was even more impressive than the books.

Then he returned to the States and I didn't hear about him for a long time until one day, years later, I saw him in *Time* magazine as the guru of the hippies, with a long beard. . . .

When he was here, he looked just like any other psychiatrist, nothing physically impressive. But he made an impression upon me, not so much as a psychiatrist, but as a man

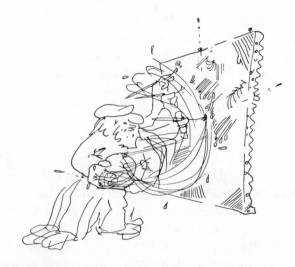

seeking a new way, in his 60s. I think if he had been a painter, for instance, he would have started a new style. The painter Tintoretto changed his style at the age of 80; he lived a hundred years.

When I knew him he looked like an aging man, but he had arrived at a point in his life where he had seen and knew everything and then went into the world to seek something new, to return to youth. I think in his approach to the hippie movement he was seeking youth; he went to the Artists' Village because he wanted to learn something new, a creative activity. If you begin something new, then you are young again. In his professional actions he was old; when he painted he was young. I think it was play for him.

He evidently succeeded in rejuvenation. You know, he gives a great optimism by his example for aging people. He was a Faust. I don't know whether he thought he sold his soul to the devil or not; I do think that his professional work was only part of his life, just part. The accent was on the transmutation, the rejuvenation. What some call depression, I think, were the pains of a birth. He wanted to be reborn. It was a crisis, a crisis of life. But a personal crisis, not a pathological one. I liked him because he dared to do it, to leave his career, to begin something new.

JOHANAN PETER

We went several times with him to Haifa and once Sonia Sadron, a woman painter, came with us. He was driving in his car and on the way, they had a quarrel and he wanted to throw her out in the middle of the way. She said she never would go again with him.

SONIA SADRON

Dr. Perls, Peter, Peter's wife and I all went to Haifa together to see Martha Graham, the American choreographer who created a modern dance school. We were all her admirers many, many years back, and now we enjoyed seeing her again at the concert with her students. That evening Martha Graham performed "Herodiade." It is a ballet about aspiring to grandeur in the theater and becoming worthy of it. It deals with one of Graham's great themes— the attainment of selfhood—and in it is her genius to demonstrate choice, to show being and becoming. One can only guess Dr. Perls' response to this performance of the commitment to the unachievable.

On the way back in the car I said that Martha Graham should stop performing herself because she was already old, and that she ought to give her best students an opportunity to participate in her shows. I felt that she did her reputation a great harm and that she spoiled the impression we all had of her when she was young.

I also belong to the stage people. I, myself, was a professional musician, my father was a viola player and orchestra conductor, and my mother was an opera singer. I know how she also had these problems when she got older. I am convinced that stage people don't know when to stop. They can't give up. Even when they are in their decline, they still continue to perform. For stage people, an opera singer or a dancer, after forty, she's already old. I sincerely believe that Martha Graham should stop performing because it is harmful to her prestige.

When I said this, Dr. Perls suddenly jumped on me in a very aggressive way, "You say that because you yourself

would like to be in her place and because you are jealous! Jealous!'' I was surprised by this attack and his lack of tolerance for a different point of view from a stranger. He hurt me very much. How can he say that to someone he didn't know? I know my value, I know who I am.

I tried to divert the conversation with a joke and artificial laughing, to break the embarrassment of everybody in the car—but I didn't succeed.

Of course, I did not answer his remark. I didn't know who he was. We met just because of our mutual friends. He was not introduced to me. I was not presented to him. I suppose he knew that I was an artist because he was living in this village.

JOHANAN PETER
A few days later we spoke about the village and he said there was only one good and sensitive painting in the gallery that he liked. He described the painting and I started to laugh.

I said, ''That painting, 'The Musicians,' is from this woman, Sonia Sadron.''

''Impossible,'' he said, ''that can't be. That woman cannot make such a painting.'' Then he said, ''If Sonia Sadron painted that then I'll go and beg her pardon in the middle of the village.''

Next day he went to the gallery. He saw that the painting is from Sonia Sadron and when he knew that the post is coming—when half the village is here. . . .

SONIA SADRON

I was sitting in the Village Square, not far from the gallery. I saw he was coming . . . I just looked at him. Then when he came in front of me, he fell down on his knees in front of everybody,—I jumped a little—kissing my hand and asking my forgiveness! He apologized. It was quite unusual, funny and even ridiculous.

I was once again astonished and embarrassed. I did not know how to react to this strange behavior of an old man. I said, "That's OK," and I went away.

It was a very nice gesture, of course, in front of all those people who didn't understand what was happening. . . .

Peter and I had a hard time explaining the matter.

Other impressions of him? Well, I think he was a man full of the spirit of culture, a little bit eccentric and with a good humor if he was in the mood.

In my opinion, Dr. Perls also belonged to the stage people. When he was lecturing, he needed an audience to perform and communicate his ideas. Maybe with my remarks about old age, I hurt him personally. When he learned about me by looking at my pictures, I was, for him, an artist, having the right to criticize another artist. I think he was really great to force himself to recognize his mistake and come to apologize. Doing this, he unconsciously proved that an artist, even old, can still be good and creative.

GIDEON SCHWARZ

I didn't know Fritz when he was in Israel (I'd met him in California) but I knew people there who did. A lady from a gestalt group I was leading brought a painter, Gershon Davidovitch, from Ein Hod to my home. At some stage, Davidovitch had become the teacher of a Fritz Perls who had wanted to paint. The woman had told him about my knowing Fritz Perls. (I had been talking about Perls in terms of . . . well, he had become my guru, so to speak) and Davidovitch had told her it couldn't possibly be the same person, because the man he had met was an idiot.

Davidovitch said, "He knew absolutely nothing about painting, and he was a lousy pupil, but, more important, the guy was crazy, obviously crazy. I'm willing to believe anything about him except that he could have had anything to do with therapy or dealing with people. This is impossible!"

At that time we had a portrait of Perls on the wall that he had given my ex-wife as a parting gift. Davidovitch looked at the picture and said, "This is the same man."

Two months later, I visited Ein Hod myself, and I ran into Davidovitch. He invited me to his place. When I brought up the subject of Fritz Perls again, he said, "You know, 'idiot' may not have been precisely the right term. But he was a strange man; he did things that made people angry. For example, at a party in the village coffee shop, people were having a good time, some getting drunk, a typical party. All of a sudden Fritz groaned, held his chest, and fell to the ground. He seemed to have had a heart attack.

"Everything stopped dead; people were hovering around him, when he turned over and said, 'I was only kidding.' People got very angry, and when they asked why he did such a thing, he said, 'Somehow I felt that was my role in this gathering.'"

It may have been some sort of comment about what was going on there. I can just speculate that he felt everybody was trying to get attention by phony means, and he decided to outdo them all, to get more attention than anyone else, knowingly, by the phoniest means.

SARAH HILLEL

He was very much worried about his family. He didn't get any letters from his wife. He said he sent her presents and he never got an acknowledgment about these things. It hurt him very much. He was always thinking about the family, even sometimes homesick, talking about how he hasn't heard what the children are doing, what they are studying, how they are. For many, many weeks, he was always expecting letters from them and was very much upset when nothing came. His wife left him because she wanted to be in New York, and he didn't. That is why they parted. The thing I am mostly sure about is *she* left him and went with the two children and *not* he left her. He was so depressed about it. She had the training I understand, and has a clinic and earns very well, and she doesn't need his money. She had her interest and took good care of the children—of course, she always welcomed him back on account of the children.

New York/Los Angeles

Some of those who saw Fritz upon his return said he came back relaxed, obviously refreshed, and ready to resume his work. Among them, Fritz Faiss. . . .

FRITZ FAISS

He came back relaxed and feeling good. The tension was less, his heart condition had improved. He began to take more care of himself. The prolonged evening sessions were shortened. He was able to cut down smoking.

However refreshed and relaxed, Fritz returned to a strained relationship with his daughter, Renate, and her husband, Art. . . .

RENATE PERLS

When Fritz got back from Israel, we were living in the other house and I was doing some painting. Fritz and I were showing our art to each other. I thought his painting was really wishy-washy but I pretended to admire it: We didn't have the courage to tell him it was all crap. But he said, "You know, you have something that I don't have. You have the courage to use color." It was one of two compliments I ever got from him in my life.

The other time was when I was thirteen years old and dancing. It was right after World War II, in Johannesburg, and I was taking lessons from a woman who had been a prima ballerina in Russia and we had this tremendous cabaret going. We staged a very large to-do at the City Hall. The mayor and the ambassadors and anybody who was anybody was there. And Fritz was there. Nina Runitch, my teacher, was the star but I did a couple of solo parts. I happened to be a good dancer. In fact, I was the best jumper in the class. I had all the lovely big leaps across the stage in this grand production and I got marvelous compliments from everybody. Also, afterwards I was wearing my first evening gown, you know. An exciting, fantastic evening. Of course, Fritz was very proud of me, bragging about it to everyone: "My daughter blah, blah, blah. . . ."

Art Gold

It seemed he only reacted to success in both of us, and if we weren't successful he was very negative toward us. Unfortunately, during the time it just wasn't a meteoric rise to the top. It was one long uphill struggle for me in my professional life. He was very intolerant about that.

He was responsible for my going off to California. Ren and I weren't getting along very well; Alison was a year old. It was difficult. Fritz spoke of the wonderful opportunities in Los Angeles, and he suggested that I go out there. He was beginning to commute at that time. I didn't have any idea of going out there before, so he was really responsible for my going.

Renate Perls

We went up to Provincetown and I got pregnant with Leslie, so we decided I would stay and have the baby because I had my mother and my doctor here, and I had nobody there. Art didn't see Leslie until she was nearly six weeks old.

Art Gold

I was looking for art jobs, which were almost impossible to find. In those days it was much worse than it is now. I wound up with odd jobs—silk screening and window dressing, all kinds of things.

The people he knew that I stayed with when I first got to L.A. were all homosexual, and very friendly with Fritz. He came back to New York with rumors to Ren that I was rapidly going gay. Later I found out Fritz was bisexual at that point, and screwing around a lot. He was by no means a queen or anything like that, and I'm sure he would have defended it as experimentation. Maybe he was getting the suspicion off himself by talking about me that way, I don't know. He never accused me directly, but he did his best to split us apart.

RENATE PERLS

I believed what he had said, because Art and I had parted on rather difficult terms. If I had gone along with Fritz, I would have had no love relationships with *any*body. I did not get this love at home. Whatever Fritz and Laura had, it was not the kind of relationship that I want for me; I don't need a man who is traipsing off here, there and some other place and fifty women on the side and so forth.

ART GOLD

Fritz removed himself from any kind of involvement with Ren and myself. The only time we really communicated with each other was shortly after Ren and I were married; I was a kid in my early twenties in art school, and Fritz was painting again. He had fixed up the third floor of a brownstone for a studio, and many times he called me over there to ask what I thought of his work.

I was very noncommittal because I was terrified of the man. But I'd give him what I considered to be valid criticism and he listened. He respected my opinion and I valued that. But otherwise, and from that point on, it was all downhill between him and me. He was very belittling, and very, very sarcastic toward me. He was only interested in my helping him with his work. For the most part, it was pretty crappy but I couldn't find it in myself to tell him it was garbage. . . Well, look, we were in a compromised position with him from the beginning: We were living with him and I didn't have a dime.

Fritz was looking down his nose at me the whole time. It wasn't that I wasn't good enough for his daughter; he wasn't selective about that: He called us *both* leeches.

I was in L.A. about eight months before Ren joined me.

RENATE PERLS

When I got out to Los Angeles it was *very* tough. We weren't getting along at all and neither of us could find work. I finally got a job at the Hollywood Ranch Market, of all places, and only because the woman next door had to quit her job. I worked every day except for Saturdays. That was fine with me because that way I could be home weekends with Art and the kids.

It was 1957, Art couldn't find a job for love or money. There was a period of a couple of months where we had no income whatsoever and I had to ask Fritz to pay the rent. In fact, we were so broke that for six weeks we ate corn flakes. Luckily we had an account with the Carnation milk people and so we just put everything on their bill. I remember we ate cereal morning, noon and night. Whatever else we could buy we gave to the children.

After three months in California we decided to come back to New York. But we had a big blow-up with Fritz. Because we were too afraid to tell him we were leaving, we did a very stupid thing. He had bought us a stove and refrigerator and had paid our rent, and when we put an ad in the paper to sell our furniture, Fritz, who was looking for furniture for his own place, saw the ad and called up and told us if we sold the stove and refrigerator he would have the sheriff on us.

My brother Steve is completely unlike Fritz. He is a strict father but he cares about his children and does things with them. But then, Steve was never Fritz' "baby," so to speak. I had a father for the first four years of my life, but Steve says he never had a father so he never missed him. Steve was strictly my mother's baby, because Fritz didn't want him and my mother refused to have an abortion. Fritz said, "Well, all right, I'll send him to college when he grows up." When Steve got to college age and my mother said, "Okay, now take over, you send him to college," Fritz damn near dropped dead. He'd forgotten about that completely.

STEPHEN PERLS

Most of the time Fritz was generous, but not *really*. It was a contest we had throughout life: He was very generous with money if he was asked for it, but he would never offer first. Laura says that at first Fritz didn't want to pay any of my college expenses and she was going to pay it all. Then apparently they got into a big argument—so I'm told, though I wasn't there—and she insisted that he pay at least tuition and she would pay living expenses. That's how they did it. I don't know the facts for sure but he *would* have balked at it. Then, pushed a little bit, he would have said okay.

When I needed some money to get my family from Chicago to Oregon where I intended to work for my doctorate (I had a counseling assistantship which paid fifty dollars a week or something like that—not a hell of a lot for a couple with two kids), I asked him for a loan to help buy a car. He said, "Sure, no problem" and wrote out a check. That was about 1961. And when I tried to pay him back he said, "No, you don't need to pay it back." He had plenty of money. That wasn't the issue.

Another time I needed $500 to pay moving expenses after receiving my doctorate. Again, he came through just on request. And it's a fairly significant amount of money, in my opinion . . . I think those are the only two times that I specifically asked him for money.

My assumption was, "I shouldn't have to ask. You're my father, you should offer. Talk to me, see where I'm at and what I need. I don't want to come begging." A major reason for not asking was based on his attitude toward my sister, who he felt was a taker. Takers annoyed him greatly. So, by asking him for something I would wind up being a taker and he would have no respect for me. So I didn't ask and I didn't beg, and most of the time I didn't get.

JIM SIMKIN

Fritz wasn't much into making money. When he invested, it meant nothing to him to just cash in and leave. In 1965, he and I bought some land in Los Angeles and planned to set up a therapy training building. He put up most of the money but on the deed we were fifty-fifty partners. We put in well over

$30,000 and made plans . . . and then he just pulled out; he was willing to dump it all for $15,000, if he could. It was typical of how he operated. He would get tired of something and just get out, finish with the thing.

The part of Fritz that was child-like and a con artist got sucked in. I never heard him acknowledge that he was in touch with that.

He had money. When we bought that lot he had a net value of a little over $100,000, and most of it was in cash. He had been compensated by the German government for some property in Germany. He used to do very well from investing. He usually bought conservative, solid things—something like Florida Power and Light. The big thing then, in the late '50s, was the 10 percent return. When some of them started to sour, he pulled out.

Whenever he experienced that something was surplus for him, he could loan it or give it away. When he voluntarily loaned money or gave a gift, he was very generous. He became anything but generous if somebody asked him, or tried to take. . . .

> . . . I feel I am being taken advantage of. Actually and factually, I am justified as far as the agreement and the financial situation is concerned. But I cannot allow myself to be generous and to experience myself as a sucker.

. . . as always there are differing views of how Fritz dealt with money.

On the one hand. . . .

SARAH HILLEL

He was a little bit—I don't know how to say it—stingy—very hard with money. For instance, he was eating at a restaurant here. At the end of every week, when it came to paying the account, he said "Make it round," and always cut it down. If, for instance, they said he owed thirty-five pounds, he said, "Cut it to thirty." They were really fine people, but they had to put on higher prices to him. What could they do? He also bought several things he needed for painting. He took everything, the brushes, paints, the paper, and then when they gave him the account, he insisted, "Cut it down."

Another time he was with my husband; he needed some batteries or something. He had no money so my husband paid for it and other things for him. He knew what the amount was, and when he came to pay up, he said, "Cut it down."

WILSON VAN DUSEN

He didn't actually need money. I know that he had planned to work a certain period of his life and stash it away so he would never have to work again and he had solved the money thing. He did not need money although he was stingy about it. If he got any he hung on to it. I was not terribly surprised to learn later that this man who mooched whenever possible was relatively wealthy.

BERNARD GUNTHER

Fritz was paying me less for working with his professional group than anyone else was paying. He was giving me fifteen dollars an hour and I was getting twenty-five from other people. He then wanted me to start teaching massage, and I told him I wanted twenty-five dollars.

"I don't want to pay you that much," he said, "because you're not worth it," and added that I was getting three times as much as most craftsmen got.

"Look, Fritz," I said, "I'm not a craftsman, I'm an artist."

The gist of his reply was, "Don't do it if you don't want to." I thought that one over and figured, "Why shouldn't I do it." Obviously it was important to me, so I said, "In the interest of harmony, I'll do the massage and do it for whatever you want to pay for it."

"I figured you'd come around."

Things were never quite the same after that.

And on the other hand. . . .

BOB SHAPIRO

Fritz, was an excellent yet frugal businessman and he was very generous financially to Esalen. He also contributed by charging relatively much lower fees to Esalen than he did for a workshop in Chicago or New York. He probably gave away hundreds of hours of his time to members of the staff. That's what I mean when I say he donated substantially.

ARTHUR CEPPOS

We never discussed royalties in all the years when there was money coming. By now the estate is getting quite a bit.

ROMILLY GRAUER

I became acquainted a bit with Fritz' trip about money.
Sometimes he was very generous. He'd throw a big party or
take us all out to dinner and have a nice time. And sometimes
if a person would ask for one week's delay he'd say, "No,
you have to pay." With one person he'd say, "No way," and
with another person he'd say, "OK."

KEN STEVENS

He was a patron of the craftsmen and the artists, too, here in
Big Sur. I know he bought a painting from Roland Hall for
$1,500. He would see people doing creative things and he
would support them.

ELLEN STEVENS

He donated a lot of bread to the Barn. He donated $4,000 to
the Barn. . . .

GIA-FU FENG

In 1965, soon after Fritz came to Esalen, Karl Lee, a potter
in Big Sur, needed a wheel. Fritz said, "Here is $100."

STEPHEN PERLS

My father did come to my high school graduation and he
did come to my college graduation. I was amazed. I was
amazed and pleased, very pleased. He also came to my wedding in 1956 at Antioch in Ohio. He was doing quite a bit of
consulting at that time in Columbus so he was only sixty
miles away. It was good to have him come. He didn't really
say very much that I can remember but I did get a hand-
shake. His way of congratulating, I think, was to give a
check.

Japan

Whatever Fritz' ambivalence towards money, he seemed always willing to finance his wanderlust. . . .

> *. . .Japan—Tokyo and Kyoto. Impossible to describe the contrast of those two cities, merely a night of high-efficiency train service apart. In contrast to Tokyo, I fell in love with Kyoto.*

JIM SIMKIN

I have lots of fascinating correspondence from him during a trip he took around the world. He had this child-like enthusiasm, for example, about a taxi ride costing a nickel. And the Zen sanatorium, where they were going to cure him of his smoking, cost only three dollars a day! He was enthralled by bargains and he got conned by bargains.

> *I got a woolen overcoat that cost only $30, but it was skimpily made. I got a white dinner jacket which I used on board, but it has been hanging unused for years now in my closet. . . .*

WILLIAM QUINN

He had a friend in Japan who was the abbot of a Zen monastery. The abbot put him in a hospital. He was there for several days, and he made a serious effort to stop smoking. Each day the abbot would pay him a formal visit in his formal attire. Fritz felt very serene. Then, after three or four days, he suddenly exploded—smashed up furniture, just went completely berserk. And as he was watching himself do this, he thought "What? What? Is this me, tender little Fritz?"

115

I was always fascinated by Fritz' smoking because I'm a heavy smoker myself. He did it with such a peculiar absorption. He smoked, literally, three packs of Camels a day. But he smoked with extraordinary intensity. It was as if his whole being was focused on the act. I often had the feeling—although I never asked him about this—that it must seem to him the negation of all his philosophy of awareness. What was reflected in his gesture as he smoked was acute frustration, acute consciousness, which he did not transcend.

Looking . . . not sure what to do with himself. Seeking a new way. He had come from a kind of waiting in Miami to a sort of psychological resurrection; in confusion. But Fritz was one with his confusion, with his disgust for the restraints of conventionality, with his unpredicability, and with his kindness and warmth, too. The old encrusted curmudgeon had a soft heart. Carol Marshall bears witness . . .

CAROL MARSHALL
I was 27 or 28, about twelve or thirteen years ago on a British ship which stopped in Tokyo. He boarded it there, wearing this very flashy Hawaiian-type T-shirt, in sandals, his hair flying.

It was about four o'clock, tea time, when I first noticed him. He'd come up to these very conservative little British people and come out with, "Oh, that's a fuckin' lie," or,

"The trouble with you is you have verbal diarrhea." Absolutely terrible. They'd shake their tea cups. They'd see him coming and they'd run the other way. I was sitting there and he came over and pinched me as hard as he could on my cheek.

"Hey! what's that for?"

"Listen, that's all you need to know. That's it." Then he said, "What you need to be is like a window—looking out—as opposed to being a mirror." From that point on we became good friends.

On the ship they had an old dance band type of thing. The old Lawrence Welk type of music and stuff. Anyway, Fritz loved to dance, and he would have a great time flying all over the dance floor.

It was a lot of fun, but I always considered him an eccentric. I loved him, but he was just kind of a loony tune.

I called him Fritz. That's what everybody called him . . . just Fritz.

One day he came in and asked me to wash some clothes; he didn't have any one to wash them for him. So I remember taking all these huge Hawaiian shirts and stuff, and I washed and ironed them and gave them to him.

And then one day he asked me to type some manuscripts for him . . . he was recording these experiences, sending them to New York to somebody. I remember that in the manuscript that I typed he was talking about going through some "usual" state; It was as though the person receiving the manuscript would know what he meant. part of the manuscript was about his experiences in Japan. One of his pastimes was to just get off a train and wander around and see what he could find. And I remember one part was about a Japanese woman who had shined his shoes. He commented that after she had shined his shoes she looked up at him and he noticed this intense satisfaction in her eyes; it was an incredible realization for him at that time.

Anyway, more of the people than not just considered him an absolutely . . . you know, crazy person. As I said, I thought he was a little bit eccentric, but I'd kind of go along with it. He did swear a lot and, you know, you never quite knew what he was going to do next, but there was also something very lovely about him. I remember one time when we were dancing, he looked over at me and he said, "The trouble with you, Carol, is that you're not demanding enough. You need to be more demanding. . . ."

Years later I was over at Stanford with this friend of mine and she's reading this book called *Gestalt Therapy* by Frederick Perls and she was ooohing and aaahing about it, but I made no connection at all until I was over at Kepler's bookstore one day wandering through, and I saw this book with Fritz's picture on the thing! It was *In and Out the Garbage Pail.* And I said, "My God! That's Fritz!" And wouldn't you know, I opened the book up and there was the same passage about this woman in Japan! He had put that vignette in that book.

> *In Tokyo . . . I had a peak experience: the loving eyes of an old woman, squatting in the gutter, polishing my shoes. I threw a cigarette stub away. Greedily she picked it up. Then I gave her my half-full packet. She turned her head towards me. Dark eyes melted and shone with love that made my knees weak. I still see those eyes occasionally. Impossible love made possible.*

I always considered him eccentric and I think the thing that impressed me the most about the whole experience is the way that a person like Fritz is put on a pedestal. It's absolutely as if he's been made a god and yet they forget the human dimension of him.

He was on the ship just wandering around the world . . . he didn't quite know what to do with himself. I'm not sure those were his exact words, but it was more or less that he was going through a confusion and he was willing to be very anxious about things: He'd been in Germany and some of his cohorts, psychiatrists and psychologists, had been imprisoned, persecuted and killed by the nazis. He went to New York, had a family, but he wasn't happy with all that . . . something was missing. It was really like he was going about the world looking for some answers.

Re-Entry

Finally I returned to the States, still dragging my dismay with my profession as a heavy burden on my hunched shoulders. There was a meeting of the American Academy of Psychotherapists . . . that stand[s] out. I was heartsick and had an angina pectoris attack that was rather disturbing and kept me in bed for a day . . . and . . . an outburst of despair I had during a group session. That outburst was for real. Violent sobbing, not minding the presence of strangers, de profundis.

NATALIE MANN

He had just come back from being around the world when I met him at an American Academy of Psychotherapy meeting someplace in Ohio. The organization met once a year for five days. We worked in a mental hospital with a group of maybe five therapists to one patient. The idea was for each of us to show our style and to share our work with this group. This was long before group therapy became popular, and we did therapy for ourselves and for each other.

It was a very intense, moving experience. People at the conference didn't know Fritz, but he was the star patient of the whole group, because he was so needy and such a giant! He was a giant even though he was terribly depressed, deeply depressed; he was seen as a giant who was bleeding and dying.

I remember we were sitting with Ruth Cohen and Rene Nell, after he had come through working with the three of us. He wanted a cigarette; he realized that he didn't have to have his own cigarettes—he could take from other people. It was important to him to know that he could take from other people, that people would be there for him. He was just in anguish.

Before that, in many ways, he was a man who had to take out his own appendix!

*This outburst did it. Afterwards I was able to reassess
my position and was willing to take up my profession
again.*

JIM SIMKIN

As soon as Fritz got back into harness he started feeling irritated again and had trouble with his heart. That's when he
first started going to Esalen. He got back in the summer of
'63 and in the fall he was already doing some lecture-demon-
strations. That's where he met Bernie Gunther . . . Fritz
always arranged to have a *shick-yingle*—a shick-yingle is a
servant.* So Fritz would get Gene Sagan—he was one of the
hangers-on—or Bernie, to drive him.

BERNARD GUNTHER

There had been times when Fritz would come to me and
tell me his problems. After a workshop, you know, when the
people have left, there's a let down, a loneliness. He talked
about it in terms of whether the seminars were worth doing
and why he was doing them. One day he told me, "I need a
therapist very badly, someone I can unload on."

There were other times when he wouldn't talk at all. One
time I drove Fritz from L.A. to Big Sur, which is a six-hour
trip, and he didn't say one word to me. I tried to talk to him
but when Fritz didn't want to talk, you could talk to the wall.
He had the capacity to just chop you off. You didn't exist
any more.

NATALIE MANN

He was very depressed, and he was looking for a place to die.
Afterwards he found Esalen, but during that period he was
looking for a place to die; he was just roaming.

*Christmas, 1963 [Gunther] suggested my participation
in a workshop at a place in mid-California, called
Esalen. . . .*

---

*It has nuances beyond that: *Shick-yingle* in Yiddish is a kid you send to
fetch things.

BERNARD GUNTHER

I got out of weight lifting and into psychology as a result of a friend of mine doing gestalt with Jim Simkin in L.A. I started therapy with Jim privately and in a group once a week. One day Jim went on a vacation and Fritz took over the group for a couple of weeks. I was very taken with him, and I asked if he would work with me. He said he didn't feel he could because I was Jim's patient. When I asked Jim, he said he didn't care. So I began having private sessions with Fritz.

In those days he was pretty isolated and lonely. He had a little apartment down on Robertson Street. He used to do his sessions there. Everything was all over the place in that apartment. I worked with him over a period of time.

Then one week there was a conference at Esalen of leaders of humanistic, existential and body teaching, which were unheard of then. Gene Sagan put on that particular conference and since Fritz and I were both invited, I drove him up in his gray Volkswagen. That was the beginning of a series of trips to Esalen with him. Fritz ran a couple of sessions and was not particularly impressed with Esalen. In fact, he was glad to get out of there when the week was over.

Back in L.A. I arranged for some lectures at *Books in Review,* where Alan Watts used to speak. I put out a lot of postcards to various therapists, took care of the cor respondence, and got the thing set up. We got a marvelous response—250 people. That was quite a lot for Fritz in those days. Although people had read his book, nobody really knew he was around. So, in a way, this series of lectures was the kickoff of his popularity. I remember he said to me after one of the lectures, "The shitting goes well," because for him talk and concepts were bullshit.

It was my idea to set these lectures up. Fritz had a slogan: "You organize, I function." He had reservations about his ability to convey verbally what he was trying to show people in experience, since he was really dealing in process. Words about process were always something of a contradiction to

him. Yet during those years, Fritz grew in his strength and
his command of what he was doing.

After the success of these lectures, Fritz and I began to
fantasize about training gestalt therapists. It was an idea very
close to him and something I wanted to do because I wanted
to be trained. I made a deal with him: I would get free training if I got a training thing going for him. He agreed to that.
I would organize it, set it up, get the people and the place,
promote the whole thing and he'd do it. So I began sending
out postcards to various therapists, and putting it together.

We started talking about where we should have it. I suggested coming back to Esalen but he didn't want to do that.
He didn't like the place. It was way out in the sticks, it had
funny vibrations and so forth. Actually I had fallen in love
with the place. The minute I saw it, my feeling was that I
wanted to stay there. I urged Fritz to consider it. I pointed
out that it was a good location and the clincher for me was
that it was available. Finally, he consented.

Big Sur, California

The route from Berlin to Amsterdam, Johannesburg, New York, Florida, Los Angeles, Mendocino, Israel and Japan, led inexorably to Big Sur, California, where in 1962 two young men fascinated with the synchronism of various teachings had started Esalen Institute.

There are as many versions of how Fritz and Esalen fused as there are of almost every other aspect of Fritz Perls' life. That they were fated for one another is indisputable. . . .

> *How did the target Esalen hit my arrow, poised towards it years before I knew of the target's existence?*

WILSON VAN DUSEN

I think I was the one who suggested he try out Esalen. I saw it as a freer life. The hotel room he had been in wasn't appropriate for him. My nut house wasn't appropriate for him either. Everything was too uptight. This man needed a much looser space to enjoy himself.

EUGENE SAGAN

Later I organized a conference at Esalen which was Fritz' first contact with Esalen. . . .

JIM SIMKIN

Fritz was still using my office for the study group, and in early '64 he asked if I would be willing to do a gestalt training thing at Esalen with him and Walt Kempler. I said yes. Bernie Gunther was the liaison person who was doing the leg work on this and he became very angry because he had put in lots of work and I wouldn't let him in since it was a professional training group.

Did you and Fritz agree on this?

Fritz didn't take those kinds of stands. He never set standards; then he would get pissed because he was taken advantage of, or when people would write in and say they wanted to be in the directory of gestalt therapists. He'd tell me, "This guy isn't a therapist—he's a patient."

BERNARD GUNTHER

I organized the whole thing! It was the first annual training series for therapists. Yet when Jim Simkin heard that I was going to be in the training sessions, he said he wouldn't be in it if I was because I didn't have a Ph.D. It was either him or me. (I don't think it had anything to do with my dropping him to work with Fritz, but who knows these things?)

Anyway, after I'd organized the whole thing, Fritz came to me and said, "Look, you can't be in the workshop."

What did I get out of it? I just got thrown out of it, that's what I got! It was a little harsh. I was very pissed off at him.

JIM SIMKIN

I have to take a stand somewhere: My stand is I'm unwilling to train people who are not licensed.

Obviously Fritz had standards, too, but he wasn't willing to make them explicit until much later. He would chide me for being rigid. I believe that it did matter to him but he was unwilling to put himself out on a limb. Fritz was not honest in that regard. He played both sides. Fritz would sabotage. The minimal education requirements and clinical experience for gestalt therapists which I had been arguing for in '52-'54 in New York (there was a big split then), Fritz finally accepted in '64-'65. Then he would bring in somebody he was sleeping with, like his girl friend from Florida: She teaches psychology courses in a junior college and has a master's, and has had some therapy with Fritz and he insisted that she come into a professional training workshop. At that time she was someone who was a technician and not a clinician.

I believe it's important not to go beyond one's support level and not to send double messages. I don't think it's fair to confuse the public in this way.

Fritz evidently was willing to give preference to even under-qualified psychologists in his desire to get acceptance by the community of professionals. Yet he evidently believed that a strong adherence to standards of qualifications, or of techniques, was intrinsically alien to the practice of gestalt therapy, which allows for the evolvement and freedom of the individual and of life.

The question of whether gestalt therapists should adhere to specific training standards and techniques continues to evoke a variety of opinions. . . .

SEYMOUR CARTER

Gestalt is an art; it's a very complicated art. In Fritz' later years his position, I think, was to not limit it to people with clinical degrees; he was more interested in the human being who was learning more than the one with the degrees. A lot of people who were close to him during those last few years didn't have a clinical background. I don't think it mattered to Fritz as much as it did to Jim Simkin.

CLAUDIO NARANJO
Fritz was not attracted to the idea. He went along with Jim's organization of accreditation meetings. I talked to Fritz and he said, "You are certified by me to do what you like. I don't care about these things anyhow. These are Jim's things."

I think Fritz perceived Jim's concern with credentialing as a lack of trust in life. To Fritz, the principle of non-manipulation went to the very end.

BARRY STEVENS
Fritz wanted to get gestalt accepted in professional circles and he cultivated professional people. He also let me and Marie Berg stay because he approved of us as therapists although we had no "background" at all. . . .

JOHN STEVENS
Fritz was doing gestalt back in the '40s and '50s, and he kept developing it. He was so far ahead, it took the rest of the world a long time to catch up with him, to realize what a genius he was. He had a real ambition about getting gestalt therapy legitimatized and one of his ways of trying was to get certified, card-carrying psychiatrists into his groups. He was so eager he would take psychiatrists and therapists with three heads and two assholes if they were at all interested.

WALT ANDERSON
It seems to me that one of the things gestalt is about is learning to take responsibility, develop your own support. And what accreditation is about, as I see it, is letting society—a fairly small segment of people really—decide who is qualified and who is not. Jim seems to me, frankly, kind of hung up on this.

ERIC MARCUS
I agree with Fritz that many people who don't have "proper" qualifications are nonetheless good therapists. I consider some of my professional colleagues essentially incompetent because their training (which was initially *my*

training) is inimicable to effective psychotherapy. I was stultified by psychoanalytic concepts: "Don't touch the patient, don't reveal yourself," etc. The result was a spouting of "insights" which passed for psychotherapy. In a training workshop Fritz told us that as trainees we first needed to reduce ourselves to "nothing"; then raise ourselves to the level of "human beings"; and then we may become therapists.

ABRAHAM LEVITSKY
My background in psychoanalysis was ultimately to prove a very serious obstacle for me to learning gestalt therapy . . . it took me years to get over it.

RICHARD PRICE:
Gestalt is really a framework, the means, the tools, a starting point for each individual's approach. What Fritz did was to define and give tools to people who wanted to use them.

He was very ambiguous about credentials. He wanted to get in and make his impact on the "legitimate" psychological and psychiatric societies while standing very much in opposition to them. To the end, he remained willing to train the competent, rather than just the "qualified." Anyone who thinks he's a successor to Fritz can't be. Gestalt cannot be assigned to a successor—it's not that type of thing.

WILSON VAN DUSEN
Fritz didn't see any use in the professional hierarchy or degree business at all. The system he used was very much like the Zen: You become recognized by your guru for your skills; the master recognizes it and others recognize it. It is an informal rather than a credential system. Fritz would just find anyone, from anywhere, it could have been a cook in the kitchen at Esalen. If he could do it, Fritz would give him the mantle. It was as simple as that. I don't think there was much technique or set of techniques for Fritz. Fritz fell into those certain ways because it was his nature. It would be entirely appropriate for other therapists to do things differently.

ABRAHAM LEVITSKY
One time the chief psychologist of Israel sat in on some of
the workshops and, of course, he was there to find out about
Fritz' work. At one point he asked Fritz, "Do you know why
you are a great therapist?" And Fritz said, "Because I have
eyes and I have ears and I'm not afraid." What he was saying was, "I trust my own judgment and rely on what I observe at this moment. I don't have to have all the textbooks
of psychiatric theory to tell me what to do. I see and hear and
that tells me what to do."

BETTY FULLER
I think Fritz was excited by anyone who expanded the gestalt
process to include dance or theater or art or crayons or the
way you could relate to a garden of flowers or whatever. He
just simply wanted us to have the *awareness* of what is. He
never intended gestalt to be stuck in techniques or methodol-
ogy, and yet he wanted those of us who were leading groups
and such to have some basic understanding of the way things
work. Actually, though, I think you might count fewer than
a dozen fundamentals to hit on the things that you need to
know about gestalt.

CLAUDIO NARANJO
Fritz had that kind of real authority that was evoked not by
any technique, but simply by Fritz' *presence,* by the ring of
truth in his being and his apparent level of mastery. I've seen
others imitate his style, but it never evoked the same response
in me. He simply knew what he was doing to an uncommon
degree, to a degree that a spiritual teacher of very high rank
or a shaman might know.

WILL SCHUTZ
. . .a search for standards for inner purpose rather than
outer authority. We imitate the founding saint. Freedom ex-
ists in going against the style of the master.

JACK SCHWARZ
Any technique can be as detrimental to us as it can be helpful

if we let it dominate us. That is why it is important for us to remember to use the techniques but never allow them to use us.

STEWART EMERY

People observe someone like Fritz work and they conclude that it's what he does that produces the result. They don't seem to realize that it's who he is. And so they imitate what he does. In thinking that it's the form of what they do that produces the results, they are in fact denying themselves as a source. That is the problem of the patient also: One is working on the other's psychosis and neurosis, and both doctor and patient are busily denying themselves as creators working together, and that's a pity.

JIM SIMKIN

Fritz would surround himself with second- or third-rate people and then complain that he had second- and third-rate people around him. There were some exceptions: I think Erv Polster was an exception. I think Paul Weisz was an exception. I think I'm an exception.

It is not quite accurate to say Fritz surrounded himself with second- and third-rate people.

GEORGE I. BROWN

It didn't take more than ten minutes of watching one of his dream seminars to find out how out of it I was. In half an hour, he was doing the work that an analyst would take ten years to do. He was going very fast and was very efficient. It was just incredible how he would get those things and at first I thought it was because of his medical training. But that's absurd. It was simply because he had this incredible sensitivity and insight.

Abe Levitsky was in that group and Abe and I would sit there and in subsequent workshops and Fritz would do something, and we'd just look at each other in amazement. Once, for instance, a girl whom Fritz hadn't had anything to do with sat in the hot seat. He just took one look at her and he said, "Did your mother try to abort you?" She was startled. She said, "Yes, how did you know that?" I remember feeling in that first workshop that I was seeing a series of miracles.

It took me a while to realize that these weren't miracles at all. It was like. . . if you're in a dark room, and somebody lights a candle, that seems like a miracle. But if you open the door and go out into the sunshine, that's really where it's at. Fritz was able to let a lot of sunshine into some very dark rooms. He did it from a place of knowing—he lived in the sunshine and he knew what it was like to be there.

One time he gave someone three chances to say something real. He said, "I'll give you three strikes."

"But I don't know what you mean."

"That's one."

"Fritz, you could at least tell me what you mean."

"That's two."

"God damn you!"

"You're in," he said then, and the guy was "in" because that was an honest expression of frustration and of real feelings.

JULIAN SILVERMAN

I have a background as a scientist and a writer. I've worked as a clinical psychologist and was very *un*impressed with the kinds of technology that we had for treating and helping disordered minds.

When I met Fritz, and began to get involved in gestalt work, I was just greatly impressed with the intensity that he could develop in a therapeutic contact. His work was geared towards providing a context for the individual to regulate himself in an experientially safe environment where there *was* support.

When I saw Fritz work, I thought, "That's the guy I want to learn from!"

I had spent years listening to and reading some of the

greatest psychotherapists, knew them cold, and believed there were lots of major flaws in their techniques. To see the way Fritz would come through time and time again! Just like Toscanini.

I remember a woman who was in a group I was in with Fritz. She was a small, tiny woman. Maybe late 30s, early 40s. She was mousy and shy. She had a very soft voice and was sweet all the time. That kind of thing. One day she was working with Fritz when he sat her down in front of him, between his legs and put his hands like this over her head. He said, "OK, now push." He had her push and work hard to get through the opening. It was about a 10-minute thing. She was working hard to get out. He was holding his elbows tight and making it difficult for her to get through. Really exerting pressure, a great deal of pressure! Then she "came out!" She ended up on the floor and she lay there for a few minutes, breathing quietly. All of a sudden, she exploded—really came alive and became vital! And she stayed like that, alive, all the time I saw her.

There were times when I'd say, "Wow! How'd you do that?" The excitement of just watching him. Yeah!

To a clinician, somebody who has seen people in many different kinds of clinical settings, the way he worked was, for me, like an orchestration of great music. That's what he was doing, through my eyes.

I saw him do some beautiful work with Dick Price. He had worked before that with some girl. There had been a lot of crying. It was a rainy day. Then he worked with Dick. Just when Dick finished working—and really great work—the sun came out.

I remember George Hall, one of the guys who was working with him, said, "Hey, Fritz, I can dig what you do with Dick, but how did you get the sun to come out just at the end!"

Fritz says, "I got a little button down here by my seat."

The people who loved him, man, *really* loved him! I mean that was deep love.

John Stevens was a junior college psychology instructor. . . .

JOHN STEVENS
I saw Fritz do a lecture-demonstration in 1967 when he was
launching the Gestalt Institute in San Francisco, and I was so
turned on by it that I signed up for my mother and myself in
one of his first workshops. I thought I really knew where it
was at, as I had a lot of background in psychology, dream interpretation and stuff like that. So I just jumped right into
the hot seat—nobody was in it and I was going to use it. I
started doing those "little boy" games, and Fritz started shitting on me something fierce. I took it for about an hour, and
then got off the hot seat. Everybody in the room was paralyzed, and the hot seat was empty for about fifteen minutes,
so I got back for another hour and he shit on me even worse.
He pointed out how I was playing helpless and stupid and
not coping—and every bit of it was true.

It was just what I needed, though, of course, I didn't think
so then. I felt awful all week. I was talking to myself, saying,
"He can't be right, he can't be right. Yet, look at what he
does with all those other people, so maybe he is right." I was
so out of touch, I didn't know what was happening or how
he did what he did, but I was certainly impressed, and towards the end I began to get glimmers. He'd say to me,
"You're sabotaging. You're not doing what I ask you to.
Shit or get off the pot."

That workshop was quite an experience for me . . . I was
so blind, and he seemed to have radar. I could see how much
I had to learn, so I went to Fritz' four-week workshop in the
summer of 1968. The first week, he started to do all these
little awareness exercises, and I didn't know what in the hell
was going on. I was into my little-boy stuff still, feeling like a
six-year-old coming into college with all the "big people,"
talking to myself—"What are we doing this for? When is the
therapy going to happen?" I was petrified of him. Through
most of that workshop I didn't really understand, but that's
when I really started to get into gestalt, to see it.

The title of Barry Stevens' book, Don't Push the River *(which was Fritz' working title for the manuscript that appeared as* In and Out the Garbage Pail), *somehow epitomizes Barry herself.*

BARRY STEVENS

Steve, my ex-son, sent me an application form for a week with Fritz in San Francisco. I didn't know what I was in for at all, but I went. It was held in the Dancer's Workshop, and it was cold. It was a completely bare room with no outside light except from a doorway into another room which had windows looking out onto the street. We had little folding chairs to sit on and Fritz had a wicker rocker. The first thing he said was, "I find it difficult to be intimate in these circumstances." Then he asked us how we felt there, and each of us expressed ourselves in some way. One woman said it was so miserable, she wanted us all to go to her apartment. Fritz asked the rest of us and nobody wanted to do that, so we stayed.

The first couple of days I didn't know what was going on. I had had no previous exposure to gestalt and I was fascinated. I could see the results were good, but I had no idea how he did it. By the end of the week, I was getting on to it—not altogether, but some glimpses. I told him that much of my life I had been way out in isolated places where there was no help, so I did things myself, but as soon as I came to town I thought I should go to someone else for help.

He said, "Tell me, 'Fritz, I don't need your help.'"

I said, "Fritz, I don't need your help."

Just saying that made a complete difference inside me. Then I added, "And so you have helped me." Instead of thinking of needing his help, I continued with him just to learn from him.

It seemed to me that it might seem a little ridiculous to the people who were in that group for me to have said, "Fritz, I don't need your help," and then go on with him, but inside me it was totally different.

This is one of the things I think so many people watching gestalt don't realize: how much goes on inside. It's very different. It's the difference between saying, I see a house and seeing a house with all its architectural style and color and materials and the landscape setting that surrounds it.

You know the trick of noticing a song that is going on in your head? Well, at the end of that week what was going on in my head was "Hallelujah I'm a Bum!" I felt just great.

JOHN ENRIGHT

I met Fritz in spirit before I met him in the flesh, in the sense that I met his work, his ego. A person who has really gotten in touch with himself and is doing his own thing, *is* his work.

Before I knew that Fritz even existed, I was assisting a fellow doing psychodrama in Los Angeles. I was rather enjoying it, though it didn't seem quite what I wanted. Every now and then, he would do something that just stood out from everything else. I'd say, "Where did you learn that?" and each time, he'd say, "From Perls." I got the sense that whoever Perls was, his way of working just spoke to me beautifully. When I asked where he was, I think he told me he was then in Japan. Anyway, some months later he called to tell me that Fritz was back.

So I went to the Metropolitan State Hospital and joined a group of nine psychologists there who were meeting two hours a week with Fritz. As soon as I sat down with him, the first five minutes, I had this kind of delicious comfortable feeling that I'd found what I was looking for. He had each of us report what we were aware of. This *awareness continuum* was Fritz' basic tool for many years. All the fancier stuff in later years was built on that. It was startlingly new to me. I was in a very, very head-tripping part of my life and I decided then that this was the right way to go.

A lot of my basic learning of gestalt was in that group. There were so many incidents where I really learned some of the principles very deeply. I remember one about projection, for example, where I looked across the room and said to this guy, Norbert, "You look like you're looking down at a bunch of insects through a microscope." The guy drew his breath to say something but Fritz motioned him to be quiet and asked me to take responsibility for that feeling. I said, "*No!* That's ridiculous. *I* don't feel that way. *He* does." Fritz persisted and to get him off my back, I finally pretended to look down a microscope at people and, sure enough, a minute or two later, I realized that *I was* putting them down, looking down on *them* contemptuously. Since I was the only one in that group who didn't work at the hospital, I felt like an outsider, and was kind of touchy about it. I thought they might reject me, so I was rejecting them.

What really made it so powerful was that the next week, this guy started off the group by saying, "You know, John, you were absolutely right last week; that's exactly what I felt." If Fritz had let him say that at the time, I never would have gotten in touch with my own projection. I just would have said, "Fritz, what do you mean, *projection?* He's admitted it, goddammit. It's not me. It's him." But Fritz had the wisdom to stop him from saying it then until I could claim it for myself. I got a double learning from that: I really experienced projection for the first time in my life, and also I saw the value of not letting it get confused with perception. Even if the description is absolutely accurate, it's still projection. I've seen it a thousand times since.

The first time I ever saw him do dream work was in that group. It was very touching. There, this gray-haired, somewhat depressed, 55-year-old psychologist had had a dream about seeing some friends off at a railroad station. Fritz had him go through the dream as himself, as the friends, and as the railroad train. None of it seemed to produce very much. Then Fritz said, "Be the station."

"What do you mean 'be the station'?"

"Just describe the station, only keep saying 'I'."

"Well, I'm old and dilapidated, not very well cared for, and actually out of date. Please just come and go and use me and pay no attention to me." And he started to cry. I was very touched by that, feeling it as part of me also, I guess.

There were many moments like that. The vignettes—every

one of them—were personal, clear, learning situations. I remember one fellow was telling a very boring dream, and a gentle snore came out of Fritz. The guy said, "Damn it, Fritz, I'm paying good money for this workshop." Fritz sleepily got up, took out his wallet, handed him a ten-dollar bill and went back to sleep again. I had the impression that could have been one of the most useful things that every happened to that guy.

I really became a gestaltist during that nine-month workshop. I'd lectured on projection for years and never understood it, and I learned it in that five minutes. I learned the dream approach in five minutes, and I've done it many times since. After that group, I moved up here, so for the next couple of years while Fritz was still in L.A. I only saw him when he came to meetings in northern California.

Fritz himself couldn't stand being in a group of people without being the center of attention. He used to tell the story that since Freud didn't like being looked at by people, he arranged the couch; and now you can find hundreds of articles showing that the couch is necessary and inevitable. In the same way a lot of people copy Fritz' mannerisms and the format, and apparently don't realize that the format is entirely independent of the principles. The principles of gestalt are very simple and basic and can be manifested in many different ways.

Fritz was always changing. I'm sure he would be the leader of some new wing of gestalt if he were still around. He wouldn't agree with what I'm doing to some extent, but I think I really grasped the principles of awareness and responsibility very deeply and I think Fritz would see that, though he might not like all the ways I'm manifesting them.

I never felt close to him—I did feel a little awe and respect and fear. I would find it hard to tell him some things about him I didn't like—his loneliness and isolation and his moodiness.

Esalen Institute—In Residence

JACK DOWNING

When Fritz first went to Esalen, it was a pretty raunchy place. There was a bar and the Big Sur heavies would come in and get drunk and there'd be fistfights . . . and here's Fritz in his jump suit in the midst of all of these people living out their wild-west karma, just getting along perfectly well— sitting there playing chess. He loved it, he really dug this atmosphere.

KEN STEVENS

Everything was a lot different then. It was really wide open. Having gate guards hadn't yet been instituted and anybody who came down the road came down the road. There was a parking lot outside the lodge; and there'd be anywhere from twelve to twenty vehicles parked. At night it would be like a big gypsy camp.

It was a wild place. There was just a lot more characters in that day. In these days the lodge was a happening place at night. Every night there was a mini-party and about two nights a week there would be a maxi-party where everybody would be in there dancing and everything. At that time this was the center of action on this coast. There was a bar, then, too. And at night there'd be people drinking rainwater and port and getting torn up . . . there'd be a fight about once a week.

A lot of nights there would be a whole lot of people in various states of consciousness and Fritz was just part of the circus. He was like the ringmaster. The psychedelic era was just coming into full tilt at that time, and Fritz was part of that in a way, too. His way of relating was a much more expanded way of relating than people were used to. That was part of his charisma. He was his own man on his own trip.

We'd discuss the situation a lot in the general meetings held there at the time. Everybody who worked there was invited to them. Fritz was conveying a lot through Dick Price then; he said there needed to be some way of cutting off that element of just anybody coming down here. And that if we were going to work, we were going to work. He proposed—and we accepted—that we keep the other elements out. He pushed that a lot.

HUNTER CULP
He had a couple of confrontations I can remember. One he had with Omar. I won't make any judgments about Omar, but when he got drunk he got a little far out. He's a pretty big guy, and one night he was drunk and yelling at Fritz, calling him an old jerk and saying this and that, just one of those heavy scenes. Fritz remained pretty cool the whole time, but after that night, the word was out that Omar was out.

ELLEN STEVENS
I can give you an idea of his way of handling things: One morning, during the time I was breakfast chef here, we were all in the process of getting it together and cooking—which at that time entailed getting loaded on hash. Fritz always liked to get up early and he'd hang around the kitchen wanting something. Evidently, that morning he could hear all this coughing and giggling, so he opened the door and said, "Aha! This is vy breakfast is not getting done!" And he slammed the door. We were all in there shivering and wondering what could come down behind this, because here is the guy who has a lot of influence on what's happening at Esalen. And, you know, nothing came of it. It was cool with him. He was very good-natured.

HUNTER CULP
When he was feeling good, man, there wasn't anything in the world could come down and cause a bad vibration; and it would just start spreading. So when he felt good, everybody felt good. There would be parties and dancing.

*Several years ago, during the mostly unlamented fall of
Richard Nixon,* Time *magazine ran a cover story listing the
two hundred young Americans most likely, in this leaderless
time, to become the future leaders of America. Michael Murphy was one of those two hundred. He and Richard Price
founded Esalen Institute. He is a writer, a runner and a remarkable guy. His relationship as the young "land owner"
to the take-no-shit-from-anybody Fritz was unique. Mike
and Dick and the Esalen they created were key steps in Fritz'
metamorphosis from the old crocodile waiting to die to the
bouncy, feisty fun-loving brilliant therapist.*

MICHAEL MURPHY

In *Garbage Pail,* Fritz says, "Mike and Dick were innkeepers
when I came and Esalen Institute was famous when I
left . . ." By the fall of '64, when Fritz moved there, we had
been going strong for two years. We had a momentum: the
gestalt had formed, and the gestalt has carried us ever since.
Esalen gave a gestalt to existential and human potential idea.
It dramatized how these things are connected, and the richness of it. But Fritz added luminosity and brought in more
new ideas and excitement.

We began with an idea that was both intuitive and abstract. We ran seminars to discuss what we called "The Big
Vision" and all its implications, with leaders like Aldous
Huxley, Paul Tillich, Norman O. Brown, Arnold Toynbee
and dozens of other people. The next period was a shift to
the experiential—Fritz was part of that. It was an attempt to
provide situations in which people could explore personal
realities and experiences. In this phase gestalt therapy became one of the fundamental disciplines.

We already had quite a lot going and a reputation before
he came; however, my conviction is that Esalen had its destiny whether Fritz had come or not. Fritz, too, had his destiny
and he was bound to make an impact one way or another. It
was a happy confluence because it gave him both the platform and the laissez-faire atmosphere for this to happen
Dick and I—Christ, we gave him carte blanche! He could do

whatever he wanted. We had it all set up for him. He did the workshops the way he wanted to and people came.

Fritz just loved Esalen. He'd always had an incredible Bohemian side to his character. He was the doctor, the therapist, of course, but his secondary personality was the artist. He loved Big Sur, and it was very healthy for him to live there. He also loved the platform Esalen provided. He loved it!

At first, he was very much a narrow-faced, dramatic guy. I think he usually saw me as naive and inexperienced. To him, I was the young aristocrat who owned the land, an amateur who had started this thing; and he, Fritz, had come along and given it stature. He wanted Esalen to be a particular kind of trip. He was extremely judgmental. There was always talk of "I do my thing, you do your thing," yet he made a definite effort to shape what I was doing. He wanted Esalen to be a particular way—his way.

Since I did most of the programming, he would mobilize people to come and compliment me for what was in his direction and be critical of what was against it. Sometimes he would do that himself. "Oh, you're doing great, Mike. You're getting rid of all that elephant shit," and all that. And, of course, it was great to get a compliment from him. He was such a powerful character . . . a lot of contact with him was just painful.

I remember one time I came into the lodge and Fritz was sitting there with some women. "The trouble with you, Mike," he pronounced solemnly for all to hear, "is you fuck too much!" Usually he did these things because he had something on his mind, he wanted something. . . .

I could have enjoyed Fritz more, but I was too intimidated by him. I wasn't used to fighting back. When he deflated me, he'd enjoy it—he was beyond caring to a large extent. And then he'd laugh. It was like he was some kind of Zen master, always challenging. But who needs it? We actually thought it was good for us in those days . . . I don't know why we gave him all that authority.

As I got on more of an even footing with him, then I could fight back in these things. Once, I was sitting with Virginia Satir and a circle of people at the Mark Hopkins during some convention. Fritz puffed himself up (he was impressive—God!) and said, "Mike, because you associate with phonies, I have decided you are a phony," probably smarting about some programming decisions I had made that he didn't approve of. And I said, "Like Virginia? Like you?!" And he could see I was ready to take him on and he actually blushed. People usually didn't call him.

I think Fritz was very good for people who had to learn to stand on their own two feet. I must say, whenever I discover some pocket of me that is not my own man, I give Fritz a little bow of gratitude for direction to that point of recognition.

He was full of the juices! He had a lot of the Old Testament prophet in him and a lot of rage. His style was highly challenging to the end.

JOE WYSONG

I think on a lot of levels, Fritz was a mirror—our mirror. We put all kinds of stuff into him that had to do with us. That's why I'm so interested in Mike Murphy's question, "Why did we give him all this power?"

What do you think the answer is, Joe?

I only have theories for me, a couple of them actually. First, I think it's important to recognize what was going on politically and culturally, and how, on some level, Fritz was addressing himself to the kind of desperation we're all feeling now (in '72). My desperation was on honesty—being free to be honest. I'm just a Wasp who grew up in southern Indiana. All my life everybody had told me to always be concerned about the other guy's feelings, not to hurt people, to be good, to be nice, etc.; in effect, they were telling me never to be honest. I was desperately looking for somebody to tell me it was OK for me to tell the truth.

Fritz used outrageousness—or whatever you want to call it—as a technique or a tool. And the thing was that for me, this crazy son of a bitch was saying, "It's OK to tell the truth!" and, in effect, that *I* was OK. I needed the kind of morality that Fritz put down. I needed Fritz and I needed Groucho Marx. I know that what I'm feeling when I tell the plain, blunt truth is nice and it is right, but frankly, socially, it's outrageous.

And what Fritz did is go around being socially outrageous. It was like Fritz knew. He really recognized that the time for the kind of Western intellectual tradition of being calm, of "Yeah, let's talk about this . . ." was over. Fritz knew that was crap; what he did was go around saying, "Look, I'm not going to do that, man, I'm going to hit you between the eyes with a hatchet." Fritz *was* a hatchet, and a really good one.

William Quinn was a member of the three-person staff of Esalen in the early days. . . .

WILLIAM QUINN

I was the secretary-treasurer of Esalen when Fritz first came here. My relationship to him was somewhat like that of an impresario. I had to watch him and see that he didn't get into some dreadful mischief. He could be quite a problem. He was capable of being outrageously unkind and thoughtless and arbitrary. With the force of that man, a cutting remark could be shattering. I saw him in a social situation once where there was a young woman of a rather rigid type who was very elegantly mannered. She so lost her poise confronting Fritz, that she did something completely idiotic: She was chewing gum, and she took it out and stuck it in his beard! Crazy reaction. It was panic, I suppose . . . and he viciously slapped her in the face. Really, just as quick.

I published his first paper here; in fact, I think it was the first Esalen publication. It was a mimeograph thing, and I remember the initial quotation was from Krishnamurti. The idea was that when you realize the futility of conflict you can call that the grace of God. Stylistically, his writing had a kind of Talmudic complexity. His literary style and his command of English were beautiful. He had a very deep feeling for words; he used them with precision and a kind of simplicity that I suppose only comes with great maturity, in a sense of poetry, really.

Fritz had extraordinary eyes. Sometimes he'd look positively incandescent—very, very beautiful eyes, which could be full of baleful fires, too. This reminds me of a comment he made once about Freud, whom he'd met and didn't like. He said Freud invented the couch because he could not look people in the eyes! Freud started off as a hypnotist, but was not particularly good at it, you know. . . .

KEN STEVENS

He controlled the vibes around here, all right. He was that dynamic. Everybody's energy was tuned into his. He'd radiate that energy out and then someone else would pick it up and he'd sit back and watch it all go down after he got it going.

He'd walk into the dining room and start hugging all the chicks. I mean, just putting out vibrations that you couldn't believe an old man could be putting out like that. Really sensual, a lot of high energy love-type vibrations, you know.

HUNTER CULP

He definitely jacked up the sex energy around the place.

KEN STEVENS

He always had a lady with him. When he was feeling good, he was like Santa Claus, he had that vibration.

ELLEN STEVENS

You know, I don't think there was a time, except maybe when he was really down, when he didn't go and pinch somebody on the ass. . . or he would just say hello by pinching someone in the tit, you know. That was his way. He liked a lot of sexual contact.

KEN STEVENS

When he did that a lot of different things can happen, but what is going to happen for sure is that people all around feel the vibes and they are all going to start relating. . . . He was sort of the patriarch.

HUNTER CULP

He did what he wanted, he did what he wanted.

I never saw Fritz try to cheer anybody up who was down. If you were cheery, you were cheery. I never saw him manipulate a scene other than in his workshop, but there he was trying to get people to see into their mechanisms.

Fritz had a poster on his door on which an old man is dancing with a young girl; that was his attitude most of the time.

Shanghai-born Gia-fu Feng who was also a member of the early Esalen staff, was both an admirer and rival of Fritz Perls. . . .

GIA-FU FENG

I came back from Japan in '64; I was studying with Namikoshi who was an expert on shiatsu. Fritz came after that.

I was then on the front desk. He was giving a workshop, just staying in a little cabin. Nobody knows about him. There were not enough people. Fritz said, "Goddammit! My workshops always fill. How come nobody signed up? There must be wrong publicity." He was raving at the counter and I let him rave for half an hour. But anyway some of the workshops had to be cancelled.

I found he was interested in Oriental religion. He actually went to a Zen monastery in Japan and came back in the early '60s.

He stopped in at one of my workshops and cornered me.

"What do you know? Try it on me." He wants to have body work on his breathing. I was not far into that. But anyway I gave shiatsu treatments to him. He was very prompt for five times straight.

Then I made a mistake—actually Bill Quinn made a mistake—he charged Fritz $50 for my services when, according to the custom then, he should have free service because I did sit in his workshops. The money thing is very heavy with him.

Eventually he started gaining momentum, lots of followers. One month Bernie Gunther was there. Me and Bernie and Fritz were the only three residents listed on the brochure. Anyway, I have some people coming to take Fritz' workshop who also want to work with me on a body massage. And Fritz said to one guy, "Don't go to Gia-fu!" He was so mad about the $50. And the guy actually cancelled the appointment! Afterwards, Ida Rolf arrived, so he said, "Everybody go to Ida Rolf, forget this Chinaman."

I don't feel bitter. I took him as he was because I understood his background so well. His parents and brothers were all burned to death and he was still able to come out of it. I'm a member of a minority myself, so I can understand. I think he had guts and he was honest; and besides, because he forced the group not to come to me, and sort of kicked me out, I moved out and got my own center in Los Gatos Hills. So he actually helped me to have my own trip.

Once Abe Maslow, Dick Price, Mike Murphy, Joe Adams, Fritz and myself had a meeting. Red Thomas and Gordon Tappan, both professors of psychology at Sonoma State, were there too. Maslow was the chairman. Fritz was just one of the members. Maslow says, "We want something respectable here at Esalen." And Fritz says, "Fuck it! Let everybody take off their clothes. We have to disregard the social customs. We are in the movement. We have to be way out. . . ." and he stomped out! I think everybody present thought Fritz was crazy to say anything goes, like nudity. But we didn't think Maslow was too real, either. He was more of a preacher.

Tappan, Thomas and I sided with Maslow. We wanted to be respectable, and Fritz was off the wall. But to think back, Fritz was very courageous. He didn't give a damn what anybody said!

Richard Price's regard for Fritz is best expressed in the Esalen catalog, where among the brief, often impressive, biographical sketches of the leaders, Dick writes simply, "Co-founder and Director of Esalen, student of Fritz Perls."

RICHARD PRICE

Fritz first came here the Christmas of 1963 through an old student of his named Gene Sagan. He liked it here and decided to settle in April 1964. It was very much on his own initiative, and not on ours.

At first I was negatively impressed by him, thinking him bitter and not a nice old man. Watching him work was very unpleasant; he seemed unnecessarily cruel. In the early days here he would sit by himself and whoever came and sat with him generally felt repelled. He didn't feel to me like someone I could trust and I just didn't want to expose myself to him.

In fact, at that time he was very sick; he was very spiteful and fearful. He felt his work had not come to flower in the way he imagined it would.

I've just been re-reading his 1944 book, *Ego, Hunger and Aggression.* I'm amazed at how much of the essential Fritz was already there, and with a great deal of clarity and precision, free of the bullshit of most psychological writings. Yet in 1963, twenty years later, his flower hadn't yet unfolded. Or, it had unfolded but it hadn't been recognized.

So he was difficult. Personally, I didn't care if he stayed or left. He felt he was dying of a heart condition. He only became easier to live with as his health improved, through his work with Ida Rolf and as a result of a more settled and generally healthy life here.

Fritz progressively developed a softness and a warmth which, so far as I could see, was not part of him before. At first he would sit down and tear a person apart without that touch of kindness—in a way that isn't in order, isn't good at all. It was only later that his incisiveness grew with greater and greater kindness.

His first workshop drew maybe four or five people, and he almost left; his next workshop, maybe seven or eight. And so there was just enough to keep him here. By the time I started working with him, in '66, he was drawing thirteen or fourteen people. So it was very slow.

Once I was in his workshop, I was tremendously impressed. He had become a lot warmer and was able to receive more and more warmth, as far as I could see. Part of that was his own enthusiasm. He was finally at the ground where he felt his work could emerge substantially—though very gradually. My respect for him grew. I got to know him in a very, very subtle and steady way. Yet my business and my personal relationships with him remained very difficult. In the workshop situation he was patient, incisive, kind and insightful: He didn't push his trip. In business, however, he was not kind.

I'd go to Fritz after a workshop and say, "Here's your check for fifteen people." He'd say, "I had sixteen. I know there were sixteen." And I'd say, "OK, Fritz, before I pay you out, you or your secretary come with your own list, check it out, and we'll pay you out." This was a drag; most of my relationships at Esalen have been on trust. In going over it, you know, my figure usually would be correct: He would be counting the cameraman or something!

Yet, I think one of the really important things Fritz taught me is to be selfish, rather than continually driving myself "unselfishly"—giving out and giving up. He taught me to have a little more respect for my own organism. I feel primarily what he's given me is tools. Fritz wasn't into playing the good guy, nor were there any pretenses of love and support. This was his total position.

Fritz was very, very close to the ground. He really saw how awareness works. There is a great antipathy towards esoteric nonsense in his world. His effort was to clear away the bullshit which most religious systems are just full of. In that way, I couldn't have more appreciation for him. Fritz was Fritz. He was like the story of the Zen master dying in a scream of agony. Very unbefitting, we think . . . we expect there to be a sweet smell, a great peace which all saints should exude at their death. Fritz was simply not that kind of "holy man." He was bitter when his work was not recognized or not fully appreciated. His sense of responsibility to himself was deep.

I remember one time at one of the "circus" things (a circus was his weekend performance; it wasn't just a group of fifteen or twenty, it was however many people we could get in that room), he was on stage. By this time he was getting quite famous. There were about a hundred people there. He would say, "Who wants to work with me this weekend?" In a smaller group, he'd work more patiently in process with whomever wanted to come up. But in this situation he would say, "Who wants to work with me this weekend?"

Of course, people would be petrified of getting up on that stage before eighty to one hundred people, particularly with this very formidable man they'd heard so much about. They would be torn between, "Well, I don't want to get up there because I'm scared shitless!" and "This is my only opportunity to work with the great Fritz Perls." So gradually hands would rise. And Fritz would count out, "One, two, three, . . ." until the hand raising became more and more hectic, and stop at, say, fifteen.

Then whoever was number one would come up and work with Fritz. And number two. These things generally would work a lot faster than in a smaller group, where he would show a lot more patience.

I remember one woman coming up and presenting her case and Fritz gave her a direction, "OK, talk to your mother."

And she said, "Oh, doctor, I don't think that's relevant."

Fritz turned around and said, "Number 10."

He was a *great* performer! I remember in still another circus performance, a woman came up and did this bit of leaning forward just slightly . . . kind of sucking Fritz into lighting her cigarette, and Fritz not doing anything.

She was presenting this very manipulating game where she could expect to get a particular reaction. Of course, Fritz refused to fall into the usual game of automatically obliging: "There you are, my dear."

Fritz was a master at discerning manipulation . . .

EUGENE SAGAN

I tried to give Fritz things all the time. His attitude was always that if I could outflank him he would be pleased. But if I just walked up to him slowly when he could get himself organized, he would say, "Why are you bothering me?"

MICHAEL MURPHY

After a while he began to expand. He'd come up from the baths and he'd stand erect, and he'd prance around the grounds, preening. He'd puff up. He would beam. He was kind of like royalty. He'd look around as if to say, "Look how great I am!" He was enjoying it. And he always had young women who loved him. You could just see him filling out. He was, I would say, shameless in showing the girls his incredibly marvelous body. Panache! Just put on your body and strut around! He must have grown a couple of inches, I would say from about 5'7" to 5'10". If you see early pictures of Fritz, the change seems amazing. Fritz twinkled or glowed and had either a wicked or a marvelously luminous look, but I can't remember him laughing. He just glowed all over when he was happy. He had a very malicious wit; he was very creative with language and was a very tough old man.

"Ed the Mailman" brought fruit and vegetables, nuts and cheese, and special-order items that often included medicine and chickens and sometimes horse feed and hay. He also had candy and cigarettes. But mostly Ed brought the mail. He was always a welcome sight. . . .

EDWIN CULVER.

I put in ten hours every day, six days a week. I make 150-200 stops over a total of 145-150 miles. Esalen is my longest and biggest stop; there's more people there buying groceries and picking up mail than anywhere else on my route. The whole route is fun. I've had it for twenty-two years. It's not a job, you know, it's like a vocation. The whole coast is my backyard.

I've seen a lot of changes take place in the local people in the years since Esalen has been in Big Sur. They were what you might call "stand-offish"; generally, you know, they don't get in close. But after a while they began to see people touch each other, hold hands, hug each other. It began to spread around and gradually it spread along the whole coast.

It was something I had always wanted to see happening to people. Even as a child people would come up and I would have liked to hug them or be close, but you couldn't touch anybody. I've always had that feeling toward people but I couldn't express it until Fritz and the rest of them got things started around here. It's like a little boy standing on the corner . . . he has a dog on a leash and people come along and they pet the dog and the little boy stands there—nobody is petting him— some people would like to but they don't dare. Anybody touches the boy, you are molesting a child.

Fritz wasn't a young man, so people weren't going to be afraid of him, and after a while people accepted his touches. They knew he didn't mean anything because it was a nice, loving touch.

So many times I'd come in the office and catch a glimpse of Fritz patting someone's rear-end—a little friendly, lovable pat—and all of a sudden they'd turn around and give him a hug. It was nice. It was accepted as a gesture of love.

When I stopped at Esalen, Fritz would come by my truck to buy little goodies and cigarettes and things. He impressed me as not being really concerned about what other people were thinking about him. I believe he didn't care like a lot of the younger folks did—the "health kids" I call them—who eat what they are supposed to. I remember one day some of these younger kids were standing around buying apples and things and here comes Fritz. He looked in the truck and, the first thing, he went to my little ice cream box and brought out an ice cream cone with nuts and chocolate on it and started eating it. Right then everybody else liked the idea as though suddenly it was all right to do.

Fritz always looked relaxed. To me he seemed to be a quiet man. He had a quiet way of going about things, not to attract attention but just concerned with people in the immediate vicinity. I know the ladies, young and old, loved him. That's one of the good things about a person like Fritz. He was happy because everybody else around him was happy. He could walk up and hug a young girl or an older lady. It made them all happy, because people want to be hugged as much as you do.

ROLLO MAY

The next time I met him he was very much in residence at Esalen. But he still seemed to be mean. At that time Mike Murphy was running Esalen. I thought for a while there that Perls was the Mephistopheles to Mike Murphy's sainthood. You see, each saint, like Gandhi, has to have Mephistopheles to express that side of his life, and Gandhi had—what was that guy's name? Rattakrishna something or other, a very ornery Indian. Now, Mike was in the saintly role at that time. Perls seemed to have the function around there of being the negative aspects of Mike's over-positiveness, I would say.

MICHAEL MURPHY

Fritz argued with Dick about money and with me on programming, but he never really abused me. In *Garbage Pail,* he said, "Mike Murphy is anxious to let people do their own thing. Consequently, all these turner-oners came." At that time Fritz was very antagonistic to Will Schutz and Bernie Gunther and others who were sharing the limelight. He wanted this to be his stage.

There is, of course, some validity to his criticism, but *he* was the greatest turner-oner of them all!! Though he would sometimes humiliate people, they would gladly participate in his dream workshops which were fantastic! It was the damnedest thing! There was often a lot of learning, and usually a lot of humor, but it was certainly show biz.

One time we decided to have a "Being" laboratory where everybody would get together and talk the "Being" language. It was a disaster! It ended with Fritz crawling across the floor challenging people and telling Henry Drake to come down and wrestle with him! Here was Abe Maslow headed toward the heights, imperial, while Fritz was crawling around on his stomach making up things about Popeye being a dirty old man, and something about farts! At the height of all this, Abe Maslow leans over to me and he says, "This begins to look like sickness . . ."

Everything Abe proposed was lofty and beautiful and Fritz would come in with this earthy, vulgar, raunchy stuff. His intentions were clear from the very beginning: Whenever we had anything that seemed overly idealistic, he wanted to shoot it down.

Fritz' genius left him when he met certain kinds of people—his prejudices got in the way; if you came in a religious guise, he'd be against you. He was against the whole deification of personal experiences, and generalizing them. Many people give a kind of allegiance to classifying people. That tendency to construct a world philosophy out of bits and pieces of experience, or out of some scraps of ancient scripture, is too easy. I'm with Fritz in that. You don't need that fancy stuff; you can do it playfully.

There were particular people that he hated. Like Peter Hurkos, the famous Dutch clairvoyant. We invited him for a weekend during which we were going to have a demonstration of his powers and it was going to be studied by a group of psychical researchers, a couple of professors from Stanford, and some others. We had arranged an experiment of Hurkos' powers, but Fritz demolished the entire weekend! There were about forty or fifty people and right at the climactic moment, he stood up and said, "Mr. Hurkos is a fraud and a charlatan!" It was the most timely moment for the hit! Hurkos was awful that weekend! He collapsed at the end of the weekend in a kind of epileptic fit. The stress had been too much for him. If Fritz hadn't been there, it would have been a lot easier for him.

GIA-FU FENG
Everybody was just raving, "He is a great psychic . . . can tell everything," and so forth. But Fritz got up and said, "He's a fake! He's a fake!" Everybody booed him, but Fritz

said, "Oh, that's bullshit. That's nonsense!" He kept saying that, in spite of the whole auditorium saying it was not proper. It turned out one of the architects who has a house in Big Sur had had a robbery and had asked this psychic to go there, and he wanted a thousand bucks before doing anything. That very weekend, the psychic broke down because of the opposition from Fritz. Esalen was in turmoil until he was shipped out of the property.

I admire Fritz' guts for standing up against the whole audience. He turned out to be right. There was no bullshit about him.

MICHAEL MURPHY
But this was typical of Fritz. He had a great sense of theater. He could sit in a room so as to intimidate the speaker. Occasionally, George Leonard would come and give talks on the visions of the future. I love that kind of thing.

GEORGE LEONARD
I would come to Esalen in '65 and give workshops on new directions in education, and on the possibility of utopia in America. I had a feeling that the world could be improved, that things didn't have to be this bad. I think that perhaps now I am more in touch with process and with the dangers of utopia. I think to Fritz, with his European background and his understanding of the nazis, my proposals seemed naive and programmatic. He would come to my workshops and sit there and bug me. He had a marvelous way of doing that.

"Your trouble, George," he would tell me, "is that you want to give people blueprints. I give no blueprints." I don't think I gave blueprints as much as he thought I did, but in any case, his warning and his importuning did influence me. Without question, Fritz was an influence on my work.

At that time, all the workshops were given in what is now the lodge at Esalen. Fritz had a big easy chair that no one else would sit in. He'd position the chair exactly in the left periphery of my vision—I saw him do this to several people—so I could not actually see him without turning, and yet, with my peripheral vision I would be aware of his movements—impatient movements, or anything like that.

He really loved to undermine the leaders who came in to give seminars, especially if they were into what he called "elephant shit."

I think Fritz liked to scare people. I remember the first time my brother-in-law, John Poppy, went to Esalen. John was a reserved, elegant young man. He happened to get in the food line with Fritz and bumped into him. He said, "Excuse me," and Fritz turned and looked at him—these huge brown eyes—and said, "Why should I?" And John said, "Well, I-I-I don't know."

Those were days at Esalen in which marvelous, theatrical, wonderful things happened, days in which there was always the promise of a miracle. Major discoveries were turning up at the rate of three or four per weekend. It seemed to us that the transformation was imminent. In that same sense of exuberance, at a time when I was giving one of my workshops, I told Mike Murphy at lunch that Fritz was really making it difficult for me to give the seminar.

"Mike, if Fritz does it again—if he bothers us in this afternoon's session—do I have your permission to get four of us and go over and pick up the chair with Fritz in it and carry him out?"

Mike said, "Sure, you have my permission," He was even willing to help.

MICHAEL MURPHY
He was really such a marvelous old fart, in his seventies and

just as feisty! So he comes in and George was going to make a big proclamation about the future. Fritz sits at an angle so that when George looks forward he can just see him out of the corner of his eye. He'd sit just on the edge of the audience so the speaker would be aware of his presence . . . this way you get a sense of this hovering presence. This was one of Fritz' favorite tactics; he would usually assume the seat of dominance.

George gave an inspiring speech that just made my hair stand on end. I was really thrilled and Fritz started a few of his torpedoes coming in from the side. I can't remember exactly what they were, but it never got to the point where we had sufficient excuse to carry him out bodily. Was he sensitive to this? Well, I'm positive he was; he had the most incredible radar. He probably knew we were gunning for him.

GEORGE LEONARD
Fritz would have loved it . . . he loved legends, myths and theatrical things. But unfortunately, that whole afternoon he was extremely polite. He must have picked up something in the air, because he never bugged me the least bit! He made some nice comments. I think he even put himself more in my vision where I could see him. I was disappointed. It would have been great fun carrying him out, chair and all. I never told him what we had planned.

MICHAEL MURPHY
. . .but actually, you know, maybe we wouldn't have been men enough! I mean even four against one! We still might have chickened out! He scared the shit out of a lot of us! He had us all intimidated.

Fritz had such personal authority that his insights stuck in our minds. It wasn't so much his intellect, although he was very smart; he had a great command of the language. He was great with little phrases; he was constantly coming up with new ones, like, "It's not so important to save yourself; spend yourself."

I think Fritz has been misunderstood by a lot of people. His phrases, for example, are often used out of context.

Fritz' house was built in 1966. . . .

MICHAEL MURPHY

We built that house for him. He was going to live there throughout his life, then the house was to go to Esalen. We agreed on an advance payment of rent—it was like $200 a month and he'd given us $10,000. He was in Europe at the time and we needed more money to finish the house, so we sent him a telegram asking him for it. He replied, "IF YOU DO NOT FINISH THE HOUSE, I AM INSTITUTING A LAWSUIT. I AM SENDING YOU NO MORE MONEY." So we had to pay $50,000 and he paid $10,000. It wasn't his fault that it cost more. He was tough! But that was fair enough. We had put it to him that it was that or nothing, and he fired back . . . we took it.

VIRGINIA SATIR

He offered me that house. He said, "Maybe you should have this house instead of me." He meant it. There were going to be two houses. I never did build mine. He told me he'd always wanted a house that faced the ocean, where he could write his poetry and do his painting, a place where he could see and hear the ocean. That would just be perfect. And that is what that house was.

WILL SCHUTZ

When I first got here, I went up to his house and I was just entranced with it. I could just feel that this could be a permanent home. I told him that was the first house I had ever seen in my whole life that I would be happy to live in. He was very touched by that.

MICHAEL ALEXANDER

. . .adulation was something Fritz needed. He had to have it. He set himself up there and he was subtle and very creative about doing it. Everybody else was down there on the flats with the lodge, physically and otherwise. When you went up to see Fritz there was a very special sense of climbing the mountain to get to him.

FRITZ FAISS

The house has a marvelous view over the Pacific Ocean. The rugged coastline extends north and south; below, the main house, cottages, pine trees, eucalyptus trees. . . a picture of calm and quiet. Right under the house, far down on the cliff, is the bathhouse with its old hot springs. The place was known by the Indians and used as a health spa. The rather flat part where the main house stands is where the Indians used to live. There was a strong belief around Big Sur that the last natives put a curse upon the place. Many times I heard people saying they felt uneasy . . . tormented . . . hunted. They left. Fritz acknowledged the Indian spell, too. Whenever people complained about the disturbing atmosphere, their negative feelings about Esalen, he told them about the old myth.

I called him the "Old Man of the Round House." He lived there without any kind of comfort. The house was used for his group meetings, it was filled with stale smoke, and it was never aired. The furniture consisted of a couple of old, dilapidated chairs and a dirty rug with black holes from cigarettes. The bookshelves along the back wall were empty of books, with some empty wine bottles and heaps of cigarette butts. The rooms looked forbiddingly messy, smelly. It was difficult to believe that this was the way Fritz liked to live.

JACK DOWNING
The house is a lot like Fritz. You know how you walk in and you're faced with this blank, curving corridor? To go around that corridor is really an effective way of modifying your perceptions. In terms of design and space, I think it's wasteful but not in terms of drama. You walk along that corridor and suddenly you turn and your sights open up. He and Selig designed it. It is like Fritz. It's built like a gun emplacement. You could put a cannon up there. I used to call it the "West Wall Bunker."

ABRAHAM LEVITSKY
The walls of the bedroom were redwood; it was small and sparsely furnished. There was a bed, a bookcase and a bowl of vitamin pills. I just assumed that the bowl was filled with vitamins; he seemed to dip into them fairly often. Perhaps the most interesting thing in his room was a cleverly designed arrangement of bits of glass shells and sand encased in plastic on the top of the bathroom sink. It was colorful and tastefully done.

RUSS YOUNGREEN
Don Juan talks about a circle of energy and a circle of power. So did the ancient Indian philosophies. That's why Fritz had that room built like that. It was circular, and whenever he had a workshop, people were more or less in a circle.

PENNY YOUNGREEN
When you bring all that energy and that power to a focal point, something's going to happen there. It takes an awful lot of negative strength to work against that sort of positive energy.

He would say, "We are not really very unique. There's not that many problems," And when he said that you would feel a lot of empathy for the person he was working with because you knew that trip. You'd been there yourself.

The first time I worked in that room, I worked on a dream and for me it was the most valuable work that I've ever done. It was as though people in the room just faded out of sight and I was really in the dream. I had dreamt that I was standing with my mother and there was a conveyor belt going by with little babies on it, and the babies were turning into chickens and we were wrapping them up, like in a market. I ended up standing in the middle of the room screaming for my mommy to come pick me up.

Then Fritz gently guided me back into the room and said, "Find a mother in this group to pick you up, to hold you." And it was funny—I picked a woman with big boobs. My own mother is a small angular, bony woman—she's all hard surfaces. This buxom, soft woman rocked and held me for quite a while. I came through that one. Before that time I couldn't stand to be alone. Russ and I had recently been married and he couldn't go to the shithouse without me. I would follow him everywhere. But after that, I no longer felt that need to be right on top of him, to be right on top of anybody. It took a while. It didn't just happen overnight. But I found that when Russ wanted to go somewhere, though part of me wanted to go, I was beginning to feel that there were other things *I* wanted to do. I could be alone and on my own, which was a new experience. That came out of working on that dream.

I watched video tapes of it later. It was almost a hypnotic thing that I was in. I had lost focus of the people in that room until Fritz brought me back into the here and now. That room *does* have a hypnotic circle of power.

*Hunter Culp, who became Fritz' butler, got to know Fritz
from the ground up, and from the skin out. . . .*

I came to Hot Springs (it wasn't called Esalen then) about the
winter of '65-'66, when Fritz did. Fritz' house had just been
built, but there was something wrong with the septic tank. I
was working for Selig* that year, and it was my job to dig it
up. Every day for a week I was out there digging deeper and
deeper. I used to have buckets of dirt taken up and Fritz
would walk out in the morning and look down, you know,
without saying anything. The day I finally got down to the
septic tank, he looked down at me, the guy in the hole, "Vell,
Hunter, you vork hard. I thought you only played, but you
vork, too."

"I work as hard as I play, Fritz."

"Me too," Fritz laughed.

In my personal experience, I could feel him strongly. I
went to a few of his dream sessions. They were especially interesting.

I never saw anyone that old who was really that sharp.
There were no flies on Fritz' back! I kept watching him,
thinking, "There's something I can learn from this man."
I've always been a seeker in my way. I decided I'd like to get
close to him but not on the level he was dealing with other
people.

Like everyone here, I was really feeling a strong love for
this man. It was just the feeling when Fritz was here, everybody was right. I observed his habits and noticed that he just
never got it together to take care of his own personal scene.
He was great with doing his thing, but his room was funky
and messed up, and he wore the same jump suit for weeks,
you know, with food spots all over it. And I was getting sort
of tired of digging ditches. I had been doing that and working hard for about six months. So I sort of invented this job

---

*Selig Morganrath was the man most responsible for the construction, the
exquisite detailing and landscaping at Esalen Institute.

and one day I went up to him and said, "Fritz, you have a need."

He looked at me kind of funny, "Vell, vot do I need?"

"You need a butler, Fritz."

"A butler!"

"Yeh, you need somebody to take care of you. Look at your room. Look at that jump suit!" and I pointed at the three-week-old egg on it. "Look at you, you're a mess! You need somebody to take care of you—not a woman who is going to try to put her thing on you but just someone to make sure your place is straight."

He went for it right then and there. "Ok, you start tomorrow."

"No, I'm starting today!"

He laughed and so I went right up to clean his house. I straightened it all up, made his bed, and just started work in that capacity. He'd come home in the evening and his room would be made up—that kind of thing.

He had three jump suits and they were all exactly the same. He would just wear one, the other two were brand new. I made him change jump suits. I'd slip in at night when he was asleep and I would take his jump suit and put out a new one and go get that one washed.

Then he had me doing a lot of things. I started to build a meditation garden for him, terrace the land (it's all overgrown with weeds now), plant grass and bushes and put in a ditch. He asked me to build him a chess table, which I did, a nice inlaid redwood one. And I framed his paintings. He liked to paint; he had some weird paintings. I thought they were like "Are-you-kidding-me?" I wouldn't say that to him, of course. He thought they were something important. I'd do a good job, you know. I was a framer here on the coast for a long time for a lot of artists, and I'd take each one individually and frame it in the style of the painting. Fritz had one that was sort of a Picasso abstract, it had big holes in the people, so I made a frame with a big knothole so it didn't quite join—it looked just like the picture, not quite together. He liked the frames.

When I offered myself for the job, it was obvious that there was going to be some pay involved but we never discussed it. Anyway, the first week went by and it was Friday and the weekend was coming up and I needed some money. I was broke. So I went to him and I said, "Well, Fritz, this is Friday and I need some money."

"How much do you vant?"

"Well, whatever's fair."

"How much money do you need right now?"

Well, at the time I was in the process of building this house in Pioneer Cove and I needed a couple of hundred bucks to get some materials. So, I just scratched my head and said, "Well, Fritz, I really need $200." He didn't even blink an eyelash, he just reached for his checkbook and wrote out a check for $200.

"OK, thanks," I said and walked off, thinking to myself, "Wow! two hundred bucks a week! Man, that's great! That's good pay!"

Well, the next week came and I didn't see any money and then the next week.

And that went on for five weeks! I was working and I got no money. So, it worked out to be about $30 a week! Finally, I had to sit down with him and come to terms.

I went to Fritz, "Well, Fritz, I need some money."

"Money? Vot about that $200 I gave you?"

We decided on $75 a week. He gave that to me in cash.

At times appropriate to him, he was quite light with it. . . .

JOHN HORLER

He lent my old lady a hundred bucks one time because we were broke. My old lady just went up to him and said, "Hey Fritz, we're broke, could you lend us a hundred bucks?" Fritz knew what was going on. I don't like borrowing money. I paid it back. I did it by putting in some vines below his house; I cleared the slope and planted onto it. I think he helped out a couple of other people, but mostly he was straight biz—nothing for nothing.

I was at Esalen off and on for about nine years. When I came here it was still Big Sur Hot Springs. The Esalen thing happened on occasional weekends. I was working as a cook when Fritz started giving seminars at Esalen. I wasn't in charge of cooking at Esalen. I managed to stay away from that trip. I've never been in charge of anything. Hopefully, I never will be. I started as dishwasher, then when the cook eloped with the waitress, I was made cook. Just like that. Then every once in a while something happened and I became dishwasher again. I was also bartender.

Fritz would generally choose a wine that went well with the meal. He really knew his wines. If he didn't come himself he would send somebody over for some rosé, which made everybody happy. Fritz was always cool. So far as I know, he drank as a moderate man.

He was pretty much resident guru when I was cooking, although he still hadn't moved into his house. I'd seen him around—we just sort of passed each other. One evening one of the waitresses told me that Fritz was surrounded by starfuckers again and he just wasn't getting any eating done.

Starfuckers are sycophants, drones, groupies. They are the ones who want to fuck the rock-and-roll musicians, The Man. They were after Fritz, and if they didn't want to fuck him physically, they wanted to fuck him mentally . . . they just wanted to be around. Fritz really didn't dig it.

I walked out of the kitchen and indeed his table was surrounded. He barely had room to get the fork to his mouth. I caught his attention and said, "Hey, Fritz, if you get crowded, you can always come to the kitchen. I'll keep the people out." He looked at me and said, "Why have I never seen you before?" I went back to the kitchen and was doing my thing. About ten minutes later he came on back and sat down in my chair.

He had a bigger ego than a lot of people; and he had a lot going for him. People want to get into that, to try to get some. I mean, he was a very wise man. I understand he was also a good fuck. Besides that, he had a very controlled tongue and gave a damn good massage, and the ladies loved it. With one thing or another he was constantly crowded, but you can get too much guava jelly. So he'd come into the kitchen occasionally. He'd give me recipes. He gave me a recipe for stuffed cabbage, which I tried and it was really good.

Fritz was a good cook. He had been eating in restaurants for years—a lot of really good restaurants—so he had his food down. He knew what he liked and knew how he liked it. When I was the cook I figured I was cooking for him and Selig, and when either of them would walk in and say, "That was a good meal," man, that was it—that *was* a fucking good meal!

When I first saw him, he was a wreck. It was when he first started coming to Esalen, and people were all talking about Fritz Perls. "Who the fuck is Fritz Perls?" Then I saw him, and there's this tottering old cat, who could barely make it from the car to the lodge. He was really gibbled, could hardly make it down to the baths. I mean he was really hurting. Dark, scraggly eyes, bags under his eyes.

KEN STEVENS
He'd drive down the hill in his little car. . . I think it was a Messerschmitt or something like that.

HUNTER CULP
It was one of the smallest cars you could get. . . it looked like a mason jar on wheels.

He'd drive a car to save his heart, but then he would smoke all the time. He was always smoking. He was really inhaling, too; and you're see him literally lighting one off the other. He was trying to quit by smoking all kinds of. . . .

ELLEN STEVENS
. . .it smelled like burned garbage. You could tell when he was around because he was burning garbage.

HUNTER CULP
He carried four or five packs of different kinds around and he'd smoke one after another of different kinds, you know.

JOHN HORLER
But he got rolfed and he got massaged; he laid in the baths and he really dug the country here. There were only two places in the world for him. There was Big Sur and then there was someplace in Israel. Both had the same sort of feeling. And he really got healthy. It took a while but he ended up dancing and lightened up. You know, he was very, very straight when he first came here: He was wearing a jacket and a tie. Then he started getting into wearing nothing but jump suits and chicks would make him necklaces. He was always wearing necklaces and beads, and he let his hair get long.

Fritz and I were never close. We knew each other; we had a cup of coffee; we played chess a few times; we talked. It's hard to say about Fritz . . . he would really get onto some people's backs, he would hassle and harass them. Some of the chicks who worked for him just got driven up the wall. He was a hard cat to work for, very demanding; things had to be done just so, his way, or nothing. He drove out a lot of chicks. It's not that he was stubborn so much as he knew what he wanted. He got where he was and he did what he did, and if you didn't like his trip, well, it was like he said, "If we get along, fine. If not, get the fuck out of my life."

He was so straight; really very gentle and loving and kind. He was very generous in a sense, but he would not allow anybody to come to him and say, "You're the only one who can help me." He threw some people out of his workshops. He would say, "You just demand too much; I'm not a magician . . . don't come to me looking for some sort of dramatic rah-rah because that isn't my trip." He tried to teach what he knew, but he wasn't a do-gooder and he wasn't greedy.

ANN PARKS
When I was living and working as a waitress in Esalen, I served him many times. In those days we served at the table in the dining room. He was very demanding and obnoxious, really. He could also be kind of flirtatious and lecherous. I did not really know him well, at all. I was just someone working there. Yet, I never felt him open, I never felt him at peace. I never felt him radiating. I felt him as a very powerful man on a power trip.

Doug Madsen is an architect, a Big Sur land owner, and a horseman. . . .

DOUG MADSEN
I was repulsed by this hideous hunk of vulgar flesh chasing pretty girls around at the baths. . . .

One time at the opera, I think it was *Manon,* I bumped into Perls. He really was gross. I was there with one of the

most beautiful women you've ever seen. She's like a fine pearl. She is a Spanish Jewess and they have a great class distinction about it. She was beautifully dressed; we were both dressed up, you know, collar buttons and the whole deal. And *he* came up in the most *godawful* bunch of dirty clothes, with this filthy hair; he just looked repulsive. When I saw him coming, I tried to run. We were having champagne and he just insisted upon coming over. She and Fritz talked in German or Jewish, I don't know. I just found him repulsive—his manners, his attitude, his food, his thought. I couldn't imagine them even letting him in the Opera House.

JAMES FADIMAN

I was married at Big Sur Hot Springs. Fritz was on the property at the time. He was not invited. He came anyway and had a perfectly wonderful time, the most delightful part of it being his dancing a kind of exhibitionistic duet with Gia-fu Feng. I have a wonderful photograph of the two of them facing each other, kind of like strutting cocks, each outperforming the other in kind of wild, dramatic and exhibitionistic dance movements. It has that feeling, that they were both striving to outdo the other.

Fritz also managed to frighten and alienate most of the guests who were there by his usual good-natured, easygoing, charming manner of finding something wrong with their psyches upon contact. People would come up to me and say, "Who is that man?" And I'd say, "That's Fritz Perls." "Boy, he certainly, uh, put me off." These were mainly relatives and friends who were not too familiar with Esalen.

GIA-FU FENG

I feel a great similarity between Fritz' ideal and Zen Buddhism. In 1965 before every session he'd say, "What I'm going to do here is to assist you to have a sudden awakening." And a sudden awakening is, of course, satori which is Buddhism's main point.

The Esalen brochure always said, "Meditation, meditation, meditation." And he said, "Fuck meditation. Get off your fanny. Start working! No more of this sitting-on-your-ass trip!"

Confucius said, "When you are fifteen you start to learn; when you are thirty then you stand up; at forty you are out of confusion; and at fifty you know the destiny; at sixty you are so desireless you can really listen, you are untemptable; and by the time you are seventy then you do whatever you want without worry about right or wrong." Fritz is a living example of a man at seventy acting without worry.

He was absolutely committed to simplicity; so many of us are intimidated by it. We could call the quality "Fritzness."

FRITZ FAISS

Fritz was very upset by vague minds. He would tell people, "Make up your mind—now and forever." Actually, he was against all final theories. For him, there existed no finality, everything was in constant change.

GIA-FU FENG

Very early, '65, he set a standard for the borderline case. One of the workshop people, a professional of some kind, suddenly one night can't sleep, and he is raving all around the compound, and his roommate says, "Fritz, do something for him!" And Fritz says, "Call the ambulance. Take him to the hospital." The whole staff was against it. You know, "You have to be humanitarian; you are responsible for him; he's not that bad." But Fritz insisted, and the man was driven by the sheriff to the hospital. So after that we realized there's such a thing as a borderline case, and Fritz insisted the ones we admit to us have got to be on *this* side of the borderline.

BARRY STEVENS

One evening in the kitchen, sitting at the table, Fritz took a woman's hand and turned it over and looked at her palm. He made remarks about various lines in it, calling attention to this one being long, that one deep and this one broken and so on, sounding perfectly serious about it. I didn't know if he had studied palmistry and I asked him, "And what does that mean?" He said, "I don't know."

JAMES FADIMAN

Within about four or five minutes of working with me, he indicated that my verbal facility was like watching a swordsman who was so good that he could keep himself dry in a rainstorm.

JIM SIMKIN

There were times he was sentimental. He liked people to sing "Auld Lang Syne" at the end of a warm workshop. People would stand around in a circle and he would burst into tears and leave. . . . He called me when Paul Weisz died. Paul was a close friend, a psychiatrist, who died of a heart attack at Paul Goodman's house. Fritz was in tears.

There was that soft side of him, but he could become arrogant and demanding any time he felt that somebody crossed him.

JANET WULLNER FAISS

The "kindly father" was a role Fritz Perls played just as skillfully as he did the "lecher" or "reprobate." It was almost entertaining to watch him shift from one role to another. He enjoyed a good duel of wits, but unless an opponent was very alert to the fast changes of Perls' personality, what began as a duel ended as a bout of shadowboxing, with Perls laughing in the wings.

JOEL KRAMER

Sometimes one would get the feeling that Fritz felt obligated to be real at all times. Being "real" is always being a little bigger than life, as it were. It gets into the interesting question of the whole nature of image. You begin to build an image structure of yourself as what it is to be real, and that image structure becomes what you are. Then you begin to learn to play at being that, but that play is also what you are. In a way, that was the dance Fritz was doing.

NATALIE MANN

In the very early years, he took a lot of acid and always by himself—never with anyone else. I remember once he told me he took it and he went into his own heart and gestalted what was going on there, and in that way avoided a coronary. He was full of tremendous emotion that he had had this deep contact with himself.

GIA-FU FENG

I found that Fritz was a part of a tradition of Maoism. Mao said to the Red Guards: "The key word of a cultural revolution is *loan* . . ." *Loan* in Chinese is "rabble-rousing"—the word actually means "confusion, turmoil or chaos." So, he says, "The more *loan* you have the better it is. Now, you Red Guards, go out and make more rabble-rousing. . . ." Mao is a rabble-rouser, and I found this element in Fritz Perls, too.

WERNER ERHARD

Fritz had class, if one defines class as the ability to graciously not give a damn.

ANNA HALPRIN

He was witty and sharp and intellectual, and often an outrageous ham actor. I loved that about him. One time at a conference with an audience of over a thousand people, Fritz was part of a panel with a group of distinguished psychiatrists. He was so bored, he just closed his eyes and fell asleep! He had said one or two things that sort of demolished the whole group and then went back to sleep. It was obvious he wanted everyone to know he was bored with the bullshit.

JACK ROSENBERG

I was thirty then, an established professor and well thought of, and I couldn't get up and kiss girls and dance around. Fritz was doing it, and that kind of gave me permission to do it. I started to try it. Man, it was like I had permission to be alive because he was alive!

TOM SHANDEL

I come from an ethnic ghetto, you might say. The sort of middle-European mongrels that I grew up with were all like that old man—intemperate, irascible: boot you out of the way when you were kids. It's like grandfathers were . . . certainly the kind I knew.

RICHARD PRICE

He was one with his lost temper: There was no sense of losing it. There wasn't that split in that particular way. He says it in *Gestalt Therapy:*

> *The straightforward tendency to retaliate is seldom encountered . . . Most adults display their pleasure in vindictiveness vicariously: by reading crime stories, or following court proceedings, or indulging in righteousness, or pushing the execution of revenge onto God or fate. Admittedly, revengefulness is not one of the pleas-*

ant characteristics of humanity, but being convicted at one's own expense produces inhibitions which leave situations incomplete; where retaliation, if it is taken in the form of gratitude or revenge, definitely closes an account.

I never felt Fritz was at all hypocritical. Nor that he was preaching. Rather, Fritz was Fritz.

JOHN STEVENS

. . .one evening we were looking at the proofs of *Garbage Pail,* and he was looking at the page where he talks about Will Schutz, because he thought maybe he might've been too hard on him. He looked at the page. He thought about it for some time. He read it, and he just sort of withdrew with the taste of it, and said, "No, I think that's fair."

> *I was glad to hear that Bill Schutz was to be in command at Esalen. And I mean in command. He is something of a Prussian officer, but he is also observant and skillful. He is an intellectual sponger, but deep inside suffering and desperate for growth. He tries to be hippish, but is more of a square. If he does not feel observed he looks somewhat morose. No wonder that he wrote a book on* Joy, *the usual psychiatric externalization.*

WILL SCHUTZ

We had a rocky relationship. Prior to moving to Esalen, I talked to senior people here—Virginia Satir and Bernie Gunther and Fritz—and asked them specifically how they would feel about my coming. They were all very positive, especially Fritz. I would not have come if I wasn't wanted. Fritz and I were together at Esalen just about two years. He came a year before I did. I came in '67 and then he left in '69. We had one good year and one bad year.*

The first year we were very friendly. I wouldn't say we were intimate, because I doubt if Fritz was very intimate with

---

*Actually, Fritz came to Esalen in 1964.

anybody; but whether he was or not, *we* weren't. But we were colleagues. It was us against the world. We were the two mavericks trying to fight the establishment and we supported each other. We were alike in ways, too, being prima donnas. I like to do things my way. I'm not an idolator. I don't have any heros except Lou Gehrig. Fritz may have been like that, too. I don't think he had idols in particular; I never heard him talk about anybody else in that way. When he would come back from a trip he'd show me his clippings and tell me of all his triumphs and we would "tsk, tsk" at the opposition and say how stupid they were. We had that kind of camaraderie.

Then something happened and we didn't get along well. I felt this change was primarily Fritz' initiative. He started to put me down and be critical of me and was just generally negative about me. In fact, there was a television program about that time—"California Girls," a Canadian program— to film me running a group. So I started rounding up a few people out on the deck when Fritz came by and said he'd like to be in the group. So Fritz became a member of my group for the film. Of course, it soon came down to Fritz and me confronting each other. I would say something like, "Fritz, I don't want you to be opposed to me; I want us to be closer." He was saying, "No," adamantly. He didn't want to reconcile and it didn't matter to him.

NED HOKE

While the movie is being made, Fritz is sitting regally in a deck chair. Will is squatting on the floor talking up to Fritz. It is the casual, California kind of throne Fritz occupied with great pleasure, and Schutz is looking up at Fritz and saying, "But why don't you acknowledge my presence?" And I remember perfectly Fritz saying, "Why can't you stand a little rejection?" Will was just getting his *Joy* together. He was beginning to get a pretty big following and was a star in his own world. But he was always an insecure star, like a new member of an exotic country club giving his first party. And yet he's the kind of man who has the feeling for power but he never seemed to have the guts for it. Fritz had the guts for power. I'm not patting him on the back, but some people have the guts for power and some people don't. Schutz didn't seem to be much of a risk taker, not from what I saw. And anytime you'd do that with Fritz—sit on the floor and talk up to him and ask him to encounter you—he'd just shit on your face.

ILANA RUBENFELD
He was very rough on what Bill Schutz did, and on the kind of people he was training. He really believed gestalt was it and although Bill uses a lot of gestalt now, Fritz felt that the kind of encounter work that was going on at Esalen was devastating. They were having twenty-four-hour marathons and using the crudest techniques for getting defenses down. Fritz saw this going on, and he'd blame Bill.

WILL SCHUTZ
People have pointed out that his opposition to me came at about the same time that *Joy* was getting popular. I suspect that had a lot to do with it and, in a way, I can empathize with that feeling. Here was a man who for forty years was denied recognition and now finally was making it. Then just as he is making it, someone else—a relatively young kid— comes along and begins to take on some of his glory. I can see why he didn't like that so much.

I think I was a threat to him, and anybody who was in that category had a lot of trouble with him. I was his most direct competitor because for much of the time when I was here, we were the two major figures at Esalen. Another thing: He anticipated that I would become a gestalt therapist. I think that was one of the reasons he was so happy to have me come here. After a year, it was clear I wasn't going to do that. I like to go around and find somebody I can really learn from, learn and appreciate, and then move on. I think it affected his feeling about me. He did like people to do *his* thing and I didn't do it. Yes, that does make more sense. I think my rise in popularity aggravated the fact that I wasn't going to be one of his boys.

My star was ascending here at the time. I used to compare our drawing power—how many he drew and how many I drew. I remember it began to lean in my favor and once I drew more in a week-long workshop than he drew in a weekend. I must admit I felt pleased at that.

I tried quite a few times to get closer, or at least not to have this opposition which I felt was foolish. Fritz didn't like it that whenever I had a workshop, the dining room was always very animated and people were having a good time. He thought that was "instant joy" and he didn't like it. We had one direct confrontation about it. I said, "Fritz, why don't you come in and watch what I do? You are making all these comments about my groups and you have never seen one and you really don't know what's happening." And he said something that was in a way charming and in a way not. He said, "Sometimes I'm not being rational," which allowed him not to do anything further about not being rational. . . .

VIRGINIA SATIR
I feel certain that Fritz didn't come because he couldn't stand what Schutz classified as therapy. He didn't like the way Bill worked: screwing in public and calling it therapy in the therapy group. (Fritz loved to play, but he didn't mix therapy and play.)

In '68, Esalen got to be really messy for a while. Fritz couldn't stand it. He was very blunt and very sharp. I remember at the Christmas meeting, Fritz and I were sitting together, and he said to Bill Schutz that he was really a crook. What Fritz meant by that was Bill was a phony. Bill made believe that he didn't hear it as far as I could tell. Incidentally, he never asked me about his coming to Esalen.

Fritz, however, was supportive. . . .

HAROLD OAKLANDER
I remember one piece of work I did with him that made a big impression on me, because it was very supportive. I volunteered to work as a therapist in his workshop, with him sitting in as supervisor. The guy who offered to work as a pa-

tient was a close friend of mine who had come to Esalen with me. I don't remember what was going on, but I said to him, "Look, Tom, I don't have any power over you to work with you. If you want something from me, if you have good will, if you're willing to say what you want, then I can work with you. If not, I can't."

Fritz stopped the work at this point, and he said, "It's very important that a therapist have power with the person he's working with. Oaklander demonstrated real power as a therapist here. He demonstrated it in the best way he could, by taking his stand. By saying what he did, he demonstrated the essence from which a therapist has power over somebody."

I was taking care of myself in my way. Fritz never would have done it that way; his way would have been very different. But it was an affirmation that I could do my own thing.

WILL SCHUTZ

I came to him once when we were getting along and told him that I was getting very tired of running groups. He said, "You must understand the meaning of the word *tired.*" So I thought, "Oh, Fritz, for Christ's sake, another bullshitty smart-ass comment." But I thought about that comment for several months afterwards. Every time something would come up I'd have another definition for "tired." Once I thought it meant getting cancer and another time I thought it reflected my fear of younger competitors. . . I knew then that he had a bigger impact on me than I had realized or than I wanted him to.

Sometimes Fritz would really hit it like that. He would say wise things that would make me think a lot—sometimes reluctantly.

When I started in encounter I used to make what I considered dazzling interpretations. Later on I realized that I was trying to compensate for my own insecurity. I found that as I got better as a group leader I said less and less. In the best groups I ran they hardly knew I was there. I would just come in and do what I had to do and allow them to go where they had to go rather than being a big, flashy leader with all these clever insights. I suspect that same need underlies some of the big interventions in gestalt.

The Fritzian model is a bit show-offy. On the other hand, I've picked up something important from him—the idea that you're responsible for yourself. I believe this is a vitally important principle. I've adopted it and elaborated on it and made it one of the keystones of encounter. I got that primarily from Fritz. But I don't like the way he handled it. I think he carried it to extremes. When somebody wouldn't do anything, when they were in the hot seat, Fritz would fall asleep or kick them out or something, which was very dramatic and usually effective, but I think, debilitating.

On the other hand, self-responsibility is extremely important, something that I never handled well and that traditional "I'll take care of you" therapy doesn't do right.

Fritz said, "You come here if you want to and if you don't, you don't." I thought, "That's too extreme," but it's basically right. As I began to do a little more of that, I did indeed elicit the strong parts of people. I was also saying to them, "I feel that you are strong. I trust you to deal with what happens." The less responsibility I take, the better, because it allows them to do more. So I really think that was a very big contribution Fritz made to me—making me aware that being a responsible therapist is a real trap.

It's hard for me to have a warm feeling about Fritz. I think almost everybody close to him both loved and hated him. I didn't get close enough to Fritz to feel that strongly. I neither loved nor hated him. I liked him and didn't like him. Almost everyone else was a student of his, but we had a different relationship. I came in as a colleague and equal.

Stanley Keleman

We were just talking one time, and I said something to him about experiencing some confusion in my own life, and he said to me—very warm, very gentle, very friendly, very helpful—"When I see you work, Stanley, I see loving guts and reality. Sometimes when you talk, you bullshit. What I would like to do is teach you to deal with some of the conflicts you see."

WILL SCHUTZ

I'm not sure how much the honesty principle, which is a key-note of encounter, meant to Fritz. I had heard that Fritz never paid taxes and they were finally after him so he had to leave the country. I also heard that Fritz really wasn't a Ph.D. or an M.D. Now, there again, you'd have to check with people who know more than I do, but I suspect it's true. I suspect that's the bullshitty part of Fritz. Responsibility without honesty doesn't work. If honesty isn't inherent in gestalt, then that's a real flaw.

LAURA PERLS

. . .the M.D. is quite legitimate. Somebody wrote somewhere that he got his medical degree in '23. I think he got it much earlier. Because he came out of the war—the war was finished in 1918—and in '19 and '20 he was in Freiburg. I think at the latest in '21. He got it from the Frederick Wilhelm University in Berlin. . . certainly, I have the diploma.

JIM SIMKIN

In Frankfurt he did postdoctoral work with Kurt Goldstein at the Frankfurt Institute. I'm sure he couldn't do post-graduate work without an M.D. His medical background was impressive. His M.D. was fine. I think he got a Ph.D. under kind of strange circumstances, I'm not certain what.

GIDEON SCHWARZ

Once someone who was typing a letter for Fritz while I was in the room asked him, "Fritz, is it 'Frederick S. Perls, M.D., Ph.D.'?" Fritz replied, with a naughty boy smile, "Frederick S. Perls, M.D., Ph.D., L.S.D."

HAROLD OAKLANDER

I always saw him as being honest, direct, and so I always approached him in the same spirit. I've seen him so moved by some work, he'd leave the room.

WILL SCHUTZ

I guess my real feeling about Fritz and honesty is like everything else—ambivalent. There are some ways in which he was excruciatingly honest. I mean, he could say negative things to anybody at any time and that was admirable in a way. So he was a "real" person, as they say. There were other times when I suspect he wasn't really honest. For example, I think he wasn't facing up to how he really felt about me and what the reasons were for his big change. He didn't seem to want to think about it—he wanted to keep himself in the dark, not to tell me. Somehow it wasn't clean.

NED HOKE

Fritz was in the business of generating power, and Schutz appeared to be in the business of trying to placate it. He would let you throw your energy away, while Fritz seemed less interested in just exposing and turning over "inner rocks." I felt Will often asked me to throw my energy to the winds while Fritz' whole thing was to teach me to bring my energy home.

Fritz' personal fascination with the quality of energy went beyond teaching. He led people so far into that energy that they could experience it in themselves. It's true, Fritz was a priest and a garbage collector. And it's very far out for someone with that much intellect and that much *chutzpa* to go down into the garbage, literally, and say, "That other wonderful stuff out there is all trivia. What you are experiencing right now IS IT!"

All of us who were at Esalen in the '60s were part of a whole drama that was going on and in one way or the other were driven there by our culture. Perhaps Fritz, too, like some of the old men of India, who give up their wives and their houses and the whole business to go into the woods and look for knowledge, was seeking the truth and learning to "see." But Fritz' woods took him through *my* woods. . .

As the *Teachings of Don Juan* speak of the "therapeutic theater," Fritz appeared to stand as the aged warrior giving lessons to the younger or less vigorous seekers, sharing encouragement, strength, leading the student away from being constantly overcome by fathomless fear. He understood the necessity of courage to "throw off the chains," as he called them, the chains of neurosis.

Often, as Fritz looked into and through us, I imagine he, too, like an old Indian warrior, had reached the spiritual stage of "seeking."

KATHLEEN NUGENT

I was living in a little house near Nepenthe. One morning I got up and said, "I must dance for Fritz." So I hitchhiked all the way down to Esalen. He was taking a nap when I came in and he was very surprised. He put music on for Zen meditation and then put it at different speeds, back and forth. . . I got to a very centered kind of place where I was kind of on the ground and he slowed the music down. Then he sat me down on his knee and put a cigarette in his hand and said, "You've died already, haven't you?" I said, "Oh yes, I died a year ago."

NED HOKE

At one point or another in his work, Fritz would recognize that the impasse was death—a death that occurred within a person, within the person's heart. To this person Fritz would say, "When did you die?" and the person would just go, "Wwwaaaaahhh. . ." a primal reaction, you know. They'd remember the precise moment when that feeling had hit them, when they'd rolled over and died inside. They'd have to go through that experience again and again with Fritz and sometimes it would take six months. Fritz would keep pushing the button, and there'd be that incredible moment that someone found out, "Oh, my God," they had died: Their bodies were still moving and they were talking and everything, but they were dead! And they knew it! And Fritz knew it! In a way, Fritz and the whole room had come to their deathbed, and he asked them if they wanted to live again. No one else had ever seemed to care—or even notice. Tremendously dramatic.

When Fritz would do one of these everyone would just come apart. The whole audience would gasp within their own little place that had died, that no longer lived. How many people walk around like that? Death has occurred in the heart. And of course, "I don't want them to know, so I'll come on gregarious," or "I'll be withdrawn," or whatever. And Fritz would break up that game. Right in the middle of it, he'd have the person talk to the body laying on the ground. Fritz was at a place of seeing in many of the same ways Castenada gets right down to it—plus he was a psychiatrist.

The Buddhist term *skillful means* seems appropriate here. For me, Fritz was certainly a practitioner of skillful means.

As a practitioner of skillful means, Fritz gave lectures to whomever would listen. One of the places he went to was the University of British Columbia in Vancouver. Sol Kort had invited him. . . .

Sol Kort
Phillip Reiff, Benjamin Franklin Professor at the University of Pennsylvania, noted that Fritz had lectured here, and asked, "Why do you sponsor a man like him? He's evil." He wouldn't elaborate, but, listening to his lectures later, I understood why he felt that way. Reiff talked about two kinds of charismatics. There are those who exercise great power over people in an interdictory fashion, like Moses who said, "No, thou shalt not. . .," they draw the lines—the boundaries beyond which we shouldn't trespass. Then there are the remissive charismatics who push aside the boundaries and say, "Well, the limits are broader than you've been socialized to perform within. You have my permission, I encourage you to try new things, to do things that maybe are not socially acceptable." Reiff gave Hitler as the most flagrant example, with whom anything is true, and everything is

possible—to kill and humiliate and dehumanize: the concentration camp ethic. He didn't put Fritz in the same category as Hitler but he did claim that Fritz gave people permission to abandon certain restraints on social behavior, and Reiff felt that this kind of license was dangerous, that society had to be constrained within certain rules and regulations.

I have mixed feelings about this whole business of transcending the ego, achieving unity with the cosmos—this kind of thinking is alien to our Western culture. And I suppose that's why a lot of people felt threatened by a man like Fritz. . . perhaps Reiff was one.

I think many very able and great people are very humble, approachable, and gentle. Others are somewhat megalomaniacal. Fritz had a lot of the megalomaniacal/egomaniacal in him.

JIM SIMKIN

One of the problems gestalt therapy had was Fritz Perls. He was the megalomaniac who almost destroyed gestalt therapy. He was also the founder. It was sometimes almost impossible for Fritz to permit the growth without holding on, so when something would begin to show signs of developing he would get angry or split or something. My guess is that's part of what accounted for his nomadism.

He had in him the attitude that if he couldn't have his way, he wouldn't have any part of it. This is true of most geniuses and innovators. They're egomaniacs, very self-centered. They need or want constant adulation, and if they don't get it they go into temper tantrums. I've known at least a half dozen brilliant people who were like that. They all contributed tremendously in their field and were personally obnoxious people—very difficult to get along with.

Julian Silverman, co-director of Esalen Institute, is widely known for his work in the field of mental disease.

JULIAN SILVERMAN

People called Fritz paranoid, people called him a god, people

called him a saint, people called him a sex maniac. I don't
know what the hell they called him; it all depends on who
they were.

From a nonjudmental point of view, the terms *paranoia* or
megalomania refer to a particular way a person is in the
world, a particular way of organizing the "out there" so it
makes sense to him. You see, a megalomaniac or a paranoiac
is one who *constructs* the world for himself and then says,
"That *is* actually what is going on in reality." He makes up a
story and then that story re-presents his world. Now, if a lot
of people believed him, then that becomes a concept or a
shared re-presentation. So if a being like Hitler says, "We
are the master race," and people agree that *that* re- presentation is *their* re-presentation of the universe, too, we're in
trouble.

On the other hand, there are constructive re-presentations.
For example, Einstein took a re-presentation of his own central nervous system activity and then generalized it to the
"out there" and said, "This is what's going on in the universe." It was an excellent re-presentation. His notions of
time and space are biological re-presentations that are shared
by a lot of people.

> *All theories and hypotheses are fantasies of models
> about how the world functions. Once they are verified
> and applicable to physical reality they themselves
> assume reality character.*

Fritz was a system builder, and in a sense, he taught an aspect of megalomania and paranoia. Actually, I'm a bit uncomfortable with such psychiatric language, yet one *could*
say, "Fritz was paranoid." But he made his paranoia into a
beautiful story of the way the world could be. Using any kind
of psychiatric term, including paranoia, *in a negative sense,*
really limits the understanding of the process of what is going on when a person is doing his trip. Does that make sense
to you?

Paranoia, in its descriptive form, is simply putting an internal story outside of you. Basically, it is only a way of

making sense out of the world; which is, I take what's going on inside me and I put it out there. This is called *projection.* I put a fantasy out there and then I say, "It's real." That's what any good theoretician does. He says, "It's not this way; it's another way," and by doing something in this new way people benefit, develop emotionally, change their point of view, etc. Fritz theorized that Freud was limited to such and such an extent and he said, "Now look what we can do if we do it *this* way." So if you want to call Fritz "paranoiac"— that's OK with me, but if the name limits you by pigeonholing him in some negative aspect and doesn't do justice to the way he experiences his world and what his contributions are, then you've diminished him and yourself.

How does that differ from megalomania?

That's a name again. Anytime you name someone, in terms of categorizing him, you limit your appreciation of what he is in the world. You don't understand him anymore, you don't hear him anymore, you don't see him anymore, except in terms of the names you call him. We've got to stop pigeonholing if we want to really understand someone.

The problem with the whole field of psychiatry today is that it's so messed up with theories about what people "are" rather than just describing their behavior.

JIM SIMKIN

I think Selig, the real guru at Esalen, knew what he was saying when he once said, "A discipline disappears if the disciples love the guru; a discipline can grow only if the guru loves his disciples." Fortunately, there were a few people Fritz was able to love and was proud of and whose success he enjoyed. That's what allowed gestalt therapy to grow—the fact that he did love. I think that he loved me. I think he loved Erv Polster. I know he loved Paul Weisz. Each of these people who was loved grew beyond Fritz. You see, if the disciples do not grow, the discipline dies.

MARILYN ROSANES-BERRETT

Jim didn't love him. He wanted Fritz to love him and Fritz

never did. Fritz said that he was a good worker, a good therapist and that's all he ever said about him. I feel Jim's not a courageous man; he's not a great innovator; he's too stuck in his own myopia.

JULIAN SILVERMAN

If you loved him, you really loved him! When he'd come down to the lodge, I didn't want to sit *any*where or hear *any*body's rap if I could be sittin' by *him*. *All* the time I knew him was like that! To me, he was just such a beautiful person! Just to touch him, to hug him. . . .

RICHARD PRICE

I was around when he first met Bob Hall. He took an immediate liking to him. Then Bob became his student and there was a real thing together. Fritz really wanted his work carried on, and Bob had the credentials.

ROBERT HALL

I was in the audience once as Fritz was doing one of his workshops. I was a psychiatrist in the Army at the time. I had never before seen anyone who could really do anything in therapy and I had been getting discouraged. When I saw Fritz work, I realized that this was somebody who could teach me something. It was the first time I'd ever seen anybody who really knew what he was doing. He was working with a very shy girl who had had a dream about being on stage and singing "The Rain in Spain." Before she finished,

Fritz had her singing that song in front of the audience. It was very beautiful. She broke down and sobbed afterwards. I was sobbing, too.

I had just spent three years at Fort Knox. I hated the Army. My time was up but they wouldn't let me resign because of the Vietnam situation. I was really frustrated. I was teaching first-year residents in San Francisco. Alyssa and the children and I were living in Mill Valley.

A friend of mine, Ed Maupin, was at Esalen and I went to visit Ed. It was during Christmas week of 1966 and we were having lunch in the dining room. Fritz was across the room eating alone, and I kept feeling him staring at me.

All of a sudden I realized he was standing right next to me. He was just standing there looking down at me. I thought he wanted to talk to me. I got up and we just looked at each other's eyes. We had never met before. We had never exchanged a word. We didn't say anything. We were just staring into each other's eyes and the next thing I knew we were embracing. And then the first words he said to me were, "I want you to come down to work with me."

He didn't even know I was a psychiatrist! He told me that I could come down there right away and that in six, ten weeks I would be his assistant.

I said, "OK, yes, I will."

At the time, I didn't even know I could get out of the Army. I went home, boy, up in the clouds! I contacted a general I knew in the Surgeon General's office, and he helped me wangle a discharge!

I got out of the Army on the 28th of February and the next day, March 1, we were in Big Sur. We moved into one of Jan Brewer's houses. I had no income, no way to make a living. I told Fritz when I got there that he had to give me some money to live on but he wouldn't.

"How do you expect me to live?" I said. Then in a few days he got me a job at the County Mental Health Clinic two days a week and that way I could support my family.

He was a perfect and a very hard teacher. A very hard

teacher! I had never done group therapy before and actually I hadn't really had much experience in therapy at all. He told me later he recognized that I was alive. And we sort of fell in love with each other at first sight.

Fritz had collected a whole bunch of really hard-core people around him. A lot of them lived around the Big Sur area. They were really heavy and some of them were pretty crazy. They went to all of his groups and his workshops. He had collected thirteen of them together as a group. Then he gave me this group of thirteen people, presented them to me and said, "Here, this is your group." That was a horrible experience. I was frightened to death, I hated it, I was practically immobilized. God, they were hitting each other, beating each other up! Yet, I opened right up, snap! He would come in maybe once a week.

Anyway, what Fritz said to me that first day was right. In six weeks my name was on the program and I was his assistant, giving workshops with him. I had to go through a lot of hard times the year I was there. . . .

Almost everybody fought with Fritz. He and I never had fights. We really got along. A lot of it, I suppose, was that I was very obedient. I saw him as my teacher and realized that I wasn't going to learn anything unless I did exactly what he said, so I did. I loved him.

Though Joe Walsh's contact with Fritz was far less direct than Robert Hall's, it nevertheless had a profound effect. . . .

JOE WALSH

My family situation wasn't good. I've had the old-fashioned view of the family. Catholic—not strict, but serious. The word *divorce* just didn't exist in my dictionary. So our separation was very traumatic. It upset all my preconceived ideas of a family. It was a shocking experience for me. Here I was, at sixty, a grandfather, and everything fell apart.

I got interested in the growth movement through the

Perls-Hefferline book, *Gestalt Therapy*. Then I found the Gestalt Institute in Cleveland—which had been there for eighteen years—and got involved in it. I found the idea that you can actually, physically, do something different than you always have—that a person *can* change through vicarious contact with Fritz—very exciting. The exercises are simple: sit on a table and eat off the chair, instead of the regular thing, for example. Something clicked. I discovered that if I didn't try to figure everything out, or try to figure the consequences of what people would think, it would turn out beautifully!

I'll give you an example of what I mean: About that time, seven or eight years ago, a couple of days before my birthday, my sister called. She lives in Detroit. She said, "Why don't you drive over for your birthday?"

It just happened that I'd sold a truck I owned which wasn't worth anything to me, so I had this nice wad of bills in my pocket; and when I stopped by the Automobile Club to get a map from Cleveland to Detroit, there was this big poster in the lobby: "Air Canada/Daily Service/Cleveland to London."

I'd always dreamed of these trips. Now, suddenly, without any planning, I went to London! On the morning of my birthday I had the best bacon and eggs I ever tasted, in a little hotel *in London!* On the table was a little placard that said, "London to France, Air France Every Thirty Minutes— You'll Never Be Any Closer." So I went to Paris! There was nothing rational about my going there, so I decided I was insane. And I stayed insane for a weekend!

It was like a dream! Here I was peeing in a stand-up place, out in the open, made of stainless steel, made in Cleveland! Crazy!

I got a room in a little hotel like you see in movies with a circular stairway and a tiny little circular elevator, right in the middle of Paris!

I got back Tuesday. I was embarrassed to tell anyone about it. For two or three weeks after I got home, nobody knew I had gone! They didn't have a chance to say, "Hey, how stupid can you get!'' But what the hell, it didn't hurt anyone!

That was the beginning. It was one of the first times in a lifetime that I'd allowed myself to be somewhat spontaneous before I figured everything out. It was one of those crazy things that rationality and economics had nothing to do with.

I think those are the real things. Whenever I go ahead and act with love in a situation or a relationship, ignoring my rational worries, there is no anxiety. I just feel like everything is as it's supposed to be.

That was my initiation into gestalt, and it led to an extraordinary meeting I was to have with Fritz. . . .

HARVEY FREEDMAN

It's 1965. Two innocents from Toronto are going to a seminar on family therapy at the invitation of Virginia Satir and we arrive in this strange, strange place that eventually got to be known as the Esalen Institute. But at the time it was unknown to anyone we knew.

And after the usual journey into the place, the cliffs and the queer people with earrings and long hair, and girls without brassieres, my wife and I sit down for a meal, and this stranger with a beard and a jump suit joins us—commanding, commanding presence. Remember, I had never heard of gestalt therapy, never heard of Fritz Perls. Three minutes later I'm doing a dream; while the waitresses are clearing the table, Fritz is working me through a dream. And that's my introduction to gestalt therapy.

I hardly attended any of the sessions on family therapy with Virginia. I spent the rest of the week watching Fritz work, talking to Fritz and learning about gestalt therapy. It blew my insides out! my head right off! I spent the 48 hours having 35 years of catharsis. That was my introduction. And my good wife saw me through it all.

I guess everyone has heard the usual, extraordinary changes that take place in a person's life after an experience like that. Meeting Fritz was the turning point. I'd been look-

ing and searching, but gestalt and the work I did with him
gave me the orientation. I felt clear and solid, both personally and in my work. I dropped out of the university where I
was an assistant professor of psychiatry on the faculty of
medicine, and got out of administrative work for the first
time. I started doing the kind of work that was honest and
meaningful to me. Until then I had felt a fraud. I never felt a
fraud again in my work. I felt very clear. For the first time in
35 professional years I felt I knew what I was doing, *really*
knew what I was doing and could be honest about it instead
of playing the usual shrink game, puffing on a pipe and the
whole business.

ABRAHAM ELIZUR

We live in Israel. When we came here we lived in the apartment of Robert Golding in Carmel. They were so kind to us.
Golding's family was away at that time, and there we knew
his daughter who was eighteen years old. She told us, "Don't
miss Fritz. It will be great experience for you; you shouldn't
miss him." And this is the first time I'd heard about him,
and with such enthusiasm from a young girl that was taught
something.

She drove us to Big Sur. The way there was very difficult;
it was along cliffs and narrow roads and it was a very interesting journey. Ultimately, we got there and we saw him: the
beard and the hair—he was very impressive. He welcomed us
very warmly and invited us to stay during his seminar.

Before that he said, "Let's go to the baths." And we all
went naked there. My wife was the only one who didn't want
to go in naked, even though Fritz said, "If we can be naked
in our emotions, why can't we be naked in our bodies?"

Then we went to a week-long seminar with him. In that
seminar I wanted very much to participate—he didn't force
any participation—and when he asked, "Who wants to
work?" I immediately raised my hand. He counted one, two,
three, four, five, and I came out number ten or so. He
worked with all the people who wanted to work.

I worked on a dream. He asked me what was my dream. I said, "Well, I had a dream but I don't remember it."

"OK, put your dream on that chair and speak to the dream."

I started to speak to the dream. I said, "Dream, why are you evading me? I want you back; I want to catch you."

Then Fritz said, "OK, go over to the other chair and speak for your dream."

I sat there and said, "I don't want to come back to you and I'll never come up to you, leave me alone!" And Fritz told me to go back to the first chair. So I did, and said, 'I'm so sorry that you left me."

"Who left you?" Fritz asked.

And somehow I came to my father, and I remembered certain situations; though my father never left me physically, I didn't have the feeling that there was closeness.

And Fritz said, "OK, let me be your father." He let me sit close to him and he said, "Do whatever you like to." And I started touching him. I touched his face all around and his beard. It was the first time I have done something like that to a man: to touch a face, going around with my hands and exploring the facial features of another man.

He just let me do it; I experienced that he was willing to accept my exploration, whatever I want, my closeness. He did it silently without speaking. Somebody said in the group that I'm going *around* the face. So that gave me some courage to go to all the features in the face—on the face—not only around the beard. For me—what can I tell you?—it was like re-experiencing a closeness that I never had with my real father. I learned a little then about what gestalt therapy is.

In a sense, gestalt is an integration. It aims at integrating the various aspects of the self, but it does so in one way: only in an experiential way. Gestalt is mainly an experiential approach. It's interested in how a person experiences life—how he perceives, and the way he's coming out just now before our eyes.

Gestalt is also interested in one's childhood. In my case, as I described it, we went back to my father. But here, too, there's a difference; the past is made present, brought into the room—"Here is your father."

I mentioned that at times I felt inferior. I didn't have the courage to participate in things, but that sometimes I feel I am above others.

"OK," he said, "be above us. Stand up on the chair and talk to all of us." So I stood up on the chair and I made some bombastic talk to the audience. I smiled when I did it, but apparently it did something to me. It wasn't just a play; I felt that some hidden impulse, some hidden desire was getting its way. Then he told me, "OK, now come down to earth." And I came down and he said, "Look around and say how do you see everybody now?"

I looked in the eyes of everyone and I saw them warm, understanding, accepting, and it was very appealing to me. I felt the warmth coming to me from all the people in the audience. It was one of the greatest experiences in my life.

GEORGE LEONARD

Fritz Perls loved publicity. Several times I went down to Esalen with *Look* magazine to do stories about what was going on there . . . Fritz would do anything to have his picture taken. We went down to the baths and he insisted on being in the pictures.

One time I said, "I hope it doesn't disturb you that pictures are being taken here." He said, "No, I love to have pictures taken of me and I love to be in magazines."

His picture did not appear in any of the things we did and I always had a feeling he was a little annoyed with me for that.

Although Fritz loved and wanted publicity, he received very little notice from the media. One of the few to interview Fritz was Walt Anderson. . . .

WALT ANDERSON

I was publicity chairman with the Center for Human Development in L.A., and Fritz was going to do a one night lecture-demonstration there, so in order to publicize the thing I went and interviewed him and wrote an article for the L.A. *Free Press.* I'd seen him do a lecture once before in Beverly Hills. The interview itself was a very satisfying experience. Fritz is capable of turning on the warmth when he wants to, and he was very warm to me, though I was a little scared of him. It's easy to fantasize that he's omniscient and judgmental, and I knew he was capable of being rough with people.

At the lecture at Beverly Hills High School, there was a guy who made some kind of a big wordy statement to Fritz and Fritz didn't say anything. The guy was kind of embarrassed, so to get beyond his embarrassment he made another big wordy statement; and again Fritz said nothing. It became a very hilarious scene. It's hard to describe, but Fritz' whole way of dealing with him was not to deal with him, and the guy was like somebody trying to wrestle with a judo master. He just kept falling and falling and falling. It was painful and it was the funniest goddamn thing imaginable.

When I sat down to interview him, he said, "Turn off your tape recorder." Actually I was having trouble with the thing and he said, "Just don't use it, it'll help you get in touch with your memory." He was doing a little gestalt therapy on me.

One of the things I recall about the interview which seems typical of Fritz was somehow we were talking about marijuana and I asked him, "Do you think it should be legalized?"—a typical interviewer's question—and he said, "I don't know."

Fritz was Fritz consistently.

MICHAEL ALEXANDER
I remember Perls as a bastard. I have an inherent distrust of gurus, and he was the guru around there. He fit the mold all the workshop leaders at Esalen seemed to fit: They were reflections of the things they worked with best. Virginia Satir was a family therapist, gone through a couple of marriages, no family—her family is her workshop. Schutz, the apostle of joy, was a joyless man who never laughed. Gunther, the touchy-feely guru, mostly stood around encouraging others to touch. And Perls, the apostle of the integrated personality was the most disintegrated person you ever saw in your life! Read *In and Out the Garbage Pail* . . . he's a schizophrenic, bouncing from one thing and one idea to the other. He was always working to get people to see both sides of themselves but I never had the feeling that he integrated at all well. He was neither here nor there.

I was a photographer for *Life* magazine when I went to see Fritz, but I was also a participant in his group. I originally went to Esalen because I thought it would make a good story. I was doing a lot of shooting for *Life* at the time. I was the classic Beverly Hills Jewish liberal magazine photographer. I'd been to Selma and to Watts and I'd worked for the San Francisco *Chronicle* for a year. Photography is what I do with my life. I photograph the things that interest me and use photography as a way of getting involved in something myself. Instead of just saying "I want to take a Fritz Perls workshop," I could photograph, publish it, spread it around, get some bread for it and, at the same time, be a participant . . . except I wouldn't talk too much about wanting to be a participant. It was a way of staying slightly apart. As

a photographer there is always a certain emotional distance between me and my subjects. To an extent, that's always true of photographers. You've *got* to step back physically, and very often emotionally, just in order to push the button.

Fritz would come in and be very emotionally involved and then he, too, would step back. Looking back, I see Fritz must have thoroughly enjoyed the feeling of power and domination he had over the assholes who came to him—idolatrous and ready to spill their guts and absolutely terrified of doing it.

When the story was nearly complete for *Life,* Fritz came to me and said, "Listen, can you get my picture in the magazine because I have a sister in New York and she's not well and it would do her so much good to see my picture in *Life.*" All I could think of was, "You motherfucker, all you want to do is get your puss in *Life.* And what a bullshit way to try to wheedle in and do that—you, the guy who gets people straight!" I felt he had a special obligation to live what he was talking. And he didn't. In many ways he lived the opposite way of what he preached.

I'm not so ready to condemn him now, but he wasn't always on. He was still a human being, and he sure had that incredible ability to go right to somebody's core.

BETTY FULLER

I remember one sad, painful time in 1968 when Jane Howard and that bunch from *Life* came to do an article. It was centered on Will Schutz's groups. Jane was in Will's workshop, so the focus was on encounter. And here was Fritz, who had been the one bringing the big crowds to Esalen, being bypassed by the national media. We were in the dining room and I remember Fritz pleading to be put in the article. Michael Alexander was the photographer and he was pissed off at Fritz for some reason. He sat across the table from him at the lodge while Fritz begged to be in *Life*. His words were, "I deserve to be in *Life* magazine. My work deserves recognition and there won't be another opportunity like this. I want to be in *Life*." His picture appeared but the article was centered very much around Schutz and encounter, instead of Fritz and gestalt. Fritz had worked all his life evolving a new therapy form, a new way of dealing with human beings, of putting them on their feet and making them independent. And a lot of us who built on his foundation got a kind of national recognition very early, that came to him only late in his life. The *smallness* of us at that moment not to have recognized and been willing to acknowledge the man who was the source of an awful lot of our strength and ability to get results with people! It would have been so easy and so small a thing.

Fritz and Will Schutz had a break in their relationship about that time. I know that Will loved Fritz and that he tried to communicate with him. But, there finally comes a point of embarrassment—an impasse—where neither party can move. There was a moment where they came together at the end of our resident program. We met at Fritz' house and in effect he gave us his blessing. I know he loved us all. I had a great snapshot of him and Will arm in arm and feeling good about it all.

ANNA HALPRIN

I did something in a session with Fritz that I wouldn't have done with anybody else . . . It began with a man who was dressed in a suit and oxford shoes, black stockings, shirt and tie—he just represented everything I couldn't stand at the moment. We were having a lot of trouble getting the kind of recognition in the theatre I felt we needed and I thought, "I'll show this uptight man!" and I stood up in front of him and started slowly stripping all my clothes off until I stood stark naked in front of him and he started to cry. I was so proud of myself for being so brazen. It didn't startle Fritz at all that I would just take all my clothes off and stand in front of the man. When I sat down, his only comment was, "So what are your legs crossed for?" I was totally reduced.

Fritz was intuitive. At times, his depth of perception was unbelievable. One time we were sitting in a group and I was looking into the fireplace. Somebody was working and I was not paying attention to what she was doing. Without thinking I drew a circle around myself in the carpet. I wasn't saying or doing anything but looking into the fire. The next thing I knew Fritz had walked across the room and put his hand on my head and said, "I am your guardian angel." I had actually been fantasizing that the fire was the burning bush. I'll never know how he knew.

He would come to the theater and watch our company rehearsals. When we'd get stuck on a piece we were working on, he'd set up a situation in which we would relate like actors responding to a direction. He loved that. He loved working in the theater in that way. He was an artist and I could really identify with that. He was using gestalt, and he used it in an exciting and creative way.

He did a series of workshops for our dance company. He loved it, because everyone was so responsive. We actually did the whole gestalt workshop as dancers and as theater people. We'd dance and act out and everything. He would do gestalt therapy by getting us up on our stage and saying, "Now be this . . . now be that . . ." and everybody would be it by dancing it. Every time he worked with somebody it was like a performance. They were so good at getting in touch with their feelings through movement. They could role play.

As I look back on it now, having been in other therapy situations, I realize how rare that was, how high that experience was for us. Fritz loved being the theater director. He loved it.

George Leonard

In '66 or '67, Jennifer Jones Selznick gave a fabulous party to introduce the human potential movement to Hollywood. There were ten of us and eighty of them. Just name anybody in Hollywood—they were all there—Rock Hudson, Dennis Hopper, Eddie Albert, Jason Robards . . . It was an incredible party. We drove up to the mansion which was in Beverly Hills or one of those townships, and the cars were met by eight red-jacketed car parkers. Then we walked up to the house under a long aisle of Japanese lanterns. We were all dressed rather informally except Fritz, who came in a tuxedo. He had the long beard, and a biblical look about him . . . he really looked like something out of Sunset Boulevard. . . .

It was a weird party. Fritz had a great time. He sent at least three people home in a snit. He sat out by the swimming pool sort of holding court, an informal gestalt thing, and people were gathered around him. He was playing havoc with Hollywood that night, and enjoying it because he did love films and he knew very well what he was doing.

The first person who came under his scrutiny was Natalie Wood. She started doing a dream and talking about what she was into. Fritz said, "You are a spoiled brat who thinks about nothing but herself." She flounced out, snubbing Jennifer Jones at the same time. Tuesday Weld stamped out, shaking her head. Oskar Werner got into some kind of a rap with Fritz and came out in a huff.

I think what really blew the minds of the Hollywood community that night was the fact that we didn't ask them for anything. Mike Murphy, Dick Price, and I and the whole bunch decided that we wouldn't ask them for money or support because we did not want all of Hollywood coming to Esalen. If it became an "in" spot for the Hollywood crowd it would have spoiled the ambience; Esalen would not be Esalen any more.

It was quite a party. It went on until dawn. Fritz was on the highest level of dignity. My impression of him that night is one of a prophet or a famous wizard.

ROBERT HALL

One day during the summer Fritz told me I would be opening the Gestalt Institute in San Francisco in October. Up to that point there was no indication of such a thing . . . he just picked October. I couldn't figure it out. I didn't want to leave Big Sur, Alyssa didn't either; I'd assumed I would stay at Esalen with him.

I put up a lot of resistance. But somehow or other, October 23 was the opening night of the Institute. There were about 2,500 people there. I was backstage with him, about to give a little introductory speech and I was really, really nervous, I said, "Don't you get nervous?" He said he'd gotten over his stage fright, and he added, "What do you risk?"

I worked constantly for about three years.

He used to get quite upset with me because he wanted me to travel around; he had things he wanted me to do in Europe and that sort of thing, but I was really comfortable at home and I didn't like to travel. I wouldn't go. So we started to disagree a little bit about that; out of this friction I began to see that gestalt therapy was really a great tool but that it wasn't the final answer for me and I began to go more and more toward meditation.

I saw meditation as really an extension of gestalt—gestalt turned inward. It was just a more refined, much more subtle, way of working. I tried to tell Fritz this on many occasions, but he would not listen. He saw gestalt therapy as final. His thing was action. Being alive is action; meditation didn't seem like action. He reacted against it without listening or discussing or trying it or anything. He used to make fun of me for meditating. He always called it "neither shitting nor getting off the pot."

One morning he came to our house and threw a very bad scene. This was the last time he was ever in our house. He had gotten up early; Alyssa and I were meditating, and there was no one to make him coffee or to cook his breakfast. We usually did that. We came out and he was in a rage, just in a rage, that no one was there to make him coffee. He threw a tantrum, stamping his feet and everything. It was really frightening for me to see him like that. He said he was going to leave my house. And he did. He called Anna Halprin and she came and took him away.

Before he left, he embraced me. He was just shaking.

JERRY ROTHSTEIN

It wasn't the coffee. To Fritz, there was something very peculiar about Bob's becoming a disciple of a spiritual master. To Fritz, it was shocking beyond mere disappointment. How could a man who was a gestaltist—someone who really understood gestalt (or so Fritz believed)—be so completely oblivious to the basic *premise* of gestalt? Fritz' teaching is that he/we have it all within ourselves—yet paradoxically, Bob took a way that was foreign to this. Fritz believed that submitting to a "master" is the avoidance of looking within yourself and completing yourself from your own resources; it was alien to the concepts of gestalt.

Anna Halprin

Fritz called me and said, "Come and get me," and I had to go down to Mill Valley. Bob was his protege, and he couldn't understand it. He felt it was like removing yourself from the reality of the world. Bob had all these pictures of his guru on the wall—that's what got Fritz. "How can anyone really understand my work and accept a master? There is no such thing." From Fritz' point of view it was a total contradiction. That's a Jewish point of view too: you experience God directly; you don't have any intermediaries between you and God. Fritz' way of experiencing Bob was that Bob hadn't really grasped what he was doing. It was disappointing and frustrating to him and it made him angry.

Jack Rosenberg

I'd been close to Bob before he got a master and went into spirituality very strongly. I remember I went to Bob—it had upset me—I was working on my own feelings about him having a master: "What right have you got to have a master? What right do *you,* whom *I* look up to, have to allow someone else to tell *you* what's going on?"

Of course, I knew that those were really irrational feelings and I was working on them, and when I finished and got settled within myself, he said to me, "You know, Fritz feels the same way."

Pamela Pomeranz

He didn't take any games from anybody. I was straight from the suburbs, a housewife at Esalen with my husband. I'd never been into any of this kind of stuff. The first time I sat down to work in a group, I giggled and did other kinds of numbers. I was embarrassed and Fritz said, "What's that?"

which made me even more embarrassed. It was very hard.
After a few minutes more of my awkwardness, he said,
"Leave the chair. I don't want to work with you". . . he
wasn't being supportive of my number . . . it was like he
wasn't going to take my bullshit. I ended up leaving the chair
crying and feeling really humiliated. It seemed *very* cruel, yet
obviously it wasn't.

The next day, he wasn't there and somehow or other I got
into a fight with this older man in the group. I got furious.
I'd never been so angry in my life. It wasn't a game. I was
really out to get him.

By the time night came around, in the group again, I was
really shaking. I had been learning about working with the
energy of that, so I got in the chair again and Fritz said,
"You here again?"

"Fritz, I have something to work on this time."

"Get outta the chair."

"No, Fritz, this is not foolin' around. I want to work on
my shaking."

"Get out of the chair and let someone else work!"

I don't remember anything else but just . . . my arm
. . . my fist just banging into this arm. Then the guy I'd beat
up on in the afternoon jumped me . . . and Fritz got furious
at him for interfering with what was going on. He really tried
very hard to work with me but I was just too scattered. I had
never done anything like that. I'd never expressed any real
emotion, especially anger, in front of anybody.

After that I just couldn't talk to Fritz at all. Every time I
would say something it was always dumb. I was very uncomfortable around him. I was really in such a heavy place I
thought about killing myself. But I knew that would be a
number, too.

Then I got involved in a massage workshop. One day, they
all decided to meet at the baths at dinner time to practice.
Fritz was going to come down to be practiced on. I said OK
and went down at six and there was no one there but me and
Fritz.

I said, "Well, do you want a massage?" Up until this time I hadn't been able to say a word to him.

I gave him a massage—it was a lovely massage. I was really paying attention to Fritz and did all the things they told me to and towards the end he had a hard-on. He kind of chuckled and said (with his heavy accent), "You zee vhat you do to me."

I felt funny, like with his reputation of being a dirty old man, "Uh, oh, what do I do now?" In fact, I thought he was going to accuse me of being a cock teaser. All kinds of stuff was coming through . . . apparently he saw that on my face.

"Don't vorry," he said, "I von't fuck you."

It was a very tender moment. It was like I had given him something. I had related to him in a way. This was apparently at a time he was having trouble having an erection. It was a lovely sensual moment without that dirty-old-man number going on.

After the massage we walked out holding hands. We didn't say a word. We parted when we got to the top of the hill. Then he told everybody in the office that he'd had the best massage he'd ever had.

I'd met Betty Fuller in a couples' workshop she gave eight or nine years ago in upstate New York. Now we sit in the living room of her spacious house in Marin County looking out at the San Francisco skyline. When we started to talk I realized that she wanted so badly to talk about Fritz that she thought perhaps she shouldn't. She speaks out of her love of Fritz of this love.

BETTY FULLER

You know, Jack, I experienced an enormous amount of resistance meeting with you and doing this interview. There was the fear that I would pretend that my relationship was more significant than it was. And also, it's like treading on the memory of a very great person.

Gene Sagan had said, "I am giving you an afternoon with Perls." That didn't mean anything to me at the time. I honestly had no inkling of who this guy was; suddenly, in walks this exquisite old man! I'd never seen anybody so beautiful. He just absolutely knocked me out.

He was wearing one of those jump suits of his and he leaned forward, smoking, and he started talking right to me. He said how tiring it was to play the role of therapist, to mobilize a group and help heal others when he hadn't handled his own neurotic symptoms. "Ze smoking," he said, "I'm not handling ze smoking." I totally withdrew. I just leaned back and closed my eyes.

After the group got going, Juanita Bradshaw said, "I resent Betty Fuller because she's not giving anything to the group, and she's pushing me away, too." I snapped back, "Tough shit! If you're being pushed away, you're letting yourself be pushed away. Don't lay that on me!" I came out with that! I'd never been so *there* before in my life. It must have been Fritz' influence on me. Up until then, I thought responsibility meant, "Did you do the dishes and empty the garbage?" The idea that I was responsible as the cause of my experience was totally foreign to me.

I took off after that . . . literally! That afternoon I became a whirlwind! Fritz had been tickled by my "tough shit!" and he seemed tickled with me, maybe because I was so willing to be such an asshole.

Anyway, that afternoon I played every role Fritz writes about—tragedy queen, crybaby, dumb butt. I ran the gamut.

I was such a mess! He just kept making me look at my experience of who I was. I kept saying, "I don't want to be fat." And he'd say, "But you *are* fat." There was no judgment, no put down, just straight reporting of what was.

Now, the next big thing was his asking me, "What does your fat *do* for you?" And I protested that it didn't do a thing for me. He just kept smoking and asking, "What does it *do* for you?" and blowing smoke and asking, "What does it *do* for you?" In years of therapy and the theater and education and getting degrees in college and all the rest of it, I had never truly experienced another human being simply being *with* me, with nothing going on with them. I'd been in therapy for a number of years, going in twice a week reporting how my life was working fine, and everything was great and I had it all together. Then I'd get in the car and sob all the way home, but I wasn't going to cry in front of the therapist, by God! No one was going to see *me* cry. What Fritz was getting me to look at was just so simple I couldn't accept it.

It took me a year and a half to get what Fritz was teaching: that if I didn't want to be fat I wouldn't be fat. And while I'm moaning and groaning about being fat, it's just perfectly obvious that I am fat, so I gotta want to be. We can want some very nutty things.

The key was simply this: When you examine your behavior, you realize that as long as the advantages are greater than the disadvantages you will not alter your behavior one iota. Period. I decided right then that I could learn a lot from this man.

He did a whole raft of workshops in the Bay Area, especially at Janie Rhyne's place in the Haight-Ashbury back in the heyday of the Haight. She had an attic in an old Victorian that was set up as a gestalt art workshop. Fritz came there several times . . . I can still see him huffing and puffing up those three flights of stairs. A lot of outstanding therapists who are now practicing in the Bay Area were sitting in the circle up there in that room. We were a close-knit, informal group of maybe twenty, and after a workshop some of us would pile into a movie. I remember after we saw "Marat Sade" in particular Fritz walking out and smiling this beatific smile and saying, "Ooohhh, I've been sitting on that fart for 45 minutes and it feels so good just to let it go."

In those days—'64, '65, '66—Fritz was incredibly benevolent and warm and funny. He was beginning to make appearances at San Francisco State College and involving himself with the students and young people. He loved the Haight and loved to just walk around. He was becoming a counterculture hero and was incredibly happy and fun to be with. He radiated love. Yes, I got love from Fritz more than anything. And for all his disappointment at not having realized or consolidated more of his own contribution to psychology before the end, in those days there was just love.

* * *

> There is a place like Eden
> Where you have miscellaneous
> enjoyments like the maiden,
> The baths, the sun, and wisdom groups
> It's truly Esalaneous. . . .

The window is wide open. Faintly threatening murmur of the surf. Gently blowing winds lift papers on the desk, too weak to make them fly. Like my soft beard

stroking a maiden's face and breast and making them
shiver with silent delights, making their nipples stand up
in proud erection, patiently waiting to be bitten.

DENISE FREY

When I knew him, Fritz was about 70, yet he led an extremely active sex life. What was unique about him was the fact
that he came at it with total freshness and eagerness. He was
the pasha of the baths. He would go down at five o'clock
every day and hang out there and just want to kiss everybody
in the place.

He was so genuine, and it was such nonpossessive sex. He
was just so eager. He was like a little kid who had just found
out there were all these nice people to touch and all these
groovy things to do—and he could go out and do it! He had
great vanity in this respect—I think he just discovered he was
all right to look at, that he was attractive.

I think his description of himself as a mediocre Jewish
psychiatrist in New York was probably extremely accurate.
And then he came out here and got turned loose, you know,
all of a sudden. He got turned loose in the sense that suddenly it was all right to be a kid, and it was all right to be
whatever you were and go out and do it.

I went to bed with him once, during a workshop up here—
the first time I'd ever been to Esalen, and got into making
love. And it became fairly obvious he couldn't sustain an
erection long enough to go through with it. I don't know if
that was universally true, but we played along and had a
good time. What was nice about it was that I could feel
everything happening in him—the panic that he wasn't sus-
taining an erection, and his worry about me—what did *I*
think of him. It was the least amount of avoidance I've ever
met in anyone. To me that was very lovely. He was very
beautiful.

BETTY FULLER

My first four-day workshop with Fritz at Esalen was in '66 in
his Big Sur house. At one point, a Harvard type with a pipe

was coming on with the whole Ivy league bit, and Fritz fell sound asleep. He began to snore! That was another valuable thing I got from Fritz: You can withdraw from unnourishing situations; you can go with your preferences rather than getting stuck in "shoulds." If anything interesting happened, Fritz would always wake right up. Someone in the group would say, "What the hell!" or "Bullshit!" and Fritz would be back. He was the first therapist I know who gave himself permission to live with preferences instead of "shoulds."

One night Fritz said our group was all going down to the communal baths and anyone who was uptight was going to be disappointed because it's so easy. Well, I didn't believe him; nobody was going to get *me* in those baths! But, somehow I got into the shuffle of the herd down that little path . . . and pretty soon my clothes were off and there I was in the water! I looked around and thought, "You're absolutely right. There's nothing to it!" I was actually disappointed that it wasn't any big deal. I couldn't believe that you could walk out of one universe and into another one with that ease! The whole business of getting your clothes off and just being with yourself; wow! It made all the difference!

He also taught me the necessity to chew every single bit of food until it's only spit, and swallow it before putting anything else into your mouth. And that is more than a dietary prescription—it's a way of living life. He believed we must destructure whatever we take into ourselves of the environment; that it has to be broken down and assimilated into our personality and the useless eliminated, or there can't be a whole person.

And I had to handle my "sacred cow" thing with him. If he sat at my dinner table, for example, I went right into my awe trip, staring worshipfully at him. I was so overwhelmed by him. Ooohh, I wanted to sleep with that man so much!

I even ran a number at one time that I wanted to have his child. One time, on a "trip," I really felt totally at ease with Fritz. I came down to dinner glowing and our eyes just kept meeting and melting and blending. The only words spoken were when he said, "You're radiant." There wasn't any need for words. I've seen that look in his eyes many times. They'd grow a little wet and misty and soften . . . they melted. His melting was exquisite to behold.

I *loved* him. I loved the way he looked and talked and the things he did. I loved his work, his way with people. There's no getting around it, I was incredibly in love with Fritz.

MARGARET CALLAHAN

I got into the tub with everybody else and was feeling a little shy because it's not quite my number to undress in a group. But I was curious to have the experience. It was very beautiful out there—the rocks and the ocean are absolutely gorgeous. The minute Fritz saw me, he grabbed me by the hand and took me away from the others into a separate little pool where he proceeded to play with me for about an hour in a very childlike fashion, rolling around in the water and rolling over me. It was apparently sensual to him. I didn't have any sexual interest in him and so I limited our play to non-erotic activities. It was very fun and very special. He was enchanting and childlike and playful. I was very taken with his mind and his fame; I felt as though I was with a great innovator: The father of gestalt therapy was playing porpoise love with me in this pool. He didn't try to kiss me or get too close. But there were sensual overtones. After a while everybody left the other pool to where we were playing like dolphins. They watched us and laughed. It was a moment in time with this bony old man. But the incongruities got me: This old child shouldn't even have been alive; he had no chest, he had no stomach, he had no legs, he had no neck, he had no arms—

he had nothing. He was caved in everywhere; he looked like a corpse. But he had this *enormous* erection! It was not to be believed! I thought, "This is absolutely unreal. How could this old man possible have an erection?" I didn't know whether to be flattered or terrified by his interest in me.

When he walked me home that night from the baths he asked me to share his bed. I think I'm the only woman in the world who hasn't been in bed with Fritz Perls.

HARVEY FREEDMAN
Seminars always mean that we go down to the baths. On this particular evening an extraordinarily attractive woman (if she walked by now we'd all turn our heads to look at her) who was also a psychoanalyst—orthodox right down to the very marrow of her bones—arrived. And, of course, Fritz and she immediately found each other.

Prior to the baths we had all been sitting around while they had tangled, Fritz obviously enjoying himself, she trying desperately to put him down, accusing him of sexuality, acting out, the usual kind of thing. She was quite articulate, representing the respectability of the profession and responsibility and so on. She was the last person in the world that I expected to see at the baths after this intellectual discussion.

Three o'clock in the morning. There was no moon that night. I go down and in the dim light of the baths I see Rodin's statue of *The Kiss* on the edge of the tub. Who is it? Fritz and this woman, in the l o n g e s t kiss. They were frozen in this. Not a stitch of clothing on except for, I can still recall, a yellow hair band.

A clergyman who was in one of Fritz' groups was concerned about whether Fritz was using his position and power as therapist for his personal sexual needs. He posed a number of questions to the Esalen Board, one of which was. . .

Is the in-residence Fritz Perls therapy program a form of institutionalized seduction, in which the therapist has such powerful instruments of persuasion at his disposal that it is unethical for him to subject even more or less normal persons to their impact? Is (Esalen) . . . a trap for innocent persons seeking to strengthen their personal and married lives? Is Fritz Perls exploiting the power of the "cultural island" for his own personal needs as well as using his skills to help some people?

He also made this comment:

Someone is bound to tell me to look into myself and see my own lusts, insecurities, etc. Fine; glad to; but this is another subject.

Another voice. . .

My hands are strong and warm. A dirty old man's hands are cold and clammy. I have affection and love—too much of it. And if I comfort a girl in grief or distress and the sobbing subsides and she presses closer and the stroking gets out of rhythm and slides over the hips and over the breasts . . . where does the grief end and a perfume begin to turn your nostrils from dripping to smelling?*

JANET WULLNER FAISS

I first met Fritz Perls at Big Sur Hot Springs in July of 1964 when he came to one of Fritz Faiss' workshops. I found Dr. Perls rather unsettling. In fact, after that initial meeting, I went back to my cottage and did a brush and ink sketch of my impression: Perls is represented as a cloven-hooved figure and two serpents are eating at his heart . . . Fritz Faiss is standing at his side and looking away, his hand lifted. I saw

---

*Reminder: all indented italicized quotes are from Fritz' *In and Out the Garbage Pail.*

Perls as a satanic figure. If there hadn't been a streak of humanitarianism in him, Fritz Perls would have been an extremely dangerous, destructive man.

Today, I sense that I was not entirely above the feminine dream: Possibly, through me, even this man will find more of his true self. I would never have confessed to such a thought or hope eleven years ago, but in retrospect, and at 42 years of age, I can risk candor with myself.

Fritz Perls always had an entourage of females around him. They couldn't seem to worship him enough, and he seemed to find it difficult to believe that I didn't want to join this group of admirers. I didn't have anything in particular against him, but I'm not a joiner. I don't care to be a keeper of the godhead. What I did not say then was that, although I admired his intellectual abilities, I was not sexually attracted to him.

And sexuality played an important role in the assemblage. The picture of a worn-out satyr surrounded by would-be nymphs was just too offensive for me to even consider. Today I might judge less harshly—or not at all. I suppose they counteracted a certain Puritanism in themselves through these sexual encounters.

I remember quite clearly the morning Fritz Perls complained that he felt in his art class, Fritz Faiss had peeled away layer after layer in order to get down to the skeleton or the base of art. He, Perls, didn't care for that. When I pointed out the necessity for a skeleton or a foundation in the spiritual, the intellectual, the physical aspects of man, Perls remarked that if he took me to bed, he wouldn't be interested in my skeleton. This ruse was so typical of him, and females evidently found it irresistible most of the time. I told him that, interested in it or not, my skeleton goes where I go—at least while I'm living. Well, we exchanged a few more thrusts and parries until I said that this was futile bantering because even if he had any intention of taking me to bed, I certainly had no inclination or intention to go with him.

"Oh, I know," he said, "you're the kind who thinks 'never on Sunday and only in the dark.' " I said, "Why not on Sunday or any other day; in the sunlight, under the moon, in the forest, on the sand? But I will not go with *you.*"

ILANA RUBENFELD

My introduction to Fritz was a long line of people waiting to kiss him. I didn't know anything about him except that people said he was a dirty old man—not an admirable reputation—and it made me very uptight. It was the first time I'd ever seen him: a huge, bearded man with gargantuan hands and knees, a big nose, long hair and a messy beard. He didn't look the least bit sexy to me. I didn't know what the fuss was about, but they were all lining up to kiss him—long ones, two-minute kisses with the tongue, both men and women! And they were coming back for seconds!

Fritz said later, "She was an uptight, proper lady," because I wouldn't kiss him. I sat down in that room, my arms and legs crossed, protecting myself. Fritz looked at me and I said, "I don't know what I'm going to do here for a whole month, six to eight hours with you! Every day! For a whole month!" He said, "Exaggerate your body position." I crossed my legs tighter. "More and make sound." I held myself tighter. "More," and I made more sound until finally, I broke my arms open, uncrossed my legs and screamed, "You're all a bunch of jerks! I hate it here!"

And when I let all the anger out I looked around. He's sitting there smiling. And the colors and the people look very clear to me. Fritz said, "My dear, you have had a mini-satori! You will do very well here, very well."

Right from the beginning it was apparent that he liked me. I had made a very deliberate decision that I did not want to be with Fritz sexually. I was with Frank, but the married part didn't make the difference. I didn't feel that way about Fritz, and I wanted him to be my therapist. I didn't want to screw around. To this day, I knock on wood for the fine decision I made.

We became very good friends, and he had a feeling for me that was much nicer than it would have been if we had been lovers. I'll give you a flavor of the way he worked: One night a group of us were standing in the doorway watching a video feedback of a session. I had on a long towel dress that we all wore in '67 with a zipper up the back. I felt someone unzipping me and I turn around. "Fritz! What are you doing?"

"Oh, I'm just seeing how you are."

He was like a kid. That was what was so beautiful about him. I said, "Fritz, zip up my dress!" He zips it up right away. Three minutes pass, and I feel this pair of knuckles going into my side. "What are you doing?"

"Giving you a little rolfing."

I take his hand away. And I say, "Please, Fritz, leave me alone. I want to watch this thing. Cut it out! ! !" Five minutes later he's back again, unzipping my dress and massaging my neck. I let him massage my neck for a while.

In a husky voice he whispers, "What else would you like? I like you so much, I could do this all over to you."

"No, please. Stop it. Don't do it." He was like a very young person and it was hard to reject him. He didn't know how to hear no. Finally he said, "OK," and looking sort of chagrined, turned his back and left.

There is a syndrome in this field where a lot of the women go from group to group and see if they can make the leader. Women went up and wanted to have sex with Fritz all the

time. I'm sure he couldn't get it up—which disappointed them and frustrated him. . . .

One thing I'm sure he could do and probably do very well is touch. His hands and his lips were beautiful. The second summer, I kissed him—and Frank kissed him too—and I know how really beautiful and sensuous a pair of lips he had. Once at a workshop he was with a woman he liked a lot, Asa Kadish, a woman in her seventies. She had broken her leg skiing and was *kvetching* about it. "Oh, Fritz, I'm getting old." He put his hands on her and said, "Asa, we're all getting older. You know, I can't get it up so much anymore. . . ." In front of the whole group! So the stories about fucking night and day are bullshit.

I don't blame those young girls, though, because he gave them such double messages. Two or three young girls would walk into my house because they'd heard that Fritz was there. I'd introduce them, and they'd look at him, starstruck. He'd take them in his arms and give this tremendous-

ly sexual soul kiss. The girls would leave but a half hour later the phone would ring. Once he was at my house having coffee with me when Mari called up. They had been together a few times and she wanted to see him. "Again?" he said.

The key to my relationship with Fritz was that I didn't put him on a pedestal. We got very close. We transcended and broke a lot of rules through our humor. I said a lot of things to him that other people wouldn't say. It's like the court jester who says things that nobody else dares tell the king.

Fritz loved jokes and riddles. Once at breakfast I said, "Fritz, what did one strawberry say to another?" He looked at me blankly. "Listen" I said, "if we weren't in that bed this morning, we wouldn't be in this jam tonight!" He roared.

He knew I was with the Alexander technique, and one day he said, "I would like to have an Alexander session with you, Ilona." He called me Ilona, not Ilana.

"What time?" I said.

"I'll be free at 11:00 tonight. Let's do it at the baths."

"OK." And I said to myself, "Am I crazy? I'm going to give Fritz Perls a session at 11:00 p.m. at the baths? What if he thinks it's awful? My reputation will be ruined!"

There was this fear inside me, but I was alone in my room and I put Fritz in his chair and I said, "Man, you're lucky

I'm even going to touch you, you son of a bitch!" And I when through a whole thing and took my power back.

By the time Fritz came down to the baths that night I yelled, "Get on the table!" And he was like a kid! He was wearing this blue terrycloth outfit and he started to unzip it. I said, "Oh, no, zip it up!" He says, "Vat? The Alexander technique is with clothes on? Everything at Esalen is with clothes off!"

We had a session. He was not easy to work with but he was very willing and very responsive to my hands and to my instructions. A lot of his trouble came from smoking. He had a lot of congestion in his chest. There were places that were very, very heavy. He had about ten or twelve sessions with me. Once someone kidded him and asked, "Who's your therapist?" and he turned around and said, "Ilona."

SUSAN WARD

I had enrolled in a Fritz Perls workshop with a woman who was a close friend of mine, and just after we arrived at Esalen the two of us were standing in a corner of the dining room talking. It was all new to me and I was feeling kind of anxious. Fritz was there and he walked right over to me and said, "Do you always take the back seat with your friend?" We did have that kind of relationship. Whenever we were together I was always the reticent one. Fritz knew this just from watching us across the room. I felt he could see right through everything and it scared me.

This was Friday, and that night I saw him in operation in the workshop. I really respected him; I was very impressed with his professional skill. I'd never seen anything like it. Somehow it made me feel a few inches shorter than I already was.

After dinner that night he came over and said, "I would like to be the one to take you to the baths." I was flattered that he, God, would want to take me to the baths, you know, and I said, "That would be very nice." God got me a towel and I went down to the baths with him, my friend sort of trotting along behind us. I was very frightened.

I envisioned some kind of huge Japanese bath where you go into a dressing room and emerge stark naked. Then when I saw this little place where I had to stand and take my clothes off, I was terrified. Fritz stripped his clothes off in seconds, climbed into one of the tubs, and sat there about two feet away, watching me. I actually thought of jumping over the edge of the cliff but I decided against that. So if I wasn't going to jump, I had to take my clothes off—there was no other way. It was torture. I'd come directly from school, and in those days I wore stockings and underpinnings and stuff. It seemed like hours. I was just mortified, thinking, "What am I going to do when I get them off?"

Then, finally, I had my clothes off, and Fritz, looking up at me, beckoned with his fingers, you know, "Come in here next to me." I was in sheer terror but God was calling me and I wouldn't think of not obeying. I got in. Instantly his hands were all over me, fondling my breasts, my genitals, everything. If it had been any other man I would have said, "Stop it!" But God? No. I looked down and he had this huge erection. I was impressed with that, at his age. But he kept pawing and fondling and wouldn't leave me alone. There was no conversation, nothing. Silence. I just sat there. Terror. I couldn't enjoy it; I had strong feelings that I was being used. It was repulsive to me. All I could think of was, "How can I escape? I've got to escape." I stretched my legs, but as soon as I moved over, he pulled me back. I tried to scoot over and make my friend sit next to him, just thinking she'd be more experienced and could deal with him, but I couldn't. I don't know how long this was going on.

All this time I never said a word to him. It began to get crowded in the tub, and suddenly a naked guy jumped in the bath, and started making very funny remarks. Though I don't even now know who he was, I'll always remember and be grateful to him. He was a very funny man and everyone was laughing. Fritz, too, and as he did, he stopped fondling me and I managed to get away from him. I jumped up on the edge of the tub, pretending I was laughing hard with the rest of them.

I avoided him after that. I was in his workshop but I didn't work with him at all, and he made no reference to the episode. In fact, the very next morning he saw me in the dining room at breakfast and I was worried about what I would do if he came over, but he ignored me!

I realized he was so perceptive that he nailed me the moment I came in. He knew he could take advantage of me and I wouldn't do anything because I was scared to be at Esalen, scared to be in the baths, scared to be with him. I'm sure my fear was showing all over my face—it always seems to—and he saw it and picked me out. It was like picking on a cripple or a weakling, like stepping on the littlest flower because he knew he could squash it. I thought, "You bastard! You knew I would act exactly the way I did."

But I learned something: "You stupid fool! Why did you let him do it? Just because he's up there as a therapist doesn't mean it's his prerogative to. . ." I learned it's my own fault if I can't take care of myself.

Jack Hurley called me one day when I lived at Stinson Beach and said he heard I was writing about Fritz and would like to talk to me. He came over with his wife. They are quiet, unassuming, pleasant people.

JACK HURLEY

I worked for Fritz for a period when he was developing his movies. Most of the time I was playing with his equipment. I also arranged for a few of the reels of his movies. That part was discouraging. It wasn't a paying job . . . theoretically, it was "if it ever made any money," and it never did.

One year I helped him with his calendar; he coordinated his activities with the opera schedule in San Francisco. Once he got the opera schedule, he filled in the rest of the slots on his calendar. You know, "I vant to go to this vun, so I'll go there then. I can see this vun when I come back and this vun on my way," and that's how he did it.

Rae started working for Fritz when I was in charge of the Esalen cabins.

RAE HURLEY

Fritz wasn't a hard man to clean up for. During his work-shops it was difficult because I had to get over there when the seminarians weren't working and do it quick! The rest of the time it was a very easy job. The only difficulty I ever had was with his desk, because there was always all kinds of junk on it; I didn't know what I could move and what I could not move. Fritz was not a very neat person and he lived in a clut-tered place, so cleaning consisted of picking up his pajamas and hanging the towels and washing up the bathroom and making the bed and, if he was there, of lying in the bed for awhile with him and enjoying life. . . .

That was part of the job, although I never felt that I had to. I mean, I wanted to. And then there were times when I didn't want to, and Fritz was never insistent. There have been all kinds of stories about the dirty old man aspect of him, but I never felt that. Fritz had presence and he knew how to turn me on. It just happened. It was very lovely. And he would usually take a nap after.

One time, Fritz asked me to come and help him catalogue his records. I went and had a perfectly lovely afternoon, in-cluding a fuck, and at the end he said, "How much do I owe you?"

"Fritz, I had such a good time, I don't need to get paid."

"Ach! That's vat you have to learn: to get paid for doing vat you enjoy."

I always felt it was an even exchange of energies. It was something very beautiful, from which we both got some-thing. And I came to feel over the years that energy ex-changes like these were one of the ways Fritz kept himself young.

I was always so turned on after being with Fritz. The morning after the first time I went to bed with Fritz, Jack and I were sitting in the lodge at breakfast and all of a sud-den there were all of these young men sitting around. Men, *young* men, who I'd been drooling about yesterday. It was my first experience of being "in heat" and I attribute that to Fritz. He released something in me which had not been there before. I don't know how he did it. He brought me to a new level of response. He was able to touch certain spots on my back and turn me on. . . .

I've learned something that Fritz knew about what's behind all that—the allowing and the exchange is done to build. He could put his fingers in the right places, see the response, allow that response, allow the allowing and build on that response. I would see him do this. It would be different places with different people. It's an energy transaction, and when you keep the energy transaction on a balance and flow, it's not possession.

How did you feel about that, Jack?

JACK HURLEY
I appreciated the wonders Fritz did with Rae.

Gentle, conniving, sexual virtuoso, inept, male chauvinist, impotent, dirty old man, charismatic, man of incredible virility: Fritz. Everything but a child molester. . . .

MICHAEL MURPHY
I hear a lot of rumors that he was supposed to be great with women. He once said to me, "You've got to let go to the top of your head." How he handled this, a man into his seventies, I don't know. He was a man of many moods—a lot of ambition, and also the pains of sensuality when a woman turned him down. He used to love the waitresses—they'd wear these long dresses, and he'd call them "floating maidens." He would always react to them. He liked big, handsome women—full-bodied, quiet and *zaftig**. He was an archetype of male chauvinism.

JACK DOWNING
Fritz was sexually active from an early age, and he loved to fuck. I once asked him how he remained so alive, and he

---

*Zaftig describes in one word what it takes two hands describing an hour-glass figure to do. (From *The Joys of Yiddish*.)

said, "I get just to the point of orgasm, but I don't have it."
I don't think it was Tantra; he figured it out for himself. He
would become aroused, he wouldn't ejaculate, and then he'd
walk around in that state through the day. He would only allow himself a few orgasms a year.

FRITZ FAISS
He liked to play the harmless, innocent, misunderstood man.
He knew by experience that this was a very effective tactic to
capture female attention or sympathy. He was without doubt
a master in that field. He could shrink, belittle himself, and
in no time change into a monster.

CYNTHIA SHELDON
He had me role playing every type of female he could think
up—a tough little girl, a sweet little girl, a baby, a mother;
then he said, "Now I vant you to play the whore," at which
time I came out of my trance and just froze. I looked at him,
and he had this twinkle in his eye. I went back into my
trance, and started playing a very seductive role with some
guy on the sidelines, which broke up the whole group. He did
not ask me to play a woman—only a little girl, good and bad,
a mother, a baby and a whore.

During another workshop, Fritz was working with a
woman in the group, and Jim Simkin got very angry, yelling
at him, "Fritz, you really hate women! You talk as if ninety
percent of them were all bitches!" Fritz turned around and
grinned, "No, that is not correct. It's that eighty percent of
them are whores."

WILSON VAN DUSEN
Fritz gave me a whole history of impotence going way back.
He told me a funny story about his last analyst—I forget
which of the three it was. He had been talking about his im-
potency and inadequacy for a long time, and the analyst
said, "Well, let's look at the damn thing." Fritz was
stunned. The guy said, "Let's look at your penis. That's
what we've been talking about, isn't it? How big is it? How

adequate?" Fritz got it out, they looked at it, and it looked adequate. Fritz told me that he was shocked that it was possible to get the "real" out, and when you did that, it killed all the fantasy about it. He said this was the incident that led to his conception of gestalt therapy.

LAURA PERLS
Ever since I knew him, he was highly potent and sexually adept; we had a lot of very good sex. But while Fritz was in analysis with Reich, he had a short period of impotence. I didn't take it very seriously because I knew it wouldn't last, but Fritz was seriously concerned.

NATALIE MANN
When he was older, there was a period when he was impotent, but never with me. He made love like a virtuoso, like someone playing the violin. It was a beautiful experience.

GER AGREY
He was one of the sexiest men of any age I've ever met. He was beautiful, lecherous. He really liked women, and he didn't play the game of breaking down a woman's ego in the process of seducing her.

WILSON VAN DUSEN
His dependency on lovemaking always seemed to me to be a bit of a weakness. I would almost think he would perish if left alone.

CYNTHIA SHELDON

In the '60s I never had the feeling of him being out to misuse contact. A friend of mine spent quite a lot of time with him during that time. Rather than only being into pleasuring himself as many saw him, he focused on her pleasuring herself. They did not have a sexual encounter, though he helped her become aware of her vaginal feelings with both her own touch and his.

WILSON VAN DUSEN

An incident I hesitate to describe occurred late in our relationship. My wife had left and I was sitting alone in the living room. Fritz came in with his blood coursing through his veins so sharply that I could see it. He was terribly excited, and implied that I should do something for him. I got the impression that it was sexual, that he wanted me. I said I couldn't. For one thing, I wasn't sure what he wanted, nor am I now, but he was visibly aroused and the only thing I could think of was sexual.

RAE HURLEY

I think he brought a lot of women in touch with their bi- or homosexuality. He'd be in the baths with a woman on each side making up to him, and then he'd quietly slip away. He did it to me once. He suddenly withdrew his energy and I found myself embracing another woman. That had never happened to me before, and I felt, "Hey, wait a minute . . that old bastard, what's he up to now?" Since then I've gotten into other places—I like women, but at that time I wasn't there yet.

JACK HURLEY

Fritz didn't draw artificial lines between where therapy stops and love begins. I saw the number of women who came and went for their private sessions with him.

People who came to the Big Sur would comment on all the kissing. Have you ever seen two bearded men kissing? If I happened to be walking by, he would call me over and we would kiss, and boom! All sorts of pieces would fall apart in people.

Fritz didn't claim to be the best fuck because he didn't always get a full hard-on, but the kissing, yes. Rae said it had something to do with presence . . . not aggressiveness . . . a delicate balance, just enough push for the override button to get into the next response.

STELLA RESNICK
Well, it's hard for a seventy-seven-year-old man to be sexual and not be a dirty old man. He was a sexual, sensual man who loved beautiful people. He was in touch with his energy, and he came on to women a lot. Very early in the game, he asked me to come to his cabin, and I said, "No," and that was that. Fritz would say he wasn't a dirty old man, because dirty old men sneak up on you. That was a fact; he never snuck up on anybody. He was direct. . . .

BEVERLY SILVERMAN
A young, intense guy, who had read all Fritz' books and was really impressed by him, got up on the stage to work with Fritz, hesitated, and then said, "I gotta say it. I read your books and I really feel warm and good about you, but I see the way you are with these young girls and I just feel dirty inside watching you do this." Fritz said, "Even dirty old men need love."

PENNY YOUNGREEN
A friend told us about this seventy-year-old man who could be a sexual turn-on. The first time we ever saw him, I said, "Oooh, you've got to be kidding! God, look at that old man with that pot belly and those baggy clothes . . . Jesus, he looks . . . ugh!" Then, after about the second day of the workshop, just to be touched by him was . . . whew! . . . just a mind blower. I wouldn't say he was the typical dirty old man, and I've seen a lot of them. He had power in the Don Juan sense, he had charisma.

JOHN STEVENS
Fritz had a woman on each side in the baths, and they were both feeling him up. He had an enormous erection and I was in the tub on the opposite side, feeling uncomfortable. He was glorying in the sensory stimulation, grinning from ear to ear he was so happy—and I imagine he was also glorying in my discomfort.

BETTY FULLER
Fritz was partly a stern old man, and partly a soft gentle man who loved his kids—the people who worked with him—very much. He really loved young girls, too. In fact, it was mostly young girls he took to bed. He was totally male, not that machismo thing, just an incredible virility. God! He knew how to touch and how to be with you. That's all a woman is looking for anyway, someone who can touch and be with her.

> *When I was four, I fell in love with a circus horseback rider who seemed to belong to another, wonderful world. Her golden costume, her elegance and self-possession—the princess of the fairytale incarnate. My first goddess to be put on a pedestal.*
>
> *Was such a world beyond my reach?*

SYLVIA BEHRMANN CONRAD
He said that he was contemptuous of most people, but most of all of himself. I contrasted our ways of approaching people, saying that I tended to love people. Then I added that it had its difficulties as it laid me open to hurt.

"Ah, Sylvia," he said, "If you can only love, then the pain doesn't matter."

NATALIE MANN
He had this deep love for himself. I don't believe he ever had this sense of caring in a continuous way for anyone else in this world. Even his supposed love for Marty Fromm . . . I know the contempt he sometimes felt in speaking of his feelings for Marty. I was always struck by what I thought was his incapacity to love, and he recognized it too.

JOHN ENRIGHT
Fritz wasn't able to maintain a really close human relationship. My wife and I saw him for a few sessions, and he obviously didn't value marriage very much. The unit of existence for him was the individual—there was nothing more than that. I don't think he ever accepted that it might be possible, to give up some part of yourself to form a small group of two or three that might be an even higher unit than the individual, without being neurotic.

CLAUDIO NARANJO
His love was full of narcissism. As soon as the role was challenged, love was withdrawn. Ginny Sutton was one of the best of the earlier Esalen trainees. Her heart was set on building a community, and she was very possibly the inspiring force behind the idea of the gestalt kibbutz. She was Fritz' lover at the time, but when it developed that it would be too much of a work-oriented community, with no place for the children and the animals, she wouldn't go. He took it very much to heart, and wept, but then he turned against her. He had devoted long pages to her in *Garbage Pail*. When they had that falling out, he closed his heart to her and removed

her from the book. This was Fritz in his classical, vengeful style.

GEORGE I. BROWN

Judith was in a workshop with him, where he was talking about the manipulation games between husbands and wives, how they do things for one another with the expectation that the other will pay back, or with the feeling that they're fulfilling some kind of obligation. As he was talking about this, Judith began to feel uneasy. She kept silent for a while, but finally felt she had to speak up. She said, "Fritz, I disagree with you. There are times when I do things for George just because I want to do them, or because I know he needs them." Fritz turned to her and said without hesitation, "Oh, that. That's love." It's sad that you don't hear that kind of thing very often about Fritz, because he was at times a very loving man, tender and caring.

LEO ZEFF

I remember one time Fritz was deeply hurt when a woman came from New York to see him. He told us the next day, his voice quivering, that he was very, very disturbed and wasn't sure he could work that day. He was deeply hurt because this woman he loved very much had told him she did not love him and wanted nothing more to do with him; but after a little while he was in his chair working with us with no more signs of distress. He shared his hurt with us, and once the parting happened there was nothing more to it.

GABRIELLE ROTH

He had a profound, an incredible ego. He took great pleasure in being an old man, and he knew exactly how much he could get away with behind that cover. Fritz was very mutable, always changing. I saw him in all those spaces. He could be so soft, love vibrations emanating from him, just coming out of his eyes and his pores and his smiles. His essence beamed through all his dishevelment.

Edward Rosenfeld is the author of The Book of Highs, *the editor of* The Gestalt Journal, *and a teacher.*

EDWARD ROSENFELD

Marty Fromm had been a lover of Fritz' and I was a lover of Marty's when I first met Fritz.

In 1967, Marty and I drove across the country with another friend, and when we got to California, Fritz invited us to be his guests at Esalen. Looking back on the meeting, it was like three generations, with Marty in the middle between the two of us.

I was a little awed at meeting him. I had heard a variety of stories from Marty—in essence, folk wisdom—that had to do with her relationship and interaction with Fritz, how as a result of her being in therapy with Fritz, and being his lover, her whole world view had changed.

That was the only time I met Fritz socially. Marty and Fritz spent some time alone together—they hadn't seen each other for about two years. There was a warmth I could see between them, a true bond and a true affection. There may have been bad times in the past, but the time that we spent together there was a real charge that flowed between them.

ARTHUR CEPPOS

It was a different time, when I first published his book *Gestalt Therapy,* after all, by the time he came to Esalen, he had a certain amount of recognition; when he came to me he had none.

Fritz, unquestionably, had all the talent and imagination that any great man should have. He was very, very articulate and the quality of his articulation had a great deal of color. The thing that he was fighting then—and the fight went on for a very long time—was to achieve a certain type of professional recognition. He had some. Berne for example, was a great admirer of Fritz and, I think, made great use of Fritz' material. But recognition didn't occur until much later.

In terms of gestalt therapy, only Fritz does it because he

created it. And regardless of what Laura may claim, Laura applied it as a relatively academic therapist, with none of the real feeling and appreciation for it.

ALAN MARTIN
He was really advancing in his work and developing. The New York crowd pretty much stayed where they were. He kept adding new things and trying new things.

Laura was more the theoretical guide, he was the experiential, as I see it.

NATALIE MANN
I was in a workshop in Laura's apartment with Fritz and Laura, and I saw how terrible he was to her. Just awful! I had dinner with them a few times and I saw how terribly he treated her. I mean, just like shit. Like Laura says, "He's like a child who leaves his dirty diapers around the house."

Laura, Laura, Lore, Laura . . . Separated for over twenty years, denounced, humiliated and insulted, Laura was never completely out of Fritz' mind. . . .

> *Lore did some writing poetry and short stories. And she had her piano. She is a good pianist and in her youth it was touch and go whether she would go in for studying law and later psychology, or become a concert pianist. . . .*
>
> *With Lore I had some on and off periods of love but basically we are co-travelers. . . .*
>
> *With Teddy, I always know where I am. I can't say the same about Lore. After all the years, I am still confused. We met over forty years ago . . . at the Goldstein Institute.*

LAURA PERLS
Only a few years ago, we were talking about South Africa and he said, "Well, you know our South African years weren't really bad at all."

"No, they were very good."

"Well, we are stuck with each other."

"I'm not stuck."

He was stuck because he couldn't go on with it and develop it in anyway, or let anything out. When he disagreed or didn't like something he simply left. At the same time he held on, but with resentment which he expressed all over the place.

BOB SHAPIRO

For twenty-two years they not only did not live together, they had no relationship. He would stay at her apartment when he came to New York. Typical of Fritz . . . he would stay any place that was free.

GREG DAVIDSON

He really treated Laura shabbily. They hadn't seen each other for a year or two, and yet he still had a thing for her— he was still married to her. He invited her to Big Sur and arranged a cocktail party for her at his place, but then he didn't show up at the party until late. It was a cold thing. She was really hurt. They never had a good visit together. Even at the dinner table he'd make oblique derogatory comments about her. I remember taking a long walk with her, just talking. She was a really warm, lovely woman, and she *really* loved that man. I mean, she really loved him and she wanted to be with him.

He would come and stay at her house in New York when he was going overseas—just drop in and expect to be received and taken care of—but she never felt welcome in his home.

LAURA PERLS

I've heard from someone who was with him in Lake Cowichan that there was not a day when he wouldn't mention me three or four times. On the same day he would talk to the same people about me in a hostile way, then kindly, and then in a different way . . . I think I was always a lifeline for him.

HARVEY FREEDMAN

He was obsessed with Laura. He hadn't seen her for years.
Yet he was constantly talking about her. Constantly.

I had never met her, and my image of her was made up of
these endless anecdotes and cursings, so I pictured a massive
football player—an Ida Rolf kind of body build mesomorph,
butcher-of-Belsen kind of thing.

ILANA RUBENFELD

I had never met Laura either, and in '68 or '69 we had a dinner for them and about eight other people. The bell rang,
and there was Fritz and this beautiful woman. She's really
striking. They looked like husband and wife, and for the first
hour of the evening their relating was really lovely. But after
a while they started to dispute, the old squabbles that two
people have. Then she played the piano. She plays very nicely
and he looked very pleased. I got a sense of what it probably
was like, and what it was no longer . . . They were in two
different worlds.

ARTHUR CEPPOS

Laura was much younger than Fritz. She was a very handsome woman and a good pianist. Almost concert quality. I
do know that Fritz could not tolerate what he would call
Laura's pseudo-academicism. He could not stay near her.

VIRGINIA SATIR

The way in which he managed Laura at times . . . awful!
But, I know enough to know that these things are transac-
tional and not just unilateral.

BARRY STEVENS

Once he said of Laura, "She is so foolish." Just easy, you
know. No resentment or anger, just "That's the way she is."
It was extraordinary how he could say it and not be caught
up in it. I think neutrality is not often heard. People don't
expect neutrality and they quickly dump whatever is said one
way or the other; they aren't neutral themselves. I've caught
myself doing this. . . .

CYNTHIA SHELDON

I remember his saying that Laura was half of gestalt therapy;
he had a lot of really beautiful feelings toward her for that.
But then, in the next breath he might turn around and not
acknowledge her.

ABRAHAM LEVITSKY

Laura played an important role, but it is not clear to me
just how much she contributed. I'm pretty sure that towards
the end of his career he felt that what she called gestalt
therapy had become rather different from his . . . .

JOEL KRAMER

One time at the baths he said to me, "The one person in the
world that I'm still afraid of is my wife."

LAURA PERLS

I knew before I married him that he was self-centered and I

accepted him. I took him as the genius he was, or could have been. And whatever he became, I think he wouldn't have become without me, but vice versa, too. He never married anybody else either. We were not divorced, although our lifelong affair was, in the last years, mostly off.

> . . .*the Posner family . . . did not trust me at all.*
> *"I guess you are now going off on a spiel with the Posner family and dodging your operations again?"*
> *So what shall I do?*
> *"Decide once and forever to finish a theme."*
> Decidere, *to cut off. The semantic significance is clear.*

Virginia Satir

I'm sure there was a lot of suffering in that whole situation; I just assumed that because in the early years Laura wasn't any more settled than he was when they came to this country. My hunch is that their love was based on the mutual survival situation that they shared.

"It was painful. I always expected something again from him, you know. . .," Laura says.

Yet to love Fritz was to give up expectations or give up Fritz. Laura knew this. She says, "Fritz was never going to be anything but himself. What he did he did." She is proud of that, even now. It says something about the lady. It says something about the guy, too. . . .

Laura Perls

I had the best years of my life with him. He was certainly the most interesting man I have ever been with. I am grateful for . . . for what I had with him.

* * *

*Walking up and down from the lodge is no strain for
most people. For me, it is. I usually drive down. From
there down to the baths is a similar distance, which I
have to walk.*

ELLEN STEVENS
He had the oxygen tanks set up by his room all the time.

HUNTER CULP
He would get into places where he couldn't breathe very well.
That's why he drove his car around all over. If he walked up
the hill, it would almost kill him.

BERNARD GUNTHER
He had had a heart attack. He worked himself very hard and
would be tired afterwards. Apparently he was having pain. I
had heard about rolfing. At the time we were down by Ran-
cho Santa Fe, I suggested he meet a woman who was a student of Ida Rolf. I got them together for lunch. Afterwards,
he said to me, "I always look at people, not from vot they
tell me but vot they're like themselves. If she's any example
of vot she does, I don't need her." So he cut it off. But later I
think the pain got bad enough where he went back to her and
in a couple of hours she helped him a little.

BETTY FULLER
Get Ida to tell you about going out and doing his ten rolfings
in ten days. Can't be done, and she did it. Saved his life and
he acknowledged that.

*What Marilyn Rosanes-Berrett did for his eyes and Wilson
Van Dusen and Eugene Sagan did for his professional life,
Ida Rolf did for his aging body. She was a major factor in
improving his health.*

> *Ida is a big powerful angel. . . In 1963 in L.A. my heart
> gave me plenty of trouble, I had such agonizing anginal
> attacks that I contemplated suicide very seriously. . .
> after, I found Esalen and improved my heart tremen-
> dously. The two main factors were: I was out of the
> L.A. smog, and I had treatments with Ida Rolf.*

IDA ROLF
The day I came up here Fritz said, "I'm in such pain I don't
want to live." And he'd already been here in Big Sur for a
while. I'll never forget the misery that guy was in. He was
giving a seminar down in L.A. One of my students was there
and she saw how much trouble he was in: "Fritz, I'd like to
show you what I'm doing." She gave this man a first hour of
rolfing and, lo and behold! his pain left him. And his pain
stayed away, but he was about to cross the country and she
knew that people often come back into pain in airplanes, so
she said to him, "You go and see Ida Rolf in New York; this
is too complicated for me."

By the time he got back he was still in pain because, of
course, Fritz is Fritz and nobody was telling him to go see Ida
Rolf—he'd say No! No! No! So he came back here and again
he was in misery. Then Dorothy (my student) called me and
asked whether I'd come out to Esalen. I thought, "What
have I got to lose? I've never been to Esalen; I've never seen
Fritz."

It was a case of the mountain going to Mohammed. . . .

Yes. I came out here specifically to do that job. I was here
from Friday of one week to Saturday of the following week;
I gave him six or seven hours of work in that time, and he
never was in really serious trouble with his heart again.

It was just a problem or organizing that neck of his. He had been under surgery a long time ago, and as he started to come out of it he said to the anesthetist, "You have injured me. There's something wrong with my neck." And the anesthetist said, "No, that's impossible." Fritz wasn't being told no by anybody, and it wasn't until I came along. . . .

The change in his neck condition was really a change in his heart condition. When I was working the seventh hour on him (that has to do with the mouth and the neck) all of a sudden I was aware the man was unconscious.

I said to myself as he lay unconscious, presumably having a heart attack and maybe dying, "My God, what a fool you are! Why on earth do you take the chance on somebody that's as sick as this?" But after I got over my momentary panic, I really looked at him and I said, "This man isn't dying of a heart attack; he looks as though he's under ether. He's anesthetized!"

He was out for maybe two minutes—it felt like two years to me, I tell you. I just hoped he wouldn't know it when he came to, because I thought he would feel the technique was dangerous. But he knew immediately what had happened. When he came out of it, he recognized this had to do with the injury to his neck. . . and he recalled being roughly handled under that anesthetic. He had apparently re-lived the whole thing, and because he re-lived it, you see, something disappeared.

And in his book he wrote:

> . . .*Ida. . . certainly helped me with the main sympton: those angina pectoris pains that made life so miserable that I was willing to end it all. In this sense, she saved my life. . .!*

He got over it, yes, he lived about five or six years after that. And he *really* lived those years; he had a great deal of satisfaction, and so much greater insight into things which interested him.

I'd like to clear something up. . . in those days I used to do the rolfing down in the massage room at the baths. I'd get ready for him. He'd have an appointment at four o'clock, and four o'clock would come, and no Fritz. Five after four, no Fritz. Ten after four, no Fritz. By that time, I'd pick myself up and go into the baths, and in the farthest tub there he'd be, soaking. And in his book he says, "I should get to the story of my health," or something of this sort, "but I'll let it wait for a while. Ida's kept me waiting many times. I'm going to keep her waiting now." He was putting it on, you know.

He also wrote:

> *. . .if one abstraction comes up, then often the total context becomes available. This is not a linear association, although it is often called so, but a comprehensive gestalt. Thus if Ida touches a sore spot, which is what the muscles remember, then the total context becomes available for assimilation and integration, including the unexpressed emotions and pictures.*

Fritz came to me in New York once or twice, in my apartment, for rolfing. This particular day we finished the session, and I went with him into the foyer. I picked up his overcoat and held it out to him—something I do with many people—and he turned around and said brusquely, "You don't have to do that with me!" I said, "I didn't think I *had* to. I just thought I wanted to. . . You know, Fritz," I said, "some people take their patients on their knee and soothe them and tell them how nice they are, and some hold their overcoats for them." It took him about thirty seconds to change from his negativism to a twinkle.

I was one of the few people with whom he just didn't ever get angry. I mean, I had quite a credit on the books. But Fritz wasn't *angry; irascible* was the word that described him. It was his habit to blow up at everybody on general principle—to keep them working.

I knew Fritz simply in a professional way, because I was

too busy working, as he was too busy working. When I first came to Esalen, we both lived in the little white house; Fritz had one of the rooms and I had another room. And we used to have lots of fun trying to figure out who was going to light the stove. It was hard to do and each of us would try to get out of it. Later, we both lived in matched houses at the top of that path, level with the lodge. And here again we had lots of games, because, when Fritz came home at night he would turn on his victrola. He *loved* good music, but it would put too much burden on the circuit, and the lights would go out. The doggone fuse would blow regularly! So either I had to keep my heater off, or he had to keep his victrola off; and neither one of us was very enthusiastic about doing this for the other guy! And then, you know, I had to sit on the bed and wonder "Will Fritz go out and fix it, or do I have to go out and fix it?" And it would be raining and blowing.

He doesn't sound very gallant.

Gallant Fritz wasn't! He had lots of strong points, but not gallantry. He was a very egocentric man, but he had reason to be. Good reason. He had done a very good job, and he was an absolute genius. I mean, it was a privilege to sit over in the corner of that man's room and watch him work.

He had a great respect for you, too, didn't he, Ida?

Well, one time he introduced me to some man and he said, "Now I want you to meet a woman who knows as much in her own field as I know in mine." I think that is the ultimate that could ever have been expressed by Fritz.

ROSEMARY FEITIS
Fritz used to get into lots and lots of trouble physically and then he'd sit around, knowing perfectly well that he ought to go see Ida Rolf, and not wanting to do it. He'd rather go to Stan Johnson, or whoever. . . .

He was just lazy, and if it wouldn't come to him, then he wouldn't go to it. Stan was easier than Ida.

But, anyhow, since I was working for Ida at the time, I carted him to see her. Afterwards I said, "Well, how was it?" And he said, "Well, she's still the magician." Later I asked Ida, "How was it?" And she said, "He's still the genius."

STANLEY JOHNSON
He loved to be rolfed. Often before each rolfing he would have a cup of creme de cacao. He'd really relax. I worked on him about twenty-five times. He's the only one I've ever rolfed who fell asleep during the rolfing!

GREG DAVIDSON

To me, he was a physically frail man. He could have taken a lot better care of himself. He was smoking, endlessly. But he was a pretty macho character, real male. He always saw himself as having a very large capacity for being, whether sexually or otherwise. He had a high opinion of himself, though it conflicted with the reality of his health.

I remember once I was going to take him flying over his house. He wanted to see his house from the air. I rented planes periodically just to keep up my skill. I love flying around. He loved to fly, too, and he told me, he hadn't since South Africa. We were on our way to Monterey, and we stopped to look at some land he was interested in investing in. There was no road and we had to walk up a hill. Fritz did part of it, and became aware he couldn't go all the way; his heart wasn't that good. But he also saw how much he could do. He went up higher than he ever thought he could go. He said, "I really am getting a new heart." It was after that he felt good about going up and down to the baths. He'd only done it occasionally before, going very slowly, but he felt a lot more chipper after that. We never made it to the plane.

No one was indifferent to Fritz. He elicited deep feelings from those he touched: hurt, disgust, fear, anger, awe and love, surely among them. . . .

JULIAN SILVERMAN

Some of us, if we're lucky, once in our lifetime there is a meeting and . . . *contact!*—those contact moments without all the bullshit that we mess each other up with all our lives. It's happiness. Happiness doesn't happen when you try to get it; it's always unexpected. It comes in a moment and is knocked over in a moment. When those moments happen with another person, you treasure them. With this guy they happened more than just once in a blue moon. But what can you say about them?

When I saw Janet and Fritz together it was like whatever the other one was doing was totally OK. They never had to intrude into each other's scene. They were just *there* with each other. There was nothing to explain or elaborate. It was just two people separate and really digging each other. That came across.

Janet Lederman was a teacher and an artist; she became Fritz' co-worker and friend. . . .

JANET LEDERMAN

It was about eleven o'clock at night. There were four of us sitting here at Esalen when I first saw him; I saw an old man. I'd never heard of him. He was passing by the table in his jump suit and looked somehow out of context here. I thought he must be very lonely, but I didn't know what to say to him, so we just looked at each other and met that way.

The next day somebody I knew was going on and on about a workshop he was in, so I went in, not knowing anything about it. Then, suddenly, there was the same old man up there! He was just beautiful!

I was working with so-called emotionally disturbed kids in the ghetto and what he was doing in connection with another person was uncannily similar to what I was doing with kids, but he had more experience and a theoretical container for what I was doing intuitively. He was very sensitive to who he was working with.

It was another meeting, watching him work.

Two or three weeks later, I was in a very fragmented place, really at the peak of a crisis. We'd never talked, we really hadn't met. I just went over and said, "Can I talk to you?"

He looked into my eyes for a long time. It seemed like two hours but it may have been about two minutes. "Yah," he said, "I see the despair. Let's sit down."

We talked for about an hour. I haven't the vaguest notion what we talked about, and afterwards, we went up to his house. We listened to music and we talked. I'm a painter. He showed me his paintings and we talked about art and music and then we lay down on the bed and he held me. He recited a German poem about a little bird who had fallen out of a tree and was injured and just needed kindness and gentleness and to be held. He was very kind and gentle.

That was our. . . first touching. It was in '66 and that was *the* relationship from then on. When I did take his workshop, I think I worked on the chair twice. That wasn't where it was at for me. It was not a technique, but Fritz, the human being; it was the relationship to the man. . . a love affair, yes.

The important, the high points, were the affection and respect; sitting in the morning, talking theory, sharing with each other. He'd take a thing in and out of focus, shooting from this angle, from that angle. It was play. We enjoyed each other. We shared; simply, we shared each other. It wasn't work.

There are a number of people now who are very close to him, and as corny as it might sound, the thing we all share is love. There's really no way of putting it in words, but somehow that's what we got.

What I'm beginning to see happening to us, like the children of the next generation, is that those who were really close to him seem to be primarily noncompetitive. This was something Fritz left, this kind of shared love that is very lovely.

LEO ZEFF

Fritz had a penchant for getting angry with people and kicking them out of a workshop. I wouldn't tangle with him, but he had fights with just about anybody who was a kind of disciple—Claudio Naranjo, for example, and Jim Simkin.

One weekend in a professional group, he kicked Jim out of the workshop, and Jim was the heir apparent, the one who was supposed to continue Fritz' work and eventually succeed him. Jim had learned from Anne, his wife, that Fritz tried to get her to go to bed with him and Jim was furious. The thing about Anne didn't come up, but Jim really stood up to Fritz. They spent half an hour telling each other, in gestalt fashion, what they really and truly felt about each other. Finally Fritz told Jim he was no longer a part of the gestalt therapy movement. Of course, the next day everything was fine again.

Jim Simkin was close to Fritz in many ways—some saw him as Fritz' heir—but there was conflict both in personalities and in working methods.

ANNE SIMKIN
I loved watching him watch Jim's growth. For example, when he was in L.A. I showed him a fir tree that was growing outside our home. And I said, "You know, that reminds me of Jim's growth." And he said, "No, Jim hasn't borne any fruit yet." About a year later he looked at Jim and said, "My young tree is in full bloom now." He felt very close with him and he very often told me that if he needed to work with someone he would work with Jim. Jim was someone he could trust. I felt that Jim and Fritz were like father and son. I used to love to watch them in the dining room at Esalen talking things over. They didn't always agree, but Fritz respected Jim and vice versa.

Another view. . . .

CLAUDIO NARANJO
Thinking back, I actually found Jim Simkin to be a better and more consistent therapist. I experienced Fritz as a genius

and a man of greater wisdom; I experienced Jim as warmer, more reliable and less willing to express his psychopathology, and, perhaps because of that, better for some people. I think he was better for me because of his clinical reliability and supportiveness. With Fritz, of course, you could expect anything, from the best to the worst. Perhaps, his creativity required the context of such open-endedness. Everything considered, I would say it was a very fruitful polarity. I love Jim and appreciate his talent in the therapeutic situation, yet I would not call him a creative genius as I would Fritz. I guess I'd also have to say that he was not able to quickly absorb or appreciate new developments. We have an expression in Spanish, *"Mas papista que el papa"*—"More pope-like than the Pope," which is to me expressive of Jim's inclination toward rules and rule-making. . . taking the gestalt rules and principles and approaching them like a policeman. Fritz was always ready to break his own rules.

Fritz was the kind of man who might have said something like Marx did:"I'm not a Marxist." Jim, on the other hand, was an implicit "Fritzist."

CYNTHIA SHELDON
In general I experienced Jim Simkin and Fritz as keeping a respectable, friendly distance from one another. Jim had his own distinct ability and style. I always experienced a consistent teaching style with Jim; he would constantly come back and refocus and get you to become more clear. Fritz was more inconsistent—sometimes perfectly on, sometimes not on at all. He would phase in and out, be prejudiced one moment and open the next. He was more into showmanship and drama. They *were* very different. The professional in the group did not necessarily prefer Fritz over Jim. I never had the feeling that Jim was second-best. He was in Fritz' shadow nevertheless by the mere fact that they worked together a lot.

WILSON VAN DUSEN
Fritz' style can seem much sharper, even crueler. I think this

was just the nature of the man. To take that as technique is a mistake made by Simkin and a lot of others.

Virginia Satir

Jim was something of a protege of Fritz and achieved some sense of peership. But they kept themselves separately and didn't tread on each other's toes. I think Fritz probably trusted Jim to do a good job, that he would be an authentic gestaltist. Fritz did not trust that many people. He often referred to them as crooks; these were people who had a little knowledge and were using it badly. He'd often warn me about the crooks.

Richard Price

Jim's work is utterly unrepresentative of Fritz'. Jim has merely taken a technique and is applying it in a very inorganic way.

> . . .*I know. . . that my motive was and is to sort myself out and to do my own therapy. There is really no one else. There was Paul and there was Marty and there is Jim Simkin, and somehow I am not ready to surrender to him.*

Seymour Carter

Jim Simkin is very one-sided about gestalt, to the degree that while he's an incredibly fine gestalt therapist, it's very hard for him to come out of that role and just be a person around other people.

Betty Fuller

Everyone I know that does gestalt and was touched by Fritz, took some little bit out of him and manifested that bit. No one got all of Fritz—the "mantle" descended on no one of us, no matter how highly trained and credentialed.

I've had more personal than professional contact with Jim Simkin, having experienced him in only two group settings—and those some time ago. Jim had come right from his heart in support of me at a time I was in great need so it was disappointing to find him so stuck on credentialing and the techniques of gestalt. Watching him work was like going to the Williamsburg Museum: All the symbols of the life that had been lived were there, but the heart and life had gone out of it.

JOHN ENRIGHT

Jim would tend to be silent in case of a confrontation and then, out of Fritz' hearing, express resentment afterwards. I heard Jim really gripe seriously two or three times about Fritz. Once, for example, Fritz had taken some people into the workshop that weren't qualified or something like that, and Jim was clearly angry. Jim didn't do anything and later on he expressed irritation. He told me later Fritz had agreed not to do that. I never saw an open, clear-cut clash between them. I heard Jim say two or three times that he thought he was a better gestalt therapist than Fritz.

Do you think he was?

I thought, "What a pity he has to worry about that one way or the other."

ABRAHAM LEVITSKY

I had a Ph.D. in clinical psychology and was in private practice in St. Louis when I met Fritz in February 1966. Up till that point, I knew nothing about gestalt therapy; I had only heard about some man who was an innovator of a new approach and who was fun to work with. One of the first things he said to me during the coffee break of the first morning of that five-day workshop was, "You seem to have an interpretation neurosis." I'd been so accustomed to relying on interpretations in my work that I was afraid to rely on what I observed.

That first day when he had come up to me, there was a more moving, an even more personal thing which occurred: When he put his arm around my shoulder in a friendly way, I made a little inadvertent move to get away. He just kept his arm there and looked me right in the eye and said, "Remain with your embarrassment." It was powerful education right off the bat. I feel it sums up a great deal of the spirit of gestalt therapy.

He invited me to come back that summer and go into intensive training with him, and I decided to take him up on his offer and I got back to Esalen in June. Since I was going to be there for the summer and he had an extra room, Fritz asked me to share his house with him.

We spent a lot of time together that summer. It was a very relaxed relationship when we weren't working. It turned out that we shared a lot of interests. I was somewhat conversant in German, so there was that. And music, which played an enormously important role in my life, was one of the other important things we shared. He was a great ballet and opera lover, and we went to the ballet together.

He had a very good musical ear. Sometimes he would give me zany instructions during a group, like, "Write a little melody appropriate to each person in this workshop." I'd go back into my store of songs and bring out things that were suitable for each individual.

Sometime during the middle of that first summer of '66, he said to me, "I would like you to be my assistant. I'm getting tired of doing therapy. You come here and do therapy and I'll make movies." I said I wanted to think about it.

I tried to make up my mind and finally, though I was ambivalent, I decided to accept. I went back to St. Louis where I had an active practice. And as time went by I began to have some doubts again, and finally I wrote to him, "I can't accept your offer at this time." He wrote back a very nice, warm, supportive letter: "You are keeping yourself from me and I'm really sorry, I would like to see you out here." Finally, after more months of doubting that I could get it together, and experiencing more self-doubt about being able to work as his assistant, I arrived back at Esalen in July 1967.

At times he could be so uncharacteristically supportive of me. I found it unnerving because I also knew how destructive he could be. In fact, the way I put it to him once when I was working with him in a group was, "Sometimes I feel that the hands that are giving birth to me are also choking me."

Not long after this, in a workshop with Fritz, I was working on a dream. In the dream I was a broad jumper in the Olympics. Fritz gave me an assignment: "Supposing you're barefoot and you have to go from here to there, but between here and there are jagged bits of rocks and broken glass. How do you get there?" I acted it out and then went back to my seat with the feeling that this was resolved for the moment. He seemed to think so too. Then suddenly, he had an afterthought and did one of the strangest things that I've ever seen him do with anyone. He lay down on the floor, face down, and said, "Can you walk over me?" I gasped. Here is this 73-year-old grandfather, not in the best of health, asking me, at 175 pounds, to walk on him. Hmmmm. Well, I decided to try it. I started at his ankles and was wobbling and afraid to put too much weight on him. Fritz was saying things like, "It's OK, you can step on me. You can build on me." I literally walked over his body as if he were a bridge.

FRANK RUBENFELD

One can think of oneself as a deck of cards: You can play this role or that, get into this feeling or that feeling. Fritz was like a whole deck. A lot of people focus on the sarcastic Fritz or the angry Fritz or the brutal Fritz. He had the power to be all those things.

I see him using it mostly as self-protection (when he felt he was getting drained or ripped off or something like that, you know). He didn't want to waste his energy. He was an old man, so he would cut things off. The other part of that, you see, was the perfect tenderness in him.

KATHLEEN NUGENT

One time I came back from the Tassajara Zen Center, and Fritz came over and said, "Where have you been?" I told him. He said, "That's the last place you need to go! You

stop meditating and you get up and dance!" He ran over and
pulled a young man up off a chair somewhere and he
brought him back and said, "Hey, you dance with her!"

WILLIAM QUINN
As time went on here at Esalen, he began to mellow in the
most extraordinary way. It was beautiful to see a man in his
old age . . . this tremendous intelligence finally becoming
harmonious with his heart. He became beautifully affection-
ate in his relationships with the staff and with many people
who were constant visitors to our seminars.

One of the visitors was Abraham Elizur. . . .

ABRAHAM ELIZUR
I suggested that he do something for our organization, the
Institute of Mental Health. In this way we could go back, as
we have done now, to start a mental hygiene clinic in Israel.

I didn't try to persuade him; I just told him about it and he
said, "Yes, I'm going to." I was so moved by it that my eyes
were tearing, and his, too, I would say. We had a very cor-
dial and lovely talk at that time.

*In Tel Aviv I met Ruth Levi who had gone to encounter
groups and Feldenkrais workshops, and was now attending
occasional gestalt weekends.*

*"Gestalt," she says, "is not like surgery or medicine or a
craft. It's not a technique that can be taught. To be a good
gestaltist, a person has to have an instinct for it; they have to
have an inherent kindness and an ancient wisdom. . . ."*

I ask her if her current therapist has these qualities.

*"No," she says, "not even close. He's a good man, but
he's not like. . . ."*

"Like who?"

"Like Gideon Schwarz."

"Is he a good gestaltist?"

"Yes, he's very good."

Many people have spoken of Fritz' work. It is Gideon Schwarz who comes close to conveying a sense of the quality of that work. . . .

GIDEON SCHWARZ

Encounter group people talk in terms of using different "techniques," including "gestalt techniques." I'm a bit of a purist, and in my view, if you do the "technique" of gestalt therapy, you really have misunderstood it, because you are using external cliches rather than the spirit of the thing itself. It's like cooking with a French flavor instead of French cooking—you put on a little mayonnaise and sprinkle some tarragon. When encounter people say, "Of course, we have been influenced by gestalt therapy, and we're using a lot of gestalt techniques"—that's mayonnaise.

Because of the influence of gestalt therapy, the therapeutic world has become more aware of the danger of slipping into abstract talking—what Fritz called, "aboutism." What matters for the group is what's happening in the group. The only possibility of something positive happening, is when it is consistently pointed out in a group that telling *about* something that happened in another place, in another time, is a cop-out.

Let me tell you the story of the girl who imagined herself as a bee. It was a unique session which will illustrate what I mean and strongly shows the fantastic intuition Fritz had. This girl, after eight days of a ten-day workshop without ever working, finally went up and sat in the hot seat, saying, "I just felt like saying, 'This year I'm trying gestalt therapy, and where will I go next year?'"

Fritz said, "Would you do me a favor? Add after every statement the words, 'And isn't that funny?'"

She said, "Sure, I can do that—and isn't that funny?"

She kept talking for a while, and, as I realized later, sometimes mumbling to herself, then addressing him for a moment, and leaving him to mumble to herself again.

After a while Fritz said, "I experience you like a bee. Does that mean anything to you?"

"A bee? Bzz, bzz, bzz—that kind of bee?" she asked.

"Yeah, go on—do that, be a bee."

So she started going "bzz, bzz, bzz" to people, and he said, "You are not using your legs." She ignored that and went on.

He said again, "Now get your legs into the act."

She said, "How? I don't know how." But she got up, walked two steps, stopped and went "bzz, bzz, bzz," and walked again silently. She seemed unaware that her legs would not participate.

Then Fritz said, "OK, now come back, sit down and go into yourself. What do you feel now?"

She said, "I don't know where it comes from, it doesn't make any sense, but I feel like saying I feel like a snail."

"OK, be a snail. Make contact with somebody as a snail."

She walked up to a big guy who was sitting there and she put one finger of each hand to her head, wiggling them.

Fritz said, "Now get in contact with him with your feet."

She started doing things with her feet, and after a moment she said, "That's amazing. I have no sensation at all in my feet, like they are paralyzed."

"OK," he said, "allow yourself to discover your feet."

After a time, while she kept trying to touch him with her feet, she said, "Oh, now I do have some sensation!" and she started to walk around and to laugh, "Oh, this is the first time I feel the texture of the carpet." She started to dance a little, and then more. She said, "This is great," and started running around.

Fritz said, "Sure! You are a human being, you've got feet, you don't have to fly or crawl."

She said, "Thank you, Fritz."

"I'm not quite through yet. Let's work on this a little more," he said. "Sit down." She did, and he said, "Now go into yourself again. What do you see?"

She said, "I'm in the back of a car," and all of a sudden it was apparent that the joy was gone.

"Are you there alone?"

"No, my sister is with me."

"What do you see?"

"You know, my sister once. . . ."

"I'm not interested in your memories, just tell me what you see."

"NO!"

"*Look* at her!"

"NO, NO!" She began to cry bitterly.

He laid one hand on her arm and talked to her, but she said, "I can't, I can't. . . ."

"Tell her you can't talk to her."

She hesitated, then she started with the statement, "You're so pretty and so gifted. It's a terrible tragedy you were born with only one leg."

We all gasped, amazed that he had sensed there was something to do with the legs. As he worked with her, it turned out that since childhood she had not allowed herself to use her legs freely. Fritz finally had her say to her sister that she would not change places with her for all her beauty and talents.

One day in that same workshop, Fritz, who loved movies, said that he wanted to cancel the evening meeting to see "The Mouse That Roared." A young guy in the group spoke up and said, "I really find that disgusting. What kind of regard is that for us? I mean, we came down here to work with you, we pay all that money, and you want to take off to the movies on our time."

Somebody else said, "Oh, come on, we aren't going to be-grudge Fritz his movie."

Fritz said, "I find it strange that the only objection comes from someone who, for seven days, hasn't availed himself of the possibility of working with me, while others who were obviously more eager to work, don't object."

The next day, the first one in the hot seat was this guy, and while he was talking, Fritz drifted off to sleep. When the guy realized it, he was furious, and sort of shook Fritz, saying, "Listen to me!"

Fritz woke up and said, "It's your droning, hypnotic voice."

"What do you mean? What did I do?"

Fritz said, "Try to do this on purpose. Play the hypnotist and put us all to sleep."

The guy looked at us, raising his hand, and said, "I am putting you all to sleep," and he started to enjoy himself very much in his role as hypnotist.

Then Fritz said to him, "Have you put us all to sleep now? Can you imagine all of us aleep?"

The guy said, "Yes," and then, "I feel cold."

So Fritz said, "Now freeze us."

The guy stuck out his hands, saying, "I'm exuding rays of freezing cold! I'm deadening you, paralyzing you, freezing you!"

Fritz said, "OK, now you've frozen us all. Now you are alone in this world where everything is frozen and dead.

I haven't told you that this guy was very conceited. He was sure everything he did was in the grand style. Suddenly, he gave a piercing scream of anguish, and Fritz said, "Ah, yeah. Now you are waking us up a little." There was some sarcasm in this.

As the session went on, the guy said that he felt that half his body was cold and half was warm. Fritz took his hands and said, "Yes, you really do have one cold hand and one warm hand." Fritz went on into a long, deep session, in which the pivotal point was a relationship, in school or college, between this guy and a homosexual teacher who had tried to have an affair with him. It didn't work, but it really screwed this kid up. Earlier Fritz had commented that the guy was paranoid, and I couldn't help thinking of the Freudian statement that paranoia is always latent homosexuality.

In another session, Fritz told a very rigid, cold, pompous man that he was very much like a puppeteer, seeing people not as they were but as he typecast them—making puppets out of them. So Fritz asked him to typecast everyone in the room, and he had something to say for everyone, "You're the nice, cozy little housewife," "You're the big boss," and for me, "You're the typical Jew." I don't think he had seen many Jews in his life.

When he finished, Fritz said, "You've left someone out."

The man said, "Oh, you—you look like some godlike figure out of the Old Testament," and Fritz, with a smile that let each of us decide for ourselves how seriously to take him, said very slowly, "Any resemblance between God *and* myself is purely coincidental."

Scott Beach: singer, actor, conductor, writer, radio announcer, raconteur. . . .

SCOTT BEACH
My success in my work wasn't in question. I made money, got applause, creative satisfaction, became something of a celebrity—in a variety of fields, too. That felt good, and still does, but it was the more ironic and bitter because I was not

successful in the thing where my innards are. My love life was all fucked up and I didn't have any anchor to windward in emotional terms at all. It was before my divorce. I can't say that I seriously contemplated doing murder in such a way that I might really have done it, but I thought about it.

Two things happened to me to help me out. One of them was, I came across a tape recording of a lecture given by Alan Watts in which he quoted Lao T'se, saying: "Govern a great state as you would cook a small fish: gently." And by extrapolation, govern yourself in the same way.

The other thing that helped me enormously was discovering the gestalt "prayer" at the beginning of one of Fritz' books.* It was "I do my thing, you do your thing. . ." It made me really stagger backwards because it gave me a recognition of the fact that maybe I was all right, and so was she, and that, as dramatic as I felt the whole thing was, the sun would come up the next day will I or nil I.

So armed with that, a new-found ability to deal with emotional storms, and to be gentle with myself and to say, "Well, if we can't get together, tough. There it is," I went down to Esalen.

Fritz prefaced the "prayer":

> . . .*To be able to become real, to take a stand, to develop one's center, to understand the basis of existentialism: a rose is a rose is a rose. I am what I am, and at this moment I cannot possibly be different from what I am.*

Gestalt Therapy Verbatim

---

*The gestalt "prayer":

I do my thing, and you do your thing.
I am not in this world to live up to your expectations
And you are not in this world to live up to mine.
You are you and I am I,
And if by chance we find each other, it's beautiful.
If not, it can't be helped.

There has been much controversy about its validity and its meaning. . . .

LAURA PERLS

It's terrible, terrible. At least I would leave out "It can't be helped." I *can't* help it means I *won't* help it.

WILL SCHUTZ

The last line of the gestalt prayer is the most un-gestalt statement one can imagine. "It can't be helped" is such a rejection. I see Fritz in that, in wanting to keep people away, and I see a lot of people picking up the prayer and using it as a way of staying alientated from people. It's almost taking up Fritz' neurosis, putting it into theoretical terms, and using the theory to justify not getting close to people. I think this is a good example of where Fritz' personality comes through and gets justified in theory. I think that's what a lot of theory is about.

MICHAEL MURPHY

I think Fritz has been misunderstood by a lot of people. His phrases, for example, are often used out of context.

Dick and I called him the Jewish Buddhist, or the Roshi of Zen Judaism. He was totally against the whole religious bit; although in another way, he was deeply religious, a mystic who wouldn't quite own it. He had to phrase it in his therapeutic language. When he coined phrases (right down to his "I do my thing, you do your thing"), behind it was a kind of religious inspiration, although he would not talk in those terms. It was a disowning of religious sham and deification and that was valid, but I feel he overreacted against that language.

STEWART EMERY

I think Fritz' prayer was misinterpreted. I think people heard what they wanted to hear. I've seen some people take it and turn it into a "fuck you"; most people do as a justification.

Fritz said it at a particular time when many therapists were coming to him at Esalen, and he realized that many of them, being in the helping profession, were deluding themselves and preventing their own growth. Everything they were doing was for their "patients"; they were not facing themselves. Seeing that, Fritz evidently considered it necessary to shake them up with "I am I, you are you. . ." In time it took on a kind of universal quality. At its worst, as you point out, it's a "fuck you." But it wasn't intended as that.

I know it wasn't. Essentially, anybody who's into saying "Fuck you" will use whatever they have available as a justifier.

SCOTT BEACH

I was to lead a week-long workshop on encounter-oriented theater games. This must've been '68, '69, somewhere along in there. I was at the pinnacle of the struggle with my wife to find a new definition of whatever it was we wanted without killing each other.

One night in the big dining hall, in came this Moses, this protean figure with a bald dome and miles of white beard. And he sat down at the table just across from me and stared out the window at the setting sun for a time.

I was rather excited, a little bit in awe of sitting across from Fritz Perls. And I decided, Jove, I'm going to talk to him; after all, we were both there leading workshops and were colleagues; and I did.

And, as a shameless ploy to ingratiate myself to him, when he asked me a question about where I came from, I claimed among other things that I'd been a singer. He said, "What do you sing?"

"I'll give you an example," I said, and burst into an old Viennese song. He loved it. I sang another, and pretty soon Fritz and I were sitting there booming away these old German songs. He even got tears in his eyes at one or two of them. The two songs that he just loved to sing with me were "Vienna, the City of My Dreams," and "The Two Grenadiers'' by Schumann. He loved it, tears came out. We were oblivious to the presence of all these other people who were looking at these two unlikely people screaming and wailing and shouting away. It wanted only great steins of beer.

He didn't sing terribly well but he could croak out some notes. He managed. He thought I sang very well but he didn't make a thing out of it. He recognized that I was a singer and he wasn't, but it didn't matter. It was fun.

Rollo May, who was an itinerant in Fritz' life, began to notice subtle changes in the man he had known, on and off, for some twenty years. . . .

ROLLO MAY

I remember I was having a seminar over the weekend when I got there. And as I was waiting for people to get seated, he came up and stood beside me; he didn't say anything. He simply stood there. And I recognized it for what it was. He was being friendly. He wanted to ally himself with me whether he had anything to say or not, and I appreciated that. He was still not at all what one would call the *bon vivant,* or affable, but there was a kind of sincerity that flowed out of him. A softening, a mellowing.

From then on, we seemed to be more friendly with each other. We began talking from time to time when I was down there. One weekend when I was down, I sat next to him at the dinner table. I remember I made up my mind I was going to talk with him come hell or high water. We talked about death. He must have been 74 or 75. He said he was not afraid of it. He told me about his heart attacks. He had heart attacks from time to time. They came with great pain. He had been driving some place or other; there had come a heart attack and with the usual pain. His first inclination was to wince and guard himself against it. Then he had thought, ''Well, why not let myself go with it. Why not let myself feel it all the way through.'' And then his pain stopped. He regarded that as a demonstration of how, if you can accept the pain and live with it, live through it, rather than resist it, then it gets much better—the pain will go away. I think that's a very sound principle, probably not applicable all the time, but by and large it's a very valuable principle for people with heart ailments, and with heaven knows whatever pain.

We had a very good conversation. The important thing to me was that he had changed so much. He now sat around. He didn't use to sit around at all. He was not abrasive any more. At least I didn't notice it in any sense. There seemed to have been quite a definite change.

Gabrielle sits in the semi-darkness of the Esalen dining hall, a candle flickering on her high cheek bones; she is beautiful. . .

GABRIELLE ROTH

Fritz and I just started playing right away and that was a comfortable space for me. In fact, he was one of the first people in my life that I could just play with, totally, without any thought patterns. We would go into mime movement or theater spaces and be absurd together. We'd make movements and sounds and faces at each other. That's how we would say hello.

Fritz was right there when I first began to do movement with groups of people. I was very insecure because I had no theories about it; I had no education in it. It was simply something that I loved to do. It was my way of expression—seeking in the body for some kind of answer. And Fritz really encouraged me to do that. He certainly supported it. He said, "Move, baby. Go ahead."

I can remember saying to him once that I had nothing to say to people, that I was afraid of speaking to them; and he said, "There's nothing to say." It was very helpful to me because I would compare myself to all these other people who were writing books and could talk for hours about what their trip was. I was really much more non-verbal, and instead of judging myself negatively, he helped me to see that.

Once I was sitting on one of the tables facing the ocean at the baths reading *Gestalt Therapy*. Fritz came up, yanked the book from my hand and threw it into the sea.

He taught me so much about movement, how pure it is, how it just comes right out of the moment. I saw him somehow get people to move. Not just talking but really doing something, going into the rhythm of their life more.

He recognized the dance in everybody. He saw that dance was going on all the time. That's what gestalt therapy is all about: that dance which your body is doing all the time when it clenches a fist or blinks an eye or whatever little things are coming through—the gestures, the tightness, the way your body moves and the language it speaks that we normally ignore. He didn't miss a thing. He saw where people were in their body. That's why he saw people so clearly.

My experience with him was more a relationship. He was not my therapist; he was my friend. He used to speak Yiddish a lot to me, which I don't understand. I do understand German; so if we spoke at all we spoke German together. That limited my speaking to very simple sentences. I used to like to listen to him. He'd tell great stories.

He did have a mean streak. He had *lots* of love, too. And he did not take care of himself. He smoked to an incredible excess—he never stopped. The fact is that smoking keeps you from the very thing which he propounded; it keeps your breathing up in your chest so you can't breathe deep in your belly and be in a really clear space, which is the "now." But that was just his process; that was just the way he channeled his energy. He had a good time.

I feel Fritz really did something for humanity. He brought back the awareness of the human body and how it is part of the entire psyche. He taught us how to blend together that mind-body split. That was his gift. It was a very important one.

CYNTHIA SHELDON

There was a special yellow-gold modern chair that happened to be sitting right in the sun. Everyone else was sitting in the shadow, and there was Fritz sitting on this gold chair in the sun with a cigarette in his hand and smoke all around him. I knew he was very special. There was a presence, a very powerful presence about him. This was in Gene Sagan's liv-

ing room. Fritz had come up to do a dream seminar for their clients. This was in 1962.

My memory of those days is that Gene was the only one doing gestalt. There was a lot of negative feeling in the profession towards anything very far out, and it was far out in those days! I ran groups and worked with clients all the time but I hesitated to use any gestalt; I feared the staff's response.

Some of us got so excited about the work with Fritz that we started meeting every other Wednesday night and practicing gestalt therapy on each other. That went on for a whole year. Then Fritz said, "I really hope you will start a gestalt institute in San Francisco." We got one started on a shoestring by inviting Fritz and Jim Simkin up to do workshops for professionals.

Then Fritz said to those of us forming the Gestalt Institute, "This is your program; I'm not going to have anything to do with it. I want you to be independent. I don't want you to imitate me. I want you to be your own gestalt people." And we appreciated that, but all of a sudden, people started arriving from all over the country acting as if the Gestalt Institute of San Francisco was their institute! And they said, "Fritz said we could be in!" We said, "We'll have to vote you in."

Well, we voted them all in—but it was difficult adjusting—including so many bright individualistic people from different parts of the country all at once.

Fritz always liked the Gestalt Institute of San Francisco because we were all so crazy. He didn't really interfere, other than to tell people, "Hey, go to San Francisco!" We listened to his wishes, but *we* decided what was to happen.

RICHARD MILLER

The professionals were very concerned about the gestalt "image," and some thought Fritz himself was a beatnik, a hippie. Larry Bloomberg and I not only weren't concerned, we loved his walking around in his costumes. . . I did my dissertation on the effect of color on emotionality, which among other things put me in touch with how walking around in a gray flannel suit is depressing. . . If you wear blue like the sky, you put some color in your world. I went around wearing colors. The way Fritz dressed gave me the support I needed to put on what I found comfortable. Although we were putting gestalt on the map, at least locally, the one thing we weren't doing was adding that particular kind of respectability—suit-and-tie acceptance by the profession at large—that a lot of people were concerned about. I had no concern about that kind of thing.

Larry and I began The Institute for Multiple Psychotherapy (TIMP) in New Mexico in 1967. In 1969 we moved to San Francisco and I changed the name to Gestalt Institute for Multiple Psychotherapy (GIMP) in honor of Larry on his birthday. (Larry had club feet at birth and had many operations until he was 20. In 1969 we did some very significant therapy with him and he fully worked out the old pain and began to walk and even hike.) It was after this that we went to Europe together and walked our asses off through London, Paris and North Africa. Prior to our work, he was afraid to travel for fear of not being able to walk. After returning from Europe we joined the board of the Gestalt Institute of San Francisco, and Fritz came to feel that I should put all my energy into it and that what I was doing was divisive to gestalt therapy.

At an American Psychological convention, Fritz saw my name tag, showing my affiliation as GIMP. He said, "A man who sits on two chairs may wind up in the middle." I replied, "A big man sometimes needs two chairs to sit on." That wasn't the way to win his heart. It's important to me to be my own man and do my own thing.

I can understand the times Fritz was angry at me. There was a similarity between us; he was a hard man to control and so am I. We're both very sensitive to being controlled. When I feel I have nothing to lose, which is most of the time, I feel secure and nobody's going to control me. We're a dangerous kind of people in an authoritarian structure. In an authoritarian world, a person who comes on like the top dog can make lots of people respond out of fear.

He was highly competitive with me, and I with him . . . and both of us with almost everyone. I didn't relate respectfully to our difference in ages. Fritz didn't like that independence. He was concerned that gestalt therapy be made respectable, and he wanted people around him who would spread gestalt. He put a lot into spreading the word.

Fritz was working out his own thing, and that was a positive demonstration worthy of what he was teaching. In addition, he was also teaching us to be caustic, to hold two-hour group sessions, to hold workshops for "x" days and seminars for "y" days, to use our professional role to the utmost. For Fritz to do as good as he could from ten o'clock to twelve and then from one to three, then an open-ended night therapy session was terrific; it was like a graduate-school experience. I didn't know then that I was learning all the time I was going to those meetings.

I'm for accepting his great contributions and leaving his personal problems with him. We don't all have to smoke cigars as Freud's students did.

WILLIAM QUINN
There was a marvelous, creative woman named Virginia Satir, one of the world's authorities on family therapy, who

gave frequent seminars here on family therapy. Fritz sat at the bar back here. I introduced them, and Fritz simply turned his head, as if we smelled or something, and walked away without acknowledging the meeting. Virginia was shattered. She wept. Well, a couple hours later, I went up to him and I said I was really appalled. He said, "You mean that queenly woman?" And she *was* queenly—a very tall, noble-looking woman, related to the German royal family. And he liked her tremendously. But his manner . . . he was completely unconscious of it. He had no intention of being rude. They became good friends.

VIRGINIA SATIR

I remember that incident when he was introduced to me. I didn't know until later that he was suffering from terrible heart trouble at the time and in pain constantly. That was before Ida Rolf came along and helped him. As you know, Fritz didn't like bullshit, and often he could be very rude; it was like that incident with me. He had good feelings about me when he was introduced to me, but his behavior would never have let me know that until later. Sometimes he'd get very dictatorial. Except for that first time, I never had that kind of experience with him.

I respected Fritz tremendously, and felt him to be a genius. We touched frequently in our personal relationship, and one of the reasons we had such a strong feeling for each other was that he knew I didn't want anything from him and I knew that he didn't want anything from me, so we could just be together. I respected him and he respected me. We had a very definitely delineated relationship—we were colleagues. I learned much from him and I know he learned some things from me. I would have Fritz in for my seminars; but after a while, I couldn't have him because he would be rude when someone would not do what he wanted them to do. He didn't have any patience with people—and yet that isn't true either. The man had many sides to him. I've often said that when Fritz was gestalting he was magnificent; when he was Fritzing, he could be a bastard. I want to tell you, it was very hard to be around Fritz when he was Fritzing and not feel totally devastated. If people didn't have a real good sense of their own self-worth, he could be really something, let me tell you. Those were times when he was lonely and he felt that nobody cared. In all my contacts with him, we'd just hug each other and I'd pat him a little. Sometimes we'd sit together in the baths. . . .

He let himself be poignant with me. We were each going to build a house at Esalen. He did build one and it finally worked out that I didn't. But, anyway, it was around that time that he and I sat down to talk about some things. He started to tell me about his longings, how he'd always wanted a house that faced the ocean and somehow that got him into talking about his disappointment with Freud. He couldn't understand that he wouldn't be listened to. How could Freud have done such a thing was his feeling, more than just rejection. "I had been reading Freud's stuff and saw there were things Freud hadn't answered. I went to see him—I had an appointment," he told me, "but Freud got very domineering and ordered me out of the house." You see, Fritz felt that psychoanalysis was interminable, and that treatment didn't have to be interminable. He felt that the analytic principle was just trying to do the best possible, but with the gestalt idea you could really break through. The gestalt principle is that you can go towards health. I think Freud opened up the possibilities that we have things in ourselves that we can connect with that might help us, but he was stuck on the pathological stuff; and gestalt is directed toward health. In gestalt, you start out with the premise that wholeness is what we're after, *and* is possible. It's very basic stuff. It's not an "if" question. We can go to wholeness because we have all the ingredients in the world. And by taking the usual ways that people have been looking at themselves to make a whole, you got gestalt. You see, you don't give anything away; what you do is transform and add so that it comes to be a whole, a whole person. In gestalt, it's like you have a ball, and in other therapies, you have a hierarchy. Gestalt is a hopeful thing; I think psychoanalysis is pretty pessimistic.

There's a story of two psychiatrists standing in front of one of Van Gogh's paintings, and one says to the other, "Do you think he would have cut off his ear if he had been analyzed?" and the other says, "Oh, sure, but he would have known why." Now, Fritz would move into, "You don't have to cut off your ear. Knowing why is not the essential part, not cutting off your ear is."

So there was a difference. Fritz worked always for new integration which would produce new action. It's a step beyond. It's an addition to. That was the essential difference. I think he was telling Freud, we can change ourselves, we don't just have to see ourselves differently. We can change the ways we live our life. He told me how he had hoped to bring this thing to the world through Freud, and it didn't work. He had hoped that Freud would understand what he had to say, but Freud didn't want to hear it. Freud treated Fritz like a naughty boy, and Fritz was very hurt by the dismissal. His eyes were misty as he looked at me, and his voice was sad. I remember the pathos and longing I got from his voice and the way he looked. That always stuck with me. At that time, I got so much the feeling that Fritz couldn't do good fathering, because he himself didn't have a good father. I often had to counsel young people, especially young doctors who wanted that new daddy. The last thing in the world Fritz would be was a daddy because it meant something I don't think he ever got straight about—what was intimacy and what was exploitation.

I often thought that he was a great man who really never felt loved by another man. He was always harder on men than women; he was very hard on men. He'd cut them off at the ankles, no question about it—as though to say, the things I hate most in myself, I hate in you. He longed for recognition from a man. There was no man who ever gave him anything. The thing that kept coming through was an expectation that he wouldn't be understood. As we talked about Freud, he told me how he hoped the doctors would accept him.

Those rare moments he would share with me made me understand that he was very lonely. He also had a lot of pride and he wasn't going to share that. He was not an ass-kisser. He went to the other extreme: "I want to be accepted on the merits of my work, not because somebody likes me."

I also saw a very shy side. I remember at a conference in Washington, he came up to me like a little boy and said, "Know what? They've accepted a film of mine." He was thrilled; I think underneath he really didn't expect that people would really care about what he was doing.

He credited Ida Rolf with saving his life. It was after that that he began to grow and make his mark in the world. Other doctors began to take notice of him, and some of the young far-out doctors were willing to come and be with him. Actually, he didn't get that recognition until very late in his life.

Fritz' students made a 75th birthday party for him. There were at least 200 people in the Miyako restaurant in San Francisco who came. I remember sitting there thinking, "Fritz, you made it. You are getting the recognition from all these people." It was like a public announcement of his being accepted. Many people, a lot of doctors among them, talked about what Fritz meant to them. He was full of smiles. He was joking. I remember the exuberance.

". . . I never thought it would happen to me." It wasn't only for himself as a human being—because he was a poet and an artist, I thought—but it was also for his work, valued by the brotherhood, the doctors. It was a lovely tribute to him. In a way, it may have seemed like a miracle to him.

Each event, seen differently is *different. . . .*

ROLLO MAY

I heard from some of my friends down at Esalen who had been to that dinner for him on his—what was it?—75th birthday, I think, and he was tremendously touched by this. I was back in New York. But they were very moved by it. He was very moved. . . .

FRANK RUBENFELD

At that 75th birthday party, we presented him with a big papier-mache lettuce because he was smoking these horrible lettuce cigarettes. They were horrible. So we made him one of paper with lettuce coming out of it as a present. We all got dressed up in costumes and we had a fantastic feast and, of course, he was the guest of honor. We had bottles of Liebfraumilch, and then it was time for him to stand up and speak to us, you know, to acknowledge what we had done. And just for a split second, he looked so young and so humble.

BOB SHAPIRO

I think the high point of that whole evening was the great dancing Fritz did. . . .

WILL SCHUTZ

It was the most painful thing because it wasn't clear what it was. First someone would say good things about Fritz, and then there would be an announcement of the next meeting of the Gestalt Institute of Cleveland! The party kept on alternating between an emotional exaltation of Fritz and some kind of mundane materialistic announcement. Fritz seemed to engender this ambivalence because as soon as you said something nice he would put you down.

GIDEON SCHWARZ

Sometimes when people ask me about the concept of "living in the now"—what does it mean?—I give them this example from Fritz' behavior: That evening, with people standing around the table in the glittering candlelight, Dale Metzger, who was a veteran of many workshops and the husband of the woman who baked the cake, got up, raised his glass, and said, "To Fritz, for being just the way he is."

Fritz looked around with tears in his eyes; I could tell by his breathing that he was very touched and excited. As we all lifted our glasses, he drank, and said, "This is the lousiest champagne I've tasted in a long time. What did you pay for it?"

Someone told him, and he said, "Oh, my God, we could have gotten so much better stuff for less money."

HAROLD OAKLANDER
I saw him very much as an artist in his therapy. I feel that doing therapy is a form of art. It's an art form, though it doesn't get recorded on canvas or clay or in notes or words.

Is gestalt therapy a science with a set of techniques, or an art that requires some indefinable, innate qualities?

GIDEON SCHWARZ
There *is* something objective that can be learned which can be called gestalt therapy. Fritz himself said that very clearly in one particular instance. At the Miyako Hotel in San Francisco on his 75th birthday, he told the audience that the question of whether it was him or the method that worked had troubled him for years. But now, looking at the various gestalt institutes that had sprung up all over the United States and at the people he had trained (or those who had been trained by his people who had become gestalt therapists), he felt he could say that there is something that can be taught to others. Not that it's enough to learn some rules and techniques, but still, there was something which could be transmitted, which was not just a matter of his personal magic.

There were other celebrations and celebrants. . . .

STEPHEN PERLS
Around 1968—I can't remember exactly when—he came to San Francisco for the American Psychological Association meeting and I talked with him there. We got into a conflict because he was having his 75th birthday. There was a big to-do and he just assumed, without consulting us, that my wife and I would go. He hassled us. I remember his exact words: "I'll send somebody to fetch you." He didn't say, "I want you to come," or "Are you interested in going?" He just

assumed that, of course, we would *want* to go to his party without consulting us, without taking into consideration that we had signed up for a couple of workshops and we had a date with somebody else. We didn't go. We didn't know any of the people and there just wasn't any need, as far as I was concerned, to go to a birthday party.

Might not his attitude have been, "By all means, come celebrate with me"?

He didn't say, "I want you to come." He said, "You will come." When somebody says *you will,* I resist the other way. We didn't go. I'm trying to remember if I saw him after that, before he died. . . no. That was the last time.

Do I regret not going? Not really. . . well, a little bit. . . since then I've met some pretty neat people, who, if I'd met them a year or two earlier would have made my life that much richer. So I do feel bad about that, but I don't feel bad about the fact that I didn't accede to his demands.

> *Basically I hated my father and his pompous righteousness, but he also could be loving and warm. How much my attitude was influenced by my mother's hatred of him, how much she poisoned us children with it, I could not say.*

The father. . . .

HAROLD OAKLANDER
I was in a very bad place when I met Fritz. In effect, our son was going to die. He had a very rare illness. I got in the hot seat and Fritz just looked at me and said, "Why don't you just talk to me, tell me what's going on?" I imagine I cried. . . I did my grieving for my kid. . . He worked with me. His concern was in his face. He gave me some advice, like everybody does, and then he got up and left the room. Our encounter was pretty brief.

I've always had a suspicion that whenever he was touched he'd get up and leave the room. This may just be my projection, I never checked it out with anybody. I suspect he had something going about fathers and sons and that he was very alienated from his own son.

PEARL SOFAER

I noticed a small baby about four months old sitting in a baby seat on one of the large blocks that overlook the ocean. His parents were sunning themselves and doing their yoga near him. The child looked about forty-eight years old. How could that child look so old? It was only a baby. I was very infuriated at the parents being so totally involved with themselves. As a mother, I was just furious with the parents. The more I looked at the child the sadder I felt; I became very upset. And at the other end of the bath, I saw that Fritz Perls was also looking at the child.

We hadn't had any communication between us; and both of us started trying to make the child smile. It was very important to each of us. We spent about ten minutes doing that: Fritz'd laugh, and make faces, and noises. And then the child smiled!

NATALIE EDNIE

I had just finished working in a small group with Barry Stevens. I was painfully aware of having missed the relationship with my father. Fritz walked into the room just as I left the hot seat. The group began to break up. Fritz said nothing, sat down and opened his arms to me. I climbed on to his lap like a child. He held me and rocked me gently, making small comforting noises. I cried until I felt comforted. Fritz said softly, "Sometimes the mother must be a little child."

STEPHEN PERLS

I think I've worked through most of my resentment toward my father. I don't appreciate it, but I can understand that what was motivating him most of his life was his need for recognition. A lot of people think the hot seat and the dream interpretation are gestalt therapy. But that's not gestalt therapy, that's Fritz Perls. Gestalt therapy as defined by him still can take a variety of attitudes, but as he implemented it, it was as the showman, the leader, the top-dog approach. Doing his thing in front of an audience was very important to him. I didn't realize when I was growing up that he had such a strong need for recognition, for adulation.

I suggest to Stephen that perhaps what motivated Fritz was his desire to contribute to the well-being of others . . . Fritz himself had said, "I am greedy both ways, to have more and more experiences, knowledge and success, and to give all I have. . . ."

I didn't get that message until the last year or two of his life. It took me a long time to make the step; I was twenty-eight or thirty; I wrote a letter to him saying that we'd been quite distant most of our lives and I wanted to take this chance to say I'd like him to come visit with us and have a chance to really talk.

It certainly got a quick response. "I'll come and visit you in Albuquerque." He made a special trip! Bought a plane ticket! Flew out within a few weeks for a weekend. Obviously, he *wanted* to make contact. His immediate response to my overture shows that. It was very rewarding. A very good experience. We talked about quite a few things, which didn't eliminate all of the past but at least helped to explain it.

I didn't know it at the time, but Fritz had a real inability to make close contact with people on an extended basis. He could make immediate contact with people therapeutically and sometimes on a friendship basis, but no long-term commitments . . . It would have been nice for his family for him to have made a commitment to them. He did a little bit, but still, it just wasn't him to have a commitment.

I still have difficulty seeing Fritz as the great man he is for so many other people. He's still father to me, though certainly not my image of what a father should be. I may have counteracted a lot of his behavior in the way I am with my own kids. I think *I'm* a *damned* good father. I enjoy my kids. I spend quite a bit of time with them (more so when they were younger than now), and they've grown up, so far anyway, to be pretty delightful, bright, all-around kids.

Chessmate. . . .

ED TAYLOR

I somehow identified him as my father and I was very afraid
of him. I was very much overpowered by. . . I was overawed
by Fritz Perls. When I was working in the kitchen, baking, I
would take food out into the dining room. One time, in particular, he walked in the door from the lounge, and my legs
just picked me up and *zooooomed* me back into the kitchen!
I was gone with no hesitation, no thought, nothing. I was out
of there.

Another time, over the bar, I told him I was scared of him;
he was really warm to me. It was beautiful. He took my hand
and said, "That's the way it is at first." And then he went his
way and I went mine. But I was still scared of him.

In his group, I would get to a point where I would resist
everything he said. So he would say, "Next," and there I'd
be. It took me a whole year to see that I was resisting him,
that I wasn't working at all. I wasn't using him as I could
have as a therapist. I was emotionally involved in battling
him.

One time I was walking down to the baths and I told him I
really needed his approval and he said, "Oh, shit." He
didn't dig it at all. He said, "You're a nice guy. You have my
approval," and I still needed his approval. It didn't matter.
Obviously, it wasn't that I needed his approval, I needed my
own approval. My fear was of myself, not him. I got that on
an acid trip later, where I really freaked out and someone
said, "What are you afraid of?" and I said, "I'm afraid of
me."

Once, I walked into him. He was so mellow it was incredible. It was almost like a cosmic feeling, really, of a very
warm old man, a mellow cat. He just hugged me and went on
because he had things to do, other people to hug and things
like that. After that, it was kind of different.

There are two things he wanted to do before he died. He
wanted to learn how to sing and he wanted to skydive. I play
the piano. I was into music for a long time before I came to
Big Sur. We talked about it. We went in and we played

around and I gave him singing lessons. It was fun. We would work on where he wasn't competent. Sometimes he could carry a tune all right. He wanted to be able to carry a tune and he didn't have confidence in himself to carry a tune, but when he got confidence he could do it. We did that for a while and that was fun. I would go up there and listen to music with him and play chess.

> *Besides Selig, I would single out Ed Taylor and Teddy as two of the few people in the world I trust unconditionally.*
>
> *Ed is . . . the redbeard, a pianist and baker. I nearly wrote he baked the bread that made Esalen famous. I love to play chess with him. Most chess players are determined to win, compulsive computers, taking up most of my time, uptight haters when they lose, forgetting that we are playing a game.*
>
> *Not so with Ed. We are playing. We have fun. To mate the king for us is just one of the rules of the game. Moves are not unretractable commitments. We reserve this for real life.*

We played a lot of chess together. He was pretty good. I don't know whether we were evenly matched; some days I'd win and some days he'd win. It was back and forth, nobody was dominating the contest. It was the excitement of the game. He was tricky, sneaky. He had lots of poise and

strategy. We played a lot at night. I was always doing something like I'd be baking and I'd have my bread in the sponge and I'd have an hour or two to play, so I'd go out and find him and we'd play chess and then I'd go back and do my thing. Or maybe he'd be gone and I'd find him later in the afternoon and we'd play. He really got a lot of chess going, there were a lot of people playing.

Once in a while he'd figure he wasn't playing good chess and he'd get up in disgust or I'd do the same thing. But mostly it was high, it was really good. When we were playing chess, we didn't talk and I didn't feel any of that fear or awe at all.

GER AGREY

For Fritz, chess was just pure fun, with no didactic to it at all, just a dance of pieces. I'd get him in a corner, and he'd sit back, wrinkle up his nose and say, "What can I do to be saved?" Then he would start playing. The first summer he was really a fanatic for it, he'd play at the lodge from eleven till four.

After he had lost about ten consecutive games to a guy who was really a pro, Fritz started his clown routine and completely upset the guy, he just psyched him out; he wouldn't make a logical move and he beat the guy very badly. He had a hard time getting him to play again because chess had been the basis for the poor guy's ego.

JOHN HORLER

He was good, very good. He could tell just by opening how you worked your pieces. He said he liked to play chess with people to find out where they were at. He played with me for a while and then he closed me down—bam!

JERRY ROTHSTEIN

He was deep in chess, but he couldn't stand orthodox play. He would do the most interesting thing for him at that moment, and usually it would be so bizarre, I wouldn't know what to do with it. But after a while I started to do different things, and then the games were really interesting. He was a much better player at that time and hated to lose, but it wasn't an issue with him.

JOHN ENRIGHT

He liked to play during breaks in the meeting, to get away from the talk and psychological work. We were very similar, quick and careless, playing essentially ten-second chess— both of us more interested in dramatic moves than in winning or losing. I was really the better player, but as soon as I'd won one or two, I'd get nervous and start losing. Looking back, I realize I just couldn't beat the master regularly.

WILSON VAN DUSEN

I was trying to compete with him, and he was just merciless. It was crushing. He was better in every possible way, better at play, better at psyching me out. It made me even easier prey that I wanted to win so badly. His attitude was kind of therapeutic, prodding me, pointing out what I was doing. Made me fairly uncomfortable. I never did beat him.

RUSS YOUNGREEN

We watched him play one night, and he was really aggressive, especially when he was losing. I swear I saw him take a piece, then stand up sending the rest of the pieces all over the place, saying, "I win! Fair, fair, fair!" That time he made sure he won. I thought, "Oh, my God, how can anybody play chess with someone like that!"

He used to do an imitation of me losing a chess game. When I'd play chess and lose, I'd throw the pieces around the room and he would demonstrate to a workshop, "Seymour losing a chess game: Grrr! Grrr!" He'd do this imitation, then, Boom! throw the game and then pieces and say, "Dat's impotence." That's the best one.

SHALOM NEWMAN

You can tell a lot by chess playing, if you're into chess. Rubin Fein, who's both psychologist and psychoanalyst and chess master, wrote books on that. There's a whole psychoanalytic thing with the king. Some teenaged kids will use chess as a vehicle in psychotherapy—the king and queen as mother and father—knocking down the king is not so surprisingly different from knocking down Freud, you know.

HARVEY FREEDMAN

It was just for fun, just for fun. But if you beat him the first game, he'd insist on revenge—"I want revenge." He would always knock down your piece, knock the king down, and then get up and walk away.

GREG DAVIDSON

On a tourist bus in Greece, I met a lady with a brochure on
Esalen that said something about the first residence program
for professional people. I wrote Esalen from Athens and was
accepted.

There were fifteen of us in that nine-month program and it
was really a motley crew, very disparate and diverse. It was
up at Fritz' house but we never met Fritz during any of the
times we went there for the selection and planning of the program. I really didn't know of Fritz. It was only at the tail end
of a disastrous marathon session—we were sort of lost—that
he appeared. Somehow I felt he didn't like the idea that we
were there in his house. He didn't particularly take to any of
the people, and he decided we were just a bunch of "greedy
phonies"—that was his term—and it struck me that he had
us pegged right.

> *The first [residence] program was rather ill-fated . . . as
> a whole, the first year Esalen bums were a poor crop.
> Mostly escapists or shithorses. They came as strangers
> and remained strangers. They expected the staff to wait
> on them and they expected to be "processed."*

I don't remember exactly how it happened but I somehow
made a connection with him and offered myself as his assistant with his recording situation, and he accepted. I just told
Fritz that though I'd never really done that kind of work, I
was trained as an electronic engineer, and maybe I could help
him. I was trained in physics and mathematics. My degrees
are primarily in engineering. I was working with computers
and missiles, creating projects that turned into satellite programs. (Some of the satellites are actually still flying. I was
really in the frontier of that particular effort in this country.)

And so, for about three months, I became Fritz' assistant.
I was with him alone a lot of the time. We'd eat together at
the lodge all the time. He talked as if he saw me as a son, yet
I felt that he never really saw me as a *person*. For example,

he zapped into certain things that were important to him and
he saw me in those terms. For at least two months he saw me
as a flyer, a scientist, then as an Israeli, and then as a human-
ist and a dancer. One time, he said, "You're a twentieth-
century man, the embodiment of the new Renaissance man."
That was heady stuff, but it was kind of hollow. I didn't feel
good about it. I wondered if he was being sarcastic.

Anyway, I was helping him get his scene together and the
immediate vehicle for that was his recording setup. He was
very much into recording and videotaping his work for pos-
terity. He had a real Mickey Mouse arrangement he was always monkeying with. The tapes that came out of it weren't
so good, and he was frustrated with it. I took it over.

I did a lot of videotaping of his groups. We talked about
forming a company, where I would put some money in, buy
equipment and market his stuff under an arrangement where
he'd get sixty percent and I'd get forty. But principally, I was
his employee; he promised payment, but he never paid me a
cent. Actually, I ended up buying equipment, like my little
television monitor, to fill out what was there. Another time I
bought some stuff that seemed too expensive for him, so I
paid part of it.

I always felt a little bit like an assistant, which I was, but I
wanted more. I wanted to be really loved by him. I must have
come at him with an "I want you. I want you!" attitude and,
of course, Fritz was so keen when that energy comes toward
him, he just evaporates. He didn't like it. He wanted me as
his assistant, helping him with the videotape.

My sense was that he always frustrated your advances. If
you wanted something from him, you obviously wouldn't get
it, but at other times it came as a gift. He was a master at
ego-reduction, and also he was ego-boosting. I don't think of
Fritz as a manipulator. I never saw him blatantly manipula-
tive, never. I think he was very crude at times, very inconsiderate, but I now see that as a virtue rather than as a fault.
Fritz was really a powerful being, both in terms of his mind
and his essence, but there were other aspects of Fritz. There
were times I'd get a real hit from him, a lot of love. Being
with him, I could really feel his pain and his inability to func-

tion, all his idiosyncratic craziness. At times he was very heavy with people. Yet he may have been a messenger, an agent. Through whatever he did, people turned to a new path, came to a fork in the road.

He was very direct; he had a sense of his own mission, and he may have been ruthless at times in pursuing it, but it was honest.

Once I was playing with a videotape of that painting in *Garbage Pail* with Freud in it, and I had the lens focused on Freud's eye. Fritz came in and he started narrating what was going on on the screen. For about an hour we played together, just scanning across his painting, and he relived all the parts of it. It was wonderful.

The beginnings of my demise with him had to do with Marcia. Marcia was a beautiful twenty-four-year-old who came zooming down the hill in her red Ferrari convertible. She'd learned to fly when she was in Australia. She was actually a stunt pilot. It was sort of like, "I am here!" Her arrival had that ring to it, and she very quickly found out where the high energy was in this place. She flew these Gypsy Moths, the same plane that Fritz flew. There was a connection. She soon got into one of Fritz' workshops and then somehow made it with Fritz.

Well, about that time we needed some parts and the only place I could get them was in Los Angeles. Fritz asked me to go and somehow Marcia decided to go with me. I was supposed to be gone two or three days and we stayed four. I hadn't told Fritz Marcia was going with me and when we got back, everything had changed. Fritz fired me! He'd never paid me for anything I'd done but now he didn't want me around, supposedly because I'd stayed an extra day but I think it had to do with Marcia's having gone with me. He wouldn't even let me get my own equipment!—my little television set I'd used as a monitor or any of my other stuff.

So after a while I went to Small Claims Court in Monterey and filed a claim against him. I was angry when I did it, but after a while it didn't matter that much. And it seemed to me a lot of time went by. I didn't forget about it, but after a time

I sort of gave up on it. I didn't think it was really going to happen, nor did I want it to. I just assumed that maybe it died, you know, like hopefully, if you forget it, if you put your head in the sand, it doesn't happen.

About a month and a half later, I'm sitting in the lodge after lunch, having tea with Selig. We like each other—he sees me as Esalen's renegade scientist. Fritz revered Selig, he saw him as a sort of saint. That day a couple of ladies from Pasadena, who I guess must have heard of us, decided to come in their chauffeur-driven Cadillac for a little adventure. So these well-dressed Pasadena ladies, all atwitter, come into the lodge, just looking around, you know, and Selig invites them to sit down and have some tea with us. And somehow, I don't know how the conversation came around to this, they had expected Big Sur to be sort of like the Wild West and Esalen to be weird (and, of course, there were a lot of interesting looking characters around)—Selig was explaining to them that "This is really a very peaceful place. We love nature, we're into our own quiet way of living here. People may look strange, but there are remarkable people here with all kind of backgrounds." He pointed to a guy who was a banker, to a doctor who was doing the gardening there, someone else who was a dishwasher and to me, an ex-scientist with the National Academy of Sciences.

While Selig was speaking I saw Fritz off in a corner of the lodge sitting by the window opening his mail. Despite our falling out, I still had that connection with him. All of a sudden, I see him puffing up his chest like a chicken, really excited, doing this very heavy breathing, you could hear him across the room. I loved him, you know, and I wanted to help him in some way; I knew he'd had two or three heart attacks. Well, after awhile, he picks himself up and comes walking very fast across the room.

I'm holding a teacup, and Selig is in mid-sentence about the placid, peaceful community, when whop! Fritz just winds up and gives me a real wallop across the face and the teacup goes flying through the air! I didn't expect it. I just didn't expect it! It wasn't a jaw-busting thing but he was very angry. And he didn't finish with one slap. He was pummeling me. So I grabbed him by his Churchill suit and ran him against the wall just to stop him from hitting me. I honestly didn't know what was happening. Then Selig got between us and separated us. Fritz said, "I'll get you, you son of a bitch!" and then it came to me—he got the summons!

CHARLES BROOKS

We were sitting in the dining room, and suddenly here's this scuffling and who is it? It's Fritz trying to punch Greg. Fritz was no prize fighter. He was not very much with his fists, you know. Of course Greg wasn't trying to hit him back. He was defending himself and Fritz was pursuing him around the room and punching away at him. Greg couldn't help but see the absurdity of it.

GREG DAVIDSON

I got another cup of tea and let Selig finish his sentence on the tranquility of the place! The women just cordially listened and then they left. It was a very funny scene.

The next day I was walking to the office when I heard a sound behind me. There was Fritz in his little Fiat, going full steam for me! I don't know if he would have hit me or not, but he was gunning that engine about thirty-five or forty feet away. I ran off the embankment into a bush where he couldn't drive. I saw Fritz leaning over the wheel, just passing me. I picked up a rock and threw it into his rear window and cracked it, I think. That wasn't right, but I did it and left.

After that I went off to Seattle and planned my return in time for the court appearance. I remembered a story my father had told me of how he had a law case in Germany, and the guy turned out to be a nazi who threatened to put him a concentration camp. My father got to the judge before the case and said, "I want to revoke it." I had a sense of that kind of thing happening to me in this thing with Fritz. I was paranoid about it. I felt once I'd started this legal thing, I had to be there, I didn't want to fool around with authority.

So I showed up at court without ever going back to Esalen. I knew that Fritz had a week-long workshop going that goes through Friday, and the court date was Friday morning, so I didn't expect him to show up. I figured I'd just say "Forget it," if I could. I didn't really want to pursue it any further.

So this Friday morning I'm sitting in Small Claims Court; I was the fifth or sixth case, Mr. Davidson against Dr. Perls. Well, after the third case, the door opens and in walks Fritz. I could've died! And I'd never seen him dressed in a serge suit, shirt and tie, hair combed and neatly trimmed. Nor had anyone I know. He didn't have that wild look. I couldn't believe it. Fritz had that same thing with authority I did. So he showed up at court and he waited around. He sat on the bench and I sat on the bench. I looked at him. He didn't look at me.

When the case came up, I was the first witness and I explained that I had been in Dr. Perls' employ, that he had never paid me any of the wages that were promised, and that I had bought some equipment that he never paid me for either.

When the judge called Fritz, Fritz went into a whole diatribe that I was his student, that he had taught me and I had never paid for any of the teaching, that I was an ingrate, and that it had been an arrangement of exchanging his teaching for my work; he went on and on.

The judge, who had never heard of Fritz, gave him a lecture about irrelevance!

"Look, Dr. Perls, there are very specific statements made here. One is that Mr. Davidson bought things for you which you didn't pay him for, and the other is that there was an agreement, presumably verbal, for wages, and you never paid him those wages. Now what about this?"

Then the judge asked me if I had anything on paper about the wages agreement, and when I said I didn't, he said that part of the claim couldn't be recognized since verbal agreements didn't hold in that court. He also said he didn't want to deal with the student-teacher relationship, but he could deal with the equipment. Fortunately, I had some receipts with me for \$38 or \$43 worth of stuff I had bought. I had made a list of them, and of my own possessions which I said added up to much more than the two hundred dollars I was asking, without the labor.

So the judge asked Fritz, "Did Mr. Davidson, in fact, buy any equipment for you? Do you owe him some money?"

And Fritz said, "Well, that's all overstated, but maybe I owe him about fifteen dollars."

Then the judge—I was a little nervous—the judge again gave him a lecture about being very explicit. He said, "I don't want these 'abouts.' You must know that 'about' fifteen dollars is not the same as fifteen dollars. It's some kind of vagary."

It was really ironic because this is Fritz' whole trip, to make explicit something unexpressed. And Fritz wilted. He became like a church mouse, his voice got smaller and smaller. I wanted to quit right then. The judge asked for the receipts. They added up to maybe \$43.

The judge said, "Would you be satisfied with that?"

"Yes."

"Do you want to contest it further?"

"No!"

So he told Fritz to pay me \$43 plus \$6 court costs, or whatever it was, and to return my property to me. That was it, that was the award. Fritz really felt like a victim, you could see it in the way he walked out of court. I really felt shitty about it, and I didn't ever expect to see him, or any money from him.

He went off somewhere for two or three weeks; so, because he was gone, I came back to Esalen for the rest of my residence program. It was like with my parents—when they were in New York, I was in California. When he did come back, I stayed out of his way, but he did pay me what the court ordered him to do. He left a check in the office for me, and I also got my stuff back.

I don't think any event is accidental in one's life. I now see all of this as important parts of the path. No, I don't feel any resentment.

A brief for humility. . . .

ALEXANDER LOWEN

Fritz lacked a sense of humility that handicapped him as a therapist. The sense of humility would make you very conscious of yourself as a human being in relationship to others. Fritz was in therapy with Reich who was really one of the giants of the century—there's no question. As an analyst of character, Fritz was very sharp and one of the best, you know, but like other people who were in therapy with Reich, he didn't develop that sense of humility.

Would you say that one of the goals of therapy is to develop that sense of humility?

Oh, it's hard to put humility as a goal of therapy, but certainly it should be considered one of the important values that therapy should develop in a person.

humility: the quality or condition of being humble.
humble: not proud or arrogant; modest; having a feeling of insignificance and inferiority, to lower in importance or dignity; abase; to destroy the independence, power or will of.

after Random House Dictionary
of the English Language

By these standards, it is accurate to say that Fritz lacked a sense of humility. He was not humble nor did he teach humility.

SAM KEEN

I felt he was very trustworthy and had an absolute genius as a therapist. He had the capacity not to let anybody bullshit him or get off the track and not to play into their games. I remember the first person who worked in his workshop was a homosexual and Fritz just crucified him; after I saw what he did to that guy, I was so scared, I thought if I'm ever going to work it had better be now. I had this whole thing I wanted to work on. So I got up and I started this program. I got about one sentence out of my mouth and Fritz said, "Aha—so you're a programmer."

He was right on. And so instead of running the program I had to deal with the fact of programming. But outside the therapeutic situation, I would try to approach him and he was very, very rude. I'd ask him something or other, start a conversation with him and he just walked away. He was one of the most unpleasant people in that kind of a situation that I've ever seen. He'd just turn around and walk away.

JANICE FOX

I had lots of opportunities to work with Fritz, and I didn't. For one thing, I was afraid of him. I just didn't feel bright enough to do therapy with him. I don't know, he was just a great person and he walked around and always acted like God. How do you speak to God? Simple as that.

SONYA FREEDMAN

I was walking through the dining hall at Esalen. It was dark. There was a group of people sitting around a table with one candle in the middle of it, and they all seemed absolutely rapt as if worshiping at a shrine. Then I noticed this old man talking. Someone beckoned me to join them. I walked up and he stopped talking for a minute. I didn't know who he was or who they were or what was going on. I said, "I have the feeling I've walked into the middle of a cult." He looked up at me and his eyes twinkled and he said, "Some people have need of cults." I laughed; after that, I got sucked into the whole thing.

I never said a word when Fritz was around. Whenever I was with him I was petrified. Anyway, once I was sitting at a table with him, I was finally starting to relax and open my mouth a little bit, and this girl comes over. She says, "Oh, Dr. Perls! I've heard so much about you! I've been dying to meet you. My girl friend told me all about you" He's just looking at her, not saying a word. She's going on and on and she's sort of running down; the enthusiasm is getting a little strained; the smile is starting to freeze a little bit. He's just looking at her and he's not saying a word. Finally she said, "And I just had to come over and say hello!" He says, "So?" And she goes on and on again, and he's not responding at all. Finally she sort of slinks along the floor and disappears, and he says, "Mosquito." I dried up again; I couldn't say another word.

DENISE FREY

For some reason he wanted to give me a piece of paper, and I wound up in his room while he was going through these acres of paper. As I watched this I said, "What you need is a good secretary." He said, "You're hired."

"Are you serious?"

"Yes, I am serious."

I said I'd be back next week, and I went home and rearranged my entire life: I quit my job, I quit school, I gave up my apartment in Berkeley, I stored the furniture. I gave myself two days for this operation, but in the meantime, I got sick. I was allergic to the medication they gave me and had an aftereffect. So I called up Esalen to say I was going to be late. I called two or three times and instead of arriving on Monday, I arrived on Wednesday afternoon. Mind you, I've got my whole life destroyed behind me. I walk in the bedroom where Fritz is lying on his bed and I say, "Hello, Fritz," and he says, "You're fired."

I thought about that for a while and I said, "Would you like to talk about it?" Which I thought was a pretty good response. Mind, I'd only known this man for a short time. And he said, "No."

I stayed around for a while, then I finally went back to Berkeley. It put me in a terrible spot. Well, actually, it put me in a very nice spot. It meant I had no life. All of a sudden, no life at all. Eventually, it all worked out. I made a beautiful arrangement with him. He needed a typist and I needed a place to stay. So I'd come down weekends, stay in the empty bedroom and type. For me, this was beautiful.

WILSON VAN DUSEN

Through all the early stages, I was the young man trying to

be "little Fritz." I became overly dependent on him. Like a stargazer, I wanted much from him—late in the relationship, there was a reversal and I needed him for nothing. Fritz seemed a little hurt about that. One time, for example, I was sitting at a table at Esalen with a nautical almanac, working out some sun navigational sights, and Fritz came by and sat across the table. Normally we would have had a lot to talk about, but this time I didn't feel like talking; Fritz waited a few minutes; he seemed a bit hurt, then he left.

He had wanted me to write a book with him; we talked a lot about that. He had a ton of notes he wanted me to work with. I should have, but I feared the difficulty of trying to read his mind and please the great man was too much to do. It was unwise, though. I would have been a helluva lot more famous if I had done it.

SEYMOUR CARTER

My strongest foreground of Fritz was really being frightened of him. He could chop me in two with a word at any moment and was very much into doing that a lot with people. I don't know what he was trying to accomplish in his bully number, by being so ruthlessly truthful.

During the time I was leading groups with Bill Schutz, and feeling very good at it—but careless, there was a lot of carelessness, carelessness that I can see now—Fritz was condemning my work. He wouldn't let me work with him on a professional level. I couldn't get into any of his workshops. He was king baboon here. He had a tremendous moral influence on the place. He made the atmosphere here crisp with the electricity of his going around banging everybody all the time.

I felt his condemnation of me changed my life. From being a worker with people, I had come to feel you must be very delicate when you cream somebody—I felt Fritz creamed people unnecessarily. Yet on the other hand, he would be so delightful, this old, ancient human being who was truly himself. I didn't realize the impact of his presence on me until after he left.

For a few years I kept away from him; I wouldn't go near

him when he was in a foul mood. He enjoyed teasing me and I got a lot out of that. We played a lot together in different ways. Sometimes I'd be with Fritz and he'd make some really insightful statement about me. Sometimes it was really playful. I worked with him only once. At the end of the work, he said, "I've released some energy for you. Dot's good." And I really felt that.

ROLLO MAY

He was often ornery.

I don't think his anger got in the way very much. As a matter of fact, I think it was partly beneficial. In the first place, he put on a good show; people would come there partly to watch him cuss everybody out.

I got an idea of how he worked from patients—ah, students—who have spent some time with him. And I must say, it always confirmed what I thought: here was a man with tremendous insight. He was very effective with human beings in trouble.

I never argued with him—I realized I could never get any place. In those days, I was . . . well, tending towards if I couldn't get any place in the discussion, then I'd avoid the discussion.

I do know that he had a very sharp insight into when somebody might go psychotic. I think it was essential if he was going to be as outspoken as he thought he needed to be. He could tell whether they could take it. I never saw him attack somebody who couldn't take it. He was always relatively sure that whoever he lit into couldn't tackle him back.

Did you ever see anyone attack him?

No . . . a bit. But I never saw it effective. He would use it for the purposes he was trying to demonstrate in the dream seminars. But no, I never heard of his being attacked. He was the kind of person we speak of who'd never pick on somebody his own size.

A 6'6" man in his mid-thirties, Richard Miller has light

brown hair, a trim moustache and a short beard that outlines his pleasant face. . . .

RICHARD MILLER

One time, I was talking to a lady and Fritz came over and started making a pass at her. Then he looks at me, gets a sort of tight look on his brow, pulls up a chair and stands on it—he was quite a bit shorter than me, right? *Then* he starts talking to me, criticizing me . . . he'd made a pass at the girl and now he's going to give me a hard time. He points his finger at me and says, "You. . . . ." She looked at him and said, "Fritz, don't you know that when you point one finger at him, there are three pointed back at you? He shut up got off the chair and walked away with a grump.

Living at Esalen in the summer of 1967, I hung around Fritz and watched him carefully. I joined one of his workshops, and whenever I started to talk to him, to make some approach in the group, he kept telling me, "You're full of shit, it's the expression on your face, the smile on your face." I said, "OK, that's mine. Now what's going on with you?" No answer . . . I had that immediately . . . he didn't want to deal with that. Fine, so I'm there to learn from him, not to figure out what's going on with him.

Al Drucker was working the camera in that group and he said, "I'll show you." He played back the camera shot, and when I saw the look on my face I got angry with myself. I had to agree with Fritz and I was pissed at myself. It was my top dog coming down on me . . . saying, "You're stupid. What took you so long to see it here?" I felt myself to be that critic, and started to yell at him. I absolutely exploded, and as I did, Fritz gave me some encouragement with his hands, which was perfect. I screamed and screamed and screamed, and then I cried and then I laughed and I felt a wonderful experience, a very important experience in my life.

Then Fritz—he always had some kind of a little lecture—looks around the room, then at me, and says, "You had rage and grief and joy. The only emotion left is orgasm." That was his theory of the four basic emotions. I looked at him and laughed some more—I had a great laugh. I was in a different state of consciousness, a psychedelic state perhaps . . . terrific . . . wonderful . . . I changed my life at that moment, and I knew it and he knew it. I experienced the understanding of a process, in a way I never had before. Ever since, I haven't felt I was compelled to listen to words to get the meaning of a process. I could tell what the communication was between me and another person without whatever our little words in English mean.

After that workshop, I was going away for the weekend and as I walked by Fritz at the lodge I told him I'd see him Monday. He said, "You had a big experience." I said, "Yes." He said, "Take some tranquilizers, wherever you go. It'll be good for you."

That was gratuitous. I didn't hear it coming out of love. I thought he was undercutting his own work, facilitating such a strong therapeutic personal experience and then trying to dilute it with drugs. It might seem like a fine thing to you but I didn't forgive him for that for a long time.

I went back to the second workshop the next week, and used it to integrate a lot of that initial experience. I told myself that I was going to accept him, that I had plenty of things to learn from him.

Fritz did the role of the authority figure very well. It was one of the things that made him very powerful. I was tremendously impressed with him, though he wasn't the kind of guy I wanted to be close to socially. He was the type who would see a person backing into a parking space and he'd race into it. I was with him once when he did that. The guy came over to Fritz with murder in his eye. Fritz didn't even acknowledge him, and the guy walked back to his car. I heard him say to his friend, "Ah, he's only an old fuck."

Fritz had a very assertive way of giving directions, too. He was authoritarian and he would say it with a little grump. Those of us who were wanting to please our fathers, and I don't know many who aren't, respond right off.

Jack, go close that gate over there.

[I turn, look at it, and start to get up. Richard smiles and puts his hand on my arm.]

Amazing how that works, isn't it? Well, Fritz was real good at that. I'm pretty good at it myself. So the next thing you know, you're going over to get him a cup of coffee or something, and there he is grabbing your girl's breasts.

He had a "Fritz diagnostic test," where he'd come over to a girl and say, "This is my Rorschach," and put his tongue right in her mouth. If she resisted, he'd say, "Don't you want to find out about yourself? The way you kiss me is very important. I'll tell you all about yourself from the way you do it." He was dynamite. He knew how to get to people—it was like he was saying be good to daddy so he can give you a gold star.

Fritz used to complain that he didn't have enough time for anything because he had to do his own laundry, his own this and that. So people started volunteering to help him. I thought there were things others could do physically easier than he, so I put down a rug for him in his therapy room. While I'm cutting it up in long slices and fitting them in place, he starts telling me how to do it. Then he wanders off and I hear him giving the woman who's doing his room some pointers about that in the same critical tone he used with me, ". . .you missed that shirt . . . you're not doing it exactly the way . . . you're not living up to my expectations of how the job is done." I started laughing, and he comes in giving me one of those looks—old top dog, with a cigarette dangling out of his mouth. I said, "You're going through this whole big complaint about how you don't have time because of all these little things you have to do, and now you don't have time because you're going around supervising everybody doing those little things for you." He stalked away.

CLAUDIO NARANJO

Fritz had a great impact on my life even before I met him. At the time I had a research job at the University of Chile and I taught at the School of Fine Arts there. I was given one of

Fritz' books called *Gestalt Therapy*. I was very impressed by the application of gestalt thinking to psychotherapy and I lived with Fritz as an influence, something very familiar, for several years, never thinking I would ever meet him.

Around that time I became interested in psychedelics. I was especially interested in yage, which is a plant used by witch doctors in the Amazon for shamanistic performances. I even went to the Amazon to look for yage and did a lot of research with it. After that, in '64 or '65, I came to California and there an anthropologist, Michael Harner, introduced me to Carlos Castaneda and proposed that we all go down to Esalen to offer a workshop on shamanism.

That was the occasion for my initial meeting with Fritz. I had a totally wrong image of what he would be like. I thought of him as a very innovative young man, a young intellectual. Yes, somebody of my type. Instead, he was—well, he was Fritz.

I first saw him coming out of a room. He was in a white sweater and looked very impressive with his beard and disheveled hair. I loved him as soon as I saw him. He reminded me of a sea wolf— *lobo del mar* — those were the exact words that came to my mind. In Spanish, this is an expression applied mostly to sea captains—men of strong personalities who are loners, not withdrawn, but strong self-sustaining men with great assertiveness.

I talked a little with him that time. I asked if he was working on another book, and he said, "No, my concern for humanity has diminished considerably." I appreciated that statement. It revealed to what extent he was not playing a virtuous role.

Some weeks later Fritz invited me to a demonstration of his dream work. He was not then so famous, in spite of his having already generated his key ideas before coming to Esalen. He didn't have anything like the workshops he led afterwards, with people coming just to sit in and be part of a performance. This demonstration did not even involve a registration or a fee. It was proposed as an experiment of a new way he had found of working with dreams that he wanted to demonstrate. First, he proposed that I explain how I, as a psychoanalyst, work with dreams. I said a few things about that. Then he asked me to tell a dream of my own. It happened to be a very long dream about seeking yage, seeking the Golden Grail. It went on from one scene to another and another and another and reflected a dissatisfaction about any closure. Fritz remarked, "You have difficulty in stopping." That was important. I realized that I felt I always had to add something more to what I had just said or done. This tendency of mine perpetrated the unfinishedness of many things that I started in my life, so that I was always wanting to improve or brood upon them . . . getting stuck and not completing them. I had talent for maintaining my business in an unfinished state.

I was very impressed with how much could be done without the conventional use of psychoanalytic interpretation. It seemed like Fritz had another kind of awareness—a psychological eye which seemed to be almost psychic. He once told me it was because he was old, but I think it was really connected with seeing in gestalts rather than in terms of detail. To perceive configurations is a subtle form of computation which constitutes much of what is called intuition. It's really *seeing* in the Castaneda sense. Fritz could see the total gestalt. He could see a certain rhythm in events and thus know what was coming and what was missing, and what a person was silent about.

Having come from a psychoanalytic background, I was really refreshed by Fritz' attitude in working with people, by his personal involvement. I had not been very enthusiastic about my life as a psychotherapist. I didn't feel I was doing something truly useful. So this is what first attracted me to him. He invited me to come back for a workshop he was doing, and I did.

During those first workshops with Fritz, I saw that there was little or no difference between the issue of psychopathology, or neurosis, and the existential issues of being a *real* person, a decent human being. He worked with you moment after moment after moment to keep you being real and not a phony. And, of course, that wasn't without risk.

I had heard Fritz was very tough on his groups, and that he believed in pain as a means toward growth, so I came ready for the hand of a surgeon who was going to cut away some unhealthy parts of my neurosis. I remember sitting there waiting for my turn, thinking that if what came out was true, it couldn't really hurt, that while I might be uncomfortable, that discomfort would be overshadowed by the satisfaction of finding out what I had come for; and, if it wasn't true, it couldn't hurt, because it had no relevance . . . This insight, incidentally, gave me a sense of unguardedness which was the foundation for much growth. For the first time I had subjective evidence of almost immediate psychotherapeutic effectiveness, and I was excited. I was just beginning to get into psychotherapy again at the time of Fritz' meeting on dreams; acquaintance with psychedelics on the one hand and gestalt on the other motivated me to return to the therapeutic domain, after years of involvement in research. When I went back to Chile I immediately started to work more loosely, and brought gestalt into the picture.

My next meeting with Fritz was in early 1966 in a two-week-long workshop for professionals led by Fritz and Jim Simkin. That was an important event in the growth of gestalt as a movement, since it was the first professional workshop done by the two of them on the west coast. People came from all over the country. After that I attended many other group sessions at Esalen and other places. Fritz thought of me as a trainee who would bring gestalt to South America, as I did.

My experience of Fritz was that he was not *doing* gestalt therapy; he was *creating* it every moment. He had a certain repertoire, but the essential element was to be with what was happening from minute to minute, *every* minute. I find Fritz' greatness reminiscent of the style of the old prophets in that he was so full of life he allowed his fallibilities to be visible. He was paradoxical in that his greatness was interwoven with his shittiness. He once invited everybody in one of his work-shops to make a brief self-descriptive statement of "Who am I?" When it came to his turn, he said, "I'm fifty percent son of God, fifty percent son of a bitch." I think that's a most fitting portrait of him. And one is no different from the other; it's the extent to which he was willing to be human that was the divine spark in him.

One time I was sitting at a table with him and somebody asked, "Fritz, what's your game?" I think the expression Fritz used was "out-bullying." I think he would always acknowledge that that was his dominant game. It was the style that made his therapy successful because he had come to a point where he could use his destructiveness to a constructive end.

My most forceful encounter with Fritz occurred when I was writing a book on the extension of gestalt therapy to the psychedelic situation. My thesis was that psychedelics don't work with an analytic approach. As a psychoanalyst I had found that psychedelics work best with a directly experiential approach, so that, in one way or another, you experience rather than reflect on the experience. I had been doing work in the field of psychedelics. In fact, I had an appointment in psychopharmacology at the University of Chile, and after a great deal of experimentation had come up with a drug called MMDA. MMDA is of the same family as MDA, but while MDA very often takes people to the past, MMDA leads to an "eternal now" trip. It was as if it was especially made for gestalt therapy.

So, I was writing a book and showed parts of it to Fritz, and he liked what he read. There was no conflict. But one day, as we sat at a table in the Esalen lodge just before one of his workshops, I invited his thoughts on a possible title after telling him I didn't know what to call it. We were silent for a while and then I ventured: "What do you think of *Gestalt Therapy Revisited*?" The words suggested the view of psychedelic extension as a quantum leap in therapeutic power, but I didn't really think of it as a suitable title, for I was not truly proposing a revision of the gestalt approach, only an application. Fritz didn't see it that way at all. He retorted, "So you want to top me." That was not my attitude: I felt like a branch of a tree in which Fritz was the trunk. I wanted the book to be a tribute to him. Furthermore, I was grateful to him for having taken me under his wing, so to say, and giving me a personal scholarship while I was still a Chilean student with limited resources. Fritz' reaction surprised me, and I said, "You know what Steckel said to Freud?" (At first Steckel was in Freud's circle but then he became independent, and when people said to him "Does a dwarf claim to see more than a giant?" Steckel had said, "Yes, a dwarf who stands on the shoulders of a giant can see more than the giant." He was implicitly referring to the process of cultural evolution in which whoever comes later has something fresher to contribute. I too, was implying that I was part of another generation standing on his shoulders. . . .)

Fritz replied with a continuation of that story I had never heard before. "Do you know what Freud's reply was?" He said, "A louse on my head doesn't see more than I." His voice was firm, with a shoulder-shrugging style.

Just before this incident, he had invited me to attend a workshop. I had come from Chile, mostly for Fritz' help. I was going through much pain in a love relationship that eventually became a marriage. He had written me, "Come to my workshops anytime," and he had confirmed upon my arrival, "you are welcome to anything I do . . ." After this brief exchange, however, he said, "This weekend is really full; I cannot invite you after all." When I told him that it was very important to me, he merely shrugged and said, "You'll have to check with the people in attendance."

Among the people in attendance were George Brown and Cindy Werthman and some others I knew, so I checked with them and was readily accepted, but I could sense that Fritz didn't want to work with me. Throughout the weekend I was aware that I was accepted by the others but not by him; I was an additional person who came last. I wanted to be sure that the others got a chance to work first. Finally, on the last day in the session, I said to Fritz, "I want to work with you."

"I don't believe you," he replied.

"I want very much to work with you, Fritz. I'm in urgent

need to work with you. I came all the way from Chile to work with you.''

"I believe in actions, not in words," he said. "You want to top me, not to work with me." He refused to work with me!

Then at lunchtime on Sunday, after the workshop had ended, I could see he was feeling bad about it. He walked up to me and asked if I would like to meet in his room with a small group of people he was training. I said, "Yes, I would."

That was a total disaster. He was terribly obstructive toward me. I can't remember more details than that he attacked me about playing stupid.

At one point, I said, "I don't understand, Fritz. I feel confused.''

"You're an intelligent man and a psychiatrist. You understand perfectly well. You make me puke! Get the hell out of here!'' And that was the end of the session for me!

That experience was very traumatic for me. I went back to Chile. For many years after that I would come back to it every now and then and look at it, but I couldn't tell whether Fritz was being a bully, whether he was right, or what was going on. I couldn't judge it, and I felt the need to . . .I had not come to closure with it. Since then I've come to think that situations which challenge one's ability to look at things clearly are a gift. Fritz challenged me deeply and I was shaken by his aggression. I finally was able to see through my idealization of him.

Now it's possible, hypothetically, that this was precisely what he wanted. At some level, I think he may have been reacting to my "good boyishness." But then many things can be true at the same time . . . even apparent opposites. Even when Fritz seemed arbitrary in his aggressive behavior, he generally put his finger on real sore spots. I believe that what was making him puke was my not getting angry at his bastardly way of treating me. Even an angry Fritz wouldn't have been angry at nothing; with his perceptiveness he would immediately channel that anger into something tangible. I guess ultimately I have to accept that if I had been more direct I would not have gone through that ritual of asking his permission.

When I came back to the U.S. again, I saw him at Esalen. He was doing his thing and I was doing mine. By then, I was becoming well-known as a seminar leader. I did not approach him, nor attempt to work with him. I didn't forgive him for a long time. I felt I couldn't trust him enough.

A long time elapsed; then one day he came over and said something that was very moving: He said that because of the quality of the work of people like Bob Hall and myself, gestalt was in good hands, and now he was ready to die. I could feel that he was wanting to come closer and that he wanted to make a bridge into contact again. But I still felt it was half-hearted on my side. I was still resentful. It took me a couple of years to digest the unfinished situation; not to be angry, and yet to be forceful . . . to maintain my integrity without defensiveness and without feeling bad about it.

RICHARD MILLER

I don't know, a man like Jack Downing, to take a lot of shit from Fritz Perls . . . Jack was already a prominent man in the field. He'd done basic research with psychedelics and so on. Interesting person. Fritz was never as tough on Jack as he was on others but he gave him a hard time. He didn't treat him like the man that he was. . . .

JACK DOWNING

I'm walking along the street in Menlo Park and here comes someone I knew, and she is just radiant! I said, "Lenore, what happened to you?" She said, "I just came back from a week with Fritz Perls." I said, "I don't know what Fritz has got, but whatever it is, I want some of it."

I came down to Esalen in October '66, and we met in what was the fireplace room then. Fritz was alive! He had life.

I think gestalt is essentially aliveness. I don't care what your technique is, unless you're alive you can't do gestalt therapy; you can neither give it nor receive it.

I'd been a psychiatrist since 1947. At this point I'd lost so much confidence in psychotherapy that I quit. By the second day of that workshop I knew this man was doing miracles, therapy miracles I'd never seen before in my life. People were just coming through their death layer and coming alive. I resolved then that my main personal priority was to spend as much time as I needed with Fritz.

He got me so that I got my sense of smell back. I remember I was working on some dream and he kept pushing at me and I said, "Fritz stop giving me all that shit!"

"Oh, you like shit. Imagine there's a big pile of shit there and start shoveling it."

So I shoveled horse manure, and was having a great time because each shovelful was going right in Fritz' face. He saw I was enjoying it too much so he says, "Use your hands." Then he says, "Smell it." I told him I don't mind it 'cause I really like the smell of horse manure. "Well, imagine human shit," he said. This took me to when I was a kid visiting on the farm in Oklahoma. There was an outhouse that didn't have a pit. The shit just fell out the back of the privy and the animals ate it which sort of turned my gorge at the time. So I smelled it and this got me back to my phobia as a kid. I went through that and I got my sense of smell back! Food tasted better. For a week I went around smelling everything I could smell. I'd go back and smell the garbage. I discovered that it's just a general social thing against bad odors and part of the training against excrement in childhood.

This experience is totally typical of gestalt therapy in that the overt content is simply the screen for what lies behind it.

I didn't understand Fritz at all for the first six months I was around him. I didn't understand a thing that was going on because he was totally out of my range of experience. I'd been at the Menninger Clinic and had had a very straightforward, conventional psychiatric background. My frame of reference was pretty much historical and analytical. His frame of reference was immediate experience and paying almost no attention to any historical antecedents, and he was getting changes magically.

Another thing: Fritz applauded when I would go to sleep in a group, because his basic concept was when you need to withdraw, withdraw. So I would go to sleep and no complaints. That was just great.

Still, Fritz basically was the conventional, structured therapist. The group was there when he came in, it began and one at a time you'd come up and work. He had nothing to do with encounter techniques. Sometimes there'd be this scrambling of people who'd want to work and they'd race to get the chair. He would not interfere. He would not help anybody. He'd work with whoever got there first. He did not help the underdog. He didn't help, period. I remember one man was very macho and pulled a knife on another man. They fought. Fritz didn't interfere. If they wanted to have a knife fight that was their business.

It was his way. It was not a technique. Compassion had nothing to do with it. Fritz did not have conventional compassion. Some people say he had none, but I saw compassion in Fritz. I've seen people weep and he wept with them.

Compassion is of the soul, it doesn't fit into boxes. With Fritz it varied with the individual, from moment to moment. . . .

LARRY HOROWITZ.
At a workshop in San Francisco, when a colleague of mine (who was a good psychologist but had a strong commitment to being helpless and being a crybaby) started to work with Fritz he stopped her and said, "I'm sorry I can't work with you." She became very upset as though, "If Fritz can't work with me, I'm lost. . . ." He said, 'It's not you, it's me, I cannot work with you. It's not that you cannot work with me."

He was such a tender man I don't think he would choose to hurt someone. I appreciate Fritz' commitment to being clear for himself and the hot seat occupant—a clarity that is usually damned uncomfortable.

ERIC MARCUS

Fritz didn't put on a mask to cover how he really felt. He wasn't worried about social conventions; when he felt cranky, he *was* cranky. He was very warm and lovable—sometimes. What really irritated people was that he could just be himself. Sometimes he was rude; if he didn't want to talk to somebody, he would say, "I don't like you. I don't want to talk to you."

One day, during the noon break of a workshop at someone's house, the host was serving lunch and kept saying to Fritz, "Do you want an orange? Do you want this? Do you want that?" and after two or three of these Fritz angrily said, "Don't take care of me!"

When Fritz was engaged in work, he was exquisitely sensitive and his sensitivity included the response of boredom. I was impressed with his incredible relaxed manner. He was not at all concerned with leading a *good* workshop, with *producing*. He had the ability to sit and wait and if nothing happened, to go to sleep! He was amazing and extremely aggravating! I felt like punching him. "I paid for this workshop, I want something!" His comment was, "Well, if you want something, then *do* something. I'm not here to entertain you!"

Fritz' genius as a therapist was his improvisational creativity. One time, for example, someone professed that he was embarrassed to work in front of the group. So Fritz said, "Just a minute." He left, brought back a stack of magazines and passed them out to everybody to read. The man looked around, shocked, said, "What's going on?" Fritz said, "Well, you don't want them to pay attention to you, do you? Make up your mind. Do you want them to pay attention, or don't you?"

Much of his work was slow and "conventional," but when an inspiration came, the effect was dramatic and potent. Once I saw him pick up on the voice tone of a man whose words were dull and boring. Fritz said to him, "Your voice sounds like a soft fart. From now on I want you to speak on-

ly in fart language, not with words." The effect was electri-
fying and hilarious! The guy came to life, and so did the
group.

Fritz said, "The patient will come for therapy and then do
everything in his power to avoid getting well." That one
sentence expresses the concept of resistance. If I ignore the
resistance and just listen to "Doctor, I want to lose weight,"
I miss the boat. If they really wanted to lose weight they
would have already! Why then are they coming?

Another thing Fritz said which I use when people ask me a
lot of questions is, "All answers are given. We torture ourselves by making up questions!" When someone asked a
question he'd have them change chairs and answer their own
question. Then he'd say, "See, you knew the answer. You
were just trying to con me into helping you and taking the responsibility."

JOHN STEVENS

Fritz once told Bob Hall, "You won't have as much trouble
being a gestalt therapist, because you're not such a prick."
In many ways, Fritz was a prick.

A woman who hadn't worked at all during the four weeks
sat on the hot seat towards the end of the workshop. Fritz
turned to her and said, as neutrally as any human being possibly could, "With most people during long workshops, I
like them more and more. You I like less and less." Coming
from him, that's a terrible thing to hear, but he said it very
neutrally, strongly and very definite, but neutrally, as a fact.
It wasn't that she was awful, just that he didn't like her. He
came up to a leader doing a group at Esalen, saying, "Your
supercilious smile is nearly unbearable," and walked away.
He would say things so neutrally. Even what many people
would take as an insult, a terribly cruel thing, he was just
stating it as a fact with no anger, no rancor, no arrogance.
He'd say, "This is what's happening," in the same tone of
voice you might say, "The sky is cloudy today."

He kept himself clean—he didn't hold on to shit when he
got incensed, he took care of himself, he let it out.

I know there are a lot of stories about how brutal Fritz was, but he was not indiscriminate about his brutality. I saw him be very hard on people, but he did it only when someone was pulling a lot of numbers, and not willing to look at how they were living their lives. With one exception, I saw those people come back afterwards and work very hard, and discover a lot about themselves. I've seen him nearly throw a good-sized guy out of a chair, pushing him until he was all bent over with his head between his knees, just struggling to stay in . . . and that guy came back the next day and *really* worked.

In my experience, he was mostly very, very straight and direct. His cruelty was really the greatest kindness to me. It got me started out of all that shit. Beyond that, he wasn't being cruel *or* kind, he was just telling the way things are.

When Fritz shit on me, he wasn't doing it for me, he was just pointing out what I was doing, telling me the way things were. Bob Hall says in the introduction to *Garbage Pail,* "You woke me out of my slumber." It took a sledge hammer to wake me up. Fritz was that sledge hammer.

Other views. . . .

MARJORIE VAN DUSEN
He had about zero drops of human kindness. He seemed to feel he couldn't achieve anything with a patient until he had broken them down. He would hammer at their frailties, their weak points, until they were groveling, destroyed. I would have found it totally humiliating. I understand the technique, but he always seemed unnecessarily cruel. Fritz was a showman who loved to demonstrate his skills, to poke around in people. Like a gourmet cook, trying out a new recipe, getting a kick out of it—no sympathy.

CLAUDIO NARANJO
Fritz hated neurosis and people who evidenced these neurotic facades. Since everybody is neurotic more or less, he hated everybody more or less. He was hard on people and would

have his psychic orgasms only at the moments of unmasking, in the therapeutic explosion. That can be done with and without love. I saw him do it both ways. There was a lot of that mixture of hardness and softness in him.

LEO ZEFF
I've seen him in social situations where he was just rotten and cruel in his responses to people. If he was feeling mean, he could look at someone and say, "I don't like you and I don't care what the hell you like." I guess he was antagonistic towards any woman who refused him. I know two women who did, and he was really down on them.

JIM SIMKIN
He was cruel and vindictive. When Fritz got burned he felt put upon, taken advantage of, and he would deny any responsibility for having set it up. It was the other guy's fault. He always looked for a fall guy.

ANNI FRAZIER
He made people see themselves in a different way, and that

could make them see him as cruel or frightening. But I see him like an enzyme or catalyst, bringing people into a more clear state. He could make them put themselves through hell. He wasn't being cruel—he saw what they needed.

MICHAEL ALEXANDER

You had to like the dirty old bastard . . . a perfect dichotomy. He was like a father, a patriarch, but you had to resent the guy too. There was that remote quality about Fritz; I think this was one of the ways he protected himself. He seemed able to be a fully human being only when he was in charge of one of those groups. On the outside he was very push-away, it was just impossible to talk to the son of a bitch.

BERNARD GUNTHER

There was a fear of losing himself, of being taken over by the role, by people. In a sense, gestalt was Fritz' defense. He was very alive when he was working, when he was directing.

BARRY STEVENS

The people who think of him as cruel are perceiving him that way. This is actually misperception, of course. What we do in our heads with our thinking makes us see everything cock-eyed quite often. One way that you really can change people is to see them in a different way.

When he would say, "Are you aware of what you are doing?" people would invariably stop what they were doing. All Fritz was asking was, "Are you aware?" and that was all. It's so easy to take that as criticism, as though you are doing something wrong.

ANDY CURRY

I only saw him bludgeon one person. This girl was obviously psychotic and just up there to wiggle her titties. The myth is that he said, "This woman is dead and I choose not to work with her." What I heard him say was, "This woman doesn't wish to work. Is there someone else who does?" He dismissed her, and she crumbled. The person next to me said,

"That motherfucker, did you see what he did?" I said, "All he did was lay it on her, right out, stone clean. If you don't want to play, take your marbles and go home."

WERNER ERHARD
People think that if I pat them on the ass and blow in their ear I'm being humane. To consider that they are less than able, to support that, is *not* humane. . . .

BOB SHAPIRO
Most of the time Fritz' position was that his energy was to be used to help well people get weller, and maybe the marginal people, too, but he'd walk away from what he called "crazy people." I understand his set of values. To spend the time and energy and effort on somebody that was that far out would require being with them continuously for six to twelve months, and Fritz was not willing to spend that kind of time.

ROSEMARY FEITIS
I once asked Julian Silverman what he meant by cruelty and he told me this story. Fritz was sitting having his breakfast and there's a woman opposite him trying to tell him about her son who's crippled in some dreadful way. I think he was mentally deficient or something like that. Some dreadful story. And Fritz says, "Go away. You're bothering me." That's not cruelty. That's a man having his breakfast. *She* was being cruel—insensitive, intrusive and cruel at the very least. Of course, one of the mechanisms of that sort of thing is, "I give you all my power, but if you use it against me, you're terrible." Bullshit!

DON BABCOCK
Fritz could be very, very hard on people because he didn't care about the repercussions. There were no repercussions as far as he was concerned. His hardness always had an objective; he meant it to bring you around to some form of reality, to stop you from playing the social games.

There is a story about a man who went to a Zen master and

wanted to be enlightened. Without a word the master walked with him into the river. Suddenly, with both his hands, he pushed the man's head under the water and held him down. The man struggled and finally freed himself and came up gasping. The Zen master said, "When you want to be enlightened as badly as you want to breathe, come to me— not before," and he walked away.

I felt Fritz' loving quality was expressed very deeply in his ability to hurt you. I see it as a manifestation of caring. He was not going to accept anything but the best in you. That's how he expressed it. He was uncompromising.

STEWART EMERY

People thought Fritz was heartless; he wasn't interested in that esoteric stuff, he was interested in results. He attacked the person's shit, not them.

BETTY FULLER

I don't know where the expression "wipe your own ass" originated, but Fritz said it out of love and knowing you are totally capable of doing that. His gift was to give you back yourself.

JAMES FADIMAN

Once Fritz was giving an evening at San Francisco State, demonstrating his gestalt dream routine, using volunteers from the audience. A young man who had organized it was a S.F. State student, about age 25, who later went very heavily into gestalt. He asked us if we would come with him and have dinner with Fritz beforehand, because he said, "I'm afraid of him and I really don't want to be alone with him. And you don't seem to be afraid of him.''

So we all went and had dinner at a lovely little Japanese restaurant that Fritz knew of near the opera. Fritz told us he used to come up from Big Sur and live in a cheap hotel during the opera season. He'd go to all the operas and then go back down to Big Sur.

We had a delightful, easygoing, charming evening so that my friend's fear was not necessarily justified. But Fritz did have a way of imposing himself that threatened a lot of people and they responded negatively to what he was trying to help them with.

SEYMOUR CARTER
Fritz, I felt, played hard gestalt morning, noon and night. Some woman said when she lived with him in his house that she got tired of gestalt for breakfast, gestalt for lunch and gestalt for dinner. To me, there were times when it's appropriate to say wipe your own ass and times not. Sometimes I felt that Fritz did it too much.

I'll say things to someone in therapy or under a therapeutic contract that I will not say as a friend. I isolate the therapeutic contract into a setting of the interview. I am not interested in taking what goes on there outside of that.

Yet, if one accepts the view that gestalt is a way of life, isn't it possible that it isn't a therapeutic moment, it's the way one lives? Fritz was Fritz, not a guy playing therapist but a guy who lived gestalt.

For him, maybe that was true, for me it was not true.

ALEXANDER LOWEN
You don't normally use your psychological knowledge in personal social relationships. You give the person all the benefit of being—and this is important in a social relationship—of being all there and responding. It's only in a professional relationship or when you're not on the level of

friends, with a certain conflict in the situation that you become more careful and size a person up more exactly.

It's a funny thing: Anybody who worked with Reich and who was strongly influenced by Reich, takes away with him a sense of the reality of human beings, which was probably Reich's greatest contribution—his concept of character analysis. You don't get pulled in by big language and theoretical or psychological ideas—you can see the reality of the person. Of course, Reich had developed this; Fritz used it very much, and we use it very much. It distinguishes these two approaches from all the others. The gestalt people, however, don't work enough with the character, as we do, but they're somewhat aware of present-day attitudes and the way you express yourself on a body level. This is where I think Perls went off—having had the exposure to Reich's character-analytic concepts—he never followed up on Reich's development of functional thinking.

LAURA PERLS

Fritz was impressed with Reich, but became critical later. Reich was still a psychoanalyst when we were in South Africa, even with all the bioenergetic stuff that he started to develop. He had been analyzed by Ferenzi, the Hungarian analyst who developed the resistance concept, but with the emphasis on anal resistance—a contraction of the rectum which prevented letting something out and eventually resulting in constipation and so on. Reich saw the character as armor, which is actually fixed through muscular contractions. Fritz and I both came to the understanding that muscular tensions are the way all repressions and inhibitions are produced and fixed.

GIDEON SCHWARZ

I once heard Fritz explain the difference between gestalt and Reichian therapy, in theory, as something the seeds of which were already in Reich but not realized fully by him—and that is that the armor is made out of the same stuff as the energies

underneath which you want to get at. Since a lot of such
energies are invested in the armor, it is a mistake to break the
armor and just throw it away. What Fritz adds to the
Reichian therapy is to have you re-identify with the armoring
part and feel it again. As I saw happen so often, he had you
go into the resistance and *be* the resisting thing. Someone
would say, in effect, "I'm trying to go into what you tell me
but all I have is a blank wall," and Fritz would say, "Be that
blank wall." The very definite logic behind this is that the
wall is like a frozen piece of that person's personality, which
you cannot just break and throw the pieces away. You have
to infuse it with life, make it pliable again, and this you can
only do by having the person identify with the wall so that he
now feels himself *as* the wall—*his* body is the wall. Then, as
the wall, he begins to soften gradually until there is no wall
any more.

Some people come to a group feeling that to tell something
about themselves is to give something, that hearing someone
else tell about himself is getting something; and so they want
to be sure that first they get, before they give. It does happen—like, "I want to sit here and see you all expose yourselves, but you will never find out about me." But in gestalt
work no one who does not want to work would ever be
forced into the hot seat. In Synanon encounter groups, they
do use the idea of ganging up on one person and "breaking"
him. This concept of "breaking" is definitely not accepted
by gestaltists, and the reason has to do with the difference
between gestalt and Reichian therapy. Reichians have the
concept of armor, expressed physically as muscular armor,
and, psychologically, as character armor. Reich says, you
cannot reach deep into a person therapeutically until this ar-

mor is broken, and this idea has been taken over by approaches like Synanon, who use this "breaking" concept.

Fritz saw this concept of "breaking" as wrong. It may seem effective when something happens to a tough guy with a very clear plastic-made external character, and he gets shook up and cries, and there's this image of breaking out of a mask to freedom. But that's wrong—it's not pieces that fall away, it's parts of yourself you want to *re*-integrate into your organism, where, hopefully, they come to life again. You see, the armor is a dead part of your own energy, a part you have disowned and frozen in some way. You have to re-own the energies that went into the armor, and turn them back into living tissue.

MICHAEL ALEXANDER
The therapy Fritz developed worked because of Fritz; it was the perfect therapy for him. It demanded that the individual take more responsibility for his or her behavior than any other therapy I've ever seen.

LEO ZEFF
In his presence and under his scrutiny on the hot seat, I absolutely couldn't lie, I couldn't deceive and I couldn't color. Whatever he asked me to look at, I looked at for what it really and truly was. Anytime I came out honest with him, I went away higher than a kite, feeling great and better able to do that kind of thing in my own work, too.

As far as I am concerned, there is only one experience in life worth having, and that's the experience of loving, not being loved. Lots of people love me. That's great, that's fine. I appreciate that but I get my kicks out of loving someone, as I loved Fritz. That's where I get my kicks. There were occasions, though, when Fritz left me dying on the vine. He could have rescued me with one kind word, but that would have been the worst thing for me. He left me swimming in my shit until I climbed out of it and could handle it. Many times I saw him bringing people out of deep holes of great misery into enlightenment, brightness and into that feeling of love.

He was really willing to share himself when it was appropriate and no big deal. He was there. He didn't bullshit at all. He shared himself a lot, but there's no question that he withheld himself a lot, too.

Fritz got people to express the reality of themselves, so that all of the other considerations and all the judgments somehow or other dissolved. And facing what you've been avoiding all the time, everything is all right again. Paranoia is the opposite of that.

BETTY FULLER

It's really fun to talk about him . . . I don't think I ever really acknowledged to myself before, the extent to which I love that man. He was a wise fool, like the fool of the tarot, just ready to walk off a cliff. He had that *total* freedom of nonattachment and absolute joy and freedom. Ecstasy is what I think he experienced much of the time, just true nirvana. When everything's gone, love is. And love *is:* that's all you can say about it. And that's what Fritz was to me.

CHARLOTTE ROSNER

He was very much like a Zen master. I was taking him out for the day; he was visiting Chicago (that's where I'm from). I wouldn't exactly say it was a pleasure to take him out. In fact, it was a terrible chore to take him out. I took him to the Science and Industry Museum. He was very much like a child there. He would try everything. What really tickled him the most: He tested his hearing and found out that he had very good hearing. "See! My hearing isn't going; I *still* have good hearing!" And he danced away—"I can still hear!" He became very much like a child.

SHALOM NEWMAN

Well, it is not exactly a child. There is the whole Faustian Mephistophelean motif of really trying again, and always renewing your youth through women. That is very much what I got out of him—the whole idea of finding your youth again and preserving it. This is straight out of *Faust*.

CHARLOTTE ROSNER

We finally went to lunch, and I started to ask him questions about gestalt. He wouldn't answer. He ignored me in a very cold kind of a way, and then he turned around and picked up a fork and put it in front of me and said, "What if two people were walking down this path, see, from either end, and it's very narrow, and they meet each other in the center and there's no way of passing—what would happen?" And I thought, and I gave a few answers, and he kept shaking his head, "No, no." And I'd make up something—"No, no." We went on for quite a while and I felt very frustrated. I said, "OK, Fritz. Tell me what would happen." He said, "Look!" I said, "I don't see anything." He says, "That's your problem, you don't see the fork." And that finished the conversation.

We left the restaurant and I realized there was no way of reaching this man with words. I took his hand and I said, "Come on, Fritz. Let's skip down the street." Both of us just skipped down, without words. He put his arm around me and I put my arm around him and we just went off. We reached that "I-Thou" place simply by the moving together.

Now: Nothing can possibly exist except the present moment and those who make a program out of it, negate it. Now is the zero point; it is nothingness . . . Fritz advocated being in the present moment of time as a way of life. In its simplicity, it has the essence of ancient and contemporary wisdom: Be here now, to thine own self be true, Buddhists' timelessness, the zero point, the fertile void, being free from the traumatic experiences that inhibit us. . . .

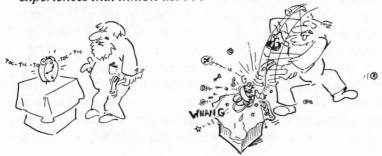

GEORGE LEONARD

One time when I arrived at Esalen Fritz rushed out in great excitement and said, "I've invented a word to describe you—*anastroph!* I took it from the Greek. It's the opposite of *catastroph,* and it's just as bad!" He talked about catastrophic expectations taking you out of the here and now. Anastrophic expectations, he told me, meant having some fixed, utopian goal that also takes you away from the now and takes you away from yourself. In his work after that, Fritz used *anastrophic* and *catastrophic* expectation as being of the same cloth; they both remove you from the existential moment.

EDWARD ROSENFELD

Living in the present, the eternal now, is where a great deal of the mythical, religious outlook toward life centers: Tibetan Buddhists, Zen Buddhists, Taoists, some of the Hindu tantric traditions. So I see a convergence there that Fritz used and was able to make very Western. We need American systems, and I think Fritz did something typically Western. . . European-American . . . and unique, tapping off some of that Eastern influence.

GIDEON SCHWARZ

One feature of gestalt therapy is that it is always appropriate to interrupt everything, and ask what is happening *now*. At any moment anyone in the group, including the patient and the therapist, can say, "Yes, but what is going on now?" and this has priority over anything else.

It's a very here-and-now oriented therapy, both in that Fritz uses the here-and-now as a technique, and in that he regards the availability of the here-and-now as the end one wants to achieve. Neuroses, or hang-ups, or blocks, or whatever term people want to use, express themselves as things which invariably diminish one's capability of being in the present. Some people are disturbed over things that happened three hours earlier, others by things when they were babies. It doesn't matter; the common thing is that they are not in the present. People who live in the future all the time, also have no present available to them. They're very anxious people. There can be pain in the present, but concern about the future is the only thing that can cause real anxiety.

STEWART EMERY

Fritz was very pragmatic rather than esoteric about it all. He was very much into getting people to live their lives in the current passage of time. He also had a commitment to liberating people from using other people's expectations of them to suppress themselves.

MICHAEL MURPHY

His judgments on the religious, mystical, Eastern dimension were negative. Fritz said, "Meditation is neither shitting nor getting off the pot," and that is to totally misapprehend meditation; but for a lot of people that's just what it is.

CLAUDIO NARANJO

Truly, he was a fallible individual who could lead you astray as well as lead you to a higher understanding of yourself. For instance, I think he misled people concerning his attitude toward meditation, which he seemed to repudiate. Not many people know this but Fritz actually meditated every day. He told me once in passing, "Today, as I was meditating before the workshop, such and such a thing came to my mind." And I said, "Do you meditate?" "Oh, yes!" "How long? A half hour, an hour?" "At least," he said.

For him, of course, meditation was no different from gestalt. What he did when he meditated was to suspend thinking and stay aware of his experiences in the ever-flowing present.

JANET LEDERMAN

I don't know if it's because of seeing him originally in the context of an old man who was lonely, but I never got into a fear trip with him. I made contact with a somebody rather than with a Fritz Perls. Something really happened in initial-

ly seeing each other. After that the roles were often reversed
between us. When he got into his terrific despair here, I had
just written *Anger and the Rocking Chair.* He read it and
jumped up and he said, "Aha! Now I know the way out of
despair!" Up he went to the top of the hill. The next day he
came down: He had started *Garbage Pail.*

*Janet, isn't that a contradiction to Fritz' teaching? Wasn't it
his teaching to go into the despair?*

Yes, that's OK if you want to be a theoretician. I think that's
been bastardized. Sure, you go in, but you can either stay
forever, which some people interpret as going into your
despair, or you can go in for a second, feel the full pain of it,
and do something, which is what he did. . . .

Anyway, that's the way we related. We talked very little.
There was a sensing as opposed to a talking-about. Somehow
with Fritz, it was always very easy to offer up my vulnerabili-
ty. That goes back to the poem about the little bird. I didn't
have to protect myself and he didn't protect himself. We
could be very vulnerable with each other knowing that those
little fragile places were not being stepped on. A trust.

*Evidently there was a moment of decision in Fritz' life
where, after some vacillation about whether he wanted to be
Fritz or to be famous, he decided to be both.*

BERNARD GUNTHER

There was a part of Fritz that feared becoming famous. I think he was afraid that becoming famous might destroy him. One day (and I remember this because I used it once in a public introduction of him) he said, "You know, Bernie, today I've decided that I can handle becoming one of the truly great psychotherapists who ever lived."

Fritz was a very egocentric man. That's not a value judgment, that's the way he was. I saw Fritz as a director even more than a therapist. He was a man who loved dramatics and he demanded legitimate responses from his actors.

John O. Stevens is the owner of Real People Press, the firm that eventually published Fritz' Gestalt Therapy Verbatim *and* In and Out the Garbage Pail. . . .

JOHN STEVENS

At a four-week workshop in 1968, I was very interested to find out that Rosemary Feitis and Teddy Lyons, who had been working on transcribing some of his weekend demonstrations, had pretty much dropped it. Rosemary was typing *Garbage Pail,* and Teddy was into something else.

I picked up the project and started transcribing tapes like crazy, and that's what *Gestalt Therapy Verbatim* grew out of. Fritz never talked long on theory—it might be three or four or a dozen sentences on one topic—maybe twenty or forty in a big lecture thing. I'd collect his mini-lectures on a single subject and try to bring them all together, eliminating the repetitions. I did have to graft sentences, but it wasn't too hard and I didn't change much.

I did that book as a labor of love with the idea that Fritz would publish it, but by the time it was done I had my own publishing business going. I told him I'd like to publish it and he said, "OK." I mailed it down to him in Big Sur and then got a letter back, "I like it. Come on down. Let's talk about it."

He had Teddy Lyons and Ginny Sutton read the manuscript through carefully. He was too much into writing *Garbage Pail* at that time to be bothered with something that was already done. But he was happy with it and, I think, a little astonished. He said it was OK for me to publish it. Both of the books we did for him came out in 1969: *Verbatim* in July and *Garbage Pail* in December. He was very pleased to see them come out, always asking, "What are the sales?"

He was like a little kid when he was writing *Garbage Pail.* He'd do two or three pages, make a few copies, and run around shoving them into everybody's hands, saying, "What do you think about this?" Just like a little kid with a new scribble, looking for attention. Everybody loved it.

JIM SIMKIN

He was very fond of bragging. He would write a few pages of his autobiography and nab everybody in the dining room to read it. He was asking for admiration. Fritz didn't ask for criticism; he didn't take criticism at all well. He was asking for admiration.

GEORGE LEONARD

I remember with great joy that when Fritz was half finished with *In and Out the Garbage Pail,* he asked me if I would read the manuscript. I took it down to the baths and spent one whole morning reading it, and I really loved it. Then he came down and we had a very warm talk. I presented all my appreciation of the manuscript. He wanted to hear my critique. As I recall, I had maybe one substantive thing to say and two or three things on typos and style.

He welcomed what I had to say. It was one of the last talks I had with him, because he left not long after that. It was a beautiful, sunny morning, and he told me again how amazing it was to him, ". . .me, a little Jewish boy, all this fame is coming to!"

Fritz himself says:

> *I am keen to have people read [the] manuscript in my presence, to experience their participation. I need much*

affirmation. If I would exclusively write for myself I would leave out much of the theoretical stuff and I want to get that across.

NATALIE MANN
He was reading at my house from the manuscript, before the book came out. He wanted feedback. It was the first time he exposed it. I was so moved by how he was reading, I asked if I could make a tape recording.

VIRGINIA SATIR
Fritz' pride and his fear of intimacy kept him from having close relationships with his children. He was to his children what his father had been to him. You can emulate a poor model without meaning to. . . .

LAURA PERLS
Fritz loved children when he didn't have any responsibility for them, the same way he loved animals. Jim Simkin's children and the children of some people in Canada took him as the only grandfather they ever had, but his own grandchildren never had a grandfather in Fritz.

Leslie Gold, Renate and Art Gold's daughter, is fair and twenty-one and smiles easily and talks comfortably and at one point I remember her dancing, spinning around and moving her arms in the tiny garden in New York where we met. She's a high-spirited, red-haired lovely girl. I liked her very much. So I'm with Fritz who wrote in Garbage Pail:

> *The fact is that I like Leslie very much, a cute and bright copperhead. There is something real about her in contrast to her mother's and sister's insincerity.*

She spoke, that day, with an underlying edge of sadness. . . .

LESLIE GOLD

I'm Fritz Perls' granddaughter. Sometimes I try to impress people by telling them I'm related to him, but many people haven't even heard of gestalt therapy. Those who have are impressed at first, but then I think, "So what? What have I got to do with that? Nothing."

I know very little about gestalt therapy myself. I think I tried to keep it away because I wasn't very attached to my grandfather. I've just let it seep in by talking to my mother and my grandmother who is so deeply involved with gestalt therapy.

I don't remember much about my childhood experiences with my grandfather, except that every time I think about those times I get a warm and happy impression. One vivid memory I do have occurred when I was six or seven years old and we were living in New Jersey. Grandfather, my sister and I put on some sort of little dance—a little play—and we dressed him up in a petticoat!

When I think about him now most of my feelings are ambivalent. I wanted a warm, friendly, Santa Claus-type of grandfather but he seemed to be very much into each person's independence, certainly his own. Personally, I like to be much more involved with people, more loving; I don't think he had that in him—or at least he didn't show it as much as I would have liked—although he seemed to care for me when I was a child. His attitude changed as I grew older. Perhaps I feel this way because there were long periods when I didn't have any contact with him.

From New Jersey, Grandfather moved to Florida and then to California. I was in the seventh grade when he came to visit us in New York. He impressed me as being very intellectual; everyone, including Grandmother and the people who came to see him, sat around talking about things that were way beyond my understanding. I felt uncomfortable and left out; in fact, I was never able to communicate with people in Grandmother's and Grandfather's crowd. During his stay in New York, Grandfather hardly paid any attention to me. It didn't seem to make any difference to him if I was his granddaughter or just another piece of furniture.

I didn't see him again until 1967 or 1968, when I was in the eleventh grade. When he was in New York he crashed at my Grandmother's place, and he seemed to me to be taking advantage of her. During this visit I tried to communicate with him but I was very uptight. His new book, *In and Out the Garbage Pail,* had just been published and he was interested in showing me the drawings in the book. I wanted to please him, and sat down to look through the book. When he left the room I asked Grandmother, "Do you think I could ask him for the book? Do you think he'd give it to me?"

I was afraid to ask Grandfather because I was still insecure about our relationship. Anyway, Grandmother told me I would just have to ask *him.* Let me tell you, it took every bit of nerve I had to ask Grandfather for that copy of his book, and all he said was,

"No, you can't have it. It's the only copy I have."

And I thought, "Fuck you, too," and that was that. That was the last contact I had with Fritz Perls.

LAURA PERLS

He had just one copy of it. Perhaps he didn't really want her to read it; after all, he had written about the family in it, but she didn't realize that. She just felt complete rejection.

RENATE PERLS
I remember when Art and I were living in an apartment in
Englewood, Fritz and the children would dress up and put on
theater productions. Art, Ma and I would sit and watch Fritz
and the two girls act out some little thing. They had a great
deal of fun.

*The French poet Baudelaire said that genius is nothing more
or less than childhood recovered at will—a childhood now
equipped for self-expression. At times Fritz epitomized this
recovered childhood. . . .*

STELLA RESNICK
Fritz was a clown. One time at Halloween, he put on a gorilla
mask and he got into being a gorilla, jumping all over the
place and hanging on the refrigerator. He was so funny,
everybody was screaming and laughing.

*And so, of course, Fritz did get along well with most chil-
dren. . . .*

NATALIE EDNIE
On Halloween someone had given Adam, who was three, a
mask and told him to scare Fritz, who was sitting at the dining room table reading. Adam walked up and said, "Boo."
No response. Adam tried again. This time, Fritz looked up
and said, "That's not good enough," and went back to his
reading. Adam paused a moment, gathered all his energy behind the mask and let out a frightful roar. Fritz then was
properly scared.

VIRGINIA HOROWITZ

We were the only people on the grounds with children. At that point in his life, Fritz didn't enjoy children. One of the people in the workshop complained at a meeting about something our children had done. And Fritz said, "I like these kids. I suggest that if you're having any trouble with them you look into yourself." He changed his rules when he wanted to . . . that's the lovely part of being in charge.

ROBERT HALL

He used to stay with us a lot at our house in Mill Valley. He loved the kids a lot so he'd be there for Christmas and birthday parties. He'd give them each a ten-dollar bill. Blew my mind. They loved him.

WILSON VAN DUSEN

He was good to our children. They both have fond memories of his taking them uptown and buying them toys.

BEVERLY KORT

My grandfather died when I was young and Fritz was like a kind and gentle grandfather to me. I found him to be a very "unadult" type of adult and I loved every minute I spent with him.

ANNI FRAZIER

He was very good with children—and that's what I was, a child, and I think he saw me as that. He wasn't forcing me to grow up, as a lot of people around there were.

Anni Frazier is a concert pianist, a professional ballet dancer, a model, a yoga master and an artist.

I was fifteen when I moved to Big Sur and I'd be at Esalen at times . . . I would come and work for my meals and stay around and help out. Sometimes, when I didn't have any place to sleep, I would sleep on the refrigerator. It was incredibly warm up there.

I got to meet and know people, and Fritz was one of the people I would see every time I came there. He was so powerful everybody had some kind of really intricate relationship with him. I knew him in a quiet way. Every time I'd see him, he'd be very warm and loving; he'd ask me how I was and if everything was OK, and he'd embrace me and be really kind. He'd just be close to me. Sometimes he would not say anything.

He loved to bake; he used to bake a lot in the kitchen and he'd make this really fantastic Russian dessert. It was like a yeast cake but it had lines going through it, chocolate or something, and raisins. He'd do it late at night when nobody was around. He'd come in and set up all his goodies. I'd end up sitting in the kitchen with Fritz, watching him go through all his baking things. He really was amusing. He'd put on this little show, like a comedian, like a chef on television. He'd be really funny and he'd bake away and then it would come out and I got to eat some of it with him. It was super-delicious. He loved it, too.

He could be very funny and somehow instructive at the same time. For example, I would say, "How are you?" just for small talk and he'd say, "How *am* I? *How* am I?" He'd repeat it a bunch of times and he'd put the question back in my own head, and I really had to examine what it meant when you asked somebody, "How are you?" How bullshit that is! Or else I'd say, "Good morning," and he'd go, "Good . . . (pause) . . . morning," and he'd repeat it like that, with a question mark after the good, or he'd come down hard when he said the last syllable of morning.

I felt Fritz was very protective toward people, like a father . . . I was a child, a young girl on my own . . . and all those trips were going down around Esalen. I appeared really naive. I was at the age where I was feeling so many things and sometimes I didn't know what I was seeing or feeling.

There were people lechering after me. He didn't. He would make me feel I didn't have to reply to all the come-ons in order to be a complete entity. He was comforting and protective in many ways.

I just felt a really loving, open thing with Fritz. Really a lot of kindness. Fritz made it appear to me: "No, you don't have to go through promiscuous sex to grow up. Growing up has to do with the spirit's evolution. It doesn't have to do with jumping in and out of somebody's bed." It was just a seed planted. He could see what people needed. He saw what I needed. He was far out, and very beautiful.

I can see his eyes and everything in my mind right now as we're talking. He wasn't afraid to look at people in their eyes. Now it's a fad to look into people's eyes and see the truth, but it wasn't a fad then. It was just natural for him. He would look into your eyes and there wasn't that much to talk about. The truth was there. He was very beautiful.

EDWARD ROSENFELD

When I was in my late teens and early twenties, I was very aware of our burgeoning generation. I mean, I come from a very powerful generation; we made great changes in the society. And I looked around and I saw a variety of dissipated old people. Then, in one year, I had contact with Fritz and with Bucky Fuller. Meeting them made me realize that you don't have to dissipate and fall apart when you get older. I was able to see in their personal life as well as the theoretical stuff that I saw on paper, there was constant revision, constant change, and constant reconsideration of what they were thinking about and what they're doing.

Tim Leary, referring to the psychedelicization of America, said in 1966, "It's over. We won." He was right, though everybody said he was crazy. An apex had been reached and from then on it was just fallout. I think the same thing happened in 1971 and '72 when all the humanistic programs being given anywhere always included gestalt. It's had a very profound, very pervasive effect on humanistic psychology. I see Fritz as having a lasting influence.

JEAN GRAHAM

To me his genius was in his understanding of the techniques of how to stay in the "now," and his ability to communicate that "now" to us. His greatness is perhaps that the therapists who follow him are more effective than he, as therapists. His genius is in the originating and the ability to communicate what he knew. For he was genius . . . Is! His genius is not past tense. It is with us yet, growing greater through the ones he trained.

JANET WULLNER FAISS
Fritz Perls was like a man who longs all his life for the "Great Experience." Toward the end of life he faces the fact that it hasn't come, it will never come . . . or it may have been here all along. In any case, he feels somehow cheated. That was how Fritz Perls looked to me then, not mellow, but as though cheated.

". . .us carnival performers. . . ."

STANLEY KELEMAN
When a girl friend of mine died and I was really distraught, I walked into Fritz' room unannounced.

"Vot are you doing here?"

"I really got to talk to you."

"Sit down," he said, and we talked for about twenty minutes.

He gave me some feeling of how to deal with the death, and then he said a very extraordinary thing to me, "Us carnival performers share a common destiny"—meaning we group leaders and wandering Jews share the pain of alienation, the pain of aloneness. We go around helping others, and yet here we are in our own pain.

So that's what I can tell you about Fritz, who I thought was a frightened, shy, scared, caring and generous person capable of feeling very humiliated, paranoiac and defensive. That was my experience with him. Whatever Fritz was, Fritz was. He was a man.

CLAUDIO NARANJO
I would say Fritz was an unusually enlightened man in spite of all his psychopathology. There *is* such a phenomenon, a

certain path of spiritual progression in which the garbage is not eliminated but it seems to shine brighter and brighter. His kind of holiness seemed to be the reverse of what we generally picture as holiness because it meant being so much more open to craziness, and encompassing it. He identified very much with the figure of the fool and the court jester. He was an example of what Alan Watts called the "wisdom of insecurity": the path of not resisting what might be termed "wrong" and, through it, attaining a more transcendent "rightness."

I experience Fritz as a divine gift, not just to individuals who knew and worked with him but, at the cultural level, as a pivot of transformation. As Alan Watts was a cultural hero at the intellectual level, Fritz was the same at the doing level of directly impinging on lives to an extent that is now being forgotten. People are beginning to give credit to everybody but him.

JOE WYSONG

Fritz was a proselytizer and what he was proselytizing was the way to live. His way of doing it was outrageous. Once, at a convention, Fritz was asked to make a presentation on Existential Therapy. His total presentation was a poem:

> *I'm not a lady performing her farts,*
> *I'm a scoundrel, a lover of arts,*
> *I am who I am,*
> *I screw when I can.*
> *I'm Popeye the Sailor Man.*

You can't get more existential than that!

To me that is the epitome of what Fritz was all about. He walks into a situation where they're expecting straight stuff, and he goes "Bompf!" It's that way of dealing with people. You put a bomb in front of some of them. That's the way you give the message. Fritz did that.

* * *

*As the '60s drew to a close, Fritz moved towards a new
beginning. . . .*

JIM SIMKIN
At Esalen Fritz claimed he had finally found what he was
looking for—a community he could identify with, a place
where he was recognized. And that lasted less than a year.*
He was fed up and angry with what was going on at Esalen.
He was also itching to change.

LAURA PERLS
I think he experienced permanence as pressure. Esalen became a kind of three-ring circus and he didn't like it anymore. Of course, he had helped to turn it on and, like the
sorcerer's apprentice, he didn't know how to turn it off! Ya,
he didn't really know what he was setting loose. Ya, it became such a circus. So big. So many people he wasn't really
interested in being or working with. Everybody wanted to be
little Fritzes. That's why he left Esalen.

RICHARD PRICE
His leaving Esalen in part resulted from his discouragement
over this place. But not completely. He felt that there was a
muddle of too much bullshit coming in here. He felt that
Mike and I were not selective enough. And he probably
wished to give a strong impetus to his work without the competition of encounter and sensory awakening and all the
other things going on here.

---
*Actually, he moved to Esalen in 1964 and left in 1969.

MICHAEL MURPHY
There was his growing disenchantment that we were a three-ring circus instead of a one-ring circus; we wanted to keep an open forum. And also he had a lifelong dream of creating his own kibbutz or gestalt community.

RICHARD PRICE
And another reason he was afraid was that with General Curtis LeMay running for Vice President on the American Party ticket, and Nixon nominated on the Republican ticket, America was becoming too much like nazi Germany in 1930; that this was the time to get out of the country. I gave him my personal support in leaving Esalen. I thought it was a good idea. It was what he wanted. He had my full blessing.

MICHAEL MURPHY
He was truly concerned, I would say semi-paranoid about the political situation. He thought that if Nixon was elected there would be some kind of fascism. He claimed he had an instinct for fascism . . . and he said it was going to happen again. I'm not convinced it's paranoia at all. Paranoia is reality in our day and age.

JACK ROSENBERG
I remember just before Fritz left Esalen I was lying in the sun down in the baths with him, and he turns over and starts talking. He had a newspaper in his hand and he read that they were going to require social security numbers be placed

on drivers' licenses. He threw the paper down and said, "I knew my hunch was right! I know that the fascists are here. They are giving numbers now. It happened in Germany. . . ." And then he went into a long tirade of how he could smell fascism. I didn't feel like he was talking to me or to anybody there, but he was really into this thing of how he could smell fascism, and he knew it was coming. I think it was before Nixon was elected. "If he's elected then we're going to have it here and I'm getting out of here; I've already made plans." And, of course, when Watergate was going on, I was aware that Fritz had told me it was happening . . . it was like he really did know.

JACK DOWNING

When Reagan and Nixon came in, Fritz was sure that fascism was coming to this country. I argued with him. "You just don't know the United States," I said. "I know fascism," he said.

VIRGINIA SATIR

I think he recognized the Hitler aspects of Nixon. Fritz was very sensitive to people in power positions that came off like Nixon did. I don't think it was anything specific. I think it was Fritz' good grasp of the national manipulation. He really felt that. This was in the whole period when there was beginning to be such a paranoid air around the country. It was also a time when there was all the talk about surveillance, phone- and wire-tapping and money being monitored. It was also during the Vietnam war. That was very crucial. Remember how much the activists were being put down?

Fritz told people that he could smell fascism coming, that he had developed a good nose for totalitarian threats. . . .

LAURA PERLS

Yes, but not perfect. Neither he, nor anyone else at the time, anticipated the destruction of the Jews, but simply the nazi takeover in Germany. He did correctly anticipate a kind of fascist regime in South Africa, and in 1968 he went to Canada because he anticipated the inflation here and the take-over by the Nixon crowd and Reagan. In a sense, he antic-ipated Watergate and all of this, not in detail, of course, but the climate. And he didn't want to stay and risk either his freedom or his money, which were relatively considerable by that time.

STEPHEN PERLS

In 1968, my father was thinking of going to Czechoslovakia. That was two or three months before Russia invaded Czechoslovakia. He thought things were becoming fascistic in this country, with Nixon being elected and the kinds of appointments he was making, and what was happening with militant activities and the suppression on college campuses. It was all reminscent of what he had been through in Ger-many, and he just wanted to get out of the country.

JIM SIMKIN

It gets a little into his paranoia—his prediction about polit-ical things. One of the so-called reasons Fritz left Esalen was that Nixon had been elected president and Fritz saw fascism coming.

CLAUDIO NARANJO

He was a very courageous person. He had what people call "paranoid" thoughts because he was concerned about the political system and about America going fascistic. But if people choose to call paranoia what is fact, it only speaks of people's blindness. Isn't it fact that America has moved into a more and more fascistic direction?

His withdrawing from nazi Germany, South Africa, and America can be called "withdrawing." It can also be called "moving towards," depending on what end. I think that was plain wisdom. I don't think that's fearful; I think it's legitimate to move to a place where you can work better.

> *"Kaleidoscope of living." Breakfast. Nixon won on the first ballot. Anybody interested in politics?*
>
> *Very peculiar morning. I felt in a desperate mood— silly, unnecessary demands. Smoked a lot, lots of heartbeats missing. Wanted to withdraw, sent Teddy away. . . .*

ROBERT HALL

He said to me he thought the country was headed toward a civil war and a fascist government. "If you need a place to hide," he said, "come to Canada." This was in 1969. He advised Alyssa and me to have a few thousand dollars in cash hidden away in the house and to have our passports ready and to be able to flee the country within a minute. We listened to him—he had been through it. We did all this. We did listen to him. We still do.

BOB SHAPIRO

This was Fritz' analysis and everybody listened very carefully, because he was the man with the most experience in how to evaluate what was going on politically and when it was time to leave., He was five years ahead of his time. Just this year (1974) the government said you can't take more than $5,000 out of the country without reporting it—another indication of the beginning of financial control. This type of regulation was one reason why six million Jews stayed in Germany. They had no money they could take out and no place to go, no way to get out. The ones who got out were the ones who did a Fritz Perls and left with whatever assets possible—or none. It was his message. It wasn't necessarily anti-Semitism. It was anti-freedom.

He had the wisdom of applying gestalt to politics and events that few people have had. For example, in August of '68, when the riots were on in Chicago, it was also the time of the AHP meeting in San Francisco. There Fritz said, in effect, from his experience this was that, the beginning of the end, that it was really the beginning of American Fascism. He talked about his experience fleeing Germany into Holland, figuring that was the place to be free, and then finding out that was no longer the place to be free, and then going down to Africa, which was kind of the golden age part of his experience. Then he fled Africa and came to America where he believed there was freedom. And now, in 1968, his keen observation was that with the riots in Chicago this was the first time in the U.S. that power became anonymous. The police took off their badges so nobody would know who they were and they broke up television cameras. The press had its films confiscated without trial by jury or anything else—just by power. Fritz said, "Ach, for me, this is the final decision. Ve must leave America."

That's when he decided Australia and Canada were the only remaining places to go, though he felt that Australia seemed very far away. Very shortly after that he went up to check out Canada, Vancouver originally. This particular incident was the trigger.

In a sense, America was on the "hot seat" that night. And when he had America act out what was going on, it came out very straight: "That's right, I'm no longer concerned about freedom and democracy. I can do away with it."

Fritz was struck with the audacity of the political people like Daley and the rest, not because of the act but that they had the intuitive certainty to know they could get away with it without a revolt.

By that time he was convinced that the next step in the growth movement was some form of community living, where people could integrate their growth. It's still an exciting challenge.

BETTY FULLER

Fritz talked a lot about how we don't have very much time. He could see the totalitarian regime increasing in this country. There was a sense of his wanting to make a safe space in the world for himself and the people he loved. One time Fritz was doing a workshop at Bucks County Seminar House and someone came up to Grenville Moat gushing about all the insight she'd gotten from the human potential movement, and Fritz walked up to Gren with tears streaming down his face and said, "Don't you realize that nothing we do makes any difference at all?"

Fritz didn't think the humanists would ever get their shit together; he thought the conservative, totalitarian way would win. I don't know if a Jew feels that more overwhelmingly than others, but it was clear to him that what you do doesn't make any difference at all, and you do what you have to do.

What about Fritz' Jewishness? Was it extraneous to his being Fritz or was it inherently relevant to who Fritz was and how he lived?

> *From an obscure lower middle class Jewish boy to the possible creator of a new method of treatment and the exponent of a viable philosophy which could do something for mankind. . . .*

Are these unrelated happenstances?

> *When . . . I first joined the University, I found that I was expected to feel myself inferior and an alien because I was a Jew. I refused absolutely to do the first of these*

things, I have never been able to see why I should feel ashamed of my descent. . .

. . .at an early age I was made familiar with the fate of being in the opposition and being put under the ban of the "compact majority."

These are Fritz' experiences. They are, however, the words of Sigmund Freud, a man whose work and person were important to Fritz Perls throughout most of his life.

Phillip Rieff had written this about Freud: "Freud found in the perennial Jewish character . . . the source of his personal integrity and above all his defensive attitude toward the world."*

I feel on the defensive. The captain of my battalion was an anti-Semite. He had withheld the iron cross before, but this time he had to put in a recommendation, and I got my cross. 1916.

I am in an army hospital. Out of the misery of the acute warfare. I had met a good man, our new doctor. We talk; he wants to know about anti- Semitism. Plenty of it, yes, even in the trenches.

Laura says:

LAURA PERLS

In Germany there wasn't that much open anti-Semitism before Hitler. I think in his first high school, Fritz got stuck for three years in a class he felt was anti-Semitic. He dropped out of school and his father put him into business and that was even worse . . . so Fritz chose a school of his own, another gymnasium in Berlin that was a better school. . . .

However, Fritz says:

The director [of the gymnasium] had a Polish name, and possibly to prove his Aryan blood he was very, very

---

*Freud: The Mind of the Moralist, Phillip Reiff.

*nationalistic. The school was new and he gathered a
staff that can best be described by paraphrasing Churchill: Seldom have so few teachers tortured so many
children for such a long time. The basic attitude was
discipline and anti-Semitism.*

*Freud took some comfort from the thought that having been
excluded from society where one could learn and practice the
usual things, the Jew could more easily be a rebel and critic.
In his last years, Freud was to say, without bitterness:
". . . To profess belief in this new theory called for a certain
degree of readiness to accept a position of solitary opposition—a position with which no one is more familiar than a
Jew."**

*Inevitably, Fritz had conflicting emotions about belonging
to a group the world had set apart for three thousand years
and marked for massacres, persecutions and expulsions. One
yearned to be completely assimilated, to live a "normal"
life. And yet, is not his unshakeable persistence in holding
firm to his bold and innovative ideas, a uniquely Jewish
quality?*

IDA ROLF
Fritz was a Jew and never anything else. Not really. He was
really a splendid example of a Jew.

Yet, he wrote:

> *My relation to Judaism and the Jews is extremely unde-
> fined. I know quite a bit about German, Greek and
> Roman history, about the history of—I can't even say
> 'my people,' so little am I identified with them—the
> Jewish people. I know next to nothing.*

Well, a Jew isn't something you define . . . it's something
that *is*. You couldn't look at that man and not place him as a
Jew. You couldn't listen to that man and not place him as a
German Jew. He was always a German Jew to my ear.

---

*Stories of Courage, Shirley Gorgon Milgrim.

Fritz' type of insight was *Jewish!* I can't imagine a non-Jew sitting in Fritz' chair and saying what Fritz said! It was just the way he *saw* things; the way he *was*.

To me, Fritz' style was typically German Jewish: kindly, paternalistic, irascible. . . .

WILSON VAN DUSEN

God, he had a mind! He was good. He was bright in all ways. But I also saw him as very Jewish, *Sturm* and *Drang*. For me, many Jews have a kind of racial heaviness in their features, in their movements, in their way of thinking, just as though the tragedy of the Jews is still there.

Isn't it?

Well, I don't know. I do know that Fritz had that quality very strongly. Whereas when I think of myself racially, or my origins, it is much different. It dragged him down emotionally. He was capable of monumental depression.

SOL KORT

He knew that we observed some of the Jewish traditions in our family, and he never made any negative comments about our Jewishness. I think he himself was beyond any major concern with Jewishness, his ethnicity, or any particular identification with it.

LAURA PERLS

In Germany at the time of the Hitler business we were not very conscious Jews. Fritz had practically deserted everything Jewish. All our parents were Reform Jews. Fritz learned some Hebrew and got bar mitzvah'd but after that he was actually more off it than I was. But then, of course, with Hitler, Fritz became aware of the fact that you cannot renounce being a Jew any more than one can renounce being black or white. You simply are, whether you like it or not.

STANLEY KELEMAN

I remember I was walking kind of dejectedly one time at

Esalen. I didn't know what the hell was going on. He walked up to me and mimicked me. It was a loving gesture—it showed me that I was walking dejectedly. So I straightened up and asked what he was reading.

"I'm reading this book about the death of a rabbi," he said. Then in Yiddish he added, "It's hard to be a Jew."

We talked about what it meant to be a Jew. He showed me the book. We talked about his own struggles trying to grow up. Something like, "I've been in this world a long time and I'm a Jew. There's no way out of being a Jew. This world doesn't let you forget it—especially the way I grew up."

TOM SHANDEL

His attitude was such that if he felt Jews had a propensity, for example, to whine more, then goddamn it, he was going to stamp out that neurosis. That is very much the way it was. He once told me, "You can criticize in the family . . ." and I think everybody was in *his* family.

ANNA HALPRIN

Fritz was essentially very Jewish, and this came out in all of his attitudes. I identified with him very strongly on that basis. He was the kind of person who could never bow down to a golden image in the sense that he would never accept a dogma and I think that's what I liked most of all about working with him. I think Fritz would squirm if I used the word *morality,* but there was one. To me, the very fact that there was no dogma is a morality.

FRITZ FAISS

Fritz approached religion from the viewpoint of science, not from its opposite, belief. Any link toward visionary, ecstatic, intuitive action was taken with great caution. The concept of souls was unacceptable for Fritz. Fritz' philosophy was directed toward the *Chabad,* which means "Wisdom, Reason, Knowledge" or the first three of the Divine Emanations.

I think it is correct to quote Baruch Spinoza and his theorem: "The love of God and the love of man are one and the same." Fritz showed love man to man. He followed the basic Judaic idea of understanding the love of God and to unify with Him in a mystical way. Fritz understood the message of his forefather, Moses, as a philosophy of ethics, without directives concerning morals or a system of precepts.

BOB SHAPIRO

He certainly looked like a Jewish rabbi. I know he went to Israel looking for the Grail, not from the orthodox Jewish approach but from the cosmic approach of trying to verify for himself that there was something spiritual and mystical that he could relate to. He felt a void about that and, if anything, probably filled that in with his music. I'm not so sure that music isn't a fine religious experience. Twice I tried to seduce him with my own mixed religious inclinations but he didn't want to go.

LAURA PERLS

Fritz had no particular affection for Judaism. He had rejected religion, in a Marxist kind of way, as opium for the people. But, of course, this view refers to the simplistic way religion is taught, which is very different from being religious.

ANNA HALPRIN

I felt Fritz was sad about the world towards the end of his life. And he felt it deeply. He was reading a book about Hitler and the rise of fascism. He said he was tired and that he was going to Canada and start a kibbutz there. He said that this country was getting too much like nazi Germany. I felt that Fritz was frustrated about not getting his spiritual, physical and social worlds integrated, and the kibbutz was his way of trying to get them together. That was his Judaism. Jewishness isn't being religious in a conventional way; it's an attitude; it's a way in which you identify with other people. He was one of the most Jewish persons I ever knew. He always had Jewish stories.

JERRY KOGAN

One of his jokes that sort of stuck in my mind because it was so incongruous was: "Roses are reddish, violets are bluish; if it wasn't for Christmas, we'd all be Jewish."

> . . .*I love Jewish stories and their pregnant wit. Israelis come frequently to my seminars, and especially if they are* Sabra *[born in Israel], I am prejudiced in their favor. I have veneration and appreciation for the wholesome Jew who is one with his religion, history, and way of life. Their Zionism makes sense. . . .*

DAVID EHRLICH

My parents used to tell me, "You can do anything." The human potential movement, which is mostly Jewish created and directed, says the same thing. The Jews have always understood that life can be good.

It doesn't matter how far a journey is. If you have crossed the borders of your country, what is it to go to another country or a city? A Jew has had to move during all of his times since Moses. Fritz was only another in this line.

Perhaps it is true that because the Jew has often had to live with one foot within the door of a society and one foot without, he has been able to appropriate the best of a culture without being bound by it. Surely Fritz owed his allegiance solely to the process of mental discovery rather than to any particular school of thought; he took freely from what excited his imagination and rejected freely what did not. He

*was at home everywhere in the world of ideas yet compelled
to lodge nowhere. Now he was about to make another
move. . . .*

ED TAYLOR

He was very warm to me that night when he left and in effect
he thanked me. He came into the kitchen while I was baking
and he took my hand. He didn't say thank you, it was just
the way he was. A really warm, beautiful old man and in a
sense saying goodbye. It was very beautiful.

JACK DOWNING

When he moved up to Cowichan, he took everything out of
the house here at Esalen, including the wiring for his TV and
the extension cords. Everything that was Fritz' went. He was
very thorough in that respect.

GIDEON SCHWARZ

At his 75th birthday party, Fritz said, "I once said that all
individual therapy is obsolete. I'm going one step further
today. I think *all* group therapy is obsolete as well." Then he
described his latest attempt (and his last, but we didn't know
it then), the gestalt kibbutz.

*Fritz Perls was many sided: a tramp, a gentleman, a poet, a
dreamer, a lonely fellow—always hopeful of romance and
adventure. Fritz Perls, too, dreamed of world peace and happiness in an imperfect and intolerant world.*

FRITZ FAISS

During those years after the first World War, up to Hitler's
time, many communes had been set up in Germany. The
young generation hoped and believed in a change to the better, from traditional forms to communes. Most were failures
or existed only a short time . . . Esalen was at first a realization of that dream that Fritz shared. Later, after some unpleasant experiences, Fritz decided to leave and set up a new
environment which would serve for his longings: to prolong

life, virility. He dreamed about forming a community: a new idealistic, or romantic, lifestyle with himself as leader. It was an exact copy of Dr. Faust's ideas played by Fritz Perls.

JOHN STEVENS

Imagine it: Here's a guy of 75. He's old. He's always had a bad heart and his body's deteriorated in many ways. He's got a comfortable set-up at Esalen—his own house, the baths, all kinds of friends, women crawling all over him. He throws all that overboard, buys a motel in Canada, and starts all over again because he wants gestalt to really happen. Esalen was such a mixed bag, so many trips, from really good things like Fritz to absolutely phony, hokey things, and everything in between. He wanted a place where he could really get gestalt together, so he did it at 75. Most people are scared shitless to do something like that when they're 25 or 30, much less 75.

Canada

Sol Kort is director of the humanistic and sciences program at the Center for Continuing Education at the University of British Columbia. . . .

SOL KORT

I was always interested in bringing people here who were making an important impact in some aspect of education. In 1968 I asked Fritz if he would be interested in coming up for a public lecture. I had gotten permission to join a gestalt therapy session that Fritz was conducting while I was at Esalen, so I knew his work. He came in November of that year.

It was around the time when there were student uprisings on various campuses and some of the radical students were in the group that flooded into the auditorium. We had one who dressed up in a jester costume with bells, and he came in with his flock and it looked like there was going to be a riot because some people had to be turned away. But when Fritz started talking, everyone quieted down: no fuss, no bother. He had a tremendous impact on his audience. He loved it.

I think that with his dissatisfaction with Esalen and his feeling about rising fasicism in the United States, the warm reception he got in Vancouver persuaded him to consider moving to Canada.

He flew up to take residence in early February of 1969. Before coming he had called to find out what the weather was like; he said he wanted to wait until the ice and snow had melted. He also called enroute from San Francisco to tell me that someone had broken into his car there, and stolen some traveler's checks and his special dental plate. It's the only time I ever heard him in distress, feeling sorry for himself.

He was really impressed with Canadian customs and im-migration. They gave him the real VIP treatment, you know, Herr Professor, like Sigmund Freud was coming to town. He really liked that. He had emphysema, I think, and in itself it could have been a cause for rejection, but they let him in. He brought many of his possessions with him: his camper, his stamp collection, and later a friend drove his little Fiat up here.

My mother-in-law was in Europe at the time, so we loaned him her apartment for about six weeks as a base for opera-tions while he looked for property. About April he moved in-to his own apartment down in English Bay. It was very spar-tan, very sparsely furnished. He had cassette tapes of operas and symphonies that he would listen to on his tape recorder. He lived simply—you, know, the car he drove, the clothes he wore. He watched his budget carefully. Once we went out to cocktails, and after a look at the menu, he said, "The prices are atrocious here, we shouldn't eat too much."

In our family he was like a grandfather; very proper, noth-ing untoward, never any kind of an off-color move or state-ment or even a suspicion of anything like that. He liked my mother-in-law's herring and most Jewish foods, though he had a thing against Jewish mothers, you, know, "Chicken soup is poison." She tried not to be a *nudnik*,* though she would have loved to consult with him about herself. But there was never any confrontation. He didn't put her down, though there could have been occasions to do so. I think he was interested in being on his best behavior while here. He was settling into new territory and he didn't want to alienate or antagonize anybody so he was very good in public rela-tions.

It was very friendly, we had him over often to dinner, and he'd visit, stop in at the drop of a hat, or we'd go out togeth-er, sometimes the theater or opera, or an evening at a restau-rant. He had a favorite restaurant on Robson Street, where they served forty different varieties of Wiener schnitzel. He

---

*A pest, an annoyer, a monumental bore.

retained his love of his European background, its food and culture. One time my mother was visiting from Detroit, and we all went to the opera together, my mother, Shirley's mother, and a couple of their lady friends, women in their sixties and seventies. We all drove over to the theater in a couple of cars and I thought, this is absurd, he's going to erupt with irritation over all this. But he took it all real cool; in fact, he was charming. He could be extremely gracious when in an expansive mood.

We had a nice rapport. We tried to make sure that people didn't intrude on him; he'd take short afternoon naps to conserve his strength. I think he considered Shirley, her mother, myself, and our daughters as a sort of surrogate family.

He liked the opera. He wore a dress shirt with ruffles, and looked very distinguished in his tuxedo. Some people recognized him in the lobby—they'd been to his lecture earlier, and this he found very gratifying. This kind of acknowledgement was very important to him. He enjoyed remarking that he had become a legend in his own time.

He was very good at picking films. He saw *The Magus* a couple of times. It's about a psychiatrist movie director, in a plot where it is difficult to distinguish between reality and fantasy. He was intrigued by the fact that psychiatry and fantasy were involved, and that a psychiatrist was also playing the part of director. He fancied himself as kind of a man of the theater. In a way, his gestalt therapy was theater, though for real, not make-believe.

There was always a tumult of people and activity around him, he was a creator of events.

STAN FOX
I am a documentary filmmaker and, as many documentary filmmakers do, I become absorbed in subjects I pick out to make films about. For various reasons, I was interested in encounter groups and sensitivity training. I was aware of Fritz Perls as a name, but hadn't read any of his books. The University of British Columbia Extension Department has a man named Sol Kort who is very aware of what is happening

in avant-garde humanistic psychology. He pointed out that Perls was coming to Vancouver to talk, and I contacted him through Kort to see if he would interview with us. Perls wrote back and said he would actually do a group for the camera, if we could assemble some interesting people. This was a terrific surprise and delight. So I selected a small group of about ten people and one morning we filmed Fritz for CBC in one of the residences. This resulted in an hour-long film.

Since it was a multiple-camera shooting, I participated as one of the group members because I wanted to have that close experience to the film. It was an important experience for me. I had had some prior gestalt experience from less eminent people.

Anyway, after the group was over, Fritz said he was terribly pleased with the people I had picked. Then when he saw the actual film, he said it was the best film he had ever done and that he had been thinking of having his whole technique filmed. Could we do that? Would I be interested? I said it would cost a lot of money and it would be a huge project.

Until then I had been very successful and had a bright future at the Canadian Broadcasting Corporation; what eventually happened was that I quit my job and assembled a few backers with money and we filmed about twelve hours over a period of a week. Actually, we filmed one evening with thirty people I picked for Fritz and then at the end of the evening—in a real Fritz Perls way—he just said, "You are in, you are out," and he narrowed down to fifteen people.

That filming experience showed interesting aspects of Fritz. For example, together, Fritz and I looked at the whole twelve hours of color film that we had exposed in the second session. I thought, "Well, obviously he is going to make all kinds of demands about the film." So I said, "Fritz, we have twelve hours of film of which we will probably end up with four that we'll show to the public. How shall we select that? How do we edit it?"

"Do you know how to do it?" he asked.

"Yes, that is my profession."

"Well, then *do* it! You're the filmmaker—I'm the therapist."

"Well, what if I pick a scene or sequence where you bomb out?"

"So, then you will have a perfect record of Fritz Perls bombing out!"

In all my experience of filming, I had never come across anyone—especially a person of some note—with that attitude.

During the filming, we were having it processed very quickly so that we could check it before the group was finished. It went on for six days, and I reviewed the films with Fritz night after night. That was really very interesting, because he talked, sometimes almost to himself, about what was happening. I don't suppose very many people have heard him give that kind of personal critique of himself. He was very frank. And, occasionally, he would see something in the film that he had missed during the actual session that would make him bring that person back.

There was a young man and his wife, for example, who were obviously having difficulty, and Fritz decided the man saw himself as Christ on the cross. He picked that out of the first day's film. He didn't tell me, he just said, "I know what's the matter with that guy," and the next day in front of the camera, he made the man go to the wall and pretend he was Christ on the cross, and he had his wife go up and do things to him. It was extraordinarily effective. Seeing themselves like that you knew by their faces that they would never be the same again.

Almost irrelevant in the face of the other astounding things, but worth mentioning, was his incredible sense of timing. Our film actually ran for thirty-three minutes. I don't know how he did it, but the fact of the matter was that whoever was being worked with was finished by thirty-two and a half minutes! I never saw Fritz looking at his watch—maybe he did when I was busy—but he *never* ended up with film running out while someone was in the middle of something important! I'd never seen that before!

At the end of the filming sessions, Fritz said to the group, "I would like you to do something for me." He had everyone get up and put their arms around each other and sing "Auld Lang Syne." He wanted everyone to do it *for him.* They did, of course. He was touched by that.

As a writer and filmmaker, Tom Shandel, made some documentaries of Fritz with Stan Fox, and also made some "demos and that kind of TV thing" for the Canadian Broadcasting Company. He hung around during the search for and the establishment of Cowichan: "We had plans," Tom says, "for film projects which would have led to exposing the ham actor in the great man."

TOM SHANDEL

I was flying around the province with Fritz when we were looking for the place for him to live. Fritz had this incredible need for a Boswell and I guess I was the nearest thing at hand at that point. And, in tagging along, I had a camera. I knew Fritz in a very specific context, primarily as a filmmaker, because at that period of his life he was really very conscious of recording himself.

Some people say he structured everything so that he would get praise and that he seemed to need everybody's adulation;

and others say that he didn't care what anybody thought, that he was autonomous. How did that come out in the films, Tom? Do you know?

I get angry when people say that. What the fuck do people expect him to be? He wasn't a saint. He was just a hard- driving kind of a man on all fronts. When he was uncertain, he was profoundly uncertain; when he was angry, he was profoundly angry.

He was arrogant and self-confident to a point, inquisitive about himself and, certainly, a person looking for something more substantial than anything he saw in his life. He used to say, "I have no future," and he'd say it with no claim for sympathy. He was prepared to push his authority as far as he dared, but, to me, he was a man with *total* compassion, such *profound* compassion that he didn't give a shit about hurting your feelings. That's why he seemed to be cruel to a lot of people but I don't think it was cruelty at all. It was the easiest way out for people to think of him as being cruel. His compassion was quite major. I think the people who came to him were supplicants, in whatever way, to get under the paternal mantle, and he cut that off.

As for me, I felt really lucky in this respect, if I ever thought of it, that I got a different Fritz: I got much more the artist, the man who asked me about things, the guy with whom I would try to figure out ploys and plots and adventures where he could make some money or star.

If he had been trained, he could have been a singer, an actor. He was show-biz personality. People with tremendous presence—it doesn't matter what the field—they are in show biz. I mean that in the best sense. He *was* a star. He saw himself as a star; he organized his life around the very rational assessment of his own stardom. He would never take on something that he couldn't do because his arrogance was too complete. He cast himself in a major role. He wouldn't see himself as a two-bit anything. So, I suppose I agree that he created situations where he got adoration. But that was his due. That's who he was.

He talked a lot to me because I wasn't in the context of his
groups, which is just an interesting difference. Remember
my attitude is different than those held by people who
worked within the context of his groups, other therapists,
people in the field. I tended to accept him for what he was,
simply because not being in the business I have a different
kind of perspective.

In the group, he was a masterful performer. That was his
thing. He took it on as a role. Fritz Perls, teacher, guru,
messiah. I think he clearly felt his work was going to last.

KOLMAN KORENTAYER
We got together one weekend in Bucks County, Pennsylvania, after he had decided to immigrate to Canada. He
invited me to travel with him while he did different workshops. I really came alive during this time. I knew then this
was where I should be and that this was the person I should
be involved with. It was about this time that Fritz had made
his decision to go to Vancouver.

He had first gone to Canada when he left South Africa. At
that time he stayed with Laura's relatives and worked with
Willerton Pennfield, the famous neurosurgeon. This was
important, later, when Fritz was obtaining immigration
papers to Canada.

He seemed completely pleased with what was happening.
Vancouver is beautiful and he liked the environment and the
kind of warm reception he got. It was a people place. He
liked the change. He was looking for a place to set up his kibbutz. He found it in Cowichan.

SOL KORT
My wife, Shirley, helped him with setting up a bank account
and transferring money. He came into the bank with something like ten thousand dollars in cash on his person. Shirley
was appalled at his casualness and carelessness; he had it
coming out of his pockets. Even the teller was astounded.
When he bought the motel which became his Gestalt Institute, he put down something like twelve or fifteen thou-

sand dollars as a cash payment—the total cost was around forty thousand.

He knew how to handle sales agents, plane charters, itineraries; he was pretty much self-propelled. He was very, very astute on land values, details of mortgages, interest and so on—he didn't want to get beyond what he could cope with financially. He thought he might find something on the mainland, but the prices were too high. He chartered a plane and with a man who was shepherding him around, flew over to the islands. He looked at another place called Yellow Point further up the island, but they wanted about half a million dollars for that. Cowichan just sort of met his pocketbook and his needs.

Cowichan Lake,
Vancouver Island, British Columbia

KOLMAN KORENTAYER
Cowichan was an interesting place. It offered ways of being alone, ways you could drift out and go away. It was an unfolding experience. You see, you went from one little community into the village, which was Cowichan, and from this little village you went into a larger village of Duncan, and then into the city of Victoria. Then the really big occasion was going across the ferry to Vancouver. Then, going back—the reverse—from Vancouver to Victoria to Duncan to Cowichan to home. It was a beautiful experience.

Fritz came in the summer of '69 with one group. There were two acres which were usable on the lower level by the lake. The upper level contained seven acres which we never got into. Previously, it had been a motel, "I found the place in the banana belt of Canada," he joked, "but I forgot that it rains a lot in the banana belt." The place was Fritz.

JERRY ROTHSTEIN
Fritz says somewhere that his first great achievement was to get from individual to group therapy, to break out of this one-to-one closed system into a group where many people's energy became available for each person who wanted to work. He then thought he was beginning to make the next jump from group therapy to therapeutic community, where the environment, the background for therapy, would not be limited. It would be the whole of your ordinary life, and you might break out of your impasse cooking a meal or hammering a nail. This expands the whole idea of gestalt to make it contiguous with life. He mentions in *Garbage Pail* that he

imagined the first such community would be what he called a "leader breeder" place. He wanted to train enough people so that they would then go out and start other therapeutic gestalt communities.

Cowichan had a certain jewel-like quality—nice lawns, big maple trees, right by the lake—but it was too small for a permanent community; I think Fritz grabbed it because he was so anxious to get going.

KOLMAN KORENTAYER

His fantasy, immediately after he got into Cowichan, was to find a larger place where we could set up a college, a humanistic college in the gestalt way, as he saw it. That's what he wanted. Cowichan was a stepping-stone. He wanted a larger place where we could plant and farm, and do a lot of different things.

A new beginning. . . .

ROMILLY GRAUER

When we heard Fritz was coming up to Canada we just couldn't believe it—it's like being into electricity and hearing Edison arrived!

He opened his doors in June of '69. I got my courage up to go over in July. I thought at the beginning there'd be a lineup of psychologists with degrees. But at the very beginning there wasn't. There was just maybe six weeks to two months for the Canadians to get their licks in before everyone starting coming up from California.

It was a motel on the lake edge with little cabins and a house. He looked as I imagined—guru-like, a beard . . . I couldn't look him right in the eye. I had the feeling he took to me. Sometimes he doesn't take to people and they feel like there's nothing they can do about it. Later, in the fall, I found out that all along he thought I was Jewish: He just assumed my whole family was Jewish, because they kind of look it. Actually they're Irish and German. I felt he had a Jewish fellowship feeling, and it stirred me a little when I found that he was including me in this ethnic umbrella. And I thought, "Jesus, now he won't like me anymore," but it didn't seem to make any difference.

Before the big meeting room was finished, we started in a little house that went with the motel. I imagine the owners lived there. Each motel room had a kitchen so they hadn't ever had communal meals before, and we had to try and make it a community. We met in a sitting room about as big as this small room for a group—that's how many people were there. When the big house was finished, nobody was going to put bread out for chairs, so we just sat on the floor and he sat on a chair.

Cowichan was his personal trip. And that's one reason why the community ran so easily. There was none of this complete democracy stuff. We'd all meet and discuss how the community would go and all the unimportant stuff, but he was there and he was interested. There had to be a garden so there was a gardening crew . . . there had to be a kitchen . . . we kept changing the method. We would have this committee or that committee—the people to fix the place, the people to make the art room, but he was *there,* the nucleus of all this: he was Big Papa.

I can remember only once when his will did not prevail. Once at a meeting, we were all gathered in this one room and Fritz was in his chair, he asked, "I think we should have no children. What do you think?" Right at the beginning there were a lot of kids. Couples had arrived, and there were three or four. In July one slightly retarded kid had come with her mother . . . she would burst out with noise for no particular reason. He was, at least at that particular time, irritated as hell with kids. He wanted to work without the distraction.

I said, "Well, it'd be silly to have a community without children. We are preparing to live in the world, and if children are a natural irritant we might as well have them in the community." And then a lot of parents spoke up; they wanted to have their kids. It seemed like there was going to be a showdown. Everybody against Fritz. He made it clear he didn't want kids. On that point nothing more was ever said.

And were kids allowed?

Kids, but no dogs, That was the rule.

There were never thousands of kids. I think, at that point he thought he'd lose a significant number of people. My impression was that he didn't argue because he wanted the process to be democratic . . . that he agreed because it was expedient to agree.

It *was* a patriarchal community and Fritz' will prevailed, yet it wasn't ever like he laid down the law. He never did. If he expressed a wish, everybody was significantly respectful of it and it was usually carried out.

At the time I arrived he really was bowed down because he'd only brought one person with him, a woman from Esalen named Kay. She had agreed to do some cooking and was needed to start a group and to get the place going. She was trying to do books and bills, and it gradually became much too much for her to try to organize, so I offered to do bookkeeping. Fritz turned around, his face lit up, and he said, "Wow, you do bookkeeping?" So I got to do that.

Eventually we did everything because there was no one person to cope with housework or other duties. I started the office which I gradually shifted on to others. I've forgotten how he set the finances up—it was $600 a month or so—but I know that whatever anybody was charged, a healthy portion of it was fee.

The June people met all the time with Fritz, in a morning group, an afternoon group and an evening session. He was in a teacher's role. I didn't realize until later about Fritz, the Savior. He was *really* into teaching others at Cowichan. He said, "There'll be gestaltists, people who will have gone through the gestalt process and be able to apply it to art or to life. Then there will be gestalt therapists . . ." He did a series of lectures up there, rather formal lectures on gestalt to us. For about an hour each morning he'd talk about all the various aspects of gestalt. He even got to the point of designing the certificate. He was also in touch with all the other gestalt institutes. They were going to devise a formal plan that would be available to people with psychology and psychiatry degrees. That caused a little ripple, because there were some very good people who were just as good as or better than some psychiatrists.

He didn't have any buddies when he started out; and there were none of those pretty little California-girl people for the first few months, anyway.

Then, in July, Teddy Lyon came up and the community formed into two groups. In the morning we were with Fritz and in the afternoon with Teddy and then we'd switch. That was for the first two weeks. Then we got to be so many— other people emerged as capable of leading groups—we'd split into three and four groups. This week you'd be with Don, and the next week with Fritz and Barry Stevens, and so on.

BARRY STEVENS
The first week at Cowichan he spent three hours every morning with us working on awareness in different ways. It was beautiful and very productive. We did the in-and-out shuttling, going back and forth from what is going on inside the skin to what is going on outside the skin. He had us become aware of our voices by saying, "As my voice I am . . ." and hearing our voices as we said that, adding after those words whatever it was that we heard in our voice, like "timid," or "harsh," or "draggy," or "joyous." He had us pair up, being aware of what was going on inside our heads while we were talking to the other person. He also had us let our awareness come out in a kind of song, or at least sound. Right at the end he had us go inside ourselves and express that inside awareness, then the outside awareness; inside and outside, back and forth, as if it were poetry but not trying to make it poetry. Each of us did this aloud so that we each heard everyone. I know that mine began with feeling very alone and it wound up as complete comfort and ease. Just a great feeling! It was beautiful the way it came out of so many people. He never did that again.

That was the way he did things, changing all the time. As

soon as he saw that we were getting our feet anchored in any situation, he'd pull the rug out by switching the situation; then we would get the wobbles again. And that was great. He was very observant in noticing when people were beginning to feel comfortable, and then he switched things.

It is so easy to get into a pattern (which is another name for a rut) and live according to the pattern instead of by observation and awareness, which is gestalt. So, in frequently throwing us into new situations, he was breaking up patterns and patterning. That's therapy in a sense, but not in the sense that we usually use the word. It is so easy in a new situation to rearrange yourself and think, "Now I know how to do this," and then wham! when things get switched it doesn't work any more. He knew all that from his own life. He had been thrown into so many new things and had had to find his way through them. What he did with us was minor compared to what he'd been through. Everything that he did came out of his own mind. It was his own work.

Fritz would say to trainees, "A technique used without understanding is a gimmick." There's an awful lot of gimmickry going around. It is really seeing, you know. Fritz saw, understood, and did something, without thinking about it. The thought process is a barrier. Once one really sees, you do it. Fritz developed tools to arrive at gestalt, which is a natural process; there are many different ways of arriving at it, but basically people who use "techniques" haven't understood what Fritz was all about.

I don't know anyone who has broken completely free of their conditioning but when you consider that he started out as a German Jewish intellectual psychoanalyst and how *much* he got out of all that, the remnants are nothing. He was so open to his own observations. When he saw something that made him change his mind, he said so. That's a tremendous thing, when you let new evidence change your views. We never know everything. Nobody does.

It was so beautiful to be able to just make statements and have them understood, not interpreted. How I enjoyed that! I could say a lot of things to him and he understood. I wasn't stuck with explanations. One night Fritz and I were driving back from somewhere to Vancouver. Cars were everywhere and he made a left turn where he thought we were supposed to, but when we got to the other side there was a dirt road. He stopped the car. He sat quietly for several minutes and then he said, "I am lost." Right then, another car pulled across the highway and drove up alongside and a young woman called, "Dr. Perls, are you lost?" She was a cute as the dickens. Gad, she was cute! And I had some resistance to it. She told us to follow her and she would lead us to the right road, and we were driving along behind her when he said, "She sure is a cutie." And I said, "Yes," because I knew it was true but my voice wasn't with it. He looked over and said, "*If* you like cuties." It was such a kind response, knowing where I was. I remember that my breath came out very deeply after that. I had been holding it when I said, "yes."

I never had any feeling of friction with him. I knew him during the last three years of his life, and I saw him changing during that time. He was *always* learning and changing.

There was a true humility in Fritz, too, which showed up in different ways. It was present when he said he'd discovered he was wrong about something. There was humility in his honesty when he said he was looking for support. Once he came to my cabin and said, "I have fired Kay" (who was his secretary and was pregnant). He wasn't at ease with this. I told him I didn't see how he could keep her on when she was so angry with him and working against him. He said, "I'm going around looking for support." When he was arrogant he didn't like his arrogance. That made a big difference to me when he was arrogant.

When he played games, they were his own spontaneous games, not the conventional ones. Once he asked the people in the group about a ride to Victoria, where he could get a plane. Romilly and Teddy started talking about their cars. "Well, if my car . . ." this, and "If my car . . ." that, "If it gets fixed in time . . ." and all that stuff, going into all these things that they didn't know about yet. Fritz sat there listening, which was unusual for him to just let it go on and on.

Then, very deliberately, every time they started running down, he would say something that would start them up again. He didn't smile at all. He was just there with them as though he was listening and joining in the conversation. When they ran down, he'd throw in some other "if" and they'd start up again. It was perfectly hilarious because there was no way to settle it, you see. Ray Walker was sitting beside me and he was laughing, too, and saying, "I don't believe it! I don't believe it!"

Most of the time Fritz didn't interpret but sometimes he did. One night I had been working with Fritz in the group and I sat down and I heard him say, "Barry thought she hated her husband. She didn't know she loved him." That's something that happens very often in psychotherapy: someone discovers that a person they've been hating they also love and they are unaware of the love. In my case this wasn't true. I didn't think I hated my husband and I knew I loved him. But this was of no importance. I left the group because what was churning up in me was very strong and I wanted to be alone with it. I went to my cabin and cried for a couple of hours, still absorbed in what I had experienced. In the days following it was still insignificant that what Fritz had said about me was untrue. About a year later I was bugging my-

self that Fritz had said this and it wasn't true. So I put Fritz
on the empty stool and in five minutes, it was no longer than
that, I suddenly was overwhelmed by the simple truth that I
hadn't forgiven him for making a mistake. This wasn't just a
head thing. It was altogether totally through my body. That
has never given me any trouble since. At the time I thought,
dear Fritz! He gave me trouble and he also gave me the
means to get out of it.

JANET LEDERMAN
When we began to work together at Cowichan, it was very
exciting the way we were in tune with each. Sometimes he
would be working with a group in another place and then
they would come down to work with me, and there was
enough in-tuneness that we didn't have to talk about what to
do. There was just a tuning-in and a going ahead. I could
read what was there and turn it into a movement. Most of my
work is through games and movement.

It's hard to put into words but there was a three-dimen-
sional quality that began to come up. We could work together without collusion. Our realities were complementary in
some beautiful, beautiful way . . . Fritz had come out of the
psychiatric context, so he was really trained to work one-to-
one. I had come out of the classroom, so I was trained to
work with a group. And that was one of the ways we worked
together. He more into the forefront and I more in the
background.

VIRGINIA HOROWITZ

I was in an advanced training session and was the only one who didn't have the proper background. One day in the big group where nobody co-led with Fritz, he said, "Does anybody who's never co-led a group before want to come up and co-lead with me?" I didn't even hesitate a minute. I just went up there and sat down. He looked at me in absolute amazement. I felt, I put myself up here and I'm just going to have to go through this. And I did.

Then he related the story of his pretending to faint at a party in Israel in terms of "you do what you need to do for yourself." He drew the analogy of what I had just done.

ROMILLY GRAUER

We'd have meetings in the evening for any resentments that might come out. But the evening sessions kind of withered because somehow it got too big.

Towards the end, when it was a big community, Fritz wouldn't lead a group. He'd go around to all the groups and sit in just as he felt. The whole point was to get people to become therapists. Even I ended up leading some groups.

He didn't make a issue about degrees and such, except that when applications came (and they came to the office so I saw a lot of them), he favored the one with credentials because he wanted it to be an accredited therapy thing. There was a basic screening process where two or three of us would read the letters that came in. He read them all through, too. And if he really liked one, or very often when someone would just drive up, which showed a great deal of persistence because it's a long way away, he'd usually let them in.

JOEL KRAMER

On a visit to California after having gone to Canada, Fritz said something to me to the effect that he thinks he's got the cure for mental illness.

I said, "Schizophrenia, too?"

"No, neurosis."

"What's the cure?"

"The gestalt community—a living gestalt community ar
rangement."

He was really feeling good about himself and about what
he was doing.

GREG DAVIDSON

He was definitely getting stronger and when he got up north
he was even further into a new bloom; he was much mellower. He had been very paranoid down here at the time Nixon
was coming in. He anticipated repression, particularly of his
kind of work. He didn't think he had many years left, and
when he got up north, he felt a new life happening for him.
He became a much more lovable person.

The Spider. . . .

JERRY ROTHSTEIN

When Fritz went up to Canada to start Cowichan, I told him
I'd like to come there, but he said, "Don't," and anyhow I
was involved in things I didn't want to stop. After a couple
of months though, I got to a point where I was free from
commitments, so I sent a postcard saying I was coming up to
visit. He replied that he was going to be in San Francisco
soon and wanted to see me about something important and
would call me. It got to be Friday of the week he said he
would be in San Francisco with no word, and I thought he'd
just forgotten about it. I happened to be walking downtown
on Geary Street, when here comes Fritz up from Union
Square! He said, "Oh, come here! I'll buy you lunch," and
we went into Solomon's.

He was totally excited and started pouring out about how
wonderful things were at Cowichan. He said, "This is working out just perfect. Everything is fine, except . . ." and then
he described all the little details people wanted him to deal
with. His interest was in training, in finding people who were
seriously willing to go into themselves to the depth you need
to to become a sensitive teacher-therapist. He didn't want to
get bogged down in how many cartons of eggs to buy, or

where does the garbage go, or who's going to live where.

He knew I was a good organizer, so he offered me the job of being what he called "the spider"—someone who saw the web of day-to-day ordinary-life details, and knows what's going on just by having connections all the way down these little wires, in the middle of the web—handling the community routines, the managerial details. I was very interested in that. I still am. In fact, I've moved closer to being fascinated by that than anything else . . . So we arranged that I'd go up and see the place, spend some time there, and see what developed. And I got into managing things at Cowichan, working with people in the ways of the community's daily life, doing groups myself and lots of different things.

When I got there, there were twenty or so people in the place, and he was doing a small group for those whom he chose. He invited me to join that group.

One night, working with him in the group, I got really lost; I turned in on myself in some kind of a dead end. I was feeling terrible, totally stuck, and I was very concerned that it would affect his decision to have me continue to do this big job here and work with him. I suffered through the rest of the group, and then, as the group broke up and we were walking out, he came over, put his arm around my shoulder, and said, "Let's have a game of chess."

I suddenly realized that I was the same person, that he didn't give a shit if I got fucked up because he did, too. At that moment, I understood how unique his way of working with people was and it's always stayed with me that he could be just a nonjudgmental human presence. That was great.

The next day I tackled the thing again, and worked it through. It was good. Ironically, after *that* group, he just walked away, he had no interest. Usually we would somehow chat afterwards, but that time he just walked away . . . there was a balance there.

We used to hug each other after our chess games. Funny, I was playing the other night and I wondered how it would go if I could have another game with him. . . .

One of the most significant things Fritz ever did at Lake Cowichan was to put a note on the bulletin board that read, "How can I get through to you that gestalt is not rules?"

He wanted to train a lot of people but he didn't want to do it in a shabby way. But how do you train somebody? This made quite a lot of demands on his inventiveness, as well as on the people who were there. A lot of the time he thought he was just getting mimicry. It would be someone's turn to play the therapist, and he would be doing a kind of version of Fritz. I suppose this is true with any great teacher or therapist or whatever—the way that the master did it becomes an orthodoxy to the followers.

This was a major issue for him. He was very inventive in his training groups. He went into areas where there was a great potential for breaking down people's almost automatic willingness to follow. He found ways for each person to contact his own originality. What do *you* really want in this situation? as opposed to what Fritz wants, or what the rule book says. Probably this is why he used the "village idiot" kind of game a lot of times. He was trying to get people to turn off all the energy that goes into figuring out what they were *supposed* to do. He nudged people out of their insistence on getting the rules right and then performing them. We're conditioned to do that.

Fritz invented certain techniques relevant to particular situations: He invented the hot seat and he invented dialogue, not so much as a technique but as a way of penetrating the layers of the personality he was working on. Fritz was trying to find a method of communicating things without being followed. "I want to make a gestalt that's not rules—not *my* rules or your rules—a way of life." That was important to me.

RICHARD PRICE

In going to Canada, he cut out what he disliked about Esalen. He defined his scene just the way he wanted it. He was absolutely in charge of everything. His word was law, which is how he liked it.

If he didn't have a group going Fritz was restless. He'd put his nose into this and that, not finding quite enough involvement. At Cowichan, he assigned me and others as leaders of three or four groups. Then in the evening he'd go from group to group; when he'd get bored, he just got up and left. It was something like going from bar to bar. He wasn't so interested in seeing what the bartender was doing as checking out the action. He was following his own lesson in seeking his greatest emerging interest.

King. . . .

ILANA RUBENFELD

The summer that Fritz went to Canada, we visited him for a few days. He walked out of the house and down the lawn like a king. Happy. He was just really happy.

At Esalen, Fritz had to share the kingdom with Bill Schutz. In Canada, he was king.

KOLMAN KORENTAYER

Fritz was involved in the community. He walked around, sort of watching the work that was going on and really loving it, really excited about it. I remember him standing there one day when a couple of dogs ran up to him. He had a rule, only cats were allowed on the property because they took care of their own shit.

"You know you're not supposed to be here," he reprimanded pleasantly. The dogs just continued on their way.

Cowichan was a small community, a small lumber town. Yet, Fritz became a major personality. "The Doctor," you know. Everyone thought that he was special; he stood out.

He made an effort to be involved with the town, too. He joined the Chamber of Commerce and actually addressed one of their sessions.

The newsstands, the corner store carried books personally autographed by Fritz. He was recognized everywhere he went. He enjoyed that.

Fritz wanted to be a part of the community, a greater community. In Vancouver, for example, he loved to go to the opera. When he went, he loved being recognized. He was known, he was seen, he was appreciated. In a very short time, he had been on CBC television attracting a lot of people.

Many of the people who worked with us were Canadians from that area. Gestalt became a part of British Columbia. And the work goes on and gestalt plays a large role in the community.

SOL KORT

We visited Fritz' school right after it was established. He played the role of the proud founder with great relish. He showed us the view of the lake and mountains. "Like Switzerland," he claimed. There were a lot of flowers already and they were going to plant gardens. He liked the fact that it was all very green and lush. He planned to clear some brush away and build other facilities across the road where there was property to which they had access. He wanted to have both a therapeutic community and a college to teach basic aspects of medicine—anatomy, physiology—to gestalt therapists so they wouldn't have to go through the whole conventional medical training. He was thinking of buying the motel next door, but the owners wanted a price that was way out of line.

He did a nice PR job with the local residents. He also spoke to the Cowichan Chamber of Commerce, explaining to them what gestalt therapy was all about, and trying to make them less apprehensive about all these bearded hippie types, all those strange-looking people coming to Lake Cowichan. What could be going on there? A commune? Sexual orgies? Acid freaks? He was interviewed by the various Vancouver media, and a Seattle TV station sent a crew to interview him.

I think he felt he was getting into his stride, he had arrived;

people were recognizing his specialness. His dream about setting up a school and maybe eventually a little college was close to being realized. He had all kinds of hopeful ideas, and talked very optimistically about the future. He was very proud of what he had accomplished thus far, and was really getting a tremendous kick out of what he was doing.

JOHN STEVENS

His response to people was never indiscriminate, it was always specific. If somebody came up and was really shitting on him, he'd just fuck 'em over. If somebody came up very real and very open, he was gentle and loving. When we were working on *Garbage Pail,* he asked me about my wife, who had been in one workshop with him then, and I said, "Most of the time she feels pretty good, but she still feels useless sometimes." And Fritz says, very softly and with feeling, "Who doesn't." That really struck me—he'd done so much for me and for so many others, how could he feel useless? It was very important for me to hear that. It's a special memory.

Something I've only recently realized is how lonely he was. Other people have spoken of his loneliness or solitude as self-imposed, but I don't believe that at all. He was so far out on the fringes of awareness, so far ahead of everybody, I know he *had* to be alone. There was nobody out there he could talk to about what he was experiencing, what he was seeing so clearly. So many people are asleep and into all their games and tragedies and not seeing, and he could see it all. Imagine being the only person awake while everyone around is a zombie. He didn't have many people he could share with, and I know how happy and warm and gentle and soft he was when others were seeing what he was seeing and were really with him.

HARVEY FREEDMAN

Though I followed Fritz around the North American continent for four or five years, I didn't really get to know Fritz as a friend, as a personal friend, until '69 when I went to

Cowichan. Whenever I would see him before that, he had no real memory of me, no continuity with me; I was just a familiar face. When I turned up at Cowichan for two months—which was the longest, most extended contact with him—we became very close.

He was for me a formidable, awesome teacher; he became a friend. When we sat around gossiping, Fritz would speak in cartoon characters. He would often create a little cartoon of people we both knew. He saw me as a red balloon, always ready to fly off; I needed my mate, my wife, as ballast to hold me down to the ground. He would often relate that way to people we knew in common as we were driving or eating together, and it was great fun.

I enjoyed him. If we didn't speak for quite a while when we were driving, he would say, "You got no tongue?"

He loved the movies, We went to the theater in a little logging town several times. One night, we lined up for the movies with seven or eight little kids and teenyboppers. He was in a jumpsuit. They were standing there with their eyes wide open looking at him and he was glowing and sparkling, full of light and twinkles. He turned around and said, "What's the matter? Never seen Santa Claus in the summer?"

JULIAN SILVERMAN
I was kind of like a starry-eyed, sitting-at-the-feet-of-father guy with him. For me, *he* was it. It was only very recently in Cowichan that I started to see him as a man. All the way through, in the years I was with him, he was just such a far-out, special guy. I just never knew anyone like him.

The last time I saw Fritz he was sitting in a rocking chair in the living room at Cowichan. There was a bunch of people, sitting, some strumming guitars, everyone was singing. And there was Fritz: beautiful voice, eyes so clear, and his face was so soft. And he just sat there and kind of rocked. It was like being at home—a celestial home. (Julian Silverman)

JOHN STEVENS
Fritz was very happy when Russ Youngreen came to

Cowichan with the original illustrations for *Garbage Pail.* I can still see him chuckling as he'd turn over a page, just bubbling in his deep, soft voice. He just loved those illustrations.

Probably because two of Fritz' paintings were on the covers of In and Out the Garbage Pail, *many people assumed that he also did the sketches inside the book. They were done by my friend Russ Youngreen, who also did the drawings for this book.*

Russ Youngreen

How did Fritz get me to make the sketches for *Garbage Pail?* Well, he saw me doing a sketch of him at a workshop in Big Sur, and he chuckled. Later, at the end of the workshop, he asked me if I'd be interested in doing some drawings from some videotapes of people he'd worked with.

Instead of paying me, he said Penny and I could come up for a week-long workshop in Horseshoe Bay—that's in North Vancouver. So we did. We went to Canada.

He was working on a movie when we got there, and he asked me to draw up some examples of various things that he wanted to convey. I did some drawings. One was of a guy up there who had a Zen center in Vancouver with his wife. They were both pretty stark people—warm, but stark. I was just doodling around with a pen and I put a rain hat on him and gave him a big harpoon and a pegleg. Fritz saw that and just cracked up.

After that workshop was over, we went back down to the States and I thought my association with Fritz was over. Then I got a postcard from Barry Stevens that said, "Fritz would like you to do some sketches for his autobiography, *In and Out the Garbage Pail.*" When the card came, Penny phoned me at work. I was so shocked I just went blank. I just couldn't believe it!

I can't describe it! I was just flabbergasted that he wanted me to do the drawings for *his* book. I guess that was payment and tribute enough for me. I still hold on to that. It's really warm; it's good. I felt like I was worth something from an aesthetic standpoint and also from a personal, deeper level as well. I'd always wanted to feel—what?—recognized as an artist, I guess. Here I felt recognized.

Then he sent me his manuscript. He wanted me to concentrate on chapter headings, or at least some definition of chapter headings. I went through the manuscript as fast as I could and got as much done as I could, then I went back over it again and bore down on the stuff I thought really needed to be illustrated. I worked on my own. I had told him I'd have it done by such and such a date, so Penny and I went on the road in our car for a couple of months. A lot of it was done while we were traveling through Glacier National Park. By the time we got to Cowichan, I had most of it done.

As soon as we got to Cowichan, we rented a room in a motel next to his. We didn't know what the situation was . . . Fritz really seemed impatient to see the drawings. He was just like a little kid, just anticipating them. I kind of said to myself, "Wow, this doesn't fit my image of this godhead." As soon as I gave him the drawings, he started going through them and chuckling. He showed them around to the people who were there. Some of the drawings didn't grab him and others did. But in general he liked them and included most of them in his book.

Many people have said Fritz was an ingrate. Since he obviously enjoyed Russ' pictures I wondered whether there had been any overt expressison of appreciation. As with everything he did, Fritz expressed his appreciation in his own unique way.

The day after we got there, Fritz was leaving for a speaking tour and he insisted that we take his cabin while he was gone. He knew that we were tight for money and he didn't want to see us spending money at a motel. He said, "Make yourself at home. Use the tape recorder. Read the books. Eat the candy. Drink the wine. Do whatever you want."

PENNY YOUNGREEN
I knew Fritz didn't like dogs and I told him we had our two dogs with us.

"They von't shit in the house?"

"Well, they're housebroken, but I never know for sure what they're going to do."

"It's OK," he said. "The dogs can stay."

I was really amazed. I felt he was really bending over backwards.

John Stevens was so worried about what we and the dogs would do to Fritz' cabin, he would come in every few hours and look around. We had our kid and Dean, a friend's son, with us, too. John would come in, and Dean would be reading one of Fritz' books, and John would say, "Careful, careful with that book. Don't get any fingerprints on the book." Dean would just look at him and say, "This guy's really weird."

Anyway, one night the kids found a box of homemade chocolate candy and wanted to eat them. I said, "Well, he said, 'Make yourselves at home.'" So the kids ate a couple and they really tasted awful. They were stale—bleh! Dean said, "Hey, Fritz used to take psilocybin. You don't think those things were laced with psilocybin do you?" I said, "Oh, Jesus, I don't know." The kids were really freaked out. They sat up half the night staring at each other waiting for one or the other to do something odd. But nobody did; they were just ordinary, stale candies.

I kept the cabin clean, I swept out all the dog hairs every day. It was probably a lot cleaner than it was when Fritz was there.

Russ Youngreen

I guess his hospitality was his way of expressing his appreciation for the drawings. I was happy to be doing it for him. I
did get some chips out of it too and I was happy about that.
John Stevens paid me for the illustrations for the book and
the copyright.

One time in that second workshop in Horseshoe Bay, I was
working on a thing with a motorcycle I had. It didn't work
and I couldn't figure out how to put it together. I kept trying; then, I said, "I can't put it together." Fritz turned and
said, "This person appears to be stupid. In fact, he actually
is stupid," and he left me hanging in the air with that comment. I got all pent up and pushed out of shape, but I broke
through some of my shit precisely because of that. It started
with this flash I had about myself: when I was about three
years old, I was feeling this intense wanting of attention and
I was not getting it. My mother was like stone; I didn't feel
any love or any great amount of attention from her. It was
all tied together: this feeling dumb and wanting attention. I
began to become aware of what I was doing with that. He
sort of straightened the energy flow out and got it going
again. It's like a form of psychic acupuncture. But in order
to do it, the man had to know how people feel and he had to
feel a lot himself because he wasn't just playing a game.
When he was there to help you, he was *there,* one hundred
percent, completely, with his energy ready to assist.

There was some communication there which I can't describe. I've never had it with any other person. I've always
felt locked in; I know I lock myself in. In fact, there's a car-

toon in his book describing the way I saw myself. It's actually a self-portrait of a chap holding some bars up in front of himself. It's his own jailhouse; the bars are held up by his hands and he's looking out from them. But you obviously can see he's not in jail. It's his own trip. It's *my* own trip! It's how I felt, something I became aware of with his help.

At the end of that workshop at Lake Cowichan, he just said, "Drawing's your language." I guess he meant it was my best way of expressing myself. I liked the fact that he saw that.

TOM SHANDEL
I remember being drunk with him once and we were talking. I was always very nervous talking with him in one sense because it was so easy to fall into a camaraderie with Fritz in which you would kind of forget the years. I liked to forget that I was 30 and he was 70, but it is crazy to forget that because then I could say some piece of bullshit, and look across and there would be this 70-year-old piece of granite. So it was hard to be completely 30. . . .

Anyway, we were talking once and daydreaming—I can't remember the context, but it had something to do with the idea of what a man achieves, his body of work, the sum of his experiences—and we got to talking about print.

We had done this series of films with him. I thought the films were important to record what he was like at the instant, but in a sense they were insignificant as a lasting work. I don't know if I really believe that right now, but my attitude at the time was that you must create a work that is greater than your actual work, so if you were going to write a book it had to be a great book. I was giving him shit because I thought *In and Out the Garbage Pail,* which had just come out, was sloppy. It was kind of rushed to completion because in some ways he was pretty desperate to get it finished and, as a result, it probably isn't as mature a book as it could have been, you know. Because I thought he was an excellent writer. He had the ability to sit down and write when he had to and when he wanted to.

FRITZ PERLS

I didn't say it to him like I really knew, since we were actually stoned. He probably told me I was full of shit or something like that. It *is* a miraculous book, really.

BARRY STEVENS

I remember one time we were talking with Fritz about things in his book *In and Out the Garbage Pail* that seemed to be mixed up. He said, "Don't read it. Just look at the pictures." He said if he read it, he'd be changing it, and that could go on forever. Later he mentioned that he'd changed his mind about a lot of things in it. So . . . for the people who use it as a bible maybe there should be a note in it that Fritz changed his mind about a lot of it.

JOHN STEVENS

Garbage Pail has sold around 70,000 in our edition and another 125,000 in the mass-market edition. *Verbatim* has done even better. It has sold around 150,000 in our edition and over 200,000 in the mass-market edition. It's still selling very well, the mass-market edition particularly.*

Other people have told me what a difficult man Fritz was to do business with, but we never had the slightest argument. He proposed the terms on *Verbatim* and they were fine with me—a very short and simple publisher's agreement where he waived royalties for the first so many thousand copies to make up for my efforts. I needed money for the initial printing costs of *Garbage Pail* and wanted to delay paying him the *Verbatim* royalties, and that was perfectly OK with him.

TOM SHANDEL

I think he saw people like me as ways to get his teaching out into the world. He was using me as much as I was using him. We are each kind of leapfrogging over one another.

I think Fritz Perls was a major figure. I think he was a genius. He had an absolutely rare ability to understand language. Fritz *really* understood. He was a master reader of

---

*Sales as of June '78: 230,000 and 375,000.

language; that is why he could sit in his group with his eyes closed. English, of course, was not his first language, yet he could express himself very, very precisely in English (given a flotilla of assorted grunts and farts along the way), but nevertheless in very accurate language. Another quality he had that made him remarkable were his ears. He was able to hear not only what somebody was saying but what they were implying, what they really meant, and he'd do that instantly. Tremendous bio-computing! The secret of the professional Fritz Perls was those ears—massive ears by the way. . . .

You might be interested in a statement he made to a group of professional therapists:

> *The main tool of a therapist is his ears. He can choose to use those ears as a computer to get the facts and the statistics and the details, or to listen and get the personality of the person.*

He obviously listened.

I feel a much stronger person because of him, physically stronger. He made it popular again to breathe deeper and bring your energy out front. I was always a bit eccentric, but I am much more of a "bohunk" now than I was. Fritz helped me become a bohunk, without ever talking about it— proudly flaunting just what you are.

LARRY HOROWITZ

At Cowichan we were in 14-hour day workshops and in the course of the day groups of us would work with Fritz. There was one man from the East, a psychiatrist dressed in all the Abercrombie & Fitch hippie clothes. He was not a very comfortable guy to be around. The second night of the workshop, this guy started to say something and Fritz turned to him. It was the first time I'd ever actually seen him enraged. He *was* able to rage. He just went, "*You!* Shut up!" The guy was already white and he got whiter. Fritz said, "If you want to stay in this room, I don't want to hear from you." That was it! Period. And he was right 'cause the guy was really toxic.

After we'd gotten through with the training session, Fritz and I sat around bullshitting. Then when I left Fritz' house to go back to my cabin, this guy was coming back. I had a sudden overwhelming fear that this man might hurt Fritz. I said, "I'll just walk back with you." He mumbled something about thinking he had left his glasses at the house. So he went into the house and found that he had his glasses on him all the time. Fritz and I exchanged a look. It was kind of a strange place for me; to be feeling protective of Fritz; the idea of his loneliness and of somebody doing something destructive to him was really frightening to me.

We were living in a communal thing, at Cowichan, trying to put the place together and trying to determine if we would all live there and find some way of doing that. I wasn't sure what I wanted to do. People had to share whatever skills they had. We all had jobs and I was the handyman. You have to know what a klutz I am to know what an incredible position that was.

One day Fritz and I were talking and somebody came up and said, "Fritz, the dock has moved away from the pier."

The pier was actually separating from the dock! He just sat there and said, "Oy ve, Larry, oy ve, Larry." I didn't know which was the pier and which was the dock. But we got it hooked back up.

STELLA RESNICK.

A month after I met him in New York, I wrote him in Cowichan saying I was ready to work with him. He wrote back, "Come ahead." I was really excited.

I became the bread baker at Cowichan, and I worked with Fritz almost every day. Fritz knew that I was seeing my lover in San Francisco. They had had some business relations, and they did not get along. One day I said to him, "Fritz, I know you don't like my friend, but I'd like you to reconsider him because he's very dear to me and I care about what you think and how you feel about him. Perhaps you could meet him again sometime." Fritz said, "We'll see."

I saw my friend in San Francisco on vacation and when I went back to Canada I told a few people that he and I talked about getting married. I didn't tell Fritz.

A few days later I was leading a group—I was already an advanced trainee—and Fritz walked in and quietly sat down. Then in the middle of what we were doing, he gave a big sigh and said, "I hear you are thinking of marrying this man." Obviously he had walked in with this. I said, "Yes, we're considering it."

Some person had been working on the hot seat and now suddenly *I* was on it. He said, "I don't want you to marry this man."

I looked at him like he was crazy. "What do you mean *you* don't want me to marry him?"

"I don't trust him; he'll only hurt you."

"Fritz, it's for me to decide. I'm not going to decide whether or not to marry a man on the basis of what you tell me. It's got nothing to do with you."

He said, "I know this man better than you do. I care about you, I don't want to see you hurt. If you marry him you'll be sorry, and you'll say to yourself, 'I should have listened to Fritz. Fritz was right.'"

And then he got up to leave and he was crying! I felt terribly sad. I can't tell you how important Fritz was to me. Then he walked out and apparently went to his cabin. He didn't come to the community meeting that night. That was

extremely unusual for Fritz. He was really upset, and everybody started giving me a hard time: "Fritz loves you and
you're not listening to him and he knows more than you
do." I felt a lot of pressure.

After that for awhile he treated me very coldly and I was
nervous around him. We didn't talk. Then finally one day we
bumped into each other and I said, "I'm very hurt by all this,
Fritz. You're very important to me, I love you very much, I
don't want you to be hurt, and I can't let you decide for me
who I'm going to marry." He took it quietly. He said, "You
love me or do you want me to love you?"

"I love you," I said, "whether you love me or not." And
he put his arms around me and he said, "I love you, too." So
we kind of made up.

Then at the end of the group he said he wanted everybody
to leave, he didn't want anybody to come back except for a
few of the advanced trainees. This was in December . . . he
was going to be away until March . . . then Cowichan would
start again in April. He said, "The people who can come
back are . . ." and he didn't mention my name. I was horrified.

I went up to him at the end and said, "Fritz, I want to
come back and you didn't mention me."

"Are you going to marry this man?" I said I didn't know.
"If you don't marry him," he said, "I want you to come
back. If you marry him, I don't want you to come back."

ED ELKIN
I had a hard time deciding what I wanted to do when I got to
Cowichan, and was feeling guilty because I didn't want to do
the carpentry and I didn't want to do the cooking. I thought
maybe I might like gardening, but that wasn't right either. I
finally wound up working in the office most of the time. I
corresponded with the other gestalt institutes to get information about what they were doing and ask them to send any
literature they had to Cowichan. When Fritz saw that I could
read and write, he dictated to me and then I'd polish his letters and show them to him and either he'd OK them or

change something. I did some of his correspondence, planning that last European trip he took. That was our closest relationship. It was an informal working relationship and I enjoyed doing it for him.

Our relationship became most difficult when he took a dislike to the woman who was there with me and ultimately he asked her to leave. I had asked him if it was OK for me to bring her to Cowichan. She had come to be with me there, not to be in the workshop; but she was very unhappy with that and asked Fritz if she could be in the workshop. He didn't like her and didn't want her in, but he allowed the community to decide whether she should be in or not. They decided she should be in and he had her in a group separate from mine. From what I heard, he really worked her hard and she suffered a lot; finally one day he told me that he had decided that she should go.

That caused me the most distress, but there was precedent for it since I knew that Fritz had interfered with a lot of relationships. Whether it was his own garbage or not, it seemed like I wasn't a unique case.

He asked her to leave. He saw her as a real bitch. In fact, to this day, I'm not sure that he was wrong. He felt it would be good for me, for my growth and development. I believe that he believed that, but I think it was his own stuff working. He said I could leave with her if I wanted. I don't even remember if that was explicit. Somehow though I knew that it was my decision to stay on with the work and send her away from Cowichan. I believe that Fritz didn't want me to see her at all but I wasn't willing to do that and I asked her to stay at a nearby inn down the road. I went to see her on weekends.

We broke up within a couple of months after leaving Cowichan. We keep in touch infrequently but my way of thinking of it sometimes, is that he precipitated in a few months what would have taken maybe a year or more. When I broke up with her, I met the girl who is now my wife. So maybe all is well. But I never knew and, of course, there's no way of knowing.

There *was* some resentment. If there's any, that's where it is and I've dealt with it from time to time and I've come to accept what is. In any event, I do not regret having spent those months with Fritz. His genius and teachings are still with me.

RICHARD MILLER

It was amazing to me that secure, professional grown men would start marching when an old man, an authority, speaks.

As we walk in the garden of Wilbur Hot Springs—a "people's health sanctuary"—owned by Richard Miller, he points out the various chickens—one that lays blue eggs that are particularly popular during Easter—and an unusually large turkey. . . .

This turkey is so heavy that he can hardly walk around. There were times when Fritz was so "heavy" that hardly *anybody* walked around. Real serious and heavy. This guy's so heavy we're not sure he's going to be able to mate. I think sometimes Fritz had the same problem. Fritz wasn't as heavy physically, but emotionally and intellectually—in the Jewish intellectual tradition—he was.

One of my mini-theories is that what I don't like in you is what I don't accept in myself, and what I like in you is what I very much accept in myself. I got into a relationship with Fritz in which I cared enough about him to like and dislike him, and by doing so learned about myself, to do my unfinished business and go on.

I had heard that Fritz didn't like Richard. There is more than a hint of challenge about him as I tell him this.

Fritz is dead six years. People have been saying negative things about me for the last five.

Once at Cowichan, he said, "Will you close that place?" He meant the Gestalt Institute for Multiple Psychotherapy. "Are you going to come into the fold altogether? If not, get the hell out of the Institute." I said, "No, I'll be in, in my way . . . that's where I'm at, that's what I'm going to do." I wasn't supposed to do that, nobody else did.

I had already bucked him in not cooperating with him with the Jewish princess I was in love with at the time. I was saying to him, I'm going to draw my territorial line. He saw that as divisive. I am a cooperative anarchist. I believe you have to check with your insides and make a decision to do the best you can and hopefully cooperate. There's space for all of us.

In '72 I closed the Gestalt Institute for Multiple Psychotherapy. I was looking for a better way to work. I found it here at Wilbur Hot Springs. We have a perfect system here. We buy and raise most of what we need. There are no clocks so people don't know what time it is, and they eat when they're hungry rather than when it's five o'clock. Booze doesn't mix with those hot baths so people don't bring booze here. We give them a space to rest and recuperate and to put together their natural resources . . . to deal with their aberrations.

LARRY HOROWITZ
Fritz told Shaw, "Now go out and be the world's worst therapist and then come back and get some more training." Now that's neat and the way it has to be. Part of the life process is to go out and try your own wings. Shaw was in his own self-doubt. He is a fantastic human being, deeply conscientious, troubled sometimes, but with a tremendous sense of joy in his aliveness, yet worrying. So to say to Shaw, "Go out and be the world's worst therapist," was kind of giving him permission to go out and make mistakes. I think that would be Fritz' statement to anybody he felt good about. It's like saying, "You've graduated, now go and try it out."

IRWIN SHAW
I was teaching at the University of British Columbia, and in 1967 or '68 I went to a conference of the American Association of Humanistic Psychology. Fritz was doing his thing in front of around six hundred psychologists, psychiatrists, social workers and educators, and when I saw him in action I

said to myself, "That's the person I would like to study with."

I heard he was making films in Vancouver, and I got in touch with him through another person who said it was all right for me to sit in and even participate. So my wife and I participated in those films. It was from that time on—from '68 to almost 1970—that I kept in contact with him.

When he came up from Esalen, he brought a "mistress" with him and her daughter. She acted as his secretary. She wasn't a bright woman. She was very aggressive. He needed this kind of helpmate to get the things going at Lake Cowichan. Aligning with a person like that, you could expect to have things done crudely. He exploited her and was real mean to her. But after a while he just shoved her out. I watched that. He just barked at her, "Get the fuck out of here." He let himself be a bastard. He often said that he would rather consider himself an "un-holy man" than a holy one.

One such holy man, very high in my esteem encountered the un-holiness of Fritz. . . .

Sol Kort

Fritz had a devastating effect on Richard Alpert—Ram Dass. A documentary producer was doing a film on Alpert and wanted a meeting between Alpert and Fritz, naively thinking that they would hit it off and that they'd create some kind of meaningful conversation with historical impact that would be good program material. The producer sent a chartered plane to bring Fritz from Cowichan. I was in the audience, and as the cameras were turning Alpert was saying to a group of kids that he had been through and had transcended "the Peyton Place" of ordinary life. "I've had my jet, my Ph.D., my chicks and that kind of stuff . . . " One of the students said, "Well, *you* might have been through all this, but *we*'d like to taste it all first before rejecting it."

Fritz walked in while this was going on, and he and Alpert gave each other an eye-to-eye greeting, looking very benignly at one another; I guess they had met a couple of times before at Esalen. Fritz didn't want to interrupt but the cameras stopped, and then Fritz and Alpert chatted. Fritz kidded him, "We look like the Smith brothers on the cough drop box—two Jewish boys with these big beards."

Too bad that the videotape wasn't saved. It was really a singular event filled with a tremendous amount of human interest. It was very dramatic. Fritz began to tease Alpert about his role playing.

"If you're enlightened and you've gone through the whole ego thing, the Peyton Place thing, why do you have to go around in an Indian dhoti, why the costume?" This miffed Ram Dass. He didn't like that at all. He appeared upset. He blew out his candles, snuffed out the incense and packed in his pictures. It all sort of collapsed at that point. Fritz said to me afterwards that if Alpert had a nervous breakdown, he could come to Fritz for therapy.

IRWIN SHAW

I was in a living room with Fritz while we watched a tape of Baba Ram Dass and Fritz talking on television. On the program, Ram Dass kept talking, playing with his "toys," dressed up like an Indian guru. Fritz just kept still, not saying one word, looking like he was very constipated sitting on a toilet seat. He realized how disconcerting he was to Ram Dass. And the more Fritz sat wordless, the more Ram Dass talked. He was very warm to Fritz. He said, "Fritz, I've heard so much about you."

The audience was composed of very sharp-tongued young people that night. And though they were more for Ram Dass than Fritz, Fritz easily held his own; he was really sharp. Fritz was happy watching the show. He obviously got a kick out of it. He dismissed Ram Dass as somebody who didn't really have anything special.

Going to the airport Ram Dass kept saying to Sol Kort, "Don't mention Fritz' name again; just keep him out of it." He closed his eyes and did his censoring thing.

SOL KORT

On the way to the airport, Alpert told me he felt Fritz had taken advantage of him at that meeting, using his seniority and reputation, and resorting to unfair tactics in putting him down. Had he, Ram Dass claimed, been further on the path to spiritual realization, he would have been able to handle it, but at that point he was not ready.

Fritz was an awesome person, and sort of formidable looking; one always had that kind of uneasiness in being around him. People were either charmed or antagonized and angered by him. If you annoyed him, then you were treated as a nobody and liable to verbal assault. He had very little patience sometimes. I imagine this was because of the limited amount of energy he had, and, I guess, also his knowing so much about the nature of human behavior and having seen so much of people's foibles.

Contrasts. . .

JERRY ROTHSTEIN

There was the Fritz who had the big ego and the pride and loved the spotlight, and then there was the Fritz who didn't want all that, the Fritz who wanted to be contacted on the basis of being an individual—not a god or some guru who had the answers. He allowed both, and it seems to me he was a pretty damned successful juggler, considering the magnitude of his energies—much more than most people. This great force goes out from him, but he could bring himself back and go the other way.

LARRY HOROWITZ

One of the remarkable things about him was his ability to be in the universe totally with people. We were in a training workshop and one of the trainees was a blind social worker from the midwest. He stopped her while she was working and asked, "Betty, how long have you been blind?" And she said, "Since birth, blind as a bat." He looked very surprised. She worked on. Later, I walked back there to the cabin where Betty was staying, and asked her about her blindness. She said, "Well, when I was about eight years old I had an operation and I could see for about six months . . ." I went back to Fritz and I said, "OK, magician, how the hell did you know that? What were you picking up on?" He said she made color references and that she didn't stay locked in that place that is characteristic of a blind person who listens—*listens* at, instead of *looks* at, you. He noticed that. Nothing went by him. Nothing. He was an exquisite screen.

He was relatively free of the need to be distracted, or the need to cover himself with all kinds of bullshit. I happened to see him for a conference up in Vancouver and I said, "Hello, nice day." And he said, "Larry, please, I'm so tired. Don't give me any bullshit. Let's go some place and talk about what you want to talk about. I don't want to handle the chickenshit and the bullshit, OK?"

That exchange with him was really beautiful and very pleasing to me. We ended up talking for about an hour, an hour and a half. We got into the concepts of toxicity and nourishment.

"I was really dragging my ass when I finished that workshop," Fritz said, "and now I feel nourished. It was like I had a good long nap and I'm OK."

DON BABCOCK

Once I saw a room of thirty-five people where nobody could work. It could have been partly due to numbers, but he was so demanding, everybody just stopped cold. It was as if we were up against a perfectionist and we were labeled this or that. He was completely frustrated. This was the first time I saw him give a lecture in a therapy situation. He talked about introjection, projection and retroflection and he summed up the lecture by saying, "Look, there is only one thing in gestalt, and that is the awareness continuum. It is the only thing there is. That's what it's all about."

All his frustration just came out and he said, "There is no need for confusion, there is *no* need for holding back. *No* need for doubt."

BARRY STEVENS

I remember his seventy-sixth birthday party. I don't know who started it, but I know I was told it would cost $2.50 and we weren't supposed to tell Fritz about it. It was to be a surprise at the inn down the road. Well, close to the time we were supposed to go down, Fritz was still wandering around in his old maroon-colored shorts, and I knew he didn't like the surprise sort of thing, so I went up to him and told him, "I was told not to say anything, but once in a while it's a good thing to ignore that. I don't know if this is one of those times or not but there's a birthday party in about an hour or so."

He stood still quite awhile; then he said, "I don't like it, but I'll go along with it." So he put a shirt on and went on down, still with his swim trunks on, and sat in the center looking very magnificent.

I told him, "I don't give a damn about your birthday party, but I'm sure glad you were born." He said, "Sometimes I feel that way, but not often."

IRWIN SHAW

I was there for his seventy-sixth birthday. We had it at a little restaurant outside of town at Lake Cowichan. I remember when he was blowing out the candles, his beard caught on fire. For a man who once said, "I'm not afraid of death," I saw real terror on his face, real fear. Fritz was afraid.

After the party we went back to Lake Cowichan. It was just party time and we were singing, although I wasn't having such a good time. He kept wandering from group to group, and then he would go back to his house. He wanted something from us, he wanted something . . . "This is a dead group," he would say and then wander off again only to come back and mutter something like this again. "Something's wrong with this group; you don't know how to have a good time; you don't know how to make a party." Finally, he went into his cabin for the rest of the night.

Jim Guinan, who is a counselor at the University of Psychotherapy in Ohio, has an earlier memory. . . .

JIM GUINAN

It was September. It was AHP . . . the best AHP . . . it was at Silver Spring. Gerry Haigh led all 1200 of us on an exciting beginning. It was the year of the "headliners" with Virginia Satir receiving a standing ovation for her family architecture, and Alexander Lowen blowing everybody's mind with his analyzing people's body and psyche simultaneously.

Especially, it was Fritz' heyday.

He was at the top. It was his show. And everybody there knew that Fritz was there. Everybody showed for his presentation. Everybody marveled at his magic. Most everybody stood aside, or backed away, or just gawked as he walked around the hotel, and somehow froze if he should catch their watching him. Truly, his presence there was that of a hero.

And on the last night of the conference, we had a party in our room, no different than every other convention party— too many people crowded into a too-small room, babbling about too many things. Fritz was suddenly there and suddenly something was different. The noise level dropped; people were trying to be serious. And, goddamit, I found myself idolizing him just like everyone else seemed to be doing.

Richard Miller was there and noticed it and began to make fun of everyone's seriousness. That only increased the discomfort. A spontaneous ritual began to ensue of individuals cautiously approaching Fritz, speaking a few questions, and respectfully backing away.

Fritz walked out.

Feeling responsible, I chased after him and apologetically stammered something like, "I guess gods aren't supposed to be at cocktail parties."

In that deep, scratchy, warm voice, he replied, "I am Fritz. I am not a god."

For a moment we spoke. I mentioned his fame, the adulation he was receiving, the fact that he was finally being heard, that gestalt was catching on. He said it was not really he that was being heard, not really Fritz that was getting famous, but only "who they think Fritz is." I was staggered with his loneliness. I was, and remain, aware of the paradox of a man seeking his entire life to be heard, to be listened to, and then when it seemed to be happening, was left isolated and alone by people only hearing and respecting their fantasies of who they thought him to be.

I was overwhelmed with a sense of recognition of him. There was nothing to say. We hugged.

I never saw him again.

ANNE SIMKIN

Until recently I was unable to say goodbye to Fritz. The mention of his name by me and others would bring up an emotional flood. Recently I was able to accept the fact that he was not always the person I had put up on a pedestal—that there were some negative aspects I found not to my liking. Only then could I see Fritz as he was: not a god, but rather a human being like the rest of us, endowed with many outstanding gifts which he shared with the world and with which he made his contribution to his period of living.

ANNA HALPRIN

At that last AHP conference, he was staying in a house next to the one where I was staying. Neither of us went to the AHP Saturday night bash; instead I went over to visit him. I had the feeling that this was our last visit. I don't know if he did or not, but I did; I knew that was what drew me over to see him. We had worked on a dream of mine for years. This time when I went to visit him I said, "Fritz, if you feel like it, I have a strong feeling about completing the dream." And he said, "Yeah, I would like to work with you on it."

Every time he worked with me on this dream, I would discover a different room in the house I dreamt about. This time all the walls separating the rooms dissolved. He said, "Where are you going?" and I said, "I'm going out into the forest and I have to go alone." He said, "I know." And then I danced for him and told him in my dance how much I loved and appreciated him. We did a short dance together, said good-bye. A month later he died. . . .

BARRY STEVENS
He knew he was running down, and he definitely didn't want to go on that way. That is consistent with Fritz as I knew him. At that time he was going around to the small groups in the evening, dropping in on different ones all the time. Then, on the break, he'd often go to his cabin to sleep. Sleep overtook him. He was getting tired from all the questions people asked him about the place, that sort of thing. Questions about this, that and the other. I mentioned in *Don't Push the River* that he'd said his ambitions were giving him nightmares.

CYNTHIA SHELDON
Fritz tried to get a lot of things done before he died. It was almost as if he had a deadline. I remember when he first said, "OK, I'm getting into videotape." And then he got into movies and then he started writing more books. You could really feel him hurrying to finish things.

SOL KORT
He established his school in June 1969, and late that year he decided he wanted to go to Europe in December. The Asian flu was going on then, the weather was miserable both here and abroad, and Shirley told him he should wait until spring to travel. But he was driven. He had to do this now because, come spring, he wanted to reestablish the sessions at

Cowichan and get going on the spring semester. So he just smiled. There was no telling him "No." In retrospect, it would have been better had he not gone, considering that he was fairly old and not that robust. But he had a rendezvous with destiny, or call it what you will. There was never any morbidity on his part. He just sort of watched himself, his energy and strength, though he kept smoking a lot and kidding about his weakness for smoking.

He was supposed to do a program for our center after he returned from Europe, in a large theater. I was a little apprehensive about it, but he said, "No, people will be able to hear me." He planned to set himself up in the middle of the stage with microphones, and the program was to be entitled "An Afternoon with Fritz Perls on Gestalt Therapy Today or Writing One's Own Life Script." It would have been a great performance. We had already sold five hundred tickets so he would probably have had an audience of at least a thousand people. He could have carried it out. The event was scheduled for April 5th, 1970.

KOLMAN KORENTAYER

Sol Kort arranged for him to do it at the Opera House he loved. It was well-organized. And even before the general announcement was out half the seating was sold. Just by word of mouth. It would have been a wish fulfilled for him.

LARRY HOROWITZ

I came to the house a few months before he left, and it was very quiet. I walked in and I felt his presence in the house. You could feel his presence. I thought he might be asleep and I didn't want to wake him up and I called very softly, "Fritz, Fritz, it's Larry." And from a back bedroom he told me to come in. I went into the bedroom. It was *very* dark. He was in bed. He had been down. I don't know if it was psychic pain or physical pain, but he was very, very down. "I wish I had another five years," came home immediately in that exchange with him.

He would say outlandish things like, "Next week I'm gonna go down and renew my pilot's license." "I could fly again if I wanted to" was probably the idea.

He used to have a lot of physical pain. He'd stayed in bed until he felt OK and then he'd go into the main room and chat, smoke—which was always his pleasure.

He acknowledged that he was hurting. I had come down to give him his pictures. John Stevens had finished *In and Out the Garbage Pail* and I was bringing back the pictures John had borrowed for the cover.

Fritz said, "Why don't you just hold onto them." I felt like he was finishing a lot of business with that statement.

JERRY ROTHSTEIN
During the last couple of weeks at Cowichan, we were talking about what his schedule would be like the next year. The first workshops were to start about March 15th. At one point I showed him a letter from Florida, from Vincent O'Connell, I think, asking him to come and do a workshop there in October. Fritz said, "Look, there's going to be a lot of requests for next year that will be coming in while I'm away. Tell them I'm not going to be available." This clashed with his wanting to do more training at that time and to travel. There was something about the way he said it that touched me.

KOLMAN KORENTAYER
Fritz always loved coming back. Cowichan was his home. I remember a moment the last weekend before we closed and Fritz was going to do a workshop. He was sitting in the corner of the living room.

"Barry, Fritz is crying!" I almost shouted to Barry.

"You know, Kolman," she said, "he is leaving his family, it's breaking apart, he's leaving now."

JERRY ROTHSTEIN
After breakfast on the day he was to leave he went to take a nap in his little cabin down by the lake. When the time came,

I went to the cabin to get him. I had been spending a lot of time with him, so I would just walk in. I went into the bedroom and he was sleeping on the bed in his new jump suit. I bent over and kissed him on the forehead, I think, or touched him on the shoulder. He didn't seem too clear, but then he cleared his head and woke up.

I said, "It's time to go." I was going to move in and take care of his house while he was gone. He gave me the keys to his stamp collection, which he kept in two trunks. He said, "This is for Steve. I'm keeping these for Steve. Here, you keep them now. Keep the keys." And he said, "You can have anything in here." He said *have*—not *use,* so I had the impression that he was somehow deciding, or whatever you want to call it, that he was finished with his work and that he wouldn't be back.

IRWIN SHAW
When Fritz left Cowichan . . . the last thing he said to us— this was the good-bye before he would start another group when he came back—the last thing he said to us, was, "If there be a God, let me live another year." I'm quoting him exactly. Well, as you know, he didn't live another year.

Europe and Back:
New York—Chicago

Arthur Ceppos

I'd seen him before he left to go to Europe, he was in my office. He always came to my office. We were friends. He came to laugh. We'd always have fun when we would get together.

In the later years I would see Fritz every time he was out on the East Coast. When we'd get together we'd just laugh at how funny things are. He would tell me things that he would share with very, very few people. He loved it when he started getting recognition and when they built that house for him in Esalen and that, finally, the pychiatrists were beginning to recognize him as being a solid psychiatrist and not merely a maverick. Towards the end this had no meaning for him at all. He realized how insecure and how unproductive these people were who rested on their recognition.

He was very pleased when Real People Press took up his things. I wasn't particularly interested at the time. He wanted me to publish *Ego, Hunger and Aggression* over and over again and I never could. Random House had published it in England. It was out of print, and I just didn't think it was worth publishing. He knew I had publishing problems, and I didn't do things out of benevolence, I never played the benevolent guy. Of course, when Fritz caught on, Random House picked it up and did very well with it.

I would never have gone to his seventy-sixth birthday party but Laura called me . . . and I'm one of his old friends. It was a snowy night and I hate like hell to go uptown . . . the trouble with parking and so forth. There was the whole group and Fritz says, "Art, it's so boring, I wish I could leave." They were all part of the old clique, Laura's clique . . . he'd broken away from them.

397

SYLVIA BEHRMANN CONRAD
I walked with him to the Museum of Natural History, as I
wanted to see Margaret Mead about something. Fritz was
quite eager to meet her and came with me. Unfortunately,
she was away. That was the last time I saw him.

IDA ROLF
Fritz' great mistake, as I saw it, was that he didn't keep in
touch with me. He went through New York, and I saw him
there on the lecture platform and I said, "Fritz, you should
come up."
    "Oh, I have to go to Europe tomorrow. . . ."
    He didn't have to go to Europe at all! And it was on his
way back from Europe that he suddenly felt so ill that he
went to a hospital. I hadn't worked on Fritz, I don't think,
for a year and a half before he died . . . he was lazy about it.

JERRY ROTHSTEIN
Part of the reason for making the trip was to hear the opera
once more in person . . . that's the way he put it. "I want to
hear it once again."
    I had that sense right then, that he wouldn't be back, and
even more when I got a couple of postcards from him—one
complaining of not feeling well in England and one complaining that the music wasn't the same as he remembered it
or as it used to be in Vienna.
    I believe that for whatever reason, he was pretty much
choosing to leave this world at the time he did.

MARGARITE GUTFREUND
He sent me a card from Europe in February; he always remembered my birthday. He congratulated me and told me he
felt fine and he was filled with music.

LAURA PERLS
In Europe, he was drifting aimlessly around, going from one
theater to another and stuffing himself with opera and
theater. He could have that here, too. Some people met him

there, by chance. And he was always by himself and looked miserable.

He stopped in New York . . . always. I saw him on his way out and on his way back. He came back through Boston and gave a workshop there but he was already very tired. He called me from there and I was just on my way out to San Francisco and he was coming here. He had forgotten that I was having my workshop in San Francisco; he was disappointed that I wouldn't be here.

MARGARITE GUTFREUND
He told me it was a mistake and that's why you didn't meet.

LAURA PERLS
Yes, I had to leave a day earlier. I offered to postpone it or just not go if he is not well. He said that it was not that bad, he just needed a little rest. "I'll be all right," he said. "I'm just so tired all the time."

"You know, you are seventy-six years old and you just can't go on like the kind of dynamo you used to be. You have to take it easy more."

"Ya, I know!"

He came here then and Isadore From stayed with him because he was so sick. Isad, of course, looked after him. And Fritz was having a workshop here also, which he then couldn't give because he got sick.

During this period of Fritz' waning health, other dramas were enfolding. Among them, Stella Resnick whose marriage Fritz had objected to. . . .

STELLA RESNICK
I was married at the end of December. Fritz was already in Europe. I worried about what was going to happen. I began composing letters to Fritz, because as far as I was concerned I *was* going back. I wanted to be with Fritz. I was in a workshop Laura was doing out here. It was the first time I'd ever met her. During that time she got a call that Fritz was sick so she left and flew to Chicago.

I don't know if he knew about the marriage. We were only married for about a year, and when we split up I went through some very heavy times. I thought a lot about Fritz' warnings . . . I've often thought about it. . . .

ILANA RUBENFELD

Fritz asked Frank and me to arrange his workshops in New York. Frank, being a clinical psychologist, and I with the body work, were reaching a whole new generation of people. So we organized the last two or three workshops for him. The last one we shared with Marilyn Rosanes. We split the four days between our houses.

Just before that last workshop, Fritz called me from Boston: "Ilona, I'm really not feeling well; but I hope I can give this workshop."

"Don't worry, Fritz," I said, "I have a bedroom for you. We'll have our dinners and everything here. Come to New York. If we need to cancel it, we'll cancel it, but come and let's see how you are."

He did, and spent the first two days in our place.

FRANK RUBENFELD

He was magnificent. This was December of '69 or January of '70. You could see he was refining and crystallizing and developing his ideas during the whole workshop. The theme was contact-withdrawal and he did wonderful things with that and, I thought, he keeps on learning; he keeps on growing.

But it was during that workshop that both Ilana and I had very strong presentiments of his death. Somebody had told me how Fritz had become quite surprisingly afraid of the dark. And, strangely, we were in our living room after dinner and the lights just went out.

ILANA RUBENFELD

It was very strange. He was doing work in my house and all the lights went out. Now I know my house and lights don't just go out. The lights went out and I got feelings . . . I looked at him and I looked into his eyes. He looked terrible. He was dying. The lights went on, then they went out again. I turned to him and I thought, "This is it. I'm never going to see him again."

FRANK RUBENFELD

He was disturbed by it. You could just see he was disturbed. He had talked to me earlier that year, and asked me to join the New York Gestalt Institute. He had also given money to Laura for the Institute. It was as though he knew that his life was coming to an end and he was trying to tie up loose ends. He wanted it to be one happy family towards the end.

That night, if I remember, Ilana and I really cried because we both had had the feeling that he was going to die. He was in pain and he looked terrible. He had a greenish tinge. He looked pale and tired—he had no energy and he couldn't eat.

ILANA RUBENFELD

The third day he went to Marilyn's apartment and got very sick. He said, "I'm not working well. I don't feel well. I'm only on half my cylinders."

Marilyn and I had our hands full. He didn't like people fussing and it was hard to put him to bed. It was hard to give to Fritz. We brought him to Laura's apartment; she was in California at the time. He looked at me and said, "Would you do me a favor?" And I said, "What?" "Get me a TV set." I brought my portable TV set up to the apartment by cab.

Fritz just sat there in Laura's apartment and talked. There were moments he was in such pain, such pain . . . And he was bitter about how people didn't know what he had been through; and then he'd come out of it and be joking again.

FRANK RUBENFELD

I remember the last night that I saw him. I came out of the subway and some guy was selling strawberries at the corner so I bought strawberries for him. He could eat those. He knew he was dying 'cause he said to me, "There's one thing I haven't done, I haven't read all the works of Goethe." He had wanted to see and I'd heard he almost did see every opera there was to see when he was in Europe for those few months and that was part of his greediness. He asked me to fill in for him in Washington. He knew he wasn't going to make it to Washington for the workshop.

ILANA RUBENFELD
He wouldn't stay in bed. He'd get all upset; and he walked into the kitchen and walked out, commanding, "Get me cheesecake!" We didn't know what to do. We called his sister to bring cheesecake. She got it together and brought it over.

MARGARITE GUTFREUND
When I called on the phone, I was told: "No, Grete, nobody can see him." They wanted to avoid my seeing Fritz so I wouldn't get the Asian flu—it was thought he might have that, or some kind of virus. He didn't want anybody. I said that I wanted to see him. Then Fritz called me up and told me I should come. He wanted all the things he couldn't eat. The cheesecake and all such things. I didn't know that he was so sick. And I saw so many things there that he even *shouldn't* have. Then I came another day . . . and he came from the kitchen and said, "I'm not happy that I can't keep it down." I think he went to Marilyn Rosanes' husband and had some X-rays taken.

MARILYN ROSANES-BERRETT
Fritz always came to see Arnold, who is a diagnostic radiologist, for his X-rays.

ARNOLD BERRETT
When I saw him I told him his heart was relatively fine for what he had and what he was. And taking his age into consideration, actually what developed was hard to say.

LAURA PERLS
He wanted to give a workshop in Washington, too, which he could not do, and still he went to give the workshop he had arranged in Chicago.

MARGARITE GUTFREUND
The day he left for Chicago he was alone. He was so stooped, but he carried all his heavy tapes and papers in his arms to the taxi. I said to him, "Fritz, how can you manage all that?" He told me he could. I went with him. It was an awful day. He had nothing on his head. I was not dressed well either. It was colder than I thought, else I would have asked him if I could go with him to the airport. He was alone. I had such a bad feeling in me that day, though I didn't know how sick he really was. He looked very thin and bad. How he could manage, I don't know.

BOB SHAPIRO

When he came in to the Chicago airport on Thursday, Jane Gerber brought him to my apartment. Fritz had stayed in that apartment facing Lake Michigan many times. He liked Chicago for a lot of reasons: He liked to wander the Art Institute, he liked to go to the opera, and to the symphony and he liked to wander about by himself.

When I got to my place Jane said, "Fritz isn't feeling well and I've called Dr. Shlaes." Shlaes was head of internal medicine at Weiss Memorial Hospital and a good friend of Jane's. Fritz was pretty sick, jaundiced, his eye whites almost completely yellow.

"I don't feel well," he said. And then, "I want to call Laura." She was in California. An interesting conversation took place; I heard only the one side of it:

"Laura, I got bad news for you. I'm not feeling well and I wanted you to know."

Apparently she said, "Do you want me to come?" because he said, "No. I don't know. But if you want to it's all right."

And she probably said, "Well, I'll come then," because as he hung up the phone he said, "Ach, I don't vant her."

I said, "What the hell did you call her for, then?"

"I don't know."

It really was not like Fritz, but let me put it this way: It's another underside of Fritz' warm, soft belly that he didn't often expose.

LAURA PERLS

Before he got to the hospital he called me in San Francisco in the middle of a workshop. I said, "I'm coming," and he said, "No! You don't need to."

Why, then, did he call me?

RENATE PERLS

At one point Laura was very bitter, especially after *Garbage Pail* came out. It was full of lies, she might deny it, but she was so angry with him she said, "I'm going to divorce that man.'' But to this day Ma says she has never met anybody who is as interesting and as intelligent as Fritz. And Fritz did not really care for any other woman except as a momentary thing. Whenever it came down to brass tacks he always wanted Laura there.

WILLIAM SHLAES

Fritz had been examined in England and Germany and various places in Europe, treated for backache and all kinds of things, but apparently wasn't doing any better. I made a house call on him at the apartment where he was staying. I examined him, and he asked me—I remember that moment vividly—a very pointed question, "What do you think I've got?"

I gave him three diagnoses: carcinoma of the pancreas (that's cancer of the pancreas), obstructed jaundice due to gallstones, and hepatitis. He asked which came first, and I told him I thought he had carcinoma of the pancreas. At this point he said, "You're the doctor for me."

I think it was the first time he'd been told what might be wrong with him, other than arthritis of the back or a little this or a little that. Evidently nobody had considered the obvious diagnosis, or if they considered it they hid it from themselves and from him. Medically, I think he'd been given a lot of baloney. He appreciated my frankness. I believe that's what led him to accept me as his physician.

BOB SHAPIRO

He was due to do a public lecture that night for the University of Illinois, but Shlaes said, "I think we have to take you to the hospital. Among other things, you're completely dehydrated." And Fritz said, "Yeah, that's right. I'll go." This was like four or five in the afternoon. We went to the hospital in Jane's car and then I borrowed it to get back to the University to announce that Fritz wouldn't be there. By the time I got there the auditorium was almost full. I had to tell them that Fritz had a prior appointment in a hospital.

He went into the hospital on Friday. He wasn't an easy patient. He disliked being confined and having to lie down for the intravenous feeding. He felt a little better on Saturday and about the same on Sunday when they finally brought in the lab technicians. By Monday they'd done all of the testing that they could do and they couldn't pinpoint what was going on, other than he was not retaining very much food; so they continued to feed him intravenously. That didn't make Fritz happy at all because that meant he had to keep his arm still. Fritz never wanted to sit still with anything.

Laura got there that Monday night. She's a dynamo. This was the first time I'd met her in all the time I'd known Fritz. The first statement out of her mouth when I met her at the airport was, "I'm Laura Perls. I want you to know he's still legally married to me though we haven't lived together for 22 years." I thought, "Oh boy, we're in for a real trip." She was probably establishing her claim that she had a right to take over. It didn't make any difference to me.

In some ways Laura was more difficult that week than Fritz was. When he wasn't too conscious there was a peaceful air in the room; when he was conscious, there was just a natural antagonism between them. Many times during the week he would tell her to leave. He'd just say, "Laura, I vant to be alone!"

When they finished the general testing Monday or Tuesday, Shlaes called in a couple of other specialists. They decided they'd better operate and find out what was going on because the tests are not telling anything definite. Fritz agreed. He said, "Fine. That's all right." They scheduled the operation for two days later.

LAURA PERLS
We tried to talk him out of being as sick as he was, but he knew. He told me he knew. He said, "I'm pretty sure I won't make it out of this hospital."

WILLIAM SHLAES
He was extremely realistic all the way through in his relation-

ship with me. Fritz was a physician. He retained knowledge of medicine and he did know the possibilities. We discussed the pathology of what might or might not be.

He accepted being the patient, and related to me as a patient, and not as a therapist in any sense. He was appropriate to the very end. My feeling about him was that this was a very great man whose brilliance never completely came through in his writing or in his movies, but rather in the personal experience of him, there came the real depth of the man.

SOL KORT

We heard rumors that he was ill and I located a number. I called him in the hospital in Chicago and they put me through. He sounded very, very weak. I asked him did he think we ought to cancel the lecture and he said something to the effect that he didn't think he could make it. Then his voice sort of trailed off and he hung up. I hadn't realized he was so ill. I was left with mixed emotions: sadness and guilt for having intruded at such a grave moment.

BOB SHAPIRO

He began to run a fever on Wednesday, and Thursday the fever wasn't any better. So then Shlaes, Laura, Jane, myself and Fritz had another meeting with the surgeon.

"Under normal circumstances," the doctor said, "we really should call off the operation, because it's pretty risky to operate when you're running a fever, and we haven't been able to do much to contain it for two days. You're not getting any stronger. If we go in and operate a week from now, on the hope that we are going to strengthen you—and you're that much weaker—it will just be impossible."

They wanted Fritz to make the decision. Any time you gave him a choice that had to do with his own being, he would always take the risk choice that promised the greatest reward. And he said, very simply, "We go. We operate."

All during this period they were giving him some kind of

sedation. But any time Fritz wanted to come back to his full consciousness, he could do that.

Laura was there and she said, "Fritz, you should tell them about when you had the operation in Africa and they gave you that anesthesia that you couldn't handle." (*Handle* wasn't her word.) You should tell them that if they're going to do that . . ." And he snapped back to consciousness and said, "Laura! 'If, if, if!' 'Should, should, should!' Self- torture, will you ever learn?" And then he lapsed back, sedated.

LAURA PERLS

. . .it was quite mechanical, I wasn't upset. It was just the kind of thing that would come mechanically from him.

Before the operation I sat with him there. I was reading and he was dozing. Sometimes we watched television or listened to music.

Once he opened his eyes and said, "You don't *have* to sit there."

I said, "I know I don't have to but it's where I want to be right now."

BOB SHAPIRO

They operated Friday morning. It was a long one—three and a half hours long. Laura was like any other woman whose husband or lover was being operated on. At times she was like a little girl, acting like a young daughter would act while her father was undergoing surgery; and, at other times, if she felt the nurse ought to know something, she became a first sergeant or fuehrer, demanding information or action.

The report was that he'd done as well as could have been expected so far as the operation was concerned. The two bi-opsies didn't show any malignancy but they were going to have to send the tissue to the lab. It would take two or three days before we'd get a final report.

He never complained about pain but he complained about being held down. He said, "What are they doing here? Tell 'em to take this stuff out. I don't vant it." Yet, of course, he knew they had to feed him that way.

WILLIAM SHLAES

He had a depth of insight into what was going on at every moment, no matter what. A nurse would come in and he would spot almost immediately what made that person tick. I selected the kind of nurse that suited him best—the no bull-shit type of nurse. He didn't have any people coming in patting his brow and saying everything would be all right.

He had some pain, which was promptly relieved. He wasn't very anxious to take relief, but we gave it to him and he accepted it. Prior to becoming comatose he was certainly vigorous enough to resent having the intravenous in, but he accepted that he had to have it. He really didn't buck that kind of thing. He was not at all difficult to work with.

He wanted to strike the same bargain with me that Freud did with his doctor, which was that if he saw fit, I would help him out of this life. I was terribly impressed by the fact that he really would have chosen death voluntarily rather than live his life incapacitated. There's no question about that. He said that clearly. There was no melancholy quality about him at all. He literally gave me a direct order, an absolute direct order. He simply did not want to stay around this world if he had a spreading cancer.

Even on his deathbed, Fritz continued to affect lives; some in uncanny ways. . . .

JOE WALSH

I got acquainted with the Esalen catalog and saw that Fritz Perls was giving a week workshop in April 1970. I signed up for it a couple months ahead. Meanwhile, Laura Perls was scheduled to come to the Cleveland Institute to do a workshop, so I signed up for that, too. The day before Laura Perls' workshop, I got a call from the secretary sayng that Fritz Perls had had a serious attack of some kind and was in a hospital and that Laura Perls was cancelling her workshop, too. I had already been considering an advanced gestalt workshop, and suddenly everything was changed. It shook me up.

When I woke up early Saturday morning I didn't have any thought about it, no plan . . . but I took the plane and was in Chicago by 8:30 that morning. I never gave it a thought. I went straight to the hospital. I don't know how I knew which hospital . . . It was real early, before visiting hours, and nobody was around. I took the elevator up, and then thoughts started coming in, *rational* thoughts: "What the hell am I doing here? I don't know this guy." I got scared. I sat there ten or fifteen minutes; then I got up and wandered down the hall and there on the door of Room 501 was his name. I went in and stood at the end of the bed. Of course I recognized him although I had never seen him before. He was all taped up with tubes in his nose. He looked in very serious condition. As I was looking at him he opened his eyes.

"Who are you?" he said. It was almost a whisper.

"I'm Joe Walsh from Cleveland." He didn't say anything. I guess I'd expected him to. So I said, "I don't know what I'm doing here. I've never met you before but I just find myself here."

Fritz sort of smiled and said something to the effect, "What do you mean you never met me before! I've known you all your life!" and I grinned a little bit. I don't know exactly what he meant. Then he said, "Thanks for coming," and closed his eyes and I could see he was out.

I stood there a minute or two, all these questions going through my head, and then I walked out into the hall and smoked two or three cigarettes. Just then a woman got off the elevator and I knew it was Laura Perls. I watched as she went into his room; I sent a note in to her saying that I was from Cleveland and was there anything I could do to help. In a while a nurse went in and Laura came tripping down the hall. We embraced. It felt very good.

She said, "You know, all the people who know Fritz are interested and involved; there are wires and conversations and telephone calls, but you're the only human being. I'm here alone with him; will you stay a while?"

LAURA PERLS

He met me in the hallway. He just said that he had to come

and he wanted to see me and Fritz. I don't even think he saw Fritz . . . or perhaps, just through the door. I may be mistaken there. He came with the intention, I think, that he would like to do some things for me . . . but there was nothing that could be done. . . .

JOE WALSH

We had a cigarette. She told me about the children. She felt that Fritz couldn't survive this thing. I left at mid-afternoon, about 3:30.

MARTY FROMM

The day after Fritz had surgery in Chicago, I called the hospital and spoke to Laura. She told me she was leaving on Monday and that Fritz was recovering nicely. She said she was scheduled to do workshops in California. She really raved about the beautiful work and vacation she was missing. I said, "Fine. As long as you're leaving and Fritz will be alone, ask him if he would like to see me. I'll come to Chicago next weekend and spend the weekend and help nurse him." She said she would.

LAURA PERLS

The doctor was in with Fritz at the time, so I spoke with her . . . not in the room, but outside . . . I asked him if he wanted her to come and he motioned with his hand that he wasn't interested . . . he just wasn't interested in anybody at that point.

. . .his last wish when he was already under oxygen was for a cigarette. I said, "You have oxygen right now and you will blow yourself up." He knew he couldn't get it and gave up. I had such trouble getting the people to give him the oxygen. He wanted it . . . he was a doctor himself. I think they were just prepared to let him die. It was Saturday, I think, and there was no doctor available at that moment . . . Then they said they can't do it without permission. And I said, "Then get the permission!" It took half an hour to get oxygen for him. He got it then and he had it for the rest of the

day . . . but it was difficult to breathe anyhow . . . it wasn't
enough anymore.

BOB SHAPIRO
Every time he regained consciousness, he wanted to have the
tubes taken out of him but we couldn't do anything about
that and he knew it. About 5:30 the doctor said, "He's probably going to stay like this for the next ten or twenty
hours." He was out, they had sedated him. So Laura, Jane
and I went downtown to dinner.

A few days before that, on Wednesday or Thursday, he
talked to us about his funeral. Anyway, that night about
8:00, we called from the restaurant and talked to the nurse.
She said, "He's about the same. He's still out. There's no
point in driving back."

The head nurse. . . .

INGE DE LA CAMP
Medically, his condition deteriorated very rapidly, but he
was a determined man. You couldn't tell him what to do. He
was just going to tell you what he wanted you to do—determined. But that's not that unusual. You see that quite often.

LAURA PERLS
Bob took us to a place called the Brown Derby. Odetta was
singing and just before she came on, at nine o'clock, I tried
to phone Fritz' room to see how he was. They said they were
busy now in his room and to call back later. About 9:30
Odetta sang something and I said, "Fritz would have liked to
have heard that," and it struck me that I had said it as if he
was already dead. And *at that moment* he died!

BOB SHAPIRO
After we ate we went back to my apartment and Laura called
the hospital. In about four or five minutes, she came screaming down the hall: "Fritz is dead!" She was hysterical. So
was I. We called Jane and took her with us to the hospital.

We got there in about ten minutes. They hadn't even touched him.

The head nurse, who had always been especially attentive to Fritz, said, "I was with him and there was nothing that you or I could have done." She also said, "He was giving us a bad time about being held down. He started to get up and the nurse said, 'Dr. Perls, you have to lie down! You're pulling out all these things.' She put him down. A minute later, he started to get up again. At this point she buzzed for me and I went in. As I came in he had almost swung his legs out of bed, and I said, 'Dr. Perls, you have to lie down.' He looked at me and said, 'Don't tell me what to do.' Then he collapsed and he was gone."

Dr. Shlaes says, "I think the story's a myth, because he was really comatose at the end." The head nurse, Inge de la Camp, does not recall it; and the nurse (Margaret Phipps) who was with Fritz at his death, says, "I was going through a rather traumatic divorce about that time and have few memories except of that. However, I do think that if Dr. Perls' death was as dramatic as saying, "Don't tell me what to do," and then dying, I would remember that, and I don't." Whether or not the story is apocryphal, it has the ring of Fritz. It is a fitting commentary on the way he lived and may have died.

LAURA PERLS
They called me later back at the house and told me he expired at nine-thirty. That was the fourteenth of March, 1970. His heart was in such bad condition; they had said if he could weather the first three or four days he would be okay, but he weathered only one and a half terrible days. His heart gave out. In the autopsy it appeared he had a deep-seated pancreas cancer and he would probably have died painfully within three or four months anyhow. Fritz suspected that he had cancer.

I'm convinced that Fritz decided to leave his body; he had the wisdom to know it was time because five days later when we got the autopsy we found that he had cancer of the pancreas and under any circumstances he might have lived another two or three weeks at the most, in agony.

WILLIAM SHLAES

In actuality, he died of an acute myocardial infarction. At the autopsy they found a cancer very deep in the pancreas, but he died of the heart attack, not of cancer. It would have been a long time before he died of that cancer.

LAURA PERLS

I think the doctor knew that he would die . . . because that morning, I had seen the doctor for a moment—I had just come in when the doctor came out of his room and I asked, "How is he?" He passed me very quickly and said, "Oh, he's a very sick man!" He didn't say anything else. I had the feeling that they had given up. He was a very good doctor. And the operation was successful, but the heart didn't hold out. It was doubtful from the beginning, you see . . . They did everything that was necessary still to do, but the heart was in such bad condition, you know, it was so terrible. *[Speaking very softly]* It was really a relief.

WILLIAM SHLAES

It's very difficult to describe a personal relationship, to describe a man in that kind of an area and give it any real substance or flavor. The only thing I can really tell you is that, in my opinion, this was a great man who met his death with the kind of distinction I would have expected from him.

> *The ability to resign, to let go of obsolete responses, exhausted relationships, and tasks beyond one's potential, is an essential part of the wisdom of living.*

BOB SHAPIRO

We complied fairly well with his wishes. He had said, "I

want to be cremated and I want a celebration in Grace Cathedral and I want Anna Halprin and the audience to dance.'' We weren't able to get Grace Cathedral, but we used the San Francisco Civic Auditorium. It overflowed with 1200 to 1500 people. Anna Halprin got the whole audience to do a dance of God in candlelight, in celebration of life and death. It was the evening Fritz had wanted. . . .

Anna Halprin

When I danced at his wake I remember thinking I didn't want to rehearse or plan ahead. I wanted to dance in the present. When I was called to the platform, the first thing that came to my mind was to form a *minyan.** I wanted to transform the stage to a sacred space within the Jewish tradition. I had ten people join me. They turned me upside down so I could get really out of my head and into my senses. Then I found myself moved by the image of the burning bush and the guardian angel that Fritz and I had experienced together years before. In my dance they merged. In Jewish tradition, the guardian angel comes and carries you on his wings back to Zion. We all danced a joyful dance. I thought Fritz would like this at his wake.

Laura Perls

He wasn't quite 77; he was 76; he didn't live to his 77th birthday. He would have been 77 in July and he died in March.

---

*A *minyan* is ten people coming together to worship. Jewish tradition establishes the number ten as a congregation.

JACK DOWNING

The Gestalt Institute in San Francisco had scheduled a lecture-demonstration by Fritz. Two weeks before we had it, he died. So we went ahead and had it as a memorial and showed some of those Canadian films. There were 750 people there. About five or six of us got up and said something about Fritz. Nobody had a sad tale. I don't know of a tear. It's exactly as though Fritz were there and we were memorializing Fritz. It was a gay thing. We all had a good time.

BETTY FULLER

Fritz was a man for these times. He might even be back with us already . . . even though he always said that once you die, that's it, there's nothing else. I like to think about that and I smile and say to myself, "I bet you know better now, Fritz!"

TOM SHANDEL

He changed my life. He changed a lot of people's lives. It is the kind of greatness that he was after, to touch many more people than you can touch yourself. Fritz really was a reformer. He was on a campaign—he was going to change the world and why not. He wasn't in there just for the personal glory.

MARTY FROMM

Even in Miami, we recognized that Fritz was an old man and we didn't imagine that gestalt therapy would make it while he was alive. That was one of the reasons he was doing his missionary work and why he was interested in training Gene Sagan, Wilson Van Dusen, Jim Simkin, the Cleveland people, and me. He really saw us as his heirs, those who would go on propounding gestalt therapy. We could not have imagined that Esalen and the human potential movement and Fritz—the right man at the right time—would mesh. But suddenly, in 1961, in California, the whole thing took off. The fact that he did achieve prominence and fame and fortune and recognition before he died is really marvelous for me as well as for him.

ANDY CURRY
Fritz was like my father. I was very shaken when he died, very shaken. It was twice, you see—my real father died in 1968 and Fritz in 1970. Two of the four or five really heavy men in my life were mortal. Now, as these people go, it not only reminds me that I'm going to go too, but that *I'm* it. If they're gone, and if anything has to be taken care of, I got to do it.

KOLMAN KORENTAYER
The night of Fritz' death I had been to eat at Nepenthe in Big Sur. I had been rolfed that day by Peter Melchior and was walking the short distance to Emil White's house. Suddenly, I sort of collapsed. My feet gave way beneath me. Getting up, I checked to see if anything had broken. A strange new strength flooded over me. I felt very different. Very, very different. Much stronger. It was most unusual. I continued on to Emil's and didn't think any more of it. The next morning when I returned to Esalen, the first person I met was Peter Melchior.

"A strange thing happened to me . . ." I started to tell Peter, but he interrupted, "Have you heard?"

"Heard what?"

"Fritz died last night."

I sat down. I was crying and then Dick Price joined us.

SEYMOUR CARTER
That was a curious time here [at Esalen]. He had been gone from here for a couple of years. It was really confused here without Fritz. The place got scattered. Then someone said Fritz had died. Right away Dick came in and he and I sat down together. We didn't cry—we just—maybe Dick cried, I don't remember. We just sat together.

RICHARD PRICE
Fritz' impact is pretty simple. It is to survive and just grow. It's like grass growing out there—simply, slowly. His work stands. Everything else falls by the wayside.

PENNY YOUNGREEN

I sure can remember the moment when I heard the news of Fritz' death—I was in shock. I felt at the time like even my own parents' deaths couldn't affect me the way I felt then. We didn't say anything; we just sat there and looked at each other. "Oh my God, we've lost our ace in the hole!"

GIA-FU FENG

Three or four months before Fritz died he was in Chicago having dinner at Bob Shapiro's apartment. Two young Japanese ladies were serving a Japanese meal to all the guests, and afterwards one of the women massaged Fritz. And Bob Shapiro said, "You know what Fritz said that night? He said to the Japanese woman, 'Your fingers almost feel like Gia-fu's fingers.'" So that's the end—a very sweet ending of our encounter.

I miss him. I came back to this place and no rabble-rouser any more. Everybody was groovy tripping and doesn't criticize anybody else. You have your trip, just lay low, just make your money and go. So I really miss him. I benefit just by his being.

He contributed to me. He was a true revolutionary. Nobody can imitate his way of digging into people. And I have seen maybe one hundred gestalt therapists after him, and nobody is like him. He will never be here again. He's evolving every minute.

CLAUDIO NARANJO

I felt a very strong connection of destiny in that I intended to meet with Fritz again at the very time he was to die. He lived up in Canada then. I kept hearing good things about him; how he had come to a mellower wisdom of age. It had been three years. During my last contact with him at Esalen he had said, "For the first time I've broken through my schizophrenia layer." For a man in his seventies to say, "I've only now defeated my schizophrenia,' is a courageous acknowledgement. It revealed the extent to which he was not fossilized. I wanted to experience him again . . . partly to say goodbye . . . so I signed up for a workshop with him that was announced for the time of his arrival from a European tour. He never arrived in Canada for that workshop, because its date turned out to be that of his death.

This synchronicity was followed by another—the most mournful of my life: The day of Fritz' memorial was also the day of my son's death in a car accident. Matías was eleven at the time. It was Easter Saturday and he was going to a picnic in the Big Sur hills with the people who were intending to become involved in what became the Arica movement. I was going to go to the picnic also, when Abe Levitsky called to ask, "Would you come to Fritz' memorial and say a few words?" I actually didn't say any words, but I felt I did want to be present at Fritz' memorial.

It's a very strange and haunting situation for me to consider. I keep thinking that if I hadn't gone perhaps the accident wouldn't have happened. Or perhaps I would have been in it. It's impossible to know. Some people who were there told me that Matías didn't want to get into that car. In his way he quoted Fritz' last words. Fritz had responded to the nurse who ordered him to not sit up in the bed with, "Don't tell me what to do." Matías had said, when ordered to get into the car that minutes later fell off the cliff, "Why do I always have to do what grownups tell me?"

STEPHEN PERLS

Much of the stuff that's happened to me since his death is not his fault. Too many people say, "Are you related to Fritz Perls?" Some people can just accept it, but others go into a whole long trip about what their experiences with him have been and do not see me as me. I don't appreciate that. I don't like being seen as "son of. . . ."

LESLIE GOLD

I didn't feel bad when he died. He'd been dead for me all those years I hadn't seen him. I had no love for him. It wasn't possible. He never lived up to my image of a perfect grandfather, and yet, I know that he has had a great impact on the lives of many people. Maybe it would be better to have no feelings towards him. Maybe it would be better to rediscover him as the Fritz other people love and admire.

RENATE PERLS
After Fritz died I went through two horrendous years not knowing who was Fritz and who was me.

In the past four years she has been through many changes. No longer afraid, no longer dependent on her husband, she has left him. "Art needed a weak woman," she says. She's discovered life. Her letters are warm, sometimes troubled and always vibrant.

As for any feelings of mine about Fritz—it's like with everything in my past. It doesn't matter any more. I have no feelings about him at all. Once I worked him through and found that I really didn't like him; he was no longer of any importance to me. He may be to others, but who I am today has absolutely nothing to do with Fritz Perls, and I find that ridding myself of him and forming a totally new personality of my own being of my own making is much more satisfactory.

Background? I was educated in Johannesburg, married at a very early age. Died. Then came back to life February 2, 1975. Not much for publication, is it? Be well. Love, Renate.

LAURA PERLS
I am not a bitter woman. I have gotten over the mourning . . . Through the years when he came and went . . . and came and went, it was always another separation and another period of mourning and resentment. Now it is final. I have lived through it and I think I am over it. I am also more creative . . . and I am enjoying my life again, much more than for many years before.

IDA ROLF
Of course there are myths about Fritz, just as there are myths about me. And when I meet those myths in the next world, I'm gonna have a bad time! But no matter how you slice it, Fritz was a good guy.

MOSHE FELDENKRAIS

There's an old Hebrew saying, "It's a pity that we lose those who cannot be forgotten." That's the kind of thing which, of course, relates to Perls. Many people remember him and many will.

EUGENE SAGAN

I was very upset by his death. Actually, I was mostly upset by the fact that he died before we had a chance to become reconciled. I wish I could run several of those years over again. I made certain demands on Fritz to be more than he was; I couldn't let him have his defects.

WILL SCHUTZ

When he died I felt very sorry and sad. That surprised me. I felt much sadder than I thought I would because at the time he died, he'd been away from here for a couple of years and I really hadn't had any contact with him. But when I heard of his illness and then his death, I felt sad. I felt a personal loss for something that might have been but wasn't.

WILSON VAN DUSEN

I felt a kind of emancipation from Fritz, which is, I think, in Fritz' own terms, a healthy thing. I didn't even go to his funeral. Someone said, "Fritz died," and I said, "Well, by golly, it was about time, actually . . ." He had had more living than most other human beings. He was square dancing and flying airplanes and doing this and that, you know. Girls galore! Goddam! He's had more girls than I've ever seen.

I felt that there went an immensely gifted man, and I would never put that down, yet one who was not very happy.

ROMILLY GRAUER

My use of Fritz personally was that this was a person I had to live up to. And in a way it was a relief but then there'd be moments when I'd feel a lot of grief. This is one of them. He could be so sweet and when he wanted he could just project love.

He got awfully tired that year. He gave a lot all the time.

JOHN HORLER

Fritz was just a guy . . . He was like a good carpenter, a good mechanic—he was a craftsman. He had a skill which he developed, and a good craftsman has a surety about himself. He'd been through a lot of trips and he'd done a fair amount of lying and what not, but he had his craft, his thing. He was fairly sure of himself, and he lived behind that. He was a good man, but he was just a man . . . he was a nice guy. . . .

JIM SIMKIN

I've never been able to see him as being completely dead. I still love him and forgive him for being Fritz. The man was an enormous genius; he could cut through bullshit so quickly and go to where a person lived in five or ten minutes, and he was very infrequently bamboozled. He was entitled to be cruel, and a bastard, and contradictory, and all kinds of things. . . .

Yet another view. . .

JACK GAINES

Fritz, who played so many roles with such relish in life, re-fused after death to be held in place as merely the subject of this book. He was present at every interview, he looked over my shoulder whenever I wrote, he led me through my own impasse—the dead point when I was blocked by an over-whelming conviction that I could not complete this book: at different stages of the work I was unable to move ahead or to abandon it. Stuck in one or another phase, a sense of un-fulfillment gnawed at me.

Then I remembered Fritz' message that inner conflicts are ". . . attempts . . . to retain the status quo; to kill the future, to avoid the existential impasse and its pseudo-agony." He spoke directly to my strong sense of discomfort in these words:

> *The tension arising out of the need for closure is called frustration, the closure is called satisfaction.* Satis -

enough; facere - *to make. Make it so that you have enough. In other words, fulfillment; fill yourself until you are full. With satisfaction, the imbalance is annihilated, it disappears.*

Fritz said that when one took care of the obvious, one was free to move on to the next experience. Gradually I realized that no matter what else I was doing, nothing short of completion would be fulfilling.

During the course of working on this book, I had met with an almost infinite variety of lifestyles and perceptions of reality. In being able to see and marvel at the many different ways people perceive reality and live their lives, I began to see that my being overwhelmed was also only a way. It took me a long time to become aware of the obvious: The only way to get through the work was to get through it. The effort to avoid discomfort or pain or failure or death is delusive. Evasion is in fact ossification and perpetuation. Fearful of an event, one lives constantly with its imminence. I began to see that I had no barriers other than those in my mind—and that they were extraneous to my life and well-being.

Each phase of this work had its own richness, and yet it was the satisfaction of completion that ultimately offered the greatest reward. I am now on the other side and it is a far better place.

For me Fritz Perls represents the possibility of fulfillment of our society's mute yearning against all odds, for a sense of wholeness. He was my doorway towards completion and wholeness. It is my hope that through this book he may also open the way for others.

BETTY FULLER:
You look around at this world and it needs Fritz Perls right now . . . we just don't have what he had. We need his wisdom for the world today. You know, if those of us who had contact with Fritz could get together and bring the piece of him that we each were able to bite off, and chew and manifest and integrate it then we might have some kind of a col-

lective gift to give the world. And maybe that's what's happened after all.

AL DRUCKER

He was really a very compassionate human being. A real
mensch*—and a reprobate, and all those other things. I respect and honor him, he is really a great being. I love him.

MICHAEL MURPHY

I must say, my appreciation of Fritz grew after he died because I was freed from the static of our relationship. He is a
genius! He was such an extraordinary man! He had to be
contended with because he was so intensely human. He had
drives. He was ambitious; he so wanted recognition. That is
really what led to a lot of the conflict. . . .

I feel that drive is the problem. It varies from person to
person. Every man wants to build his pyramid. The fire in
the soul can be translated into joy and delight and a life of
pleasure. It can also translate itself into the need for status
and recognition. We don't have to surrender to that. It becomes demonic at times in a lot of people. I've felt it myself.
Fritz more or less surrendered to it; he went all out to become
famous. For example, those big posters—he had them made
himself and distributed. He wanted to be right in there with
Marlon Brando and the others!

*But wasn't there really an inherent pride in what he was do-
ing, a certainty that his work had value? Perhaps had Fritz
received more acclaim while he was still younger and vital,
then the mellowing might have come earlier, and some of the
demonic would have been less acute.*

That could be. The acclaim came on very fast, really starting
about 1966. He died suddenly in 1970, so it came in those last
four years; with the acclaim, he mellowed very much.

At Cowichan, he became the happiest in his entire life. He

---

*Someone of consequence, someone to admire and emulate, someone of
noble character.

developed a kind of glow. His head became this big around! It actually seemed to enlarge. He and I finally came together then.

BERNARD GUNTHER
The thing is to remember him as he was, warts and all.

MICHAEL MURPHY
When Fritz died, I think there was relief, relief inside me. I can't recall the moment. It seems a seamless flow of time between the living and the passing of Fritz.

If your shade is near, Fritz, know how much we love you. That is why we talk about you all the time.

The last word. . . .

How much of the experience do you remember? How much are you biased? How much of the tone of voice, of hesitations, do you remember? Have you swallowed the incident, or do you recall and return to that event in reality—which is impossible, as the event is past while the returning is now. This returning gives us already much more—and much less biased—material than the frozen memories, which in fact are biased by the present position of liking or disliking.

Many investigations exist about the bias and selectivity of the memory of, say, observers of an accident. I wish you had seen the picture Rashomon, *and you could experience how differently each person interprets the same events, according to the needs of their self-esteem system.*

In other words, even the most reliable observation is an abstraction.

FRITZ PERLS

Acknowledgments

During the years I have spent putting this book together, I have been fortunate to have had the encouragement and assistance of many good people. It is a pleasant task to express my appreciation to a few of them:

G. Russ Youngreen is my favorite cartoonist in the world, and his drawings provide balloons for the spoken words to float around in; Joe Wysong saved me from errors and supported me when I needed support badly; Henry S. Thompson was generous with his time, his talent and his interest, somehow always being available to listen to even the most minute of my many concerns and to give me his invaluable opinion; Barry Stevens, a wise and kind woman, showed me that even when there appears to be no way beyond an impasse, with love and intelligence there is; Pam Ray helped during the lonely, early stages when I was feeling that one lifetime was not enough to complete this project; Tony Stickel, Gideon Schwarz, Louis Jones, David Morris, and Abigail Johnston helped a lot; my daughter, Nora, somehow always manages to set the pace; Peggy Fennessey, who shared my life during much of the turbulent course, provided joy and love, and was always a pleasant and necessary distraction.

And finally, to Fritz Perls, here and now, whom I came to know even though we did not meet face to face. I am glad to be the medium for others to know you.

Bibliography

By Fritz Perls:

Books

Perls, Frederick S., *Hunger and Aggression*. London: Allen & Unwin, 1947 (Random House, 1969).
____*Gestalt Therapy Verbatim*. Moab, Utah: Real People Press, 1969 (Bantam, 1971).
____*In and Out the Garbage Pail*. Moab, Utah: Real People Press, 1969 (Bantam, 1971)
____*The Gestalt Approach and Eye Witness to Therapy*. Palo Alto, CA: Science & Behavior Books, 1973 (Bantam, 1976).
Perls, Frederick, et al., *Gestalt Therapy: Excitement and Growth in the Human Personality*. New York: Julian Press, 1970 (Crown, 1977).
Perls, Frederick S., R.F. Hefferline, and P. Goodman, *Gestalt Therapy*. New York: Julian Press, 1951 (Dell, 1965).

Chapters in Books

Perls, Frederick, "Gestalt Therapy and Human Potentialities," *Explorations in Human Potentialities*, H. A. Otto, ed. Springfield, IL: Charles C. Thomas, 1966 (reprinted in *Gestalt Therapy Primer,* F. D. Stephenson, ed.).
____"Four Lectures," *Gestalt Therapy Now*, J. Fagan and I. L. Shepherd, eds. Palo Alto, CA: Science & Behavior Books, 1970.
____"Dream Seminars," *Gestalt Therapy Now*, J. Fagan and I. L. Shepherd, eds. Palo Alto, CA: Science & Behavior Books, 1970.
____"Gestalt Therapy," *Inside Psychotherapy,* A. Bray, ed. New York: Basic Books, 1972.
____"Gestalt Therapy Verbatim," *Human Development: Selected Readings,* M. L. Haimowitz and R. N. Haimowitz, eds. New York: Thomas Y. Crowell, 1973.
____"Morality, Ego Boundary, and Aggression," *Gestalt Is,* J. O. Stevens, ed. Moab, Utah: Real People Press, 1975.
____"Resolution," *Gestalt Is,* J. O. Stevens, ed. Moab, Utah: Real People Press, 1975.
____"One Gestalt Therapist's Approach," *Gestalt Therapy Now,* J. Fagan and I. L. Shepherd, eds. Palo Alto, CA: Science & Behavior Books, 1970.

Perls, Frederick, and P. Goodman, "The Theory of the Removal of Inner Conflict," *Gestalt Is*, J. O. Stevens, ed. Moab, Utah: Real People Press, 1975.

Perls, Frederick, R. F. Hefferline, and P. Goodman, "Gestalt Therapy," *Psychotherapy and Counseling Studies in Technique*, W. S. Sanakian, ed. Chicago: Rand McNally, 1969.

Periodicals

Perls, Frederick, "Theory and technique of personality integration," *American Journal of Psychotherapy*, 2 (1948): 565-586 (reprinted in *Gestalt Is*, John O. Stevens, ed.).

_____"Group vs. individual therapy," *ETC*, 24 (1967): 306-312 (reprinted in *Gestalt Is*, John O. Stevens, ed.).

_____"Notes on the psychology of give and take," *Complex*, 9 (1953): 24-30 (reprinted in *Recognitions in Gestalt Therapy*, P. D. Pursglove, ed.).

_____"Two instances of Gestalt therapy," Case Reports in Clinical Psychology, Kings County Hospital, Brooklyn, NY, 1956 (reprinted in *Recognitions in Gestalt Therapy*, P. D. Pursglove, ed.).

Perls, Frederick, and C. C. Clements, "Acting out vs. acting through," *Voices*, 4 (1968): 66-73 (reprinted in *Gestalt Is*, John O. Stevens, ed.).

On Fritz Perls and Gestalt Therapy

Books

Barnett, M., *People, Not Psychiatry*. London: Allen & Unwin, 1973.

Brown, G. I., *Human Teaching for Human Learning: An Introduction to Confluent Education*. New York: Viking, 1971.

Downing, Jack, and R. Marmorstein, *Dreams and Nightmares: A Book for Gestalt Therapy Dream Seminars*. New York: Harper & Row, 1973.

Downing, Jack, ed., *Gestalt Awareness*. New York: Harper & Row, 1976.

Dye, H. A., *Gestalt Approaches to Counseling*. New York: Houghton Mifflin, 1975.

Fagan, J., and I. L. Shepherd, eds., *Gestalt Therapy Now*. Palo Alto, CA: Science & Behavior Books, 1970 (Harper & Row, 1971).

Fagan, J., and I. L. Shepherd, eds., *What Is Gestalt Therapy?* New York: Harper & Row, 1973.

Fagan, J., and I. L. Shepherd, eds., *Life Techniques in Gestalt Therapy*. New York: Harper & Row, 1973.

Faraday, A., *Dream Power*. New York: Coward, McCann & Geoghegan, 1972 (Berkley, 1973).

Greenwald, J. A., *Be the Person You Were Meant to Be: Antidotes to Toxic Living*. New York: Simon & Schuster, 1974.

Hatcher, Chris, and Philip Himmelstein, *The Handbook of Gestalt Therapy*. New York: Aronson, 1976.

Kempler, W., *Principles of Gestalt Family Therapy*. Costa Mesa, CA: Kempler Institute, 1974.

Latner, J., *The Gestalt Therapy Book*. New York: Julian Press, 1973 (Bantam, 1974).

Lederman, J., *Anger and the Rocking Chair: Gestalt Awareness with Children*. New York: McGraw-Hill, 1969.

Levy, R., *I Can Only Touch You Now*. Englewood Cliffs, NJ: Prentice-Hall, 1973.

Leonard, George B., *The Transformation*. New York: Dell, 1972.

Loew, C. A., H. Grayson, and G. H. Loew, eds., *Three Psychotherapies: A Clinical Comparison*. New York: Brunner/Mazel, 1975.

Lyons, Joseph, *Experience: An Introduction to a Personal Psychology*. New York: Harper & Row, 1973.

Naranjo, Claudio, *The Techniques of Gestalt Therapy*. Highland, NY: The Center for Gestalt Development, 1979.

_____*The Healing Journey,* New York: Ballantine, 1975.

Passons, W. R., *Gestalt Approaches in Counseling*. New York: Holt, Rinehart and Winston, 1975.

Polster, E. and M. Polster, *Gestalt Therapy Integrated*. New York: Brunner/Mazel, 1973 (Random House, 1974).

Pursglove, P. D., *Recognition in Gestalt Therapy*. New York: Funk & Wagnalls, 1968.

Rhyne, J., *The Gestalt Art Experience*. Monterey, CA: Brooks/Cole, 1973.

Rosenblatt, D., *Gestalt Therapy Primer*. New York: Harper & Row, 1975.

_____Opening Doors: *What Happens in Gestalt Therapy*. New York: Harper & Row, 1975.

Schiffman, M., *Gestalt Self Therapy*. Menlo Park, CA: Self Therapy Press, 1971.

Schutz, William, *Joy: Expanding Human Awareness*. New York: Grove, 1967.

Shephard, M., *Fritz: An Intimate Portrait of Fritz Perls and Gestalt Therapy*. New York: Saturday Review Press, 1975 (Bantam, 1976).

Shostrom, E. L., *Man, the Manipulator*. Nashville: Abingdon Press, 1967 (Bantam, 1968).

Simkin, J. S., *Mini-Lectures in Gestalt Therapy*. Millbrae, CA: Celestial Arts, 1976.

Stephenson, F. D., ed., *Gestalt Therapy Primer: Introductory Readings in Gestalt Therapy*. Springfield, IL: Charles C. Thomas, 1975.

Stevens, B., *Don't Push the River*. Moab, Utah: Real People Press, 1969.

Stevens, J. O., *Awareness: Exploring, Experimenting, Experiencing*. Moab, Utah: Real People Press, 1971.

Stevens, J. O., ed., *Gestalt Is*. Moab, Utah: Real People Press, 1975.

Van Dusen, Wilson, *The Natural Depth in Man*. New York: Harper & Row, 1973.

Walkenstein, E., *Beyond the Couch*. New York: Crown, 1972.

Walker, J. L. *Body and Soul: Gestalt Therapy and Religious Experience*. Nashville: Abingdon Press, 1971.

Yontef, G. M., *A Review of the Practice of Gestalt Therapy*. Los Angeles: Trident Shop, California State University, 1971.

Films

Films, Incorporated, 1144 Wilmette Ave., Wilmette, IL 60091:
   What is Gestalt (24 min.)
   Awareness (27 min.)
   The Philosophy of the Obvious (25 min.)
   Madeline's Dream (20 min.)
   Memory and Pride (24 min.)
   Marriage (25 min.)
   The Gestalt Prayer (Couples) (24 min.)
   Everything is Aware Process (28 min.)

The Media-Psych Corporation, P.O. Box 7707, San Diego, CA 92107:
   Birth of a Composer (24 min.)
   The Case of Mary Kay (15 min.)
   The Death of Martha (40 min.)
   Demon (14 min.)
   Grief and Pseudo-Grief (33 min.)
   The Impasse (22 min.)
   The Mini-Satori (14 min.)
   Resurrection (14 min.)
   Relentless Greed and Obesity (16 min.)
   Self-Sabotage (27 min.)
   A Session with College Students (50 min.)
   Stuttering (12 min.)

Psychological Films, Inc., 189 N. Wheeler St., Orange, CA 92669:
   James S. Simkin: In the Now (45 min.)
   Frederick Perls: A Session with College Students (1 hr.)
   Frederick Perls and Gestalt Therapy (Film 1, 39 min., Film 2, 36 min.)
   Three Approaches to Psychotherapy: Rogers, Perls, Ellis (Perls segment, 32 min.)

Tapes

American Academy of Psychotherapists A.A.P. Tape Library, 1040 Woodcock Rd., Orlando, FL 32803:
   Eric Marcus. "Introduction to Gestalt Approaches" (#82, 31 min.)
   Frederick S. Perls. "Gestalt Therapy Seminar" (#16, 2 hrs.)
   Eugene Sagan. "Gestalt Expressive Therapy" (#18, 44 min.)
   James Simkin. "Individual Gestalt Therapy, Interview with Dr. Frederick Perls" (#31, 1 hr.)

Big Sur Recordings, 2015 Bridgeway, Sausalito, CA 94965:
   Fritz Perls. "Dream Theory and Demonstration" (#2140, 1 hr.)
   Fritz Perls. "Fritz Perls Reads from 'In and Out the Garbage Pail'" (#2300, 1 hr.)
   Fritz Perls. "Gestalt Therapy and How It Works" (#2910, 1 hr.)
   Fritz Perls. "Neurosis, Psychosis and Dreams" (#2310, 2 hrs.)
   Fritz Perls. "The Perls Encounter" (#3060, 9 hrs.)
   Fritz Perls. "Working with Dreams" (#3070, 4 hrs.)
   James Simkin. "Gestalt Therapy: Lecture-Demonstration" (#4800, 1½ hrs.)

Gestalt Institutes

New York Institute for Gestalt Therapy
7 West 96th St.
New York, NY 10025

The first gestalt institute in America, begun by Fritz and Laura Perls, and
    Paul Goodman, now directed by Laura Perls.

Gestalt Institute of Cleveland
12911 Euclid Ave.
Cleveland, Ohio 44112.

This institute was established by Fritz Perls and some of his Cleveland
    students.

Gestalt Therapy Institute of Los Angeles
337 So. Beverly Drive, Suite 206
Beverly Hills, CA 90212

Fritz and a group of his students started this institute in the early 1960s.

Gestalt Institute of San Francisco
1719 Union St.
San Francisco, CA 94123

Again, Fritz and a group of his students were responsible for beginning
    this institute in 1968.

Gestalt Training Center—San Diego
7255 Gerard Ave.,
La Jolla, CA 92037

Gestalt Therapy Institute of Canada
Lake Cowichan
P.O. Box 39
Vancouver, British Columbia, Canada

Gestalt Institute of Chicago
Oasis Midwest Center for Human Potential
Chicago, IL

Gestalt Institute of the Southwest
7700 Alabama St.
El Paso, TX 79904

Publication:

The Gestalt Journal (published semi-annually)
Center for Gestalt Development, Inc.
P.O. Box 395
New York, NY 10024

Index to Interviews

Pseudonyms were used at the request of the individuals.

AGREY, GER:
Interviewed May 11, 1973,
Big Sur, California.
Pp. 225, 278.

ALEXANDER, MICHAEL: Magazine
photographer.
Interviewed January 8, 1974,
San Francisco.
Pp. 159, 196-197, 309, 315.

ANDERSON, WALT: Writer, work-
shop leader.
Interviewed July 19, 1973,
Berkeley, California.
Pp. 126, 195-196.

BABCOCK, DON: Psychotherapist.
Interviewed July 1, 1974.
Pp. 310-311, 389-390.

BEACH, SCOTT: Singer, actor, conductor, writer, radio announcer,
raconteur.
Interviewed January 24, 1974.
Pp. 257-258, 260.

BERRETT, ARNOLD: Diagnostic
radiologist; husband of Marilyn
Rosanes-Berrett.
Interviewed January 2, 1974,
New York City.
P. 403.

BROOKS, CHARLES: Author of *Sensory Awareness;* teacher of sensory awareness with his wife,
Charlotte Selver.
P. 285.

BROWN, GEORGE I.: Director of
the Confluent Education pro-
gram at the University of
California, Santa Barbara;
author.
Interviewed March 9, 1974,
Esalen Institute.
Pp. 129-130, 230.

CALLAHAN, MARGARET: Pseudo-
nym.
Interviewed by telephone,
April 22, 1974.
Pp. 211-212.

CARTER, SEYMOUR:
Interviewed November 26, 1975,
Big Sur, California.
Pp. 125, 248, 280, 291-292, 312,
417.

CEPPOS, ARTHUR: Publisher at
Julian Press; American publisher
of *Gestalt Therapy.*
Interviewed September 11, 1973.
Pp. 36-37, 113, 231-232, 235,
397.

CONRAD, SYLVIA BEHRMANN:
Interviewed by letter, October 8,
1973, New York City.
Pp. 18, 22-23, 27, 32, 229, 398.

CULP, HUNTER: Member of Esalen
ground crew at the time of his
meeting with Fritz Perls.
Interviewed May 2, 1973, Esalen
Institute.
Pp. 138, 144-145, 162-164, 167,
237.

CULVER, EDWIN: "Ed the Mailman" drove the mail and produce truck through the Big Sur
region, including Esalen;
musician.
Interviewed January 5, 1973,
Pacific Grove, California.
Pp. 151-152.

CURRY, ANDY: Coordinator of
Humanities, California School
of Professional Psychology;
lecturer, Department of Psychiatry, U.C. School of Medicine,
San Francisco, and Graduate
School of Social Welfare, U.C.,

FENG, GIA-FU: Director of Still-
point, a Taoist community in
Manitou Springs, Colorado.
Interviewed May 1, 1973,
Manitou Springs, Colorado.
Pp. 114, 145-146, 154-155,
170-171, 172, 418.

FOX, JANICE: Group leader at
Esalen and consultant in human-
istic psychology.
Interviewed August 27, 1973,
Esalen Institute.
P. 289.

FOX, STAN: Documentary film-
maker.
Interviewed July 1, 1974,
Toronto, Ontario.
Pp. 349-352.

FRAZIER, ANNI: Concert pianist,
ballet dancer, model, yoga
master, and artist.
Interviewed August 21, 1973,
Big Sur, California.
Pp. 308-309, 327-329.

FREEDMAN, HARVEY: Psychiatrist;
associate professor, Department
of Psychiatry, Faculty of
Medicine, University of Toronto; founder of the Gestalt Institute of Toronto.
Interviewed August 25, 1975,
Estes Park, Colorado.
Pp. 191-192, 212, 234, 280,
371-372.

FREEDMAN, SONYA:
Pp. 289-290.

FREY, DENISE: Pseudonym.
Pp. 209, 290.

FROMM, MARTY: Associate profes-
sor of psychology at Miami-
Dade Community College; priv-
ate practice as a gestalt
therapist.
Interviewed September 14, 1973,
Miami, Florida.
Pp. 45-48, 55-58, 411, 416.

FULLER, BETTY: Humanistic counselor; associate director of the
Center for Holistic Studies, Antioch University.

Interviewed January 30, 1974,
Marin County, California.
Pp. 128, 198, 205-211, 228, 237,
248-249, 311, 316, 338, 416,
423-424.

GOLD, ART: Artist; husband of
Renate Perls at the time of the
interview.
Interviewed July 26, 1974,
Leonia, New Jersey.
Pp. 107-108.

GOLD, LESLIE: Granddaughter of
Fritz Perls; daugher of Renate
Perls and Art Gold.
Interviewed December 5, 1973,
New York City.
Pp. 324-325, 419-420.

GRAHAM, JEAN:
Pp. 329-330.

GRAUER, ROMILLY: Canadian psy-
chotherapist.
Interviewed in May, 1973, Big
Sur, California.
Pp. 114, 357-360, 421.

GUINAN, JIM: Counselor at the
University of Psychotherapy in
Ohio.
Interviewed by mail, May 1,
1974, Bowling Green, Ohio.
Pp. 391-392.

GUNTHER, BERNARD: Poet and
writer; former staff member of
Esalen.
Interviewed August 23, 1973,
Big Sur, California.
Pp. 113, 120, 121-122, 124, 237,
309, 321, 425.

GUTFREUND, MARGARITE: Fritz
Perls' sister.
Interviewed September 15, 1973,
New York City.
Pp. 1-4, 398, 399, 402, 403.

HALL, ROBERT: Co-founder of the
Gestalt Institute of San Fran-
cisco; psychiatrist specializing in
gestalt, body movement, and
meditation.
Interviewed June 23, 1972, Ben
Lomond, California.
Pp. 187-189, 201-202, 327, 336.

KRAUSE, GERTRUDE: Gestalt therapist; founder-therapist of the Gestalt Institute of Florida.
Interviewed August 28, 1976, Princeton, New Jersey.
Pp. 41, 43, 44.

KRAUSE, SYLVAN: Businessman; business consultant/secretary of the Gestalt Institute of Florida.
Interviewed August 28, 1976, Princeton, New Jersey.
Pp. 42, 43, 45, 52.

KULCSAR, SHLOMO: Head of the psychiatry department of Tel Hachomer, a teaching hospital in Israel.
Interviewed November 28, 1973, Ramat Hen, Israel.
Pp. 99-100.

LEDERMAN, JANET: Artist and teacher; head of the Gazebo School at Esalen Institute; co-director of Esalen Institute.
Interviewed February 11, 1973, Big Sur, California.
Pp. 244-245, 319-320, 364.

LEONARD, GEORGE: Senior editor for *Look* magazine for 17 years; former vice president of Esalen Institute; past president of the Association for Humanistic Psychology; author; black belt in aikido.
Interviewed December 14, 1973, Mill Valley, California.
Pp. 155-156, 194-195, 200-201, 318, 322.

LEVITSKY, ABRAHAM: Clinical psychologist in private practice; faculty member of the Gestalt Institute of San Francisco; co-author with Fritz Perls of *The Rules and Games of Gestalt Therapy*.
Interviewed June 21, 1973, Berkeley, California.
Pp. 127, 128, 160, 235, 249-251.

LIFSCHITZ, MARVIN: Gestalt psychotherapist in private practice in New York City; director of the Gestalt Institute of New York.

Interviewed July 31, 1974, New York City.
P. 85.

LITOWITZ, NORMAN: Psychiatrist.
Interviewed February 8, 1975, Chicago.
P. 55.

LOWEN, ALEXANDER: Executive director of the Institute for Bioenergetics Analysis; psychiatrist.
Interviewed July 30, 1974, New York City.
Pp. 36, 288, 312-313.

MADSEN, DOUG: Architect and horseman in Big Sur.
Interviewed in May, 1973, Big Sur, California.
Pp. 168-169.

MANN, NATALIE:
Interviewed January 11, 1974, Mill Valley, California.
Pp. 58-59, 119, 120, 172, 225, 229, 232, 323.

MARCUS, ERIC: Psychiatrist, gestalt therapist; instructor of gestalt techniques at U.C.L.A.; a founder and past president of the Gestalt Institute of Los Angeles.
Interviewed December 30, 1974, Santa Barbara, California.
Pp. 126-127, 305-306.

MARSHALL, CAROL:
Interviewed April 11, 1976, Esalen Institute.
Pp. 116-118.

MARTIN, ALAN:
Interviewed August 27, 1976, Princeton, New Jersey.
Pp. 48-52, 232.

MAY, ROLLO: Psychologist, author, and lecturer.
Interviewed June 14, 1978, Tiburon, California.
Pp. 35-36, 153, 261-262, 270.

MILLER, RICHARD: Clinical-environmental psychologist; founder, Wilbur Hot Springs Health Sanctuary; founding director, Gestalt Institute of San Francisco and California School of

ROSANES-BERRETT, MARILYN: Therapist; teacher of the Bates method of sight improvement. Interviewed September 10, 1973, New York City. Pp. 38-39, 52, 53-54, 80-81, 186-187, 403.

ROSENBERG, JACK: Trained in gestalt and Reichian work; working with cancer research and the transformation of consciousness at the Center of the Healing Arts in Los Angeles. Interviewed October 17, 1973. Pp. 173, 203, 333-334.

ROSENFELD, EDWARD: Teacher and editor of *The Gestalt Journal*. Interviewed July 25, 1974. Pp. 231, 318, 329.

ROSNER, CHARLOTTE: Gestalt therapist, president of the Gestalt Institute of Chicago. Interviewed August 25, 1975, Estes Park, Colorado. P. 316.

ROTH, GABRIELLE: Dance therapist active in education, entertainment, and therapy communities as well as the human potential movement. Interviewed August 28, 1973, Esalen Institute. Pp. 230, 262-263.

ROTHSTEIN, JERRY: Director, Gestalt Institute of Canada. Interviewed July 4, 1974. Pp. 202-203, 278-279, 356-357, 366-368, 388, 395-396, 398.

RUBENFELD, FRANK: Clinical psychiatrist; trainer in gestalt at the Gestalt Institute of San Francisco and the California School of Professional Psychology; private practice in Berkeley, California. Interviewed March 19, 1974, Berkeley, California. Pp. 36, 251, 271, 400, 401-402.

RUBENFELD, ILANA: Gestalt therapist, teacher of the Alexander technique and the Feldenkrais method; instructor at New York University School of Continuing Education, and New York University Graduate School of Social Work. Interviewed August 29, 1974, New Orleans, Louisiana. Pp. 176, 215-219, 234, 369, 400, 401, 402.

SADRON, SONIA: Israeli artist. Interviewed November 26, 1973, Ein Hod, Israel. Pp. 101, 103.

SAGAN, EUGENE: Clinical psychologist. Interviewed June 21, 1973, and July 19, 1973, Oakland, California. Pp. 75-78, 123, 150, 421.

SATIR, VIRGINIA: Family therapist; resident at Esalen Institute at the time of Fritz Perls' arrival. Interviewed August 31, 1978, Menlo Park, California. Pp. 158, 177, 235, 236, 248, 267-270, 323, 334.

SCHOENFELD, EUGENE: Originator of the "Dr. HipPocrates" newspaper column and radio program which appeared throughout the U.S.; physician with the Valley Emergency Medical Group. Interviewed June 2, 1974, Stinson Beach, California. Pp. 54-55.

SCHUTZ, WILL: Leader in development of encounter techniques; director, Center for Holistic Studies, Antioch University; author. Interviewed May 3, 1973. Pp. 128, 159, 174-175, 176-177, 178-179, 180, 181, 259, 271, 421.

SCHWARZ, GIDEON: Professor at the Hebrew University, Jerusalem; mathematician; gestalt therapist. Interviewed December 13, 1973, and January 20, 1974.

Photographs

JOHN STEVENS: "One evening we were looking at
the proofs of *Garbage Pail.* . . ."

MARGARITE GUTFREUND: "He was a wild child—wild, wild! Else, Margarite and Frederick Perls, Germany, 1900.

LAURA PERLS: "I had the feeling: There *he* is . . . Ya! He was *very* impressive!" Germany, 1923.

The gestalting of the Perls: Marriage, Fritz and Laura Perls, 1930. LAURA PERLS: ". . . we had a small wedding in City Hall."

STEPHEN PERLS: "I vaguely remember my father coming home on weekends in his captain's uniform. He was a practicing psychiatrist in the South African Army. . . ."

With the psychiatric staff of the South African Army Hospital, 1942-1946. LAURA PERLS: ". . . he had a lot of free time. We worked on the book. . . ."

Charlotte Selver: ". . . but I honestly must say that this man never appealed very much to me. . . ." Alexander Lowen: "He characterized himself as a dirty old man; he *was* a dirty old man." Rollo May: "I found him a boor—an authoritarian boor." New York, 1950.

Shlomo Kulcsar: "He looked just like any other psychiatrist— nothing physically impressive. He looked like an aging man. . . ." circa 1962.

SHLOMO KULCSAR: "He evidently succeeded in rejuvenation. . . ." MICHAEL MURPHY: "You could just see him filling out . . . he must have grown a couple of inches . . . he was a very tough old man. . . ." Esalen, 1964.

BETTY FULLER: He was a wise fool, like the fool of the tarot, just ready to walk off a cliff. He had that *total* freedom of non-attachedness and absolute joy." Esalen, Big Sur, California, 1967.

Russ Youngreen: "When he was there to help you, he was *there*, one hundred percent, completely. . . ."

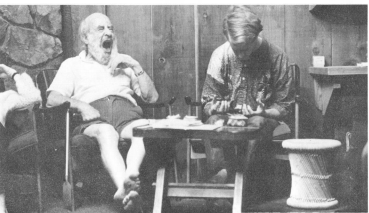

Photos by Michael Alexander

ANDY CURRY: "... commanding, almost
mirror-like, and curiously forgiving. You saw
that he saw what you were trying to be. His gift
was that he saw the truth and spoke the truth."
Fritz Perls: July 8, 1893—March 14, 1970.

LAURA PERLS

Photo by Michael Alexander

IDA ROLF

Photo By Horst Mayer

RICHARD PRICE

MICHAEL MURPHY

DR. WILLIAM SHLAES

Photo by Jack Gaines

GABRIELLE ROTH

Photo by Jack Gaines

STEPHEN PERLS

GIDEON SCHWARZ

CHARLOTTE SELVER
AND
CHARLES BROOKS

CLAUDIO NARANJO

WILL SCHUTZ

JIM SIMKIN

ANNA HALPRIN

JOHN STEVENS

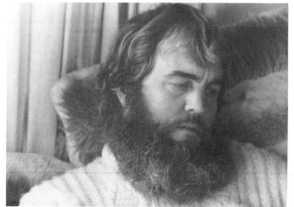

GIA-FU FENG

JACK DOWNING

JANET LEDERMAN

BARRY STEVENS

JACK GAINES

RUSS YOUNGREEN